"The one way of tolerating
existence is to lose oneself in
literature as in a perpetual
orgy."

—Gustave Flaubert,
in a letter, 1858

B·O·O·K·S
& Co.

939 Madison Avenue
New York City 10021

'phone (212) 737·1450

JOE ZUCKER

May 2–May 28, 1991

ELLIOTT GREEN

May 30–July 3, 1991

HIRSCHL & ADLER MODERN

851 Madison Avenue
New York, New York 10021
212 744-6700
FAX 212 737-2614

CONJUNCTIONS

*Bi-Annual Volumes
of New Writing*

Edited by
Bradford Morrow

Contributing Editors
Walter Abish
John Ashbery
Mei-mei Berssenbrugge
Guy Davenport
Elizabeth Frank
William H. Gass
Susan Howe
Kenneth Irby
Robert Kelly
Ann Lauterbach
Patrick McGrath
Nathaniel Tarn

Bard College   *distributed by Random House, Inc.*

EDITOR: Bradford Morrow
SENIOR EDITOR: Susan Bell
ASSOCIATE EDITORS: Martine Bellen, Karen Kelly,
    Yannick Murphy
MANAGING EDITOR: Marlene Hennessy
EDITORIAL ASSISTANTS: Meg Black, Jonathan Miller,
    Cathleen Shattuck

CONJUNCTIONS is published in the Spring and Fall of each year
by Bard College, Annandale-on-Hudson, NY 12504. This issue is
made possible in part with the generous funding of the Lannan
Foundation and New York State Council on the Arts.

Editorial communications should be sent to 33 West 9th Street,
New York NY, 10011. Unsolicited manuscripts cannot be returned
unless accompanied by a stamped, self-addressed envelope.

Distributed by Random House.

SUBSCRIPTIONS. Send subscription order to CONJUNCTIONS,
Box 115, Bard College, Annandale-on-Hudson, NY 12504. Single
year (two volumes): $18.00 for individuals, $25.00 for institutions
and overseas. Two years (four volumes): $32.00 for individuals;
$45.00, for institutions and overseas. Patron subscription (lifetime):
$500.00. Overseas subscribers please make payment by International
Money Order. Back issues available at $10.00 per copy.

Printers: Edwards Brothers.
Typesetter: Bill White, Typeworks.

ISSN 0278-2324
ISBN 0-679-73541-0

Manufactured in the United States of America.

TABLE OF CONTENTS

Memphis to Memphis
Albert Goldman

BACK IN JUNE 1968, while writing a series for *New York* titled "The Blues Today," I settled down late one night in a posh suite at the Drake Hotel in Manhattan to do an interview with Jimi Hendrix. After a little preliminary palaver, Hendrix eyed me — a middle-aged Columbia University professor with long hair and granny glasses — and asked archly: "What would you do now if I whipped out the biggest joint you ever saw and started to smoke it?" Amused by his caution, I answered: "I'd tear it out of your hand and eat it!" That broke him up and he relaxed, which was the signal for his mini-skirted entourage to resume their normal domestic duties, which commenced with the star's awakening at 7 P.M. and concluded the following afternoon, when he nodded out.

During the hours that followed, I watched the great psychedelic bluesman moving restlessly about in his exotic environment, suffused with the scent of burning incense and lit by flickering candles in red glasses. One moment he would pause to be sketched, the next he would listen to a reading of his latest review or scratch out a few notes on a sheet of music paper or spin a side or withdraw into his bedroom with one of his handmaidens. All the while, he was smoking dope or snorting coke or drinking Lancer wine, like a jazzman running endless changes on the same three chords. Just as I was starting to get groggy and nod out myself, Hendrix snapped me into rapt attention.

Clapping a pair of elephantine earphones on my head, he announced, "Now I'm gonna play you something really good." Dropping the needle into the groove, he smiled at me as I waited expectantly. Suddenly, my ears were filled with a brass chord that swelled so far that I imaged an I-beam thrusting endlong through the window. Then the chord was broken off by a funky bass that was in turn transfixed by a piercing guitar sound that quivered like an assegai. "Jimi," I cried, "that's the greatest lick you ever played!" He laughed and answered, "That's not me, man. That's the guitar player I learned from. That's the *king* — Albert King."

The next week I flew down to Memphis for the first time in my life to meet Albert King and research a piece on the Memphis Soul Sound. From the moment I stepped inside the Stax-Volt studios until I boarded my return flight clutching a couple of reels containing King's forthcoming album, *Blues Power*, I was enthralled by everything I discovered. I sat in an office watching Don Porter and Isaac Hayes (then a song writer not a performer) demonstrating for my benefit all their hits. I interviewed B.B. King as he lay naked under the sheets of the Lorraine Motel. I not only interviewed Albert King but spent the first of what became many nights watching him work, on this occasion witnessing him battle B.B. King in the musical equivalent of a rigged wrestling match at the Club Paradise on South Danny Thomas Boulevard—a converted bowling alley with two artificial palms at the sides of the stage and tough billy-wielding ushers dressed like cops. That evening ended with our driving out to a speakeasy on the outskirts of town (Memphis was the wettest "dry" town in America), where we ate heartily and drank heavily with our dates, a couple of black girls who talked exclusively about black pop stars. If you had asked me for my impressions of Memphis after that trip, I would have told you that the city more than fulfilled everything I had ever imagined about the legendary home of the blues.

Ten years later I came back to Memphis to begin work on my biography of Elvis Presley. I assumed that I would have more adventures of the same kind, only this time I would get a lot deeper into the local music scene. In fact, as day after day went by and I moved from one site or interview to another, I never heard a note of music or got the sense that there was any music left in town. The famous recording studios were boarded over and the local musicians appeared to have vanished. Gradually, I came to realize that what I had experienced in the sixties had been a rare moment in the city's history. Memphis had been full of sounds for a brief time then, just as it had briefly in the previous decade when Elvis, Carl Perkins, and Jerry Lee Lewis recorded for Sun, or earlier still in the heydey of the tent-show blues queens. Those periods, however, were simply oases in what had generally been and promised to remain a musical desert.

When I finally set about composing *Elvis*, I wrote up my findings and reflections on the evolution of the blues, intending to set them side by side with an account of white gospel as the two principle traditions that had combined in the new rock 'n' roll. My sketch turned out to be too long for inclusion in the book and so it is offered here without any effort to update it because, so far as I am aware, nothing has happened since 1980 that would alter my sense of blues history.

"Memphis" and "blues" are words that lock together with the inexorableness of cause and effect. When you reflect on the legends of Beale Street and W.C. Handy or call the roll of all the famous bluesmen who have been associated with Memphis from the early days of Bukka White and Big Bill Broonzy to the post World War II generation of Howlin' Wolf and Little Walter to the last great bluesmen, B.B. King and Albert King, all the evidence appears to add up to the anticipated conclusion. In the words of a textbook — or a tourist brochure — "Memphis was one of those uniquely endowed metropolises that afford the ideal conditions for the growth and flourishing of a famous art." It is only when you come to know Memphis from personal observation and from the study of its skimpy cultural records that you begin first to question, then to modify, and finally to discard this myth.

The natural place to begin the study of the Memphis blues is Beale Street. Just pronouncing the magic name is enough to flood the imagination with beguiling images. One pictures it on a Saturday night circa 1910, crowded with plow jockeys and parlor belles, river rousters and factory frills, pimps in box-back coats and "beautiful browns in flouncy gowns." You envision blocks lined with gingerbread palaces and clapboard cribs; sporting houses filled with creoles from New Orleans and gambling halls jammed with fancy men playing cooncan rummy. Rising like an invisible but palpable cloud around this lively tableau are the sounds of Beale — the jumbling of ragtime pianos with windup Victrolas, of shouting congregations with howling bluesmen, of strolling guitar pickers with scrounging jug bands — the South's most celebrated symphony. Then, you take a walk down Beale today.

One of the saddest sights in the United States is the vestiges of what was once "Black America's Main Street." Block after block of abandoned, boarded-over brick buildings, bare ruined choirs occupied sometimes by a dismal Jewish pawnshop in whose heavily barred window the guitars, banjos and trumpets of the local blacks lie gathering dust. Beale reminds the visitor of those ruins deliberately left standing in European cities as memorials of disastrous wars lost to superior powers. Indeed, the hollow, scabrous walls of Beale make a very eloquent witness not just to the indifference and contempt for black life which is characteristic of Southern cities but also to the active hostility of the white ruling powers of this half-black metropolis, which have sought for years to wipe out the black commercial district so that it would no longer provide any distraction from the arid and lifeless cityscape which the urban renewers have imposed on all the rest of downtown Memphis.

Considered in the light of history, the ghostly appearance of Beale suggests other, less immediate associations: for one, the precise parallel between Beale's fate and that of Storyville in New Orleans. Every lover of American music knows how the legendary redlight district that was one of the spawning grounds of jazz was abolished abruptly in 1917 at the order of the U.S. Navy, which feared the corrupting effect of the tenderloin on its antiseptically uniformed personnel. What is not so well-known is that exactly the same fate befell Beale on the eve of the second World War. Generally, it is believed that Beale was either the victim of Mayor Boss Crump's moral zeal or of the deadening effects of Prohibition combined with the Depression. Nothing could be further from the truth.

E.H. Crump, who was first elected mayor in 1910, did wage a campaign to clean up the city, which was then notorious as the "Murder Capital of America." Once he got into office, however, he never raised a finger to interfere with the prostitution and gambling, the drinking and doping, that were the lifeblood of Beale. In fact, in 1916 he was turned out of office by the Tennessee Legislature for failure to enforce the State's liquor prohibition law, which antedated the Volstead Act by nearly a decade. It was this humiliating punishment that determined Crump to build a political machine so powerful that never again would he have to fear the interference of either the state or the federal authorities. So well did he succeed that until his death in 1954, he ruled Memphis with an iron hand and even decided who would be the state's governor. As a congressman, he developed strong ties with the Roosevelt Administration; generally, however, he preferred not to hold office but to rule through his puppets and minions.

Like his counterpart, Boss Pendergast of Kansas City (whose vast network of clubs and clip-joints had become the hothouse for jazz after its decline in New Orleans and Chicago), Boss Crump had no intention of allowing his machine to be deprived of the enormous bribes paid by the gamblers, bootleggers and bordello operators.

What if every night the action cost some black man his life? The bodies were always spirited away to protect the reputation of the Street. (Hence the old Memphis proverb: "You never find a dead nigger on Beale.") What induced Crump to shut down Beale over-night in 1940 was a call from FDR. The former Secretary of the Navy told Crump that a new naval base was going to be built in nearby Millington; if the city wanted to profit from the federal treasury, it would have to reciprocate by locking up its cages full of man-eating whores, and pimps, gamblers and dope dealers. That phone call from the Big Boss to the local boss meant an end to high times on Beale.

Digging even deeper into the history of Memphis and the blues, one comes to an even more surprising realization: namely, that even in its palmiest days, Memphis was never anything more to the bluesman than a way station on his road north, east or west. Virtually none of the famous bluesmen whose names have been associated at one time or another with Memphis were born or reared in the city. Almost invariably they came from rural districts, especially from that great umbilicus of the blues, the Mississippi Delta. After years of developing their craft in the country and the little market towns, often through informal apprenticeships to older musicians, they drifted into Memphis because it was the only major city in the region.

They played in the streets for nickels and dimes; or perhaps they got an occasional job in a saloon or playing for a white man's party. If they were exceptionally lucky, they were spotted by a scout for a northern record company: Paramount or OKeh in the twenties, Brunswick or Victor in the thirties. Brought up to a hotel room and seated before the crude portable equipment, the bluesman cut a few sides for a few dollars. That was it. If he wanted to be better, he had to work up his nerve and go to Chicago. To think of Memphis as a city like New Orleans, Kansas City, or New York that fostered a particular music by providing abundant opportunities for work or the stimulating and educating company of hundreds of other musicians or regular access to recording studios is completely mistaken. Instead of being renowned as the home of the blues, Memphis should be notorious as the town that turned its back on the blues.

What, then, if anything, did Memphis contribute to the blues? The answer is *commercialization*. At several crucial moments in the history of the music, local musicians and entrepreneurs appeared who translated successfully this musical patois into the idioms of mass entertainment. These blues brokers, by virtue of their strategic position in the heartland of the blues, were able, like the cotton factors on Front Street, to act as middlemen for the commodity so laboriously cultivated in the Delta and the consuming public the world around. Memphis figures in the evolution of the blues, therefore, as an important, if only intermittently active, center of musical exploitation.

The first and greatest of the Memphis blues brokers was the man who bears the title "The Father of the Blues": William Christopher Handy. As Handy was not just the prototype but the archetype of all those composers and arrangers, music publishers and record producers, who have mined and minted the riches of black music for the past seventy years — including the creators of Memphis Rockabilly in the fifties and the Memphis Sound in the sixties — it is worth pausing for a moment to consider his cast of mind and mode of operation.

The first and most important thing to grasp about W.C. Handy is that he embodies to a remarkable degree the mentality of the "striver," the first generation of black bourgoisie in America. Born in a log cabin at Florence, Alabama, in 1873, the son of a former slave, Handy emerged from the same conditions of rural poverty and social ostracism that condemned millions of blacks to lives of hardship and ignominy. Handy lived up to his name, however: though his opportunities were few, he rarely let one slip through his grasp. Told as a young man that no "thick-lipped nigger" could ever play the cornet — the instrument that in the world of black minstrelsy was as much a talisman of success as was the fiddle to the first generations of aspiring Eastern European Jews — Handy became a cornet virtuoso and the leader of the Bihara Minstrels' band. Tiring of life on the road, he organized his own band and began to play dances for rich planters in the Mississippi Delta. The legend of the birth of the blues commences on a night in 1903, while Handy was dozing on a train platform in the Delta at the little town of Tutwiler.

Awakened by what he describes as "the weirdest music I ever heard," Handy discovered that a "lean, loose-jointed Negro had commenced plunking a guitar beside me while I slept. His clothes were rags; his feet peeped out of his shoes. As he played, he pressed a knife on the strings of the guitar in a manner popularized by Hawaiian guitarists who used steel bars. The effect was unforgettable."

Ruminating on this strange music, Handy associated it with the old work songs of field hands, who sang:

> *Boll Weevil, where you been so long?*
> *Boll Weevil, where you been so long?*
> *You stole ma cotton, now you want my corn.*

Or the plaints of lonely river roustabouts, who cried:

> *Oh, the Kate's up the river, Stack O' Lee's in the ben',*
> *Oh, the Kate's up the river, Stack O' Lee's in the ben',*
> *An' I ain't seen ma baby since I can't tell when.*

Such rustic stuff held no charm for the sophisticated, note-reading, widely-traveled bandsman. He soon forgot the country bluesman, like a figure in a dream.

Then, one night at a dance in the Delta, Handy received an ambiguous request. Somebody handed him a note reading: "Can you play some of your native music?" Handy was not sure what the writer meant by "native." His gilt-buttoned, fancy-laced bandsmen were not like minstrels who could "fake" and "jass." He decided to call a medley of traditional Southern airs that was probably right off the racks of some musical dry goods store. When the performance concluded, Handy received another request: would he stand aside while some of the local colored boys played a few dances? Handy took the suggestion as a joke. What could these clowns do that would merit them a place on the platform where he was performing? It was all he could do to restrain his laughter when he beheld his rivals: a "long-legged chocolate boy" whose band consisted of "a battered guitar, a mandolin and a worn-out bass."

When this unpromising group got into action, the music they produced justified Handy's prejudices: "one of those over-and-over strains that seemed to have no very clear beginning and certainly no ending at all. The strumming attained a disturbing monotony, but on and on it went." Even more absurd than the music were the mannerisms of the players: they thumped their splayed feet on the floor, rolled their eyes and swayed their shoulders. What a contrast they offered to the correct military posture of Handy's men! No sooner did this interminable jig reel end, however, than a remarkable thing happened.

Silver coins began pelting down on the "darkies." Quarters, halves, even massive dollars chimed on the floor. As Handy gaped at this silver rain, he experienced a revelation. "I saw the beauty of primitive music!" he exclaims. "They had the stuff the people wanted. It touched the spot. Folks would pay for it. . . . The American people wanted rhythm and movement for their money." That moment worked a revolution in his thinking. As he put it, "That night a composer was born": for which we can read — a very deliberate and resourceful exploiter of black folk music.

By 1909, Handy was settled on Beale Street, then at the height of its fame as a *"Netzenstadt"*: a city of nets and man traps. Handy was not put off by the ubiquitous crime and violence; his job was to hustle up dates for his band, which was having trouble cutting into the market controlled by two other orchestras. At this moment, E.H. Crump was running in a three-cornered race for mayor. As his opponents had hired the better-known bands, Crump was forced to engage Handy to ballyhoo the candidacy by riding around town playing music from a bandwagon.

Handy took his assignment very seriously. He felt he had been hired to swing the Beale Street vote, and, as the "best notes get the best votes," he ought to provide his boss with a catchy campaign song. Though Crump's pious campaign promises might have been symbolized best by a hymn, something gamier was needed to capture the favor of the sporting crowd. Struggling now — exactly like the rhythm and blues producers of later times — to come up with a gimmick that would turn on the ghetto, Handy decided (like the concocters of the Memphis Sound fifty years afterwards) that the best way to tickle the fancies of his sophisticated audience of "easy riders" (pimps), "players" and "hos" was to cook up a mess of steaming grits and greens. Recollecting the music he had heard years before on the train platform in the Delta, he hied himself down to the back room of Thornton's barbership. (Handy liked to compose in the heart of the milieu he was seeking to capture.) There he turned out the composition that has always been called "the first published blues." Actually, "The Memphis Blues" (so titled when printed in 1912 but known originally as "Mr. Crump") was not a true blues but a hybrid composition that combined features of the blues with the cakewalk.

When Handy took "Mr. Crump" to the streets, he created a sensation. Soon the song was being played night and day all over town. Though the tune had no lyrics, people would improvise their own words — salty, sassy street chants. When Handy put the best lines together, they added up to a rude rejection of Mr. Crump's self-righteous campaign rhetoric:

> *Mr. Crump won't 'low no easy riders here,*
> *Mr. Crump won't 'low no easy riders here,*
> *We don't care what Mr. Crump don' 'low,*
> *We gon' barrelhouse anyhow—*
> *Mr. Crump can go and catch hisself some air!*

In the published version, hackneyed Tin Pan Alley verses were sub-stituted for the original words. Along with all the other precedents established by this landmark composition went the black song-writer's capitulation to the rule that pop tunes must have lily-white lyrics.

After Handy's departure for New York in 1918 (where he estab-lished a highly successful publishing business and the first black-owned record company, Black Swan), Beale Street began a slow decline. At the same time, however, the blues soared to its first great peak of popularity. Belted out on the black vaudeville stage or ground out through the flaring horn of a Victrola by a whole tribe of sonorous black mamas, led by the fabled "Empress of the Blues," Bessie Smith, the blues became—along with short skirts, roadsters and bathtub gin—one of the distinctive fads of the twen-ties. At the end of the decade, George Gershwin summed up the infatuation with this dark, exotic music in a single gigantic blue note, drawn with the stroke of a great caricaturist's pen as the star-tling two-octave clarinet glissando that opens *Rhapsody in Blue*.

Naturally, many modifications of the country blues were made to accommodate this quirky, improvisatory and, in performance, highly individualized folk song to the mass production formulas of Tin Pan Alley and vaudeville. One of the most important and far-reaching developments was the coalescence of blues with that other newly discovered black art: jazz. On virtually every Bessie Smith record, the singer is accompanied by one or more jazz players, in-cluding such famous names as Louis Armstrong and Fletcher Hen-derson. In this so-called "classic" period, however, it is the blues which is paramount. The jazz comes in simply as improvised ac-companiment: Armstrong's cornet filling the long pauses between Bessie Smith's glacially slow phrases with bright filigree.

In the next phase of the blues, called the urban blues, the balance is reversed. Now, the musical center of gravity lies in the accom-paniment, which is ideally a hard-driving, ebulliently swinging

15

Albert Goldman

Kansas City jazz band of the type immortalized by the Count Basie Band. No longer is the singer a massive matriarch with a deep contralto voice running to gravel and growl: now he's a man mountain, like Jimmy Rushing, "Mr. Five by Five" ("He's five foot high and five foot wide") or the strapping Joe Turner—a shouter more than a singer, with a powerfully penetrating voice that rings like hard wood. The most drastic contrast is in the tempos of the two periods: the urban blues is born along so rapidly on the seething jazz current that the singer appears at times a vocal surfer riding precariously atop a surging, cresting flood of frothy rhythmic energy.

Kansas City bands accompanied blues singers by falling into short, distinctive phrases called riffs, which they repeated over and over through the performance, "setting" first one riff and then another to produce a wide range of effects, including responsorial echoes and counter-melodies (suggestive of dialogue), while always engendering the massive momentum of an organlike ostinato. These riffs were sometimes bits broken off blues lines or independent figures drawn from a large stock of conventional phrases. They were destined to play a vital part in the further development of the blues both as substitutes for melody and as background figures not just for instrumental but also for vocal accompaniments in the so-called "do-wop" groups. The growing importance of the riff, a phrase that is as much articulated rhythm as rhythmic articulation, attests to the increasing desire to make the blues "jump."

This longing was fulfilled at the end of the thirties by the emergence of the most frenzied and Dionysian of all blues: the boogie-woogie. The boogie made the blues for the second time in its history a national craze. Today, after having witnessed so many song and dance manias, it isn't difficult to account for the enormous popularity of this obsessive idiom.

All such fads have as their inciting cause an irresistible and contagious rhythm that not only drives the listener to his feet but induces in him an hypnotic and trancelike state tinged with erotic fantasy. The boogie, born and reared in the raunchy atmosphere of the "boogie house" (brothel) and the barrelhouse of the turpentine logging camp, was ideally designed to produce this effect. The relentlessly rolling bass, like Ezekiel's wheel, is enough to get anyone stoned. The powerful kinesthetic effect of the performance, which builds and builds, until it seems the whole house is rocking, is the perfect inspiration for wild dancing. But what really made the boogie an event in the unfolding of modern sensibility was its

16

boldly erotic character, proclaimed by its name, one of those cryptic black terms, like "jazz" or "rock 'n' roll," that signify fucking.

Unlike other types of erotic music, such as the tango, which evoke the sensuous or romantic aspects of sex — all those sighing, swooning violins, those predatory stalking rhythms — the boogie-woogie knows nothing about flirtation, seduction or love. It focuses exclusively on "getting down," which it mimes in dance and celebrates in song, employing earthy masculine language, sometimes leering with dirty innuendos, sometimes shouting with abandon: "Boogie my woogie till my face turns cherry red!"

To render the sex act with the utmost force and detail, the boogie employs a conventional metaphor, which generations of piano players elaborated eventually into the most extravagant feat of musical mimesis since the storm sequence in Beethoven's *Pastoral Symphony.*

The musical image of the train associates readily with all those blues verses in which railroad figures as either a symbol of release from trouble or of return to a nostalgically recollected home, but the boogie's manipulation of this image is drastically different from its use in the poetry of the blues. Instead of merely alluding to the train from time to time by suggesting its rhythm or mimicking the sound of its whistle, the boogie fastens on the train with obsessional and manic intensity, seeking by every conceivable means to conjure up the machine in all its glory. Plunging down the rails, the music summons up first the massive weight and irresistible momentum of the locomotive then it focuses upon the eccentric ball-and-sock pattern of the pistons and drive wheels, the chattering polyrhythms of the trucks on the tracks, the plaintive cries of the great whistle wailing down wind in blue notes, the huffing and chuffing of the smokestack, the dissonant clinks and chinks of the chains and couplers, piling rhythm upon rhythm. Finally, as it nears the station, the music evokes the gradual subsidence of the great beast's energies as it crawls, spent and exhausted, to a stop, signalled by a final blast of its steamy breath.

This boldly extended and superbly sustained kinesthetic conceit demands to be understood in terms of both empathy and idolatry. What it testifies to is not the black man's intimate association with machines through work (though "work" is another black euphemism for sex) or his capacity to control machines (the simple-minded notion that informs those that equate fucking a woman with driving a car). What the boogie-woogie proclaims is black

17

man's longing to *be* a machine because he sees in its irresistible strength the ideal of his own imagined sexual prowess.

The identification of sex and mechanism, which is at the bottom of this equation of man and machine, could go no further in this period of pop music. Later, however, in the age of hard rock and heavy metal, and, later still, in the robot-ridden world of disco and rap, the concept triumphed completely. If, as T.S. Eliot observed, nothing has affected modern prosody more than the internal combustion engine, think of the effects which our industrial environment has had on pop music — and on the very constitution of our nervous system.

Once the blues had been boogied, the stage was set for the emergence of rhythm and blues, the parent of rock 'n' roll. R&B marks the end of the long ride which the blues had hitched on the jazz bandwagon. By the end of the ride, the wheels were spinning at a dizzying rate and the axles were smoking hot. The idea of making the blues jump had inspired during the war years a style of jazz that was called "jump." Jump bands were scaled-down jazz bands; they played simple riff tunes, getting on a blues phrase and riding it round and round until it assumed a feverishly spinning, hard-driving energy closely akin to the boogie. The first R&B bands were directly modeled on these jump combos. A disproportionate number of instruments — drums, bass, electric guitar, piano — were devoted to hammering out the beat, while the rest of the band, which might consist of nothing more than a pair of saxophones, would discharge all the other musical duties, from playing riffs to honking out rudimentary jazz solos. When the whole band would concentrate on the rhythm — the piano rolling a boogie bass with the left hand while clinking out triplets with the right, the drums doing a fast shuffle with an eight-to-the-bar beat on the top-hat cymbal, the horns riding the riff — the rhythm of the blues became the essence of the blues, making blues, in a phrase coined later, "beat music."

Culturally, the emergence of rhythm and blues has to be seen against the chaotic background of post World War II America. This country went into the war dancing the Lindy to the sound of the big bands and came out of the ordeal communing in solitude with the intimate voices of romantic crooners like Frank Sinatra and Perry Como. No sooner did the war end than the swing bands, which had assumed the institutional status of big league ball teams, suddenly sickened and died from a complication of illnesses, which had commenced with the war-time draft and ended with the post-war retreat into the security of home, family and TV. Jazz, which had gotten further and further "out" during the war, now became be-bop, an abstract and elliptical language completely beyond the comprehension of the common man, contemptuously tagged by the boppers as "the square from nowhere." By 1947, a good year to use as the breakthrough of R & B, American music had fallen into fractions. The various elements in the population no longer had a common language.

Black people in particular were left out in the cold. They couldn't identify with white pop music; most of them couldn't understand be-bop; they had lost most of their famous dance bands; their own best singers and musicians were intent on going over with the white public. The dilemma was resolved just as it was in 1920 when the first blues records were cut by black singers. The sensational success of these records in black communities all over the country persuaded the major companies that they had discovered a gold mine. They responded by developing the institution of the "race record," the black-oriented recording catalogued, advertised and distributed outside the normal channels of the record business. Now, in post-WWII, this old institution suddenly revived. The once-honorable but now offensive word "race" was abolished; it was replaced by the stupid redundancy "rhythm and blues." (Gospel-blues would have been much better.) As the majors were no longer interested in catering to this market, a rash of tiny independent labels sprang up to satisfy the demand.

The new "indie" operators belonged to a type familiar from the earliest days of the race record. Typically *Luftmenschen*, they worked out of their hats and off the top of their heads, baiting their hooks for fresh talent with preposterous promises of fame and wealth, chiseling their performers out of their rights and even credit for their work, and seeking always to steal a march on the competition — often by stealing one of the competition's tunes or performers. The indies were just what you would expect to find in such a hot-handed, hard-hustling, highly opportunistic business where the whole idea was to find a fresh gimmick and wrap it up fast in a cheap, thrown-together product that would return a quick buck. Though nothing that has ever been said or written about the indies would cause one to feel a moment's sympathy for them, the problems these schlockmeisters faced were of a kind that would tax the resourcefulness of even the most formidable hustler.

19

Established stars could not be used because they were too costly or under exclusive contract to a major label. That meant an endless talent hunt through every ghetto in the country. One ingenious solution was to arrange in each city an amateur contest with the first prize a recording contract with, say, Black Day Records. Naturally, the new "discovery," Little Retcher or Big Little, was not likely to provide much competition to Nat King Cole or Dinah Washington. Still, scores of strident-voiced waifs in the ghetto could blat out a blues line or vocalize a riff, "do-wop, do-wop," for two minutes and 58 seconds.

As for the tunes themselves, most blues lines, both musical and verbal, were in the public domain. If someone around the studio couldn't come up with a blues, there were always other ways of obtaining material. Consider, for example, the origin of the second most successful record in the entire history of R&B: *The Hucklebuck*. This crude sax solo named after a currently popular dance would probably impress most listeners today as the product of some anonymous bluessmith deep down in the urban jungle, or, to take a long shot, some very clever, chameleonlike song synthesizer in the Brill Building with a keen ear for the going thing. In fact, the author of the tune is none other than Charlie Parker, the genius of be-bop.

In 1945, Parker arrived for an important and history-making recording session at the Savoy studio in Newark. He brought with him a new blues line, which he had probably scribbled down in the cab on the way to the date. The spooky, haunting, low-riding riff, with its startling shout at the end, was titled *Now's the Time*. Though this riff tune was just the scaffolding on which Parker would raise his ingenious improvisations, it qualified in every sense as a composition. The A&R man who was running the session offered to buy the publishing rights. The price? $50. Parker made the sale on the spot, probably counting himself lucky to score the extra bread. Three years later, in 1949, Paul Williams released a jukebox version called *The Hucklebuck* (the name of a popular dance) that rode the top of the charts for thirty-two weeks and was "covered" by Tommy Dorsey, Frank Sinatra, Roy Milton and Lionel Hampton. It was the most successful R&B song of the year.

The punch line of this story is that the owner of Savoy, the hardly scrupulous Herman Lubinsky, resisted releasing *The Hucklebuck* for a long time because he felt, quite correctly, that it was just a rip-off of the Charlie Parker original. His inability to perceive the enormous commercial potential of the piece could be paralleled by countless other instances of this same failure of vision. The truth is that the hardest task faced by the indies was discerning their audience's tastes, a job not made any easier by the fact that this public was black and the indies were almost invariably white. A great amount of atrocious music atrociously performed was recorded atrociously. (R&B was the first blues style to grow up, as it were, in public: the classic, urban, boogie, and jazz blues were all highly evolved and associated with performers of genius before they were recorded.) Eventually, R&B shook down into a number of conventionalized genres.

One of the first to achieve popularity was the hard-driving, animalistically honking tenor sax fantasia. The hero of this style was Big Jay McNeeley, who would start off playing in the conventional position, then fall to the floor, wrestling with his horn like a demon. As he reached the climax of his act, he would kick his heels at the ceiling, while wringing from the instrument the screeching and honking sounds of a trussed hog on the killing floor. This psychodrama was a great favorite with ghetto audiences and was widely copied. Doubtless it associated in many people's minds with scenes they had witnessed in church: believers falling to the floor, speaking in tongues and "slain in the spirit."

The church influence was paramount in the work of singers like Sister Rosetta Tharpe and the young Dinah Washington, the first in a long line of shouting, belting soul singers that culminates in Aretha Franklin. Though the real exploitation of gospel had to wait for Ray Charles' big breakthrough in 1955, even in the forties, R&B was starting to take on a churchy aura.

The greatest star of the early R&B, the smoothest and most accomplished performer (and the only one whose records consistently made the white-oriented pop charts), was the jivey Louis Jordan, one of those ebullient and humorous figures who have always abounded on the black musical stage, from Louis Armstrong and Fats Waller to Cab Calloway and Dizzy Gillespie. Jordan's specialty was comically phrased and jauntily accompanied vignettes of ghetto life: a teenage party doused in blue lights where everybody does the boogie *real slow* or a Saturday night fish fry down South that is broken up by a police raid.

Comedy was one of the most important elements of R&B, as it was to be of rock 'n' roll. Both the ghetto black and the white teenager were prone to view themselves as the ridiculous victims of unfortunate circumstances. Eventually, the alliance of R&B and

21

humor would come to memorable focus in the work of Leiber and Stoller, who merged the Jewish talent for doing shtick with the blues tradition and black street jive to produce the best of all possible combinations of shticks and licks.

Though R&B was sauced with the salt and sass of the streets, it embraced just as eagerly the saccharine sweetness of the "Sepia Sinatras" and the hard-edged sentimentality of those black chanteuses with big tooshes who primp and pose before their vocal pierglasses as they dream wistfully of blue gardenias. These ladies, however, were no match for the ultimate virtuosos in the art of the lover's complaint: the juvenescent-sounding male vocal groups with ornithological names: the Orioles, Ravens, Robins, Penguins, Crows, ad infinaviary. These preening birds, always haloed with the plangency of an echoing overpass, carried sweet-talking soul to such heights of latinate extravagance and narcissism that finally their song-writers burst out spontaneously in soaring violins and erotic Latin American rhythms.

R&B was, in fine, the voice of the ghetto: the music of a whole people at a particular moment in its history. If that were all, however, it would not have leaped from the ghetto into the minds of the white kids all over the country, igniting the greatest cultural revolution in American history. To understand the real import of R&B, you have to see it in a much wider perspective as the Great Divide in the cultural history of pop America.

Up to the post-WWII period, popular culture was aimed primarily at adults and characterized by increasing urbanization and sophistication. After the war, these trends were reversed in consequence of two major demographic changes: the migration of millions of blacks from the rural South to the urban North and the maturation of the products of the post-war baby boom. The first development accounts for the character and popularity of the new R&B and its revolutionary effect on first black culture and then teen culture.

What R&B did was to turn the world of pop music on its head. Instead of aspiring to the sophistication and urbanity of swing, R&B performers gloried in earthiness and provinciality, providing their audiences with the entertainment equivalent of that "ole-time religion." Instead of working to achieve ease of execution and flawless technique, the R&B singer or instrumentalist concentrated on a primitive kind of expressionism that made technique seem irrelevent. Instead of sublimating emotions into purely musical moods, R&B offered the raw, uncut stuff that came from the gut. Love

22

became lust, humor became ridicule, melancholy became despair, and excitement was driven to frenzy or ecstasy. As the twin values of ethnicity and expressionism deepened and became more closely entwined, the music began to cast up from the depths of black culture more and more atavistic elements, until its goal became the revelation of the deepest essence of negritude. At that point, R & B received a new and more appropriate name: soul.

Ultimately, R & B worked its way out of the ghetto to become as rock 'n' roll the music of a new generation of white youth. The medium through which this process occurred was radio; however, for radio to carry the new gospel, there had first to arise a new breed of DJs, who were the music's first evangelists. The most famous of these men was Alan Freed, a complex and controversial character who has never been properly assessed. In the movie *American Hot Wax*, for example, he is made to appear a benevolent, idealistic and paternal figure, given to confessorlike communings with his young fans. On the other hand, when you trace out the long record of violent commotions, criminal practices and self-destructive behavior that ended this man's career and life prematurely, you get the sense of a much more dissonant and hostile personality, who actively sought the martyrdom he incurred.

The essence of Freed — and of most of the early white R & B jocks — lay in the character of the "white nigger": the man who deliberately adopts the speech, dress and lifestyle of the black ghetto, partly out of enthusiasm for the vitality of the ghetto and partly out of an angry rejection of the values of the white world. If *American Hot Wax* had wanted to offer a realistic portrait of "The Father of Rock 'n' Roll," it would have found an actor who was small and Jewish-looking, with big cow-eyes, sleek black hair, a husky Negroid voice barking out the jivey language of the ghetto and a riveting intensity of personality that made his every appearance on mike or on stage an occasion for emotional tantrums. Like all the great white niggers, going back to the days of Mezz Mezzerow — the man who turned Harlem on to marijuana — Freed identified exclusively with the extravagant and way-out side of ghetto life. In championing R & B, he made himself a verbal R & B man.

Freed's overnight success — at Cleveland in 1951, after years of being a mediocre jock at various stations in Ohio — did not attest to any special personal talents but simply to the voracious but hitherto unsuspected appetite for the new music. It had now been nearly ten years — a cultural generation — since the heyday of the big bands. No powerfully exciting beat music of any description had made itself felt through the white pop broadcasting medium within the memory of the kids who comprised Freed's audience. Though much of the substance of R&B was traditional, it was radically new to these youngsters. What's more, in the uptight, play-nice atmosphere of the fifties, rock was dynamite. No wonder the music was soon associated with the dreadful menace of juvenile delinquency.

By 1954, the year that Alan Freed established himself at the center of the pop music world in New York City, R&B had become rock 'n' roll. Freed gave the music this name to cleanse it of undesirable racial overtones. (It's a sign of how naive he and his audience were that nobody understood the phrase as a euphemism for sex, long familiar from old blues lyrics.) Rock 'n' roll soon became, however, not just a new term for black music but a phrase that signalled its adoption and adaptation by an entirely new audience. The blues, which had always been so indelibly black, was about to be bleached pure white. The place of this radical transformation? Memphis, Tennessee, home of Elvis Presley.

Many people think that the young Elvis Presley walked into a recording studio one day and created rock 'n' roll. Others, better informed, know that rock existed before Elvis, at least in the form of R&B, but they believe that Elvis was the first singer to mix country music with blues to produce the style known as rockabilly. Still others, making no claim that Elvis invented any style, assume that he was simply the first rock singer to score a great popular success, sparking a national fad. All of these ideas are false, but they do define very well the achievement of another singer, who was really the first star of rock 'n' roll — Bill Haley.

Haley's story is interesting not just because it reveals the origins of rock but because it furnishes such a sharp contrast to the Presley myth. Haley, a moon-faced, klutzy-looking dude, dressed in a corny tuxedo and adorned with an absurd cowlick, is not the sort of figure that inspires a myth. The long, complicated, trial-and-error saga of the uninspired but hard-plugging, small-time entertainer is, likewise, not the kind of tale that translates easily into legend. Yet, if one follows the winding trail of the young Bill Haley across the musical landscape of America in the late forties and early fifties, you see infinitely more of the background of rock than you would even if you had been looking over Elvis Presley's shoulder the day he cut his first record.

Born in 1925, ten long years before Elvis, and reared in the Philadelphia working-class suburb of Chester — an area that produced
a lot of rockers: Frankie Avalon, Fabian and The Four Aces (plus
Elvis's idol, Mario Lanza) — Haley was the son of a woman who
taught the piano and a man who haled from Kentucky and played
the mandolin country-style. From the age of seven, Bill Haley was
crazy about country music. His great ambition all through his early
years was to become the country's leading yodeler. At an amateur
contest in his teens, Haley met the greatest country musician of
modern times, Hank Williams, and received the sort of encouragement that would thrill any young boy. At 15, Haley dropped out of
school and began touring the country during the war. In 1944, a
decade before Elvis cut his first record, Haley made his debut on
discs with a band called The Downhomers; their record was titled
We're Recruited.

For years Haley alternated between working at radio stations and
traveling with a variety of groups and shows on the road. He toured
with a little medicine show and a big country radio show, the *WLS
Barn Dance*, just as Elvis was to do in later years. In the course of
his travels around the country, Haley dug the boogie-woogie in New
Orleans and the early R & B in Chicago. He also heard a lot of Western swing and even Dixieland jazz. Once he quit the business completely. On numerous occasions, he cut records that received no
attention. Eventually, he wound up exactly where he had started:
back in Chester, working at a little local station as the sports announcer and record librarian.

By 1951, Haley began to move gradually out of country music into
the now mushrooming business of R & B. With his latest band, The
Saddlemen, he cut a cover version of the previous year's number-
nine R & B disc: *Rocket 88* (interestingly enough, the first hit recorded by Sam Phillips, the man who would give Elvis his start in
the business three years later). As usual, nothing came of Haley's
effort, but he kept to the same course: not just covering R & B hits
but now trying to write them. In 1953, calling his band Bill Haley
and the Comets, the erstwhile yodeler covered a record called *We're
Gonna Rock the Joint Tonight*. On the flip side, he did a country
tune, anticipating the pattern employed by Sam Phillips on all of
Elvis's Sun records. Haley was just leaving Nashville, after having
made a successful appearance on *Grand Old Opry*, when he learned
that the new R & B record was a hit.

At this point, Haley realized the incongruity of his position. He was fronting a country and western band that was making a score in the radically different world of R & B. Being a seasoned professional, he automatically changed his image. Overnight his band discarded their ten-gallon hats and cowboy boots in favor of the tuxedos that were the working clothes of pop performers. At this point, one of Haley's songs was adopted by Allan Freed. The reason was the lyrics, which ran: "Rock, rock, rock everybody/ Roll, roll, roll everybody." Haley was right on the money. His next record, *Crazy, Man, Crazy*, scored a bull's eye. As it rode up the pop charts, white rock was born.

The birth of rock out of the brain of a white country musician strikes one at first as being paradoxical: what could be further removed from the ghetto hipster than the hillbilly? In truth, there was a great gap in the two musical and cultural traditions. At the same time, however, there were numerous points of contact, similarity, and cross-influence. Even as far back as the first country musician to become a national star, Jimmie Rogers, the blues had been part of the hillbilly singer's repertoire. Later, in the thirties, when the influence of swing became as paramount as was that of rock in the sixties, Bob Wills pioneered the style known as Western Swing, whose mingling of country strings and swing rhythm dovetailed neatly with rockabilly. Finally, there was the country version of the boogie-woogie, which was called Honky Tonk and became very popular during World War II. Though the black essence did not penetrate any of these styles beyond the surface, the fact is that this essence did not penetrate rock 'n' roll any deeper. All that was required to bridge the gap from country to R & B to arrive at rock was a matching of surfaces.

Even matching surfaces, however, demands that the performer have a mastery of the idioms being combined. In the case of Bill Haley, this mastery was achieved through years of professional experience as he struggled to find the winning combination. Elvis Presley, on the other hand, scored a hit the very first time he entered the recording studio as a professional. What's more he went right on in the following years to score one hit after another, in the single greatest exhibition of chart busting that had ever been seen. As so much of his material, early and late, was derived from the early R & B style, the question arises: how did Elvis gain his mastery over this black idiom? The answer invariably given is that Elvis grew up among black people way down in the jungle of the "deep South" and that singing black was part of his birthright. To anybody who has followed Elvis's life closely from childhood to the threshold of his career, it is obvious that this customary view of his musical roots is just another portion of the Elvis myth.

The simple truth is that Elvis Presley had no significant contact at any point in his life with black people. He grew up in a white enclave in East Tupelo, lived in a white neighborhood in Tupelo proper, and divided his youth in Memphis between a white housing project and a white high school. As he was tied to his mother's apron strings until he was fifteen, there is no possibility that he had a secret life among the blacks. Once he struck off on his own and began working as a singer, he probably visited the blues bars on Beale Street, but by that point his musical sensibility had been firmly shaped by his two primary sources, the white gospel sings he attended regularly and the local black radio station to which he listened at home.

The college of musical knowledge that graduated Elvis with his degree in black arts was not some ghetto nightclub or theater or honky-tonk roadhouse. Nor was it the black church or the experience of working with black farm hands or prisoners or factory laborers — or any of the fanciful notions that fanciful fans have entertained. Indeed, this whole concept of how an artist relates to a tradition is preposterously naive. It is the cultural equivalent of saying: "You are what you eat." It is also close to saying: "All black people have a natural sense of music and dance, and if you hang out with them long enough, it will rub off on you." If this is the secret of becoming an Elvis Presley, it is a wonder that the ghetto isn't crammed with aspiring rock stars.

What Americans are reluctant to allow is the possibility that an artist can achieve something solely through the exercise of his imagination. Though lip service is often paid to the idea of imagination, what is generally understood by the term is simply fantasy. When it comes down to art that carries conviction, it is assumed there must be some model in the artist's past experience. Yet nothing is more apparent about Elvis — or the Beatles — than the fact that they approached black music not as apprentices learning a craft but as enthusiasts offering their impressions of what they had heard and admired. Elvis was not the first to do anything but be Elvis, which simply meant hurling himself on the old materials with a remarkable amalgam of energy and excitement, a good ear and a great voice, and above all, an extraordinary appearance and body language that soon made him the most imitated entertainer since

27

Chaplin — who also had an eccentric way of moving. The most revealing statement Elvis ever made about his relationship to black music was offered in the course of a luncheonette interview with a local reporter at Charlotte, North Carolina in 1957. Defending himself against the New York reviewers, Elvis snarled: "Them critics don't like to see nobody win doing any kind of music they don't know nuthin' about. The colored folk been singing it and playing it just the way I'm doin' now, man, for more years than I know. *Nobody paid it no mind till I goosed it up.*" That says it all.

The good days at Sun Records didn't last long, and soon Elvis was cutting his new sides in New York or Hollywood. It wasn't until the mid-sixties that Memphis finally put its name on a nationally popular style of music, the Memphis Soul Sound. Not much has been written on Stax-Volt records, but its history constitutes the last word on the theme of Memphis as the home of the blues. Founded by a white bank clerk named Stewart, who moonlighted as a country fiddler, and his sister, whose married name was Axon; financed with a second mortgage on Mrs. Axon's home; installed in an abandoned movie theater in the ghetto; and staffed almost exclusively with black personnel, none of whom were allowed to sign company checks because, as Mrs. Axon informed me, there was no need for it save their desire "to show off for their own kind," Stax-Volt became the last great plantation in the South. Opening its doors to the talent that had always sprung up in the region, it developed a whole series of new stars ranging from Otis Redding to Sam and Dave to Booker T and the MGs and Albert King. Even more important, it developed a new idiom that was the southern-black antithesis of the northern-black style made famous by Motown.

Instead of mining the angst of the ghetto and raiding the soundtrack orchestrations of Hollywood movies, Stax reached back into the history of its region and revived the ancient song of the South. Its festive brasses were reminiscent of black minstrelsy and the TOBA circuit of black vaudeville; its rhythms, like the shuffle and the heebie-jeebie (a dance that mimicked the movements of sufferers from malaria, who would stagger about and claw themselves) went back to the innocent times before World War I; its lyricism was the sweet, sensuous, relaxed singing of men and women out in the country on warm summer nights surrounded with fragrant crops and cutting the hearts out of sugary melons. It was all a prophecy of that longing to go back to the turn of the century, "where everythin's happen'," according to a song of the day, that led in the next decade to the great ragtime revival.

Insofar as any black music was ever "made" in Memphis, it was the Memphis Soul Sound, but when I visited the studio and quizzed its creative people, like the song-writing team of Porter and Hayes, they told me flat-out that theirs was a labor not so much of invention as of recovery. "We'll go out to a stone soul picnic [not yet the title of a song]," they told me, "and sooner or later, we'll pick up something, a phrase, a lick, a line that we can build into a song." They were hip young men who recognized the value of this old-timey stuff in the current market; their challenge was to go forth like truffle hunters to find, then skillfully package, black soul. They were, in other words, the W.C. Handys of their day. With Stax-Volt, the blues had come full circle, having proceeded in six fertile decades from Memphis to Memphis.

Always Bach
Paul West

HER WHOLESOME BREATH sweetened by violet cachous, she waddled off to hear and nod pleasedly at the bells, taken to them by Kathleen Kent, who made her livelihood by escorting well-bred children around the village, in her plaid toilet-bag a wet facecloth and some extra hankies freshly starched, as well as a compass and a whistle for emergencies. Gradually and fitfully, his mother emerged from the penumbra created by Kathleen Kent — his *infant* mother, he reminded himself, with whom he was taking undue liberties. Kathleen was a provident protectress, with a much bitten lower lip, the badge of all she wanted to get off her chest and saved for later, at home on Southgate. He guessed at the worry, the tension, the boredom of being Kathleen, of being everyone's Kath. What was she, he made her wonder. Nanny, guardian, sentry, guide, scout, retainer, or what? Here, in her charge, was a little girl who doted on bells, who seemed to hear them all the time anyway and who marched so deliberately toward the church only to gain some kind of amplified corroboration: perhaps a bulge of pressure in the air as, at ground level, the two of them neared the door. What his mother Hildred Fitzalan and Kath Kent at last stood near, their breath briefly held, when the ringing began, was not the big bells up in the belfry, marooned among windows with Gothic points and open slats, bragging and bullying, but little handbells rung on leather straps. Kath saw some half-dozen men standing between the altar and the pews lazily plying their forearms to make a sound that made her flinch and wish for other bells from a baby's harness, a Christmas tree, a cat's neck. Or a lazing cow in an upland pasture. The small boy next to her, but none of Kathleen Kent's concern, had a high color and hair black as that of the blackest dogs. He seemed not to flinch, not even during moments of emphasis when the handbells didn't so much chime as yelp and stop, their clappers quelled by a finger thrust into the bell's mouth. He appeared not to hear at all, finding her more interesting than the bells, half-grinning at her as if they two (and the other children) were trespassing in that vaulted chill where the noise of pigeons filtered down from up on high.

It was a meeting wordless and unintended, at the close of a century in which entertainment remained humble and untechnical, and people strolled for miles to hear handbells, or the church organist of a nearby parish, or just to watch larks ascending.

The boy saw an ample, resolute mouth, a grayish-green eye hue he had never seen before (and at once assumed appropriate to fishes and finches), and brown hair wrapped in too many ribbons. Older and taller than he, she "was musical"; he heard the phrase and wondered if, frail as her wrists looked, she had come there to ring a handbell or two, or even to sing in the intervals of ringing. They said nothing, not with Katherine Kent standing so close, her head hidden in a dark-brown globe of the tightest curls, but it amounted to their first tryst, by courtesy of the campanology club, to visit which during a performance was a "treat" for her, whereas for him it was an escape: all he had to do was walk through one passage, cross a path, trot through the graveyard, and enter the church, where sometimes, up in the belfry, his father let him help to mend the ropes, rolling the new knots with his bare, boy's feet. There were other mysteries too, which his father controlled, but for her it was just another temple of music: a mere extension of Chopin. They would encounter each other again here, they both knew that, and one word would lead to another, certainly before they were almost dead and brought back in here in flower-strewn boxes. To say hello to her, he yodelled once, tossing his voice to the belfry for the echo, which she answered by extending one hand and playing a rippling chord in mid-air. The pianist and her swain had met.

For days afterward, he tried to imagine what her life was like. Were there really piano stools among the well-to-do? What did the well-to-do do? Did the girl play for people or only to herself? Had she been born able to do it, like a robin or a thrush? Did she wash her hands first? What if the piano keys were dusty? Did she go to school? Not his, or he would have seen her in the playground. Was there another school, where piano players went? There was, and it was called Ruthin College, only a few hundred yards from his own school, but in a different dimension, where the girl learned grammar, read Lord Alfred Tennyson and Matthew Arnold, and studied Elocution so that she would be well-spoken whenever music failed. As for her, his yodel had made her wonder if he came from Switzerland or some northern mountainous area where he was obliged to tend sheep or goats. She wanted to play piano (pianoforte was the correct word, she knew) while he yodelled, wondering how it would sound. His jersey was torn, but perhaps his mind was whole and shone when you spoke to it without talking down. She had no idea, then, that his parents had daringly named him Hereward, after Hereward the Wake who defended the Fen country against Norman invaders. The attempt at grandeur or myth had collapsed into Herry, which had fast become Harry, as commonplace a name as a boy could have. She, named Hildreth, had fast become Hilly.

In this matter of naming they came together, both sets of parents having been influenced by the local parson, who wanted to bring old Anglo-Saxon names back into currency. So this once-Roman village in the Byron–D.H. Lawrence country had people walking around in it who, at a pinch or during a thunderclap, would answer if called upon to such names as Wulfric, Aelfric, Athelstan, Wenhaver, Winifried, and Hroswitha, which readily enough had lapsed into Rick or Rich, Alf, Stan, Wendy, Winny, and Rosy, the ancient heroic legacy lost beneath a chummy sound that put paid to anything outlandish, which was how they sounded even though they came from the heart of the land's heart. Harry and Hilly, almost vanishing into extreme informality, made virtually anonymous by similarity, wandered into life together, little occupied by their names' ancestry, more intent upon what force it was that had lured them together and taught their eyes the trick of mutual smiling even when they had no idea of what to talk about beyond My dad's a butcher (hers), My dad's down the pit. Harry wore boots whose laces dangled, whereas Hilly wore button-up boots fastened with a special hook. They met often enough at the handbell ringing or until shooed away, when the organist came to practice in an otherwise empty church, and Harry and Hilly felt they had been rolled up in some big melodic blanket she called Always Bach.

Hilly could come to see Harry only when accompanied by Kath Kent, whom Hilly's parents thought prophylactic, so she sometimes recruited her two elder brothers, Thurman and George, who in turn brought to the church (or the river bridge down the slope behind it) Edith, who had a lovely voice in the making. They two had one girl friend between them. She sang for them both, with German strain for Thurman, in a manner more French for George. Truly she sang for everyone who would listen, her gift being unquenchable and unshy. But Harry had never heard Hilly play, not until they arranged for him to pass by Number 7 Market Street, next to the fly-loud meatshop entrance, and listen at six o'clock as she tapped her way through scales, Bach, Chopin, and something by Sir Hubert Parry. Harry always tried to whistle some of the tunes while going away, but he found them hard to memorize, even to pick out, so he went away making a vague whistling sound, an honorable sound of leaking air, even as he tried to come to terms with the mystery of it, of her, whose nimble hands knew something without having learned it, whose lilting tunes at once set Edith off into a small girl's coloratura, and the two of them leaving the three boys behind in a landswill of dumbfounded admiration. Boys were for baffling, that was all. Girls were angels in disguise, tuneful phantoms who sang pure notes to purify the thoughts of boys. The five became a little gang, with Harry the only one from the wrong side of the tracks, and he learning fast to cross. Then she took to bringing her third brother, little Douglas, the weaker and paler for having been born so late. Douglas cried.

But not Harry, ruddy of face and quiet of tongue. His own mother was producing a child a year and the tiny house on Church Row (two up, two down) was filling with siblings he would rather have done without. Hilly's mother, on the other hand, was not: Douglas would be the very last. Harry, the first, and Douglas became firm friends; indeed, Harry delighted in this well-to-do clique, their big Great Dane called Ben, who always came romping with them through Reresby Woods, and watched them like a shaggy superintendent when they built leaf houses, climbed trees, paddled in the stream among the minnow or plunged their arms deep into Woody Nook spring. Nobody at home missed him anyway, and he began to wonder which family he belonged to, graft that he was. To a father who chipped coal from the bowels of the earth and came home ebony, needing to soak in the big iron bath in front of the kitchen fire with the tots trying to climb in with him, he preferred one who bought sheep, pigs, and cows, then brought them home to slaughter, this done with humane killer and a long stout rope that tugged the doomed animal's head low, with a dozen volunteers on its other end. There was more color, more drama, to the abattoir, although he could see that coal and blood had much in common. So: he belonged to two families that required a great deal of washing. Not that Hilly's brothers were destined for the trade of slaughter. No fear, they said. They were going to be metallurgists, George and Douglas certainly, Thurman just perhaps. He added steel to blood and coal, just supposing that if he mingled with enough children he would run into lead, honey, gold, and acid. It was one way of discovering the world.

It was to Hilly, pianist and reciter, however, that he clung the most, easily dreaming her into a magical creature who one day soon would go to London to take an especially hard examination. It was for her, mainly, that dusty, taciturn men visited her parents' home, *to tune* the piano (although you never, he understood, said the last bit). *To choon.* That was how you said it. When they had gone, she played all the better and felt mighty important, a monopolist of vibration, a queen of yet another ivory coast. He too, he told her, would soon be taking an examination to see if he was clever enough for the grammar school her brothers went to, and then (if he passed) the great circle of their lives would be complete, for Edith went to school with Hilly. It was as if some enormous multi-colored web were heaving into view past the horizon, with petals and jewels threaded into it, all theirs for the plucking: the promised life, the life to come, that some parents prated of, not his.

Most of all, in this realm of guaranteed magic or inevitable reward, he liked Hilly's telling him that the music she played, or even that of the handbell players, was a pale imitation of another music with which the world was full, although few might hear it. The church said it was there, though she trusted parsons little and looked to her mother, whom she believed much more. "It comes from —" He couldn't finish.

"Up there, you," she said. "In the sky, if you like, although it's under the golf links too, and in the dams, the rivers, the woods. It's inside *you*, silly."

In that case, then, it was down in the mines, in the pit, and it ran through the blood of the slaughtered cows, sheep, pigs, of her father, and it would resound along the steel of George and Douglas. He felt for the first time, at the hands of this pantheistic prodigy who played piano, in touch with something worthy of being alive — all the fuss of being born, of getting sick, of getting up early every morning, of going to school. Some things he read about at school enthralled him (history and battles, for instance), but this was different, this vast armada of light and color that sailed up to your bedroom window, full of Chopin and Bach that only she could hear as they should be played. He fell into the web of guileless adulation, at last a member of something that wasn't a family.

Harry adored to concentrate on his school lessons, most of all the Wars of the Roses and anything to do with Napoleon. He found he could do that at the same time as pondering what Hilly told him about what lay beyond what he could see and hear, almost as if he were a dog hearing what only dogs could hear. He, however, was not a musician, and he sometimes got it wrong, telling her that he could see clowns and acrobats in mid-air, sticking their index-fingers in the corners of their mouths and pulling down to make an almost permanent grimace. He saw waterspouts too, plagues of locusts and stampeding buffalo. That, she told him, was imagination, not (she said sternly) to be confused with the other stuff that was coming through from the angels or from God, or simply from amassed human memories of all the dead, including those killed in mining accidents and never brought to the surface. Entombed. There was music in the air, she said: a crude way of putting it, but it was as well to get things straight at the outset. Then, he told her, if it kept coming through, who needed pianists to play it? We need pianists, she said, to keep its confidence up, to make it feel the whole thing was worthwhile, and then he said it must be like the lightning, at which she giggled, telling him he had no *method* (her mother's word). No, he admitted it, but he was anxious to learn, to hear, to hear.

He thought he was getting the point, but he could never be sure. Perhaps he was; millions of grown-ups had died gibbering in the attempt, losing faith in their Creator as they did so. What should a small boy know of such things beyond the fact that, when you needed to cheer yourself up, you were able to do so? No, she said, tenderly instructive, it's like a current, a chorus, not interrupting the music you play, and not quite the same as it either. It was like the sky against which someone was a cloud. He dimly knew then that it was a background/foreground problem suitable for musical professionals only, though similar to what he had heard through some ricochet about the Boer War and the African *veldt*. At dusk your eyes played tricks and you failed to see what was out there while seeing what was not. Was it the same just before dawn too? He half-knew, having at an early age tried to imagine what his father's life was like, slotted into a foot-high cavity in the coal, chopping away sideways as if to embed himself horizontally deeper. This image had made him choke and cough, which his father presumably never did; but Harry knew the century was over in which they sent boys up chimneys to sweep, and bottom-naked too; so they would not be sending children down the mines either, as long as there was a good supply of older men who didn't mind getting caked with coal dust and, indeed, regarded it as a veneer of honor and courage. Harry loved music, he was sure of that.

His mind kept going back to what Hilly had told him. He knew she couldn't quite get it into words, and she certainly couldn't play it because she wasn't playing her own music, but Chopin and Always Bach. One day perhaps she would write something and then he would know. In the meanwhile he would have to make do with an approximation that went like this: All minds think more than they need to, than they need to in order to speak, for example; so some of this excess sometimes got through as music or electricity, as did what people remembered. It was an Over-Soul that he and Hilly were thinking of, or something such. She knew that music was a domain, a kingdom, not something shut away in a cupboard to be opened when company came and they wanted a little rondo to set them at ease. Not that. It was what her sense of melody splashed about in, but she wasn't going to tell Harry something as sloppy as that. It was what roamed through her mind as she was falling asleep, making her want to get up and write it down, it was so beautiful, having come out of intrinsic nowhere; but she was always too late, it came too fast, it wouldn't wait, it was too spread out and ample, like all the gold and gossamer cloaks from an enormous hunt ball. Hilly had made contact with the natural lyricism of the mind, with its steady surplus, when it not so much celebrated anything at all but merely exercised its golden mental throat, as when Edith sang by the reservoir, alone.

One Saturday, after all the pomp and warnings of the living room (Be a good boy, don't climb on things, don't touch anything, don't tap with your heels), Hilly took Harry upstairs to the music room, and he suddenly realized that the sound he had stood to hear in Market Street had been coming from above him, falling down on him, a shower. What a fancy room this was, full of fire irons, gilt-bound books, vast paintings of oxen and horses, rugs he sank into. It was a room like the soft planted earth of a queen. There stood the piano, a grand, with a vase of daffodils atop it like something that had grown wilfully upward from the lid. Might not a heavy-handed player spill the water? Look, she told him, cranking up the lid of the piano stool, revealing the big blue volumes of Chopin, Liszt, and Always Bach, nodding at him to lift them, and then together they adjusted the first one into place on the music rack, flipping up the two brass sprigs that held the pages back. She did not play, though, she just wanted him to see the piano at its best, and she was not allowed to raise the big palette-shaped lid either. She motioned him to sit on the piano stool and try to decipher the music, and he laughed, said something about metal-ur-gy (spaced thus). It was not for him, but he loved the sounds. "Play, please," he said. "It'll be better hearing in here than out there in the street." Off she went, making him wonder how hands so small could master so many keys; she played fast and with much brio, transporting him again into that enormous, vivid hinterland she had told him about, giving him the same complete, heart-stopping dream and, after a few minutes more of Chopin, making him wonder why humans did anything else with their lives when this flood of delicacy might be had for a little elbow-grease and some memory work. He decided then and there to be a pianist too. Well, in his next life, if he was asked. He had other things to do with the present one, but he would forever, in both this life and the next, be a listener, a dreamer at the keyboard, lifted or lofted to that high abyss called music, though it deserved a better name that told of its coming-from-within quality. Hilly said it came from all over the world, but Harry had begun to think it came up like a spring within you, and never ran dry.

In Nomine

David Rattray

Ranging the symptoms separately, one beneath the other, start a fresh line with each new circumstance mentioned by the patient or friends.

— Samuel Hahnemann,
Organon of Medicine (1833)

ONE JULY EVENING riding the Greyhound between Hartford and Springfield, I covered a notebook page with question marks, which I drew to look like things that hiss and crepitate: ears, waves, conchs, swans, scorpions, a poised cobra. What was that ice cold tea doing in a can, and Planter's Peanuts in a plastic pouch no bigger than a teabag? Is music the art of speaking extravagantly? That's what Ives said it is. Thinking this way is like skipping stones on a moonlit lake of a summer evening.

I notice steam on my breath. Hölderlin makes snow muffle a bell. I think about a certain ancient type of music, which the musicologist Denis Stevens refers to as "that once mysterious melange of plainsong and polyphony, the In Nomine . . ."

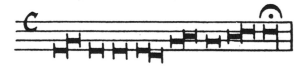

An exclusively English genre nowadays almost entirely forgotten, In Nomine is a form that came into being during the reign of Henry VIII and died out shortly before 1700. Although many of the historical questions concerning it have been answered, the genre remains (at least to me) deeply mysterious.

In Nomine gets its name from the fact that John Taverner (1490–1545) set one of his masses to a certain old plainchant tune, *Gloria tibi Trinitas*, and then he or one of his students rewrote the *In*

38

Nomine section of that mass' Benedictus as an independent piece for four viols, later transcribed for keyboard at Oxford around 1530. This transcription was the first In Nomine. The Gregorian original:

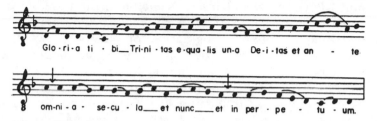

Glo·ri·a ti · bi__Tri·ni·tas e·qua·lis un·a De·i·tas et an — te. om·ni·a · se·cu · la__et nunc__et in per · pe · tu · um.

The tune works as a cantus firmus against which other livelier musical lines are added to create a web of polyphony. A variety of ancient plainsong tunes were set in the same way at this time. It was a commonplace technique in compositions for instrumental ensemble or keyboard, but none ever developed to the same degree of fantastic elaboration as the In Nomine.

According to a fictitious account appearing in Foxe's *Book of Martyrs*, Taverner was a secret convert to Protestantism and when exposed nearly suffered burning at the stake as a heretic but was spared when Wolsey said, "He is but a musician." Taverner, the story continues, remained incarcerated for a time, eventually to be released, ashamed at having "made songs to popish ditties in the time of his blindness." To rewrite one of the best of his compositions for performance sans ditty was only fitting; or rather, it would have been, if the foregoing story had been true. Since the story is not true, one can only speculate on what may have motivated this step from sacred polyphony to abstract secular composition. Maybe the motive was one of simple pleasure, the intellectual and tactile pleasure of developing, and elaborating upon, an interesting theme at the keyboard.

The words *in nomine* hark back to the Palm Sunday story. Riding in triumph into Jerusalem, Jesus was greeted as the Messiah by a cheering crowd: "Blessed is he who comes in the name of the Lord (*in nomine Domini*)."

When Taverner's first In Nomine appeared people were again looking for the Messiah, hoping for the new world that had been predicted for sometime after the year 1500. Other words associated with In Nomine, words of the *Gloria tibi Trinitas*, likewise indicated grand turning-points: ". . . before the beginning, and now, and forevermore." But from the plainsong skeleton of the In Nomine as performed in a keyboard setting, with voices flowing round it in ever-increasing rhythmic and figurative complexity, the words are absent, vanished. Only the tune that accompanied them for centuries lingers on, inaudible to any but the initiated. Still, a memory that words were once there haunts the music as it shimmers between major and minor. In Nomine does to plainsong what melismatic plainsong did to the words. It stretches beyond recognition. In In Nomine, the ghost of a word takes a shape and becomes the shape, and the shape becomes what the word means. Like an airfoil advancing over a vacuum and filled by an upward rush of air, the plainsong lifts.

In 1725 the music historian Roger North, who had heard In Nomine performances when a boy half a century earlier, confessed a distaste: "In the In Nomines I never could see a cadence complete, but proffers and balks innumerable . . . In Nomine is a sort of harmonious murmur, rather than music, not unlike a confused singing of birds in a grove." The very qualities that repelled in 1725 may attract today.

John, also known as William, Blitheman (1525–91) was the first composer to write In Nomines purely for keyboard. His set of six defined the idiom.

Following his teacher's lead, Blitheman's pupil John Bull (1563–1628), who was to become the greatest keyboard player of the day, composed a series of twelve In Nomines in sets of three. Although a Catholic, Bull may also have had affinities with the invisible order that sprang up at exactly that time, the Rosicrucians, whose members were said to share knowledge of occult and magical sciences, such as transmutation of metals, power over the elements and elemental spirits, and ultimately a vision of universal transformation. In his Great In Nomine (number 9) Bull lays out each note of the tune in the bass in long measures of eleven quarter-notes, or 22 eighths, which he changes proportionally to 33 in the concluding *tripla* section.

40

A wave: I think of a trill in which the notes blend and overlap *legatissimo.*

At Indian Wells, a six-inch-broad jellyfish, pink-rimmed with long scalloped arcs like pale green meringue. A choppy gray surf, wind northeast. Minutes ago, or so it seems, I saw wild roses still blooming behind the dunes, and it's winter.

"Snow muffles the supper bell . . ." As Heidegger explicates this line by Hölderlin, *snow* means the winter of the soul. *Supper* stands for a banquet held in the evening of time, and the poet's voice is the *bell* that summons to this exalted repast, marking the end of one era and the onset of the next.

At a dinner party I meet a German writer on art and music, Jörg von Uthmann, who deplores the cult of Heidegger. An unpleasant, evil fellow, he explains. People do always find Mephisto more interesting than Faust. But there it's a fallen angel. Here, we have a fallen petit bourgeois. "Just look at the pictures of him — a demented peasant!" Eileen Myles, sitting next to him, rejoins, "That could be something to shoot for."

According to Busoni, the sostenuto pedal is a photograph of the sky.

The In Nomine flourished at a time when — in the words of a contemporary — "many chose rather to fiddle at home than go out and be knocked on the head abroad." A time similar to the present. Like Bull and his colleague Thomas Tomkins (1572–1656), we live in an age that fulfills Ezekiel 8, in which it is written that people are sitting in darkness, "each man in his room of pictures."

Imagine the octogenarian Tomkins in his tower room overlooking College Lane, Worcester, a dissident under Puritan occupation, living in retirement with a library of manuscripts and a keyboard, copying out old In Nomines and making a half-dozen new ones that were to be almost the last ever composed.

Sometime in the 1630s, Tomkins had acquired a 100-year-old manuscript book of keyboard music in which he wrote marginal notes such as: "A good old, indeed very good . . ." Next to one of his own

David Rattray

The first keyboard In Nomine. In Nomine with ornamentation, by John Taverner: Oxford Christ Church Music MS 371.

43

compositions, an *Ut, re, mi*, he advises: "Use as many or as few as you will of these many wayes upon this playnesong."

Each in a room of pictures in the illumined shell, globus mundi, or light-filled room in a seawave. Bull's 6th In Nomine is a wave. How to undress a wave. "When major and minor alternate continuously, the two begin to shimmer and coalesce" (Busoni, *A New Esthetic of Music*, 1911).

"Floating tonality . . . a tiny cosmos of flickering iridescence and tentative stability" (Glen Watkins, *Gesualdo*, 1974).

"Your Name is flowing oil" (*Song of Songs* 1.3).

"Everything which is said or described concerning GOD is false" (*Preaching of Peter*, Hom. 2.40).

Wilfred Mellers on Bull's Great In Nomine: "Sounds rather like Vaughan Williams, only more modern."

The only In Nomine composer to lead a disreputable life was Bull. His was a flamboyant series of mishaps and misadventures not surprising in a favorite of Elizabeth I. After the Queen's death in 1603, however, Bull was increasingly out of place in King James's court. Eventually, enemies obtained testimony concerning Bull's misdeeds, and he fled to Antwerp, there to spend the rest of his life as Cathedral organist, despite English attempts emanating from the King in person to extradite him.

> "He did steal out of England through the guilt of a corrupt con-
> science, to escape the punishment, which notoriously he had de-
> served, and was designed to have inflicted on him by the hand
> of justice, for his incontinence, fornication, adultery, and other
> grievous crimes" (William Trumbull, English Ambassador in Brus-
> sels, March 31, 1614).

There are keyboard In Nomines by several other composers: Robert White, William Byrd, Nicholas Carleton, John Lugge. The White In Nomine is a bluff, clangorous piece one imagines being performed by a brass band although it was originally written for a consort of viols. The Byrd is a whimsical exercise in Design Style with a lovely ending, written when Byrd was a teenager. The Carleton In Nomine is a duet. Lugge's seven In Nomines have remained in manuscript,

unpublished and doubtless unperformed from the time of their composition, early in the 1600s, down to the present.

Amazingly, there are no biographies of either Byrd or Bull. Bull's
20th-century editor Thurston Dart announced a forthcoming Bull
biography but died without publishing it. A biography, *Thomas
Tomkins 1572–1656*, by Denis Stevens was published by Dover in
1967. Keyboard In Nomine is discussed in Willi Apel's monumental
History of Keyboard Music to 1700 (Indiana, 1972), John Caldwell's
English Keyboard Music Before the Nineteenth Century (Praeger,
1973), Walker Cunningham's *The Keyboard Music of John Bull* (UMI
Research Press, 1985), and Wilfred Mellers' two-part essay on Bull
published in *Musical Quarterly* (1954).

There is little on Lugge, apart from a short article on him in
Grove's and the pages in Caldwell describing his plainsong settings
as "splendidly resourceful examples of their type": this was how I
learned of their existence in the first place.

They were all dissidents of one kind or another. Taverner a Protes-
tant when his King was still a Catholic. Byrd, Bull, and Lugge all
Catholics under Elizabeth and James. Tomkins a Church of England
man under Cromwell.

Walker Cunningham, in his book on Bull's keyboard music, taxes
Tomkins and Lugge with a naive admiration of Bull's virtuosic manner that, he says, leads them to overload the In Nomine genre with
elaborations and complexities to the point where it collapses under
its own weight. According to Cunningham, In Nomine reached its
highest and final flowering in Bull. Tomkins and Lugge represent a
decadence, a degeneration of the form. This view is not borne out
by a closer acquaintance with the In Nomines of Tomkins and
Lugge. While Tomkins owned copies of most if not all of Bull's In
Nomines, his manner of handling the genre diverges sharply from
Bull's. Tomkins's In Nomines have the looseness and informal charm
of a masterful improvisation, whereas Bull constructs with a rigor
comparable to Bach's. Moreover, Tomkins's In Nomines, like much
of his other keyboard music, have a warmth and sweetness poles
apart from the extraordinarily sharp, energetic, often chilly fancy
that is Bull's. Lugge is another story altogether. He exhibits no influence of either Bull or Tomkins. His models go back to the age

preceding theirs, to Blitheman, and even further back, to Redford. At his most ambitious, (in his *Ut, re, mi, fa, sol, la* and in the In Nomine first published here, which I have transcribed from Oxford, Christ Church MS 49) Lugge is a composer of a most vivacious and engaging originality, an innovative, witty, and hauntingly melodious spirit. His name means *ear*. That is entirely fitting. The ear, Domenico Scarlatti once remarked, is the only organ that a musician must aim to please.

Born in 1588, year of the Armada, Lugge was only about 15 when hired as organist at Exeter Cathedral. He held the post until 1645 or thereabouts. After the Puritan occupation of Exeter he vanishes from the record. Long before that he was suspected of being a Roman Catholic, or at least of harboring Catholic sympathies. He had a brother, Peter, in Lisbon who seems to have been embroiled in political intrigue. The mere fact of receiving a letter from the brother caused John Lugge serious trouble. He was examined by Bishop Cotton on January 24, 1618 and made a pretence of submitting to the Church of England. Apart from this and a few other scraps of information, all that remains of Lugge is his music: a number of services and anthems, as well as the manuscript (probably in his own hand) containing seven In Nomines, two other plainsong settings, a short jig for harpsichord or virginals, and three voluntaries or fantasias for double organ (that is, a modern-type organ with two manuals).

I'm coming to realize that Lugge's In Nomines are the goal of my search, insofar as it has been a search for a music that no one else plays, performs, edits, or editorializes upon. To get in touch with the perennial tradition going all the way back into the black hole that is the Name of the Unnameable, I wanted a place of meditation untouched by others.

Next to his peers, Lugge was a lightweight. Compared with Bull, he is a hummingbird alongside an eagle. Size and power aren't everything, however, in art any more than they are in nature.

Bull's inaugural lecture at Gresham College on October 6, 1596 begins with the words:

> "It is written, right worshipful, that the Eagle only, soaring aloft into the clouds, looketh with open eye upon the Sun. Such a quick-sighted bird should now be in this place, who flying through heaven might fetch Apollo's harp and sound unto you the praise of the heavenly music . . ."

Thurston Dart suggests that the foregoing is simply a whimsical acknowledgment of William Byrd's presence at the lecture.

Also according to Dart, Bull served as one of Elizabeth's spies during extended tours of Italy, France, and Germany. This is only a speculation, however, and quite implausible, not only because there is no evidence to back it up, but because the same hypothesis was already put forward a half century ago in an inane fictionalized biography, *Dr. John Bull*, by Leigh Henry (London, 1937), having no prior source.

A portrait of Bull with an hourglass and skull at age 26 in 1589, now at Oxford, is framed in a rhyming motto: The bull by force in field doth Raigne But Bull by Skill Good will doth Gayne.

"(When performing a plainsong setting at the keyboard) the Gregorian tune should be as legato as possible, but it may also be detached to facilitate performance (*per più commodità*)" (Frescobaldi, *Fiori Musicali*, 1635).

Domine quam admirable est nomen tuum.

A hand raised in prayer is an upraised image of God.

In *Piers Plowman* the hand (fist, palm, fingers) is a figure of the Trinity. Wax, wick, flame.

Gloria tibi Trinitas. An orchestra of saints make a joyful noise on a mountain face to face with the Lamb and God the Father on a throne inside the cloud of the Holy Spirit. Musicians are oboe, harp, lute, clavichord. The clavichord player is in the center, directly facing the Lamb. The keyboard rests on the mountain's base. This illustration apears in the *Apocalypse of Margaret of York*, ca. 1475, now at the Morgan Library.

The Trinity: Sulfur (Nothingness, Father, Memory), Salt (Maya, Son, Intellect), and Mercury (Prana, Spirit, Will). Each of these is fundamentally androgynous. According to Wilhelm Reich, the segmented tube is a basic morphology encompassing all that lives, from jellyfish to man. Since the human form includes this, is the thing also part of the image of God mentioned in Genesis? Poe's "Conqueror Worm" comes to mind; also a line by Susie Timmons: "Love slave in tube sox . . ."

The notion that music was invented in heaven and descended to earth corresponds to the Platonic doctrine of the Ideas which in turn must ultimately go back to that Mesopotamian genealogy of kingship after the Flood echoed in *Gilgamesh*. Does the Chinese notion of celestial originals on which earthly counterparts are modeled have the same origin, Mesopotamia?

"When thou seest a most holy, formless Fire shining and sounding within the depths of the Cosmos, give ear to the voice of the Fire" (Simon Magus).

"In the Book M. as in a glass they clearly saw the anatomy and Idea of the universe" (Michael Maier, ca. 1616).

GOD = "the invoked one" derives from an Indo-European root meaning "call." Compare Germanic **gud-igaz*, possessed by a god (from which comes our word *giddy*).

In *De Fistula*, the image of the Pope drinking Communion wine through a straw, so as not to lose a drop.

"The DEITY is everywhere, but only called GOD in the light of love and in the joy love breathes. In the night of the soul he is called WRATH, and in the flames of Hell a Consuming Fire."

The Cross above the circle is the kingdom of glory which proceedeth forth in a flash of joy, and the spiritual water arising in the flash of joy is a budding, a growing, and a showing of a rainbow of colors in the flaming luster of his golden light" (Jacob Boehme, *Signatura Rerum*, the Signature of All Things, 1612).

To Palanc (the pastry cook outsider artist discovered by Jean Dubuffet in Vence about 1950) the square signified man and the circle woman. Man was straight lines, angles, "definition," "the constructed." Woman was curves, "the natural." Artemis versus Artificer.

Palanc's conception is astonishingly coincidental to that behind the famous Plate XXI in Michael Maier's *Atalanta Fugiens*: the Squaring of the Circle, with prototypical male and female figures at its center. Palanc's painting TOI DANS MA VIE shows the square and the circle separated on two inclined planes, then side by side on a single plane, and finally overlapping at the top of a vertical line, with a call-out label JOY.

Ancient China has the opposite scheme. There Woman is square and man is circular. Woman was the housebuilder, the earth, the concrete; Man, the hunter-gatherer living in a yurt under the sky, standing for the abstract. This square-circle version of yin/yang appears in the ancillary literature of the *I Ching*.

When a Taoist sage achieved liberation, the pupils of his eyes sometimes turned into concentric squares. One of those old hermits with square eyes was said to be able to see life on other planets. (One of the most distressing sights I ever saw was the eye of a friend who was dying of cancer and the eye had been operated on to remove a fungus infection which if unchecked would have spread to the brain, and the result of the operation was that square-pupilled look, only it was just in one eye, not both.)

Snakes stand for either sex because they can become both straight (as in Aaron's rod) and circular (the green-and-red *ouroborus*, or tail-devouring world serpent).

Bull constructed a circular puzzle canon titled *Sphera mundi*.

The Elizabethans spelled *in nomine* in ways indicating that they rhymed it with dominy.

To them it was merely the name for a kind of music. Nobody bothered to find out what it referred to, or where it came from.

The phrase is reminiscent either of

> *in nomine Patris et Fili et Spiritus Sancti*

or   *in nomine Domini.*

The former a Trinity invocation, the latter from the Benedictus of the mass. People always think the sing-song rhyme comical.

What does *in the name of* really mean?

"Open up, in the name of the law!"

"What in the name of the Lord do you think you're doing!"

For the Israelites, GOD had only one real name (despite many epithets) and that name was the taboo YHVH which moderns think may have been pronounced something like *Yahweh*. It may have meant "causes to exist." However, no one knows for sure.

Among the Inuit, Larry Osgood informs me, each child receives, in addition to his or her Christian name, a private name, usually that of a recently deceased relative or close family friend whose qualities the parents would like the infant to acquire. They never reprimand a child younger than ten or eleven, for fear of insulting the spirit of the man or woman whose private name the child bears. Older children are assumed to have learned all that their tutelary spirits had to teach them. If they err, they have either failed to learn properly or have deliberately chosen to do the wrong thing. One may rebuke them without fear of offending the spirits. A linguist worked for four years with an old man who was one of the only speakers of a nearly extinct Inuit dialect. One day, after hundreds of hours of working together and an increasingly warm friendship, the Inuit asked the linguist if he might impose upon him with a very personal question. The linguist assured him that he was welcome to do so. Whispering in the younger man's ear, the old man inquired, "What is your name?"

"We absolutely cannot fail to get there [to the Promised Land], that is the promised part about it, or at least sight it from Mount Nebo, because in it shines the triple image of perfection" (V.I. Ivanov, letter to M.O. Gershonzon, July 7, 1920).

I have discovered a hidden connection between the concept of Name and that of the "triple image of perfection." In Matthew 28.19 the singular *in the name of* is used with reference to the Three Persons, each linked with the other by *and*, indicating Unity in Trinity: "Baptize them in the name of the Father and of the Son and of the Holy Spirit." It does not say "in the *names* of . . ." The next sentence says: "I am with you always until the end of the age." Passages of this type, and there are many, imply presence behind seeming absence (or absence behind seeming presence: "I am no longer in the world" John 17.11). They also seem to say that the invisible is better than the visible, the unheard better than the heard.

Federico Mompou, *música callada*.

"Unheard music is better than heard" (Greek proverb of late antiquity).

"That music must be heard is not essential — what it *sounds* like may not be what it *is*" (Charles Ives, *Essays Before a Sonata*).

The proposition of Jacques Attali's *Noise* is different. He says that while noise is a deadly weapon, silence is death.

A thread connecting all In Nomine composers is that every one of them was under a cloud. "Art never thrives except under a cloud. With recognition and honors, it vanishes and is replaced by a fake" (Jean Debuffet). Schuldt points out to me that the foregoing must be taken with a grain of salt, since it has long served to justify Society's policy of malign neglect vis à vis impecunious artists.

Physical law = a passing ripple in a vaster chaos.

"Law, Lord of all . . ." Here Pindar anticipates Science. In Nomine flourished in the last decades when the learned could openly profess natural magic. It vanished with the scientific revolution, whose theological foundation is in the system of control that is monotheism.

David Rattray

In Nomine

John Lugge

In Nomine with double cursus, or full repetition of the cantus firmus, by John Lugge. Oxford, Christ Church Music MS 49. Edited by David Rattray.

David Rattray

(By kind permission of the governing body of Christ Church, Oxford.)

In the *Bhagavad Gita* it is stated that the Lord is a machine on which the rest of the cosmic mechanism turns. Further down the chain comes Shakespeare's "Majesty's a massy wheel to whose huge spokes ten thousand lesser things are mortised and conjoined."

"Praise His great and terrible Name, for it is holy!"

In this year of the disappearance of the Evil Empire I want to stand up and shout to my peers: You have nothing to lose but your Great Chain of Being!

Pagans saw the monotheism of the Jews and Christians as a *malefica superstitio*. They were right.

Love is drunk on the wine of music, James Thomson wrote. "He reeleth with his own heart, that great rich vine."

The Name has got to contain as much female as male. Obviously, the Holy Spirit is female, something female in the air.

". . . if one chooses to be conscious, which is the big 'if' in life" (Janet Hobhouse).

The dying swan witnessed by James Nares in Sagaponack last summer writhed like a white Hercules in the shirt of Nessus. The other swans formed a cortege and escorted it to the shelter out of sight behind a clump of reeds. Its contortions, having swallowed something it could neither get down nor get up, seemed an allegory of the predicament of one whose business, pleasure, and religion it is to make art.

James has been nailing tuning forks (x and y chromosomes) to a steel door in consonance with *aurea proportio*.

His family name in Latin means "power of observation." *Nares acutae*, a sharp nose.

The other day he told me about the part of Ireland he is from, where cattle and sheep make paths over the downs to stone circles in order to huddle inside, rub up against the standing stones, and shit.

The Spanish term for a dissonance was *un punto intenso*. To chromatic inflection there was a pungency suggesting that of brimstone.

From the very last paragraph of Hölderlin's *Hyperion*: "Like lovers' quarrels are the universe's dissonances. Resolution is in mid-conflict. All that was sundered reconciles. The heart's veins fork and converge."

Nomen omen est. Omina nomina sunt.

"You shall make no mention of the names of other gods in your hearts, nor shall it be named by your mouth" (Exodus 23:13).

In his *Exhortation to Martyrdom* Origen writes:

> "The subject of names is something very deep and recondite . . . if someone understands it, he will see that if names were merely conventional, then the demons or any other invisible powers when summoned would not obey those who know their names and name the names that have been given. But as it is, certain sounds and syllables and expressions, aspirated or unaspirated and with a long or a short vowel, when they are spoken aloud, by some unseen nature immediately bring to us those who are summoned. If this is so and names are not merely conventional, then the first God must not be called by any other name than the ones by which the worshiper, the prophets, and our Savior and Lord Himself named Him. . . . For it says, 'This is my name for ever, and thus I am to be remembered throughout all generations' (Exodus 3:15). And it is not surprising if the demons attribute their own names to the first God in order to be worshiped as the first God."

Inscribed in Phoenecian lettering on the temple of Astarte at Sidon: *SHEM BA'AL* = 'in the name of the Lord'

Dissonances "sting" the listener. Harmony brings happy relief.

In Nomine's very name situates it in the zone between what can and can't be said, in the sphere where apparently contradictory theologies harmonize point for point:

"That Thy Name is near, Thy wondrous works declare" (Psalm 74).

"Thou hast no name or form, even to the extent of allusion" (*Avadhuta Gita*).

According to *The Cloud of Unknowing*, the division of the nostrils (*nares*) stands for spiritual discrimination. The Devil's nose is just a hole with no division into nostrils. It is possible to look up it all the way to the Devil's brain, which is hellfire and nothing else, but all who look go mad forever.

Gregory the Great codified existing chants and institutionalized glossolalia.

In Nomine is response. Not "setting" but conflict. A resistance between two efforts, the effort to hear and the effort to make sense.

The purer the Spirit the scarier.
Who wants to be possessed?
Who wants to lose
It, meaning Me?
To let go of the difference between Me and What I See?
Between being alive and being dead?
Between Me and God?
Who wants to overflow with a joy too great for words?

In Nomine does to plainsong what plainsong did to the words — in visual terms, it's equivalent to painting a sign on a skyscraper or sitting at the foot of a wide-angle screen to watch a film.

"The abyss of music is at the body's core" (Antonin Artaud).

In Nomine has to come out of the player. To put the whole body into it. To become the crystal it vibrates in, while at the same time allowing it to become a crystal inside which one's own self may crack.

Blitheman was to Bull as Chiron to Achilles, a centaur teaching a hero music and medicine.

"Of all the evils that plague medicine, the worst is the practice of imposing generic names on illnesses in order to deduce from them generic remedies" (. . . *generalia quaedam nomina morbis imponere iisque aptare velle generalem quondom medicinam*) John Huxham (1764).

David Rattray

"The gods have become diseases" (C.G. Jung).

"What they call GOD is germs" (Artaud).

Even as I have been discovering this musical genre that seems to me a Western equivalent of raga, many people I know have fallen ill with the new plague, AIDS. The *Gloria tibi Trinitas* tune behind In Nomine was originally associated with the feast of Thomas à Becket, a patron saint of the sick. I sometimes picture In Nomine as the kind of music that Prospero might have played in his cell on the enchanted island. In Nomine becomes a country of the mind, one that is all the more inviting in that it has not yet become an officially recommended object of pilgrimage.

"Let us flee to our own country!" Plotinus turned this line from Homer into a slogan calling for retreat from the world as it is. Coming home to In Nomine, one does not have to feel like George Sand and Chopin standing in line to glimpse Mont Blanc through a telescope at Chamonix.

The main accusation against Bull in 1613 was of adultery "notable and impudent." No less than the Archbishop of Canterbury wrote a letter detailing the charges:

> "Himself and his wife lay in the upper bed, and in a truckle bed under him lay two of his maid servants. Bull, in a summer morning when it was very light, riseth from his wife's side, goeth to the other bed, raising up one of his maidens, biddeth her to lie by her mistress, he taking her place committeth adultery with the other, which the maid beholding awaketh her mistress, and biddeth her see what her master is doing. His wife beholdeth it and telleth her servant that this was no news to her, for her husband had long and often been a dealer that way, which indeed is since verified by common report. Again he was charged to come into a church a little before the beginning of prayer, and there as the minister was entering into service, in the sight of the congregation Bull pulled him violently out of his seat and despitefully entreated him. The man hath more music than honesty and is as famous for marring virginity as he is for fingering of organs and virginals."

Why does the name of God seem like that of Poe's "King Pest" nowadays? If I could only somehow step outside the fear in which much of my life is spent, I might enjoy that serenity without worship, without object whose simple truth has seemed implicit in many of the good lives that I have witnessed. I could excuse the universe for taking no interest in me or mine as individuals. I could accept the rise and fall of historical cycles with some equanimity. I might even remain undaunted by the prospect of this new pestilence that is ever so slowly eating out my friends' immune systems and brains and leaving them prey to fantastic, hitherto unimaginable ailments, as a civilization I feel I am not really a part of moves into its third if not terminal millenium.

With the triadic style, the development of polyphony at the keyboard, and equal temperament, Plato's musical theory becomes a reality exactly 2,000 years after the *Republic* (Ernest G. McClain, *The Pythagorean Plato: Prelude to the Song Itself*, 1978).

In Heidegger's lecture on Hölderlin is a statement to the effect that to set measure before that which is amorphous and to winkle simplicity out of chaos is at once the most criminally reckless work there is, and the innocentest of pastimes.

Stravinsky once said that he owned more Old English church music than any other.

I must handle this like something very delicate (and precious) that can neither be dropped nor squeezed.

Two Appreciations
Amiri Baraka

JACKIE MC

BY THE TIME I HAD GOT FLUENT in the understanding of be-bop and its revolution, and had begun to recognize the historical development of the music, I heard Jackie McLean. And from the first times I talked to my partners about him it was always Jackie Mc to the hip. He was one of the young geniuses Charlie Parker's life brought to revelation. Not only the musical innovation that will historicize Bird's life but the personality of himself as artist, and the social philosophy, the cultural explosion and introspection these elements together worked upon America. Birdland is an actual place, even to the capitalists.

Jackie came up the charismatic New York hipster, but he could play. Not only was he carrying the feeling of a generation but the sensitivity of the artist, the illogical truth of reason. What was so hip about the young Bird freaked musicians, artists, intellectuals, people was that Bird played Beauty & Truth. His life was truth, how tragic. But even that was simply Confirmation of the death rule of squares. The corniness of authority, the banality of a slow walking insensitive society in which art could be ignored, artists driven to suicide and the people beat down all kinds of ways.

Like Bird, Jackie came up as young and as wild as he had to be. As penetrating in his grasp of this world as he had to be. The music was supreme judge and purity. Life should be as hip as the music.

Jackie spoke as he grew in respectful artful admiration of the new learning, its accents and he drove his sound on alto up high like Bird's, but something more personal also developed, it was a harder, more gut shouty sound in that metallic bop alto. It was as articulate as the Parker paradigm, and in Bird there is always the homage to Johnny Hodges as well as Lester Young, but it wanted its blues street wailing and screaming.

Jackie was from his appearance part of the whole development of that music, be-bop, both in his association with Charlie Parker and

Miles Davis. The Miles connection made us understand how another younger generation was emerging. Miles & Jackie on "Dig," or "Morpheus," "Down," their look and the hard blues they pushed were carrying us into the next period of the music. Hard bop.

When Horace Silver, Sonny Rollins, Art Blakey & The Messengers, Clifford Brown-Max Roach, Bobby Timmons brought the church directly into it. Those post-cool Blue Note sides. Especially I still always listen to Jackie Mc's "Dr. Jackle." With Miles developing the ensemble style that would later lead to the Trane-Cannonball-Red Garland-Philly Joe Jones-Paul Chambers classic period.

When the Freedom Militant Funky 60s emerged Jackie had not only developed into an alto maestro but an important composer. "Little Melonnae" is another of his gems. The bands and music of *Let Freedom Swing; One Step Beyond;* his work with Grachan Moncur III, Tony Williams, Bobby Hutcherson, Freddie Hubbard and many others is outstanding, innovative yet as drivingly funky as anything in the music.

One story that indicates for me how art is related to society as intrinsically as human thought and feeling is one day during this period I wandered into a Village record shop and asked for Jackie's *Let Freedom Ring.* The squat joweled bespectacled clerk resembling a Nazi sympathizer in a 40s movie began squealing, "If you people want to be concerned with such things why do you have to put it in music?"

He was actually angry, agitated and puffing. I made some nasty remark, amazed at the hidden maniac posing as thought in the American mind, and thought for a minute about murder and explosions.

Jackie created a music that continued the Parker bop tradition and the hard bop development and restoration of blues and polyrhythms, but parallel to John Coltrane, Sonny Rollins, and the coming of Ornette Coleman and Eric Dolphy and Pharoah Sanders and Albert Ayler and Archie Shepp, Jackie McLean contributed a highly distinctive voice which told a very broad story.

Jackie starred in the Living Theater's controversial production *The Connection*, where Archie Shepp later blossomed. He played the downtown NY spots in profusion. Even made a kind of headquarters of Slug's on the Lower East Side. But there is a kind of slow death amidst lights and noise that spends the artists' energy that Jackie opposed. That he saw hurting so many of his friends. Till, finally he says when Trane died, it signalled his departure.

Now in Hartford, Ct. at the Hart Music School as Director of Afro

American Music, Jackie Mc has re-emerged as a continuing master player and innovator in the music. He sounds as swift and hot and funky as ever, his soul is certainly right where it supposed to be. Listen!

DAVID MURRAY

What makes David, his music, his approach, so important to all of us is that he has stepped back as it were to gather all of the truest tradition of soul music to him, in him, and used that as a forward thrusting recoil like a jet to propel him into the newest regions of feeling. That is the key, to keep to the hot wire of deep funk trad, the rocking, the shocking, niggers with purple stockings, yet at the same time, and because of this to a degree, to be doing the truly fresh the truly new, because the blackest tradition could never be wholly digested in the American mainstream because truth wd kill this thing outright like a funky dog. So much truth. So much of the real. Like the milk wd be cocoa or coffee or darkest night with only the smiles of slaves to light it if there was gonna be any light, if you cdn't see in the dark. Like the darkies.

The music is like that, makes you see in the dark, cause the dark be you 1st. Understand. Can you see in yr self? See the mission and the magic. The way and the cross. The hope and the double cross. The music is like that. That's why they keep black culture and art out of the schools, our children wd be too strong to handle. They are terrified of them now. Black boys especially terrify them, turn them into murderers, black girls challenge them, they have just recently found out a way to cool out some of their parents, they never discover a way to cool out the youth!

Why? Because listen to David and you will hear the whole erupted landscape of our historical lives. All our ecstasy and the heap of dead pain the weight of it like a growl, like a sudden greasy honk, like a blue moaning star leaning on an emptiness unable to pay your rent with its lonesome beauty.

Because our art valorizes, makes glorious and beautiful our lives. The lives of the slaves. How can you oppress Duke Ellington or Art Tatum — can you be believed if you want to say that Coltrane or Sun Ra are inferior? You must believe Tawana Brawley if you listen to Billie sing "Strange Fruit." You would know the weight of oppression you had to move and overcome when you hear Black, Brown and Beige. You could not think of Larry Byrd as intelligent and Dr J. as merely instinctive when you hear the World Saxophone Quartet. Louis Armstrong make an idiot savant get funky.

The art of the African (and we here are Africans, African Americans, that is our nationality, African heritage and American history) is very ancient. In that art is our whole beings, this is why it is called soul music. Soul like sol the sun, the core of all life, our jazz, is our birth replication of this life, our ideological/psychological replication of our lives on this planet. Our lives as they are are described needs laid out like notes on a page or in an hear, these needs cannot become everyone's needs or they will be answered the society altered the world changed thieves and murderers punished and homelessness or ignorance after a while would become obscure maladies of prehumans.

That's why we need the Davids, the Johns, the Eddies, the music in our schools, to reinforce the highest aspirations of our lives for our children every day. They would be intensely interested. They wd not have to be dragged to school if they did not get drugged once they got to school or got sold drugs on the way to school. If they were hearing their own lives, reading of their own history, their own escapes and triumphs, if it was their own experience reinforced they would emerge too powerful for white supremacy to handle. This is the fear. Education spoils you for slavery, Douglass' reading teacher was admonished. Dont teach em to read. The music teaches you to read even deeper into things. To discover your own face and signature at the very heart of things. Self Consciousness, a necessary aspect of Self Respect and an absolute requirement for Self Determination. That is the tradition you hear so clearly in David, Self Consciousness, and Self Determination. What does that music mean the squares would ask assaulted by our pyramidal ideas? Self Determination. "Freedom," Monk sd. "More than that is complicated."

Against Music
Robert Kelly

Utter silence

then a shadow falls on it —
how to darken silence

without an actual sound
how to let some one sound
stir in darkened or obscured silence

how to let someone sound

how
how what someone first "hears" as "a sound" sways other
sounds (performers)
is common,

and though common, beautiful
and though beautiful jazz,
and though jazz music, and
therefore necessarily sad.
If you think about it. It is sad,
the persuasions.

Words beget words beget sounds, it is common and they are
beautiful. And it is beautiful in that happens; we don't
know anything but what happens, and we call it, say, beautiful.
(We are the kind of beings who call mountains beautiful, or
weather beautiful.

How strange we are, to call what happens anything at all.)

We call it beautiful, or some variant label ("ugly," "OK,"
"ordinary," "common," "new," "traditional," "original," "dull") that

reflects some finesse of the original thing we want to find it, beautiful.

What bothers me about music right away is not that it's beautiful (or any variant, any description) but that it is realistic.

Without even being actual, music is realistic. Music, especially interesting music, especially music where intelligent musicians listen to one another as they play, and skilfully respond, weaving a text of "offer — respond — let be," music that is always answering, leading, dancing, talking, musing, commenting, being led, moving, such music is realistic, moving.

Music is a one-dimensional metaphrase of everything else, everything always happening: physics, cosmology, economics, interpersonal enterprise, history — the endless web of everything caused by and causing everything else. Pretty as an elegant philosopher, music is an exact demonstration of the interdependent co-origination of all things, the world.

By being like the world, music is part of the problem.

Tragic.

Where is the original silence from which a different music, not at all beautiful would come? It would not be realistic but actual.

Actual because uncaused uncausing.

I am imagining such a music that does not depend on the umbral dimming of the Prime Silence, that does not arise.

I am imagining a music that does not arise.

Perhaps it is suddenly there, perhaps there all the while. How can there be music all the while which is not a reference to or part of everything else that's here all the while? So while our common and beautiful music is just a phase of the "music of the sphaeres" and so on, this music I'm guessing towards would neither transitively nor intransitively move —

move neither in itself nor cause others to move or be moved.

Yes yes but could we hear it?
Imagine we could hear it. That brings it halfway home.

There are many models for present-day music-making. Whether
the model in mind is deistic (Bruckner slaving away in isolation
perfecting his massive chunk of cosmos) or angelic (Charlie
Parker impregnating with his lucid gospel the astonished
shepherds of his sleeping sidemen) or democratic (everybody
listens, everybody talks) or ecological-thrifty (Mr Glass
recycles one chord for hours, no implication is wasted), the
resultant musics will always be beautiful (how beautiful music
is!), realistic, common, unhelpful.

They will be part of, even if commentary on, the as-is world of
interdependent co–origination. Whether music is a sermon or a
lecture or a conversation, it still is enmeshed in the macro-
social, macro-linguistic event we call the world, or beauty
itself.

The more it talks, the more it's part of the problem.

And like any sign, it is a symptom.

What I am saying is difficult for me to say. It sounds clever, a
captious rhapsody disguised as an "against"; I fear cheap
whimsy and costly preciosity. I love music more than any thing
I ever know. Because I love music so, I know there's something
I'm after, some sense of an alternative. Is there a clue in what
looks at first like an ordinary romantic revulsion:

> When I heard the learn'd astronomer,
> When the proofs, the figures, were ranged in columns before me,
> When I was shown the charts and diagrams, to add, divide, and
>   measure them,
> When I sitting heard the astronomer where he lectured with
>   much applause in the lectureroom.
> How soon unaccountable I became tired and sick.
> Till rising and gliding out I wander'd off by myself.
> In the mystical moist night-air, and from time to time,

Look'd up in perfect silence at the stars.

[Whitman in 1865, about the time of the first performance of Tristan]

Is there a clue in those lines, if not towards the music I have in mind, then at least towards what my mind is after?

What my mind is up to by calling what it's after "music."

Language ("poetry") has for several centuries used "music" to free itself from referentiality. Instead of paraphrasable meaning, poetry offers at its best the sound and shape of itself passing.

> As early as 1815 (more than a century before
> MacLeish's "globed fruit"), E.T.A. Hoffmann
> has an artist proclaim: "my picture is
> intended not to *signify* anything, but to *be*."

Various eras have various standards of or tastes for the referential, and make various demands on the accountability of words. Language as music cuts the web of words by words.

No one knows if any success is in store for us in this great dereferencing. The curious looks of baffled disappointment on the faces of people leaving poetry readings are promising signs, but not without their amphibolous portent. It has been evident since at least the Buddha and Heraclitus that we are, or are in, a vast, perhaps meaningless, system. Our current whimsy tropes our hereness as: we are lost in the computer.

We have sought relief from this intermittently painful awareness by various ways we fancy rigorous: that solution-by-exhaustion we call "science," that shellgame of discutables we call philosophy, as well as by praying to the unknown programmer or technician to turn the damned thing off or let us out ("religion," apocalyptic or soteriological, respectively), but mostly by various hard to condemn quisling acts of collaboration ("ordinary life," "business as usual").

Robert Kelly

The Chinese supposed a note on the trumpet, or some note on
some trumpet, would shatter the sky. Imagine that.

   And MUSICK shall untune the Sky.   (Dryden, 1687)

I am not advocating violence. Or not yet.
Imagine a music that doesn't cooperate.
Imagine a music that is no simple or complex mimesis, that isn't
an imitation of conversation or any sort of conversation, we
being who and what we are, sleepers, sleepers;

imagine a music that is not an imitation of biological process
and not an imitation of Hegel giving a lecture or of people
walking naked in the woods or of God creating the world.

Imagine a music that does not collaborate:
that isn't Nazi or Socialist Realist or Capitalist Experi-
mentalist, that doesn't reaffirm by constant rhythmic reinforce-
ment the shabbier precincts of business: weddings and war.

Imagine a music that refuses to interact with the complex
interactions we call "reality" (but whose true name is Satan,
Lord of the World).

Imagine a music that isn't realistic.
It could not be common, hence would not be beautiful.
It would save us.
But could we hear it?

Imagine you could hear it.
Imagine you're hearing it now.

The Furies
Hilton Als

— *For Valda*

1.

LET'S SEE NOW.

What's in question here are the ways we assume we've lived so fully, through relationships we characterize as personal, in which we no longer live. This is a photograph. Aside from the emotional structure photography impels — sadness; sadness as evidence of the sadness inherent in looking at the past — it exists, and is ghastly, and refuses to know its place. Not unlike most things we prefer to forget — pets that die, unpleasant climates, people who die — photographs and their attendant memories slip from diaries and other people's tongues to find you out and reveal your shame in owning an image of someone you used to know. Always and forever: I used to know that person. How can one bear it? The ghost of "used to" rising before "know"?

And why are they like that, these people we used to know floating outside the once shared experience of friendship, of love? Every relationship we characterize as personal is doomed to the eventuality of someone absenting someone else from it. This begins when we can no longer bear our knowledge of that person, that mystery which does not deepen but thickens our sight, so used up are they by the imagination. In being used up, uninspiring, a cloying memory of love, they become a part of the larger world of everyday life, and all that annoys and disappoints and frightens in it. This is what most people call love. This is why some people can't have it.

And of the other person, the exile condemned to having once been known: he is connected to you still, in the embarrassment felt in trying to recall your name, in the photographs that slip, in the dead second where love remains.

A photograph. In "missing" someone, how best to cope with the notion you may not be missed at all? That in the hours you recall

71

as being theirs — at the office, on holiday at the shore — nothing will ever again incite them to ring you and risk displacement from the office or anything that is theirs. The point is you are no longer "theirs" — no longer a friend, nothing, certainly not a person to be "in touch with," or spend idle hours doing "nothing" with. Your violent and obsessive love of being reduced by someone also finds their reductive tendencies hideously simpleminded: You have disappointed me so therefore I must disappoint our friendship; I no longer "speak" to him/her.

Your violent and obsessive love of being reduced finds this procedure so simpleminded, in fact, that it cannot satisfy you. (In effect they are not erasing you, they are adopting a stance. This is purgatory, not hatred; misplaced love, not erasure.)

Aside from no longer being worthy of someone else's speech, regardless of the reasons — lies, theft, fear, hatred — exile is not complete until you place yourself inside the hours you recall as theirs, knowing that in each and every second of them, you exist not at all.

A photograph. What prompts the desire to be erased into being? You must begin with your body as the corporeal lie housing your fake soul; of no guilt being resolved ever and you are responsible for everyone else's, always. Each hour that we lie awake, eyes open, reconsidering the wrongs committed, the untruths told, the second chance missed — you are responsible for it; the world slips over your tongue like an oyster, foul and slippery and ultimately undigestable, but you swallow it. That's how you begin — in the digestation of what others can't imagine: swallowing the wrongs committed by someone else, which is usually accompanied by an image or two.

This is a photograph. Aside from the emotional structure photography impels in you — sadness; nausea at the guilt and anger felt at not being able to succor each and every face forgotten in the photograph — photography poses questions too. Has history only made one photograph, a record of forgetfulness? For the child who labels a photograph, citing the sitter's name, where the portrait was taken and at what time, there is only one answer: Yes. People die; places speak and then whisper away into no place at all. All of which contributes to the ineffable sense that the desire to be erased and forgotten yourself makes nothing but sense. There's nothing like it.

2.

Arias are musical soliloquies about the nature of anxiety. Anxiety is the music that governs souls if you listen carefully. Language communicating anxiety has its own timbre, cadence and phrasing. Generally, arias and anxiety are about one thing: one's war against someone's move to forget you. Not in death (no one comes back from death to sing; worms eat the chords), but in the moment the coffee has been made, moments after the throat has been fucked. There is something in the way the hat is put on, something in the averted glance or the walking stick reached for that says, Goodbye — which in itself is no consolation for having to think of future Hallos.

The aria of anxiety begins with the leap of faith into the possibility that that Goodbye could be permanent or might as well be, so gripped by the fear of permanence are you. The throat contracts. No, no. The bowels contract in a manner familiar from childhood, when the thermometer was inserted for the first time. And as regards the purpose of that insertion — to read your temperature — nothing mattered but the chill. Similarly, nothing matters while singing the aria of anxiety but the chill of desertion; the hideous calm of Goodbye, prompting the event of the temperature's rise.

The mouth is an instrument of gnashing teeth. Teeth that gnash do not masticate: that is not their purpose. The mouth is a tool, a sharp instrument, which helps to produce the vibrato for the contralto, the *basso fundo* for the baritone, and the screeching utterance of despair for the deserted. Anxiety makes a mouth of many of us. That mouth is attached to a throat, in which photographs and ashes and dust constitute a past. No one puts a hand around the throat when they should; people put a hand over the mouth when they shouldn't. This is a form of "politeness" but contradictory. Shut-up as opposed to I am/would like to kill you. In fact, one should always throttle the screeching throat of despair really insistent on the permanence of Goodbye — violence cures it and then makes love to it. That is what people are: violent and in love with the threat of being forgotten. They are that or erased, tallying events in photographs, counting the mouths in them while placing a hand over their own, dying to be forgotten.

The instruments used in constructing the aria of anxiety are The Scene (described previously) in conjunction with The Mouth and The Throat. Generally, this is best seen in the context of the opera of suffering. This form is not obsolete. This form is either lived and therefore prurient or invented and captivates utterly. This is a photograph of one production nearly forgotten, the excavation of which produced a number of paper cuts and burns but no loss of teeth, no gnawing away at the thermometer down the throat, so cold yet so inviting. No one remembers this scene very well except the archivist of it. All has been forgotten except by the archivist, so nasty, particular in detail, baroque in the execution of the mouth working — up and down, and then up — saying: They've forgotten, how many times now? This archivist is in actuality a photograph of nearly everything ever forgotten: crumbling Kodak children, a back porch, rubber lips on a cracked neck, a goodbye, an infidelity, yearning, an aria, 78s, a dance step, yawning, a recipe, Mom, forgetfulness. The archivist became a photograph due to the horror of being a self with a voice in the opera of suffering.

3.

ONE WOMAN SAID, *her voice rising*: Rather than bear the child I killed it rather than bear another version of its father.

ONE WOMAN SAID, *her voice singing*: Excuse the cunty power of the following observation. Often mistaken for something else — a different race of something else — I became something other than myself.

ONE WOMAN SAID, *singing*: Every atrocity begins with the best intentions.

ONE WOMAN SAID, *her voice rising*: Shrivelled up, it came out dead. Later on another one was born, a boy. To someone else. He's not dead, I said.

ONE WOMAN SAID, *her voice singing*: All gnatty with gnats and a closed mind and no heart but red lips. I sat on a rock resting in nothing. So disgusting, the black thing in front of me — I shield my eyes.

ONE WOMAN SAID, *singing*: The stench of others obscures myself from myself. The wrongs committed against myself. A letter written somewhere to confirm this. First the spittle, then the stamp.

ONE WOMAN SAID, *singing*: Every atrocity begins with the best intentions. The opera queen admonishes the leather queen for proferring *Opera News*, not *Opera Digest*. This is because he must follow the printed version of his master's voice: Norman, Battle, Stratas. I am his master. Will I die?

ONE WOMAN SAID, *her voice singing*: Extremely committed to the cause, I failed the individual.

ONE WOMAN SAID, *her voice rising*: I said, take this name, it's useless to me now. Take it off the dead boy and put it on the other one. So that when they play they'll know how to find one another because they're dead.

ONE WOMAN SAID, *singing*: The opera queen as friend administers information necessary for nourishing the voice: gossip; the recalcitrant sadness of.

ONE WOMAN SAID, *her voice rising*: Of course, he may become something other than what you depended on, always.

ONE WOMAN SAID, *her voice singing*: He may try to punch or rip your throat open to hear more or less. He will suck the spectacle of your voice out.

ONE WOMAN SAID, *her voice rising*: To punch and rip you off. At the throat.

ONE WOMAN SAID, *singing*: Get him before he gets you. They're not all dead, you know.

ONE WOMAN SAID, *her voice rising*: Greasy head with greasy lies in it.

ONE WOMAN SAID, *singing*: He left and I didn't.

ONE WOMAN SAID, *her voice rising*: He may harm you. You never know. They aren't all dead.

ONE WOMAN SAID, *her voice rising*: Yes

ONE WOMAN SAID, *her voice singing*: Yes

ONE WOMAN SAID, *singing*: Yes.

Up Close and Personal:
Miles Davis and Me

Quincy Troupe

1.

Like Prince says when he's talking about hitting the beat and getting to the music and the rhythm, I'm going to keep getting up on the one, brother, I'm just going to try to keep my music getting up on the one, getting up on the one every day I play, getting up on the one.

— Miles Davis, from *Miles: The Autobiography*,
Miles Davis with Quincy Troupe

IT'S JUNE, 1985, one of those sun-kissed, beautiful, blessed days, the kind that the Big Apple's political, monied leaders use to try to convince people that The City is a wonderful place to live. Scenic, pleasant, clean, crime-free. It's a clear, blue day with a lovely soft tonguing breeze. One of those days that hold out the promise of unlimited magic and seduction, the kind of a day that causes people to spill out into the streets and revel in New York's unsurpassed electric public life. And it's a great day for me, because I'm on my way to meet the legendary Miles Davis, to interview him for an article for *Spin* magazine. For me, it can't get any better than this.

I walk through Central Park, passing lovers lying in the grass, runners and bicyclists, picnickers, kids playing baseball and soccer to get to Miles's apartment. Upon arriving, I announce myself to the doorman, a tall, rotund, smiling Latino with a huge, drooping bushy handlebar moustache. After being cleared to come up, I take the elevator to the 14th floor, get off, ring the bell and wait with much anticipation.

A young black man, Miles's valet, opens the door and lets me in. He walks me across a huge living room with windows opening onto a spectacular view of Central Park. Despite the light outside, the apartment is dark, with a big-screen television running images across its face and actors running gibberish from their mouths. The walls are painted a muted gray, as are the floors. It reminds me of the inside of a cave. I see a photo of Gil Evans, clothes thrown haphazardly in a corner, blue and red trumpets resting on their sides on a table and no photographs of Miles Davis. Not one of the numerous awards he has won can be seen, nor any gold or platinum records mounted on the walls. Their absence, for me is conspicuous and already begins to suggest a little about Miles's values and character.

We turn into an alcove off the kitchen and there, in a patch of light coming in through a back window, sitting at a table drawing figures onto a drawing pad is Miles Dewey Davis, III. He's wearing sunglasses in all this darkness. In character already. "The Prince of Darkness." The one and only "bad," "mean," "voodooman" of music, the divine horseman of sound runnin' the mack down with those laser-beam eyes that can cut right through all manner of bullshit, and freeze a motherfucker dead in his tracks if he's coming off wrong. The legendary slick man of impeccable style and class, he of the kiss-my-ass attitude and stance, the black Romeo.

So there he is, laid dead up in the cut of total disarray, drawing the figure of a woman on his drawing pad, head down over his paper, in total concentration. He has paint stains all over his scruffy, torn black denims and shirt, paint all over his hands, his jet-black, smooth, wizened but handsome face, tubes of paint all over the table, all over the floor around him. Sheets from his note-pad with half-finished figures lie crumpled among the paint tubes. A total mess, but he doesn't seem to be aware that it is, like he's not aware of my presence yet, or at least he isn't letting on that he is. So, I just stand there, watching him feverishly drawing, not saying a word, shifting my weight from my bad leg to my good one, until, at last, and all of a sudden, he slowly turns his head toward me, putting down his drawing pen, takes off his glasses and looks at me kind of sideways, kind of slanting upwards, fixing on me with those beacon eyes and says: "Man, you're a funny lookin' motherfucker." Then, squinting through the darkness looking at my dreadlocked hair, he says, "How'd you get your hair like that?"

I'm not offended, but totally shocked. His response to me is so human, and, I might add, an East St. Louis/St. Louis response in that it's no-nonsense, straight to the point and kind of "country," the way everyday people from where we come from respond. Miles is from East St. Louis, Illinois and I'm from St. Louis, Missouri, the Mississippi River separating the two cities. It's something I'm used to and so I relax right away, thankful for the way he's greeted me.

"Sit down," he says pointing at a chair across the cluttered glass table from him, "what do you want to know?"

I sit down, look closer and notice he's wearing a gold and brown hair weave. This further surprises me, as does the frailty of his physical appearance. Now, I don't know what I expected of Miles, but I had heard of the cavalier and unresponsive way he has treated writers over the years. Miles was reputed to hate journalists, so I am surprised that he doesn't just bite my head off from the giddiup. I've heard he hates to be interviewed and so I'm not out of the hot water yet, because the interview hasn't started. I tell myself to proceed with caution like one does through a minefield and try not to say anything stupid.

Now the hair weave doesn't bother me but I'm kind of taken aback by its condition. It's crushed on the right side, like he's slept on that side during the night. Beyond being crushed on the right side, the weave is speckled all over with red, blue and gold paint. I discovered later this was his normal attire when at home.

All of a sudden, he reaches over the table and grabs a long lock of my hair, asking if it was "for real." Before I know it, I slap his hand away from my hair, saying: "I grew it like this."

He looks at his hand in disbelief and then up at me and says, "Motherfucker, are you crazy?!"

"Naw, I ain't crazy," I answer. "Coming here to do a story on you don't give you the right to invade my space."

He kind of looks at me funny at first, probably debating whether he should kick me out or not. Then he shrugs it off, bends back over his drawing pad and asks me where I'm from.

"St. Louis," I say.

"Oh, yeah," he rasps, not looking up from his drawing. "Now I know you're a crazy motherfucker." Then he just kind of smiles and says: "Well, motherfucker, don't just sit there, ask me some mother-fucking questions. What chu want to know, brother?"

2.

Man, I've been running the voodoo down since I was born.
— Miles Davis, in conversation

I first heard a record of Miles when I was 13 years old, a high school freshman. Since then he has been an important part of my life, a hero and a mentor in absentia. He was a hero to my cousin Marvin, an erstwhile drummer and a complete gangster: it was Marvin who turned me on to the music of Miles. Marvin was about five years older than I and was one of the people I looked up to, because he was clean as a broke dick dog, a ladies' man and didn't take shit off no one. Anyway, one day Marvin played *Round Midnight* for me, asking me later what I thought. I didn't know what to say. I did like the music — sort of. (Shit, I really didn't know what it all meant.) But I did find myself thinking about it later and the more I thought about it, listened to it a couple more times, the more I found myself liking it.

I suspect my youthful enthusiasm had something to do with Miles's great melodic approach to music, that beautiful, haunting, unforgettable sound he gets on his trumpet, a sound quite close to a human voice. His sound goes straight to the heart. Miles's music, even back then, seemed magical and mysterious to me. It always made me dream, take off inside and outside my head. I saw landscapes and birds, saw shapes and colors, and beautiful ladies floating naked. I saw ghosts all up in his chord changes, the way it all flowed was like a parade of hip people. And lawd knows I wanted to be hip, even at 13. Talking about "running the voodoo down." His music was already doing that for me, and he was still fifteen years away from *Bitches Brew!* Good God, Papa Legba, voodoo sho do work in mysterious ways.

I was 15 when I really started listening to Miles seriously. Before Miles I had been into Johnny Ace, The Dells, The Coasters, The Heartbeats, The Platters, you know, the hip doowoppers. Frankie Lymon and the Teenagers singing: "Why do fools fall in love/ why do birds sing so gay/ love is the way to make the day/ why do fools fall in love?" You know, trying to be as cool as a teenager could be back then at them blue-lighted, funky parties we threw all the time in them dark St. Louis basements, grinding down our young, hot passion, all up against a favorite young lady, who was just as silly as we were.

My other musical "homeboy," Chuck Berry, lived right up the street from me on Ashland and Fair, three blocks away. I saw him all the time in the ice cream joint me and my friends frequented; he was always in there eyeing some of the fine young girls draped over *our* arms. Though Chuck, of course, was famous, to my mind, my way of thinking back then, I couldn't imagine anyone being famous unless they lived in some exotic place like Hollywood, or New York, or Paris. St. Louis, Missouri? Who in their right mind would want to live here when they could live in some exotic place? Though I was into Chuck's music I thought of him as a "local." He was nowhere near as slick as Miles.

Soon, Miles and his music was what it was all about for me. I started to pick up on his attitude, his stance, the way he put his clothes together. He taught me what being "clean as a broke dick dog" really meant. Through the persona of Miles I acquired a new way of looking at and understanding a hostile, white world that was all around me, having just been integrated into an all-white high school. Almost all my responses to the outside world — and even, sometimes, to my own family — were filtered through the prism of how I thought Miles Davis might react to and handle a certain situation. I was reading about him whenever I could in magazines now, picking up information from people who were older than me and had first-hand news about him, because they had either seen him play or knew someone else who had. Talking to these older people, watching what they did, taught me just what being "cool" and "hip" was all about.

Besides the magisterial, deep-cool hipness of his musical language, the aspects of Miles that affected me most were his urbane veneer and his detached sure sense of himself as royalty, as untouchable in a touch-everything world. Miles seemed to be saying: "I will not ever be despoiled by any corrupting bullshit, will not ever sacrifice my integrity, will stand my ground wherever, and against whomever, will not move from here, will stand erect here as a human being, as a man, and if need be, will go down here with my life for what I believe in."

To see and feel this in a Miles Davis, a black man in a white world was very important to an impressionable, black youngster like me. Only one of six blacks attending a high school of 3,500 whites, I definitely felt beseiged, assaulted. Miles's refusal to grin in front of white audiences like many other black entertainers made a statement to me. And when I read he had gotten beaten over the head outside Birdland (where he was playing) by a white policeman who ordered him to move (he refused to move), because he didn't like Miles walking a white, female friend to a cab, that was it for me. Miles became my biggest hero.

Miles opened up the possibility of my doing anything I imagined. Miles's music is *about* conception, *about* ideas, *about* the realization of a fertile imagination. And no matter how simply or directly he plays, his music always affects me this way; it hits my heart, while never abandoning the cerebral. His voice is always a Mississippi-River-blues-based voice, achingly honest, direct and as penetrating as a train's whistle piercing the empty, midwestern plains during midnight hours. His trumpet always seemed for me to ride over the silent, dark hours and penetrate my ears, speak directly to my being as would an animal's voice, lonely, plaintive, perhaps lost in pain. It is often a sad, haunting voice, and at the same time resonant and strong.

And so as he was sitting across from me there, in his dark cave of an apartment, on this bright, clear, warm, blue afternoon in June, I admit to struggling fiercely with a sweeping sensation of awe. That is, until he grabbed my hair and made our first real encounter so human. Everything went upbeat from there. That doesn't mean we haven't had our differences since, because we have. It's just that those differences have been minor in our soon to be close relationship.

During the summer of 1986, I came to know him as almost a childlike person, delicate, almost feminine at times, much softer than what I expected, but then again, still tough. One thing is certain: it always seemed to me almost impossible to take advantage of Miles Davis because he is always alert to this possibility. Still, he is quite generous if he likes and trusts you. He would give me tapes of his live concerts with the only admonishment not to give them to anyone else, and I haven't.

I remember many times looking at him and hearing several of his tunes, but especially "All Blues" for some inexplicable reason. I would always hear it distinctly, clearly, as if it were emanating from some secret place in whatever room we were sitting in. At first I thought he might be playing it as background music. But then I knew this wasn't true because Sandra Trim-DaCosta, his publicist while he was at Columbia, told me he never listened to his old music, and in fact loathed even talking about the past.

As I got to know him better, my awe of him was replaced with a healthy sense of respect. Miles is a very unpredictable person subject to rapid mood swings. He says it is because he is a Gemini, but some of it is also due to his being diabetic. I soon learned that if I came over after his insulin shot, his energy level was low and he soon became drowsy and wanted to sleep. If you stayed around he got edgy, uncommunicative and sometimes downright hostile.

The most striking thing about Miles's physical makeup besides the strikingly beautiful color of his deep black skin is his eyes. They are riveting. You see in those eyes a resolute sense of self. They are large eyes, with a lot of white around the iris and when he looks at you it is with a direct, unflinching gaze. You see and feel genius in those eyes. Feminine, like his face, his eyes when he is happy can be very soft, delicate; when he's angry they are fierce.

Throughout the years, Miles has been willing to risk losing everything in order to gain everything. In that sense he is a gambler, one who has won and lost but won more than he has lost in his art. I think Miles has lost more in his personal life than he has won. I say this because Miles's personal life to me seems moribund, lonely and most times empty except for his involvement with his art, which is everything to him. Women come and go, as do a few, close friends and family. His younger brother, Vernon, his older sister, Dorothy, her husband Vincent Milburn, and their son, Vincent Jr. who played drums in Miles's band for a while — beyond having fun with these family members (and he really enjoys them: when they're together they're a real scream, telling jokes, playing games, eating up a storm) he doesn't really seem to enjoy himself. I once told him that I had more fun in a day than he had in an entire year. He just laughed and told me it was probably true, although he did seem shocked by my observation.

Miles likes being alone, says it is the penalty and sacrifice he has to bear to be close to his creative juices. In that light, his isolation is self-imposed, is something he controls. This isolation has kept him focused on his music for forty-five years. He has elevated jazz into a high art form, changing his style at least nine times. There have been: his "cool" period; the period of his small group ensembles with Coltrane, Philly Joe, etc.; his *Walking* album; his big band records including *Sketches of Spain*; his modal albums, like *In a Silent Way*; his seminal rock/funk albums, *Bitches Brew* and *Live-Evil*; his James Brown-oriented records, *Big Fun*, *On the Corner*, *Jack Johnson*; his rock-oriented albums, *Agharta* and *Pangea*; and his latest direction in such albums as *Tutu* and *Admandla*, which take their impetus from big-band sounds, African, Caribbean and Brazilian music. *Nine* different changes. Whew! He has told me on many occasions that music is about style. It's about the way an individual musician (influenced by regional sounds and ways of playing) approaches his instrument. Miles has learned to play in so many styles that he has ended up giving us a musical map through the whole terrain of jazz.

Personally, Miles can be a very difficult person to get along with. He is irascible, contemptuous, brutally honest, ill-tempered when things don't go his way, complex, fair-minded, humble, kind and a son-of-a-bitch. He is insecure about many things, proud of being black, totally freaked out about having to wear a hair weave, absolutely confident of his musical ability, still in awe of Dizzy Gillespie, Charlie Parker and Duke Ellington. He loves James Brown, Prince and Michael Jackson. He loves barbeque, pig snouts, chili, ice cream and Evian water. He is generous, cheap, stylishly elegant and a country bumpkin, naive about many things to the point of embarrassment. He is both one of the kindest people I have ever met and also one of the most infuriating assholes I have ever encountered. But it's like he always says: "everything's about timing." So it's about when and how you catch Miles. On the one hand he can be one of the funniest persons you ever met, or one of the meanest, he can be so humble one moment and the next moment (and I do mean the very next moment) he can turn into one of the most arrogant, exasperating, most obnoxious little tasteless bastards you ever met. He is endlessly contradictory.

3.

All musicians aren't great, creative people. They just technicians and can't hear shit. Now take somebody like you, Quincy; you got great ears and can hear your ass off. If you played an instrument you'd be a "bad" motherfucker.
— Miles Davis, in conversation

It's August, 1986 and we're sitting on the terrace of his ocean-front home in Malibu, California, near the Ventura County line. I have signed the contract to co-write Miles's autobiography, and he's happy I'm writing the book. "I got you a gig," he said laughing when I talked to him after first signing the contract. That was three months ago and we have been sparring verbally with each other ever since. On the other side of Highway 1 the mountains loom high. They look exactly like the mountains in Haiti off that country's Highway 1.

In front of us, the sun extinguishes its fiery self in an orange grave of liquid flames way out to the west. It is a wondrous sight and we are both silently in awe of nature's power. He is chewing gum and listening to the Pacific waves crashing the beach just beneath his terrace. Again, he's wearing black denims, a black silk T-shirt and a black jean jacket. As always, wraparound glasses cover his piercing eyes. He's staring straight ahead and I see a lot of native American Indian in his profile.

Miles Davis has become — or always was — a very good actor. He acts all the time, probing and testing, trying to see how strong or weak you are, and if he finds you weak or stupid he comes down hard, because he doesn't suffer what he thinks is foolishness lightly or easily. He can be cold on a motherfucker if you come off wrong. If you're with Miles and you come off wrong, you will suffer one of three things. First, he might just ignore you altogether. Two, he might turn those ray-gun eyes on you as if he were trying to execute you with a mere stare. Third, he might just curse you out and put you down verbally in such an unbelievably cruel manner that you would never ever repeat what you just have done. Already, in three months, I have undergone three fierce put-downs, three baptisms of Miles's verbal fire and I'm not about to go through it again. So on this August day I am silent, picking my words carefully.

He's sitting on the terrace in the now-yeasting darkness, gulping down great quantities of Evian water straight from the bottle. He has turned the terrace light on and is drawing feverishly, like the first day we met. All of a sudden he stops drawing, takes off his glasses and turns those scorching, devilishly twinkling eyes on me. A playful twitching jerking at the corners of his lips, he says, biting on the corners of his sunglasses, "Quincy, what do you think of McCoy Tyner as a piano player? You said you liked Trane. So what do you think of McCoy, brother?"

I sense a set-up, so I proceed a little cautiously. "I like the group-sound Trane had when McCoy was in the group," I begin.

"Answer the question, motherfucker," he breaks in, without missing a beat, his eyes flashing both mischieviously and menacingly." Answer the motherfuckin' question! Do you like him or don't chu?"

"I like him, Miles," I say, just a little taken aback by this sudden attack jumping out of a long stretch of silence.

"Why?" he says, after a long, pregnant pause. "Why do you like McCoy as a pianist, Quincy?" He says this rather sarcastically, a touch of Milesian playfulness giggling around the corners of the words.

"Because I think he plays well," I say, on the lookout now for a verbal sucker punch.

"Oh, he plays the piano well, you say," Miles says, really enjoying the game. "Well, are you sure he plays well, and how the fuck would you know he's playin' well? You a trained pianist or something?"

"Naw, I ain't no trained pianist. I'm just talkin' about what I like to hear in a piano player," I say, now a little hurt and put off by this dilemma I find myself in.

"Oh, is that what it is," he says, almost laughing at me, "you like what you're hearin'? Well, do you know what you're listenin' to? Do you know if his playin' is in context to what everyone else is playin'?"

"Well Trane must have liked it," I say, going on the offensive. "If he was good enough for Trane then he's good enough for me."

"Aw Quincy don't tell me no simple-minded bullshit like that," he says, his eyes completely on fire now. "I'm not askin' you what Trane liked — I know what he liked and why! I'm asking you what you like and if you can't tell me that from deep down inside some kind of conviction, then don't say a motherfuckin' thing, you know what I mean motherfucker?"

I start to say, "I just told you what I liked about McCoy, Miles," but don't say it because I realize I haven't told him *why* I liked him, I stop and think for a moment while his eyes burn into mine, waiting for an answer. Did I really like McCoy as a pianist by himself, or did I just like him within the context of Trane's group? One thing I do know is that I hadn't bought any recordings by McCoy as a soloist since he left Trane's group. So what does that mean? I don't really know.

"Well," Miles says, quietly now, "do you like him, or what? What is it, brother?"

He's really being sarcastic now, a little smile is playing openly around his lips. He's enjoying being the cat and me being the mouse.

"I really don't know, Miles," I say after a while. "Plus, I really don't give a fuck!"

"Oh yeah," he says in that raspy voice that tells me he knows I'm mad now. "Is it that you don't know, or is it that you know but are afraid to tell the truth because you think I might get mad at you?" He's laughing out loud, certain he's got me over a barrel.

"Naw Miles that ain't it," I say, exasperated to the core. "Anyway, fuck you man. You just playin' a game with me."

"Oh yeah," he says, "You think I'm just playin' a game with you? Well, you still haven't answered the motherfuckin' question. So what it be, brother, what do the answer be? Answer the motherfuckin' question, brother."

He spits out "brother" and turns back to the figure he's drawing.

"Well, Miles, I think he can play," I say half-heartedly, not believing my words.

"Naw, Quincy, McCoy can't play shit. All he do is just bang around the piano. Just bang around. Never played shit and never will. He's a very nice person, but he can't play no piano to my way of listening. I told Trane that, too. But Trane liked him, liked what he was doin' and kept him on. McCoy couldn't play if his life depended on it. Then, again, a lot of people didn't like Trane's playin' in my band. But I did, and that's all that counts." Then he smiles that sideways smile he does when he's about to let you off the hook and says, "Quincy, I'm surprised at someone who can hear music as well as you liking someone as bad as McCoy Tyner. Now, I'm gonna have to re-evaluate what I said about your ears, that you could hear so good and all. Yeah," he says bringing the discussion to a close, and giving me that sly, mischievous look of his, "I'm gonna have to think about what I said about your ears. You know what I mean, brother?"

This conversation taught me a lot about Miles Davis and about myself. What it taught me about Miles was that he loves to confront people to see if they believe what they say they believe. He's like a great sword-fighter parrying for weaknesses, both in your character and in your argument. If you don't stand up to him he has no respect for you. Sometimes he plays devil's advocate just to see where you are, to see if you will stand up for what you believe in. If he finds you weak he will just plunge his sword straight through your heart and keep on steppin' because he's a man who doesn't suffer from guilt. He teaches this way, in life and in music; he likes to teach what one shouldn't do, or play, and in this respect — and from all the people I talked to who played in his band — he is a great teacher.

Miles's approach to teaching was picked up from a complex group of people: Theolonious Monk, Charlie Parker, Billy Eckstine, Dizzy Gillespie, Coleman Hawkins and Duke Ellington, just to name a few. At one time or another, Miles assumed the persona of all these great musicians and leaders of musicians. These were his mentors, as were people like Humphrey Bogart, Fred Astaire and a clutch of "gangster personae" he picked up on along the way.

Much of his suspicion of the press and the way he has handled journalists — for the most part, not talking with them — came from Theolonious Monk (only Miles's approach is more hostile). His penchant for wearing sunglasses goes all the way back to be-bop and again the way Monk, Charlie Parker and Dizzy Gillespie wore "shades" as part of their hip, cool, musical uniform. As a band leader Miles is even closer to Bird and Monk in the way he chooses his bands. Like them, he likes to work his music up from ideas, fragments. He feels that if you tell musicians too much about the music they're about to play there won't be an element of surprise, a spontaneity. And Miles wants — in fact, craves, needs — surprise and spontaneity. That's why he prefers playing live to being in the studio where he feels the music easily gets pat and stale.

For that reason Miles, like Monk and Bird before him, only brings fragments of music into his studio sessions so that the musicians will have to find more interplay with each other — will be forced to play what's there, what isn't there, play what they know and above what they know — rather than relying on just what's there on the charts and arrangements. This method of recording locks creative tension into the sessions, opening the music up to improvisation.

To look at Miles in the context of the geographical space and time he came out of is to observe his personality and know his music in yet another way. St. Louis and East St. Louis were both gangster towns; white gangsters and African-American gangsters — both played a prominent role in these cities during the twentieth century. It was after the riot of 1917 in East St. Louis that African-Americans armed themselves and took on a no-nonsense attitude toward whites after scores of African-Americans were murdered. Miles's father was a hard-core African-American nationalist, a follower of Marcus Garvey rather than the integrationist NAACP. Miles picked up on these political beliefs of his father.

As for the gangster influence on his personality, Miles has admitted liking the screen characters played by Humphrey Bogart and Edward G. Robinson, the slickness and cold, hard-edged surface of their tough-guy images. He also was fond of Jordan Chambers, a prominent St. Louis gangster and politician and later, after Miles moved to New York and was hanging out in Harlem, the legendary Bumpy Johnson. He looked up to these men as independent, proud black men, and if you check out Miles's attitude closely, you will find their influence on him even today.

It is a difficult, almost impossible task to remain on the cutting edge of creativitiy for over forty-five years. Miles Davis has managed to do this, and, I might add, done it superbly most of the time. There have been failures — *Quiet Nights*, *The Man With a Horn*, and a few others — but the triumphs far outnumber his failures.

Miles has often told me that he never wanted to become a musical museum object under glass, meaning that he was required to keep on playing the same old musical thing, the same old musical licks. He told me he'd "rather die," said he had to keep on going forward. And so he has, continuously breaking musical ground.

4.

The first thing I remember in my early childhood is a flame, a blue flame jumping off a gas stove somebody lit. I don't remember who it was. Anyway, I remember being shocked by the whoosh of the blue flame jumping off the burner, the suddenness of it. That's as far back as I can remember: any further

*back than this is just fog, you know, just mystery. But that stove flame is as
clear as music is in my mind. I was three years old.*

*I saw that flame and felt the hotness of it close to my face, I felt fear, real
fear, for the first time in my life. But I remember it also like some kind of ad-
venture, some kind of weird joy, too. I guess that experience took me someplace
in my head I hadn't been before. To some frontier, the edge, maybe, of everything possible. I don't know, I never tried to analyze it before. The fear I had
was almost like an invitation, a challenge to go forward into something I knew
nothing about. That's where I think my personal philosophy of life and my
commitment to everything I believe in started, with that moment.*

— Miles Davis, from The Autobiography

Miles is what I call an unreconstructed black man, much in the
same way Redd Foxx, Chuck Berry and Ike Turner, all fellow St. Louis
area homeboys, are. They are all unpredictable, go their own way.
They don't take anything off of anybody, and will go to the mat when
challenged.

This "unreconstrucedness" can cause weird quirks in the personality, a kind of highly-personalized and self-centered way of looking
at and evaluating everything. The world revolves around the way
this person sees it. No compromises here; either do it this way or
fuck you up your ass. And in the end, it's very difficult, if not impossible, for this kind of person to see himself as wrong in a situation. So for the most part, other people involved in a relationship
with an unreconstructed black man tiptoe around, trying hard not
to upset the self-centered lifestyle of the man who is most times so
focused on what he's doing — one of the main reasons for his success
besides talent — that he doesn't realize he's giving most everyone a
royal fucking, and if he did realize it he still wouldn't give a flying
fuck. Because what he's doing is always more important to him —
and in his mind, everyone and everything else, too — than what
someone else is doing.

Miles Davis is like that. And sometimes when you work as closely with a person like this as I have there's bound to be plenty of differences. Someone has to eat crow, and since I was entering Miles's
life as a writer, a collaborator on his life story, I had to eat crow in
order to get the job done. Now mind you, Miles ate some too, but
not as openly as I did: if he was wrong about something he would
tell me in private, but never in public, or in the company of another
person. We had many memorable spats while we were working on
The Autobiography. Suffice it to say our friendship's been earned.

Miles doesn't read anything except art books, and a few magazines
and newspapers. Most of his information comes from the television,

which he has on and watches around the clock: I can hardly ever remember a time when I visited him that the television wasn't on. He was even reluctant to turn it off when we had to tape his interviews. Further, it was the biggest obstacle to my completing the interviewing process with Miles. Sometimes it was weird; me, Miles, the television and silence, that is, the silence between us.

I was also shocked to find out he knew little about African-American visual artists since he was beginning to paint every day when we started the book. He knows a lot about Picasso and Dali, his favorite painter, but he hadn't heard of Romare Bearden, or Jacob Lawrence or any other African-American painters.

His ignorance of African and Caribbean music outside of reggae and Bob Marley was also shocking. Now that's not to say he wasn't interested, because he was. When I turned him on to the music from Zaire — Franco, Tabu Ley, and others — and Zouk music from the Caribbean — mainly Kassav from Guadeloupe — he sponged it up. That music along with hip-hop, go-go and some other fragments here and there formed the basis for the music on *Amandla*.

Miles's understanding of history is also simplistic. Yet he has an intuitive grasp of what's right and wrong because of race relations in this country, because of the teachings of his father and his own experiences. But I think what disturbed me most was the way he viewed skin color. Now, I don't know whether he was putting me on or not but he said he "didn't like no woman who was darker than me." His view on skin color was for me a sign of deep insecurity, and ironic since Miles was one of the first real dark-skinned entertainment idols — even sex symbols — to come out of the 1950s; before then all of the African-American male sex symbols had been fair-skinned. Miles broke down that barrier. His chauvinistic attitude toward women and his class bias — he would deny this — toward people less fortunate left much to be desired. What escapes many people is that Miles is a product of this country's aristocracy and it shapes the way he looks at himself and at the rest of the world.

Miles and I both love sports, which was the foundation — besides the writing and the fact we are from the same part of the country — for our friendship. We would sit up and watch baseball, basketball, track and football for hours hardly saying a word to each other. He especially likes boxing and when we were watching boxing matches he would get up and demonstrate what each fighter was doing; when we watched boxing matches he talked long and heavy about boxing techniques which he knows a lot about. Another thing that bonded our friendship was the love of the same kind of food: hot links, chittlings, hog maws, pig feet, greens and fatback, cole slaw, potato salad, cornbread, sweet potato pie, you know, your basic, outta sight meal of great black soul food. Man, we've scarfed down a lot of that food together.

The first professional band Miles played in — Eddie Randle's "Blue Devils" band — was my cousin's band and this kind of cemented everything between us. Miles's love of great style and fashion — something else close to my heart — and you have the icing on the cake of our relationship. Many a time I would fall by Miles's place with something very hip on and he would tell me with that mischievous grin on his face, "Give it up, motherfucker, take that shit off you back right now and give it to me." It was just his way of letting me know I was wearing something he admired.

Miles and I have the kind of relationship where we don't have to see each other all the time to be close, when we see each other it's like we saw each other yesterday. I remember one day Miles called to ask me to ride upstate New York with him. I said yes, so he picked me up in a limo and we rode for about three hours without saying a word. Finally, the driver said, "Mr. Davis, I thought you said this guy was a good friend of yours."

"He is," Miles said.

"But you two guys haven't hardly spoke to each other."

Miles looked at me, smiled and said: "We don't have to talk out loud with each other to communicate. Plus, it ain't none of your business if we talk or not. Just drive the car, motherfucker, and mind your own business."

Well, he did and we did. That was the end of that. Again, I had learned something from Miles, the great teacher, had learned that words can get in the way, are sometimes not needed and for someone like Miles, who is a man of few words, are most times phony. It's the way he plays his horn, spare, but meaningful when he does play, and it's the way he teaches his band members to play; he tells them not to play just to be blowing on their instruments, but have something important to play, and if they don't, just lay out and be silent. For Miles, silence has its place and is just as meaningful as sound, and is, quiet as it's kept, a kind of beautiful sound.

5.

Today, Miles Davis is an international icon, feted the world over, but more so outside his own country. In this way he shares the fate of Jimi Hendrix and his friend, the late James Baldwin. If Miles had been born white and achieved what he has achieved he would already have been crowned an American National Treasure. But it's a political thing here that he hasn't and others have been so designated. All of us who really know about and love his music know the real deal, that he is truly America's greatest musician of the twentieth century, Duke Ellington and Louis Armstrong's monumental achievements notwithstanding. No other living musician has changed the course of jazz more than Miles. But then again, everyone and his mama knows that malignant racism is everywhere in these "yet to be United States" (James Baldwin's words). Throughout it all, Miles Davis just does what he's supposed to do: give us glorious, on the cutting edge, music.

He will be 65 years old in May, May 26th to be exact, and he is playing the music of someone much younger. He is a glory to behold, off and on the bandstand, a fountainhead of creative energy and grace.

I found out how much Miles hated to talk about death when I told him Jimmy had died in December, 1987. He hadn't heard and couldn't seem to get it together that Jimmy was gone. He kept saying that he had just seen him earlier in the year. In fact he told me he was convinced that among all of his friends, Jimmy would outlive him. I thought I saw tears welling in his eyes, but if they were, Miles covered it up well by going into the bathroom. One thing is certain: Miles Davis wasn't going to let me or anybody else see him cry. But I think on this cold December day in 1987 Miles Davis was crying in the bathroom for his great friend now gone, Jimmy Baldwin. He stayed in the bathroom for a while and when he came out there was no sign of tears. "Man," I remember thinking to myself, "Miles is one tough motherfucker."

"And I ain't going to no funeral," I remember him saying. I asked him if he was going. "I don't like no goddamn funeral, even if it is Jimmy Baldwin's. I want to remember him in life, in the flesh, a bad motherfucker and not some ghost of himself layin' up in no coffin. That ain't Jimmy," he went on, "but just a pile of lifeless flesh and bones. Naw, man, I want to remember him how he was: a bad motherfucker. That's all."

Throughout that day he talked about many of his friends who had

91

died — Monk, Bird, Coltrane, Fats Navarro, Freddie Webster, Bud Powell, Red Garland, Clifford Brown and many, many others. But he talked about Philly Joe Jones, his ex-drummer, the most. And every time he mentioned Philly Joe, he shook his head and chuckled to himself — Miles doesn't laugh, but kind of chuckles, sometimes emitting a raspy, throaty shaking of his voice. It was evident that Miles loved Philly Joe, and it was evident that day Miles loved James Baldwin, also.

It was on this day that I realized Miles had lost so many good friends that it had made him a lonely person, afraid to truly become deep friends with anyone because they too might leave him. I thought of this and it made me sad, for Miles and everyone else.

What does the future hold for Miles? He has mentioned to me a desire to explore the music and rhythms of Brazil and African music more, also the music of China and Japan (I mean, what would *that* music sound like?). He would like to work with the great arranger, Quincy Jones, and has tinkered around with working with Prince. They have played together, mostly in Minneapolis at jam sessions, and there are some audio and video tapes of these musical encounters. But whether this collaboration will come off, well, let me put it this way: I'm not optimistic.

Whatever it is that Miles comes up with in the future — whether it's continuing to work with Marcus Miller and Tommy LaPuma, or Quincy Jones, or Prince, look for the music to be adventurous, on the cutting edge. Because like he has said: "I'm going to try to keep my music getting up on the one, getting up on the one every day I play, getting up on the one."

It's early February, 1990, and Miles is finishing up a four-day concert tour of Pointe-a-Pitre, Guadeloupe. It's the last night — Friday — and the last set and he has already killed them dead for three days. Now, the entire auditorium jammed full with 5,000 revelers on their collective feet, screaming. I have come down to this butterfly-shaped Caribbean island at Miles's invitation to catch the last show. We are backstage, waiting in the wings for the end of the concert, waiting for him to exit. He's playing his ass off, but when he sees me out the corner of his eyes, it seems to me that he takes his playing up another notch and plays even harder. Now, maybe I can admit here that this might be a manifestation of my ego, but I would swear on a stack of bibles that this was the way it was.

When he hits his last note and turns to leave the stage, the people go crazy, screaming for more, but I know they're not going to get it because he never returns after his last hit. By this time my wife Margaret and I have moved backstage from the stage wing and are waiting for him to exit. When he comes through the double doors the first person he runs into is Margaret. He gives her a big hug. Now, what's beautiful about this encounter is that it comes after all the spats and everything, after when we have to merely tolerate each other to complete our collaboration on Miles's autobiography. But we have fought through everything to a kind of hard-won friendship, one that is solid and perhaps, lasting. I can see it in his eyes at this moment and he can see it in mine.

We hug each other and while we are embracing he says, "My man, my main man. You like the show?"

"Yeah," I tell him, "man you were burning and so was the band."

"Oh yeah," he says, happy we are together in this moment. Then he says as we disengage, smiling that sly, mischievous smile of his, "Man, you still about a funny lookin' motherfucker, and I don't care what anybody says."

He moves on smiling that quixotic, sweet smile of his when he likes something or someone, moves gimp-leg, but hip into his own great glory.

"Go on, Miles," I remember saying to myself, "go on with your bad self."

Risasi-Zachariah Dais

93

Orwell's Bells
Mitch Berman and *Susanne Wah Lee*

THERE HAD BEEN NO SIGN of martial law, not on the road from the airport, where peasants bundled crops onto flat-bed bicycle trailers, nor here on Wangfujing, Beijing's main shopping street, where women strolled hand in hand, examining cucumbers, tiny green and red bell peppers, and thin pale purple eggplants displayed on wide tables jutting into the sidewalk; where leathery shoemakers with cigarette butts and metal brads between their teeth hammered on ladies' soles; where haughty teenagers in American-style baseball caps lounged outside hair salons boasting the "Latest Faoshins"; where black marketeers hawked Camels and comic books of smeary black-and-white pornography; where flotillas of bicyclists careered lawlessly on one-speed Flying Pigeons.

Tiananmen Square was throbbing with music, propulsive pop music of some kind, so distorted that we couldn't make it out. Under white and khaki tarpaulins moored to bamboo poles, students were dozing, talking, playing cards, sucking on *bing gur* (popsicles), smoking cigarettes and listlessly strumming guitars in the heat. Wilting banners proclaimed their school names. Then we recognized it: "We Are the World." The first voice we heard raised in song in China was Stevie Wonder's.

We had walked into an air war between two sets of loudspeakers, cross talk at cross-purposes. Strung up on light standards like the product of some experiment in fruit hybridization, government loudspeakers talked down to the protesters. The canned speeches saluted the students, urging them to stop this "turmoil" and return to their campuses.

The students salvoed back from large conical speakers mounted like gargoyles on the Monument to the People's Heroes, the white granite obelisk that was the nerve center and the touchstone of the democracy movement. The national anthem was their leading weapon, played—sometimes sung—several times a day to score and underscore their demand that the government recognize their

Student loudspeaker on Monument of the People's Heroes, Tiananmen Square.

movement as patriotic. The students had turned *Frère Jacques* into a derogatory ditty about the *People's Daily*, but they took their anthem straight:

> *Arise, ye who refuse to be slaves;*
> *With our very flesh and blood*
> *Let us build our new Great Wall!*
> *The peoples of China are in the most critical time*
> *Everybody must roar his defiance.*
> *Arise! Arise! Arise!*
> *Millions of hearts with one mind,*
> *Brave the enemy's gunfire,*
> *March on!*
> *Brave the enemy's gunfire,*
> *March on! March on! March on, on!*

The principal music of Tiananmen Square was speech, free and constant and, up on the Monument, deafening. Someone was always talking; whenever it was done with an air of authority, a cluster of logo-bearing microphones sprouted like a bouquet. The students liked to address the media through gold plastic mini-bullhorns that rendered their voices trebly and mechanical without amplifying them to any appreciable degree.

A canopy of broadcast static overarched the Square, the student loudspeakers belting out a constant stream of exhortation, oratory, invective, ridicule, while from the government loudspeakers came deep, mature, mellifluous male voices, smoothly droning voices devoid of urgency, implacable in the knowledge that they would be heeded, voices that were all the same voice.

Between the frequencies, between the sheets of sound, between the crossfire, rock music could be heard from cheap boom boxes in the students' tents. Rock was a recent import, a product of China's new infatuation with the West. In 1985, Wham had become the first westerners to play a rock concert in China; though authorities had chosen the pretty-boy British duo for their clean-scrubbed inocuousness, Beijing police had still escorted dancers from Workers' Stadium. By then China had crossbred its own brand of rock, *yao gun*, and the distinction of being its first star belonged to Cui Jian.

A year after the government crackdown on the student movement escaped student leader Wuer Kaixi would tell an astonished New York audience that Chinese youths had been influenced less by dissidents such as Fang Lizhi or Wei Jingsheng than by rock musicians such as Qi Qin and Cui Jian.

Students in Tiananmen Square were still playing Cui's 1985 song "Nothing to My Name" four years after its release. Avoiding overtly political themes, Cui's lyrics articulated the students' underlying helplessness and alienation:

> *I want to give you my hope*
> *I want to help make you free*
> *But all you do is laugh at me*
> *'cause I've got nothing to my name.*

With their headbands and shirts covered with one another's slogans and signatures, with their camaraderie and rebelliousness, the students had created an instant counterculture, and Tiananmen Square sometimes seemed an extended, distended rock festival. Several rock performers did play for the students at the Square, the most famous among them Cui Jian.

Three months before the student movement had begun, an American crew had shot a video for Cui's "No More Disguises" that began with images of Beijing citizens in Tiananmen Square. After the crackdown Cui was interrogated, but not arrested; the Americans independently completed the video, overlaying the famous image of Wang Weiling, the solitary man facing down a line of tanks, with Cui's lyric, "My courage comes from me alone." The video was never shown in China.

In 1990 Cui Jian embarked on a fund-raising tour for the Asian Games, Asia's premier sporting event, which Beijing would host for the first time in September. Cui's audiences began raising their fists and flashing V-for-victory signs, gestures that had not been seen in China since the student movement. Authorities halted his tour immediately.

One sweltering afternoon, to get out from under the dinning student loudspeakers, we circled to the rear of the Monument, facing the mausoleum where Chairman Mao lay in state, preserved in a crystal sarcophagus. Suddenly a score of students and twice as many journalists came sprinting toward us, the students grabbing and pushing a young man with a bruised face as the journalists shouted questions.

The students yanked the young man into a tent and zipped the hatch. The thin nylon billowed violently, inhaling and exhaling. As the national anthem erupted from the loudspeakers, a ring of students bossed back the media, throwing hands up in front of cameras and barking at us through their little gold bullhorns. The students, who were merely doing as they'd been taught, couldn't understand why the press refused to stop questioning them. They played the anthem two or three times in a span of ten minutes, trusting in its power to maintain order, to answer all questions.

The democracy movement reached its nadir in late May, when the Beijing students who had taken over Tiananmen Square in April had returned to their schools, ceding the Square to their provincial brethren; when the first hunger strike had ended and the second hadn't begun; when the American network TV crews, weary and grumbling, were readying to pool into a single shared video feed; when only a few thousand students remained on the Square and an afternoon's rain showed their true numbers, uninflated by casual strollers, by tourists, by anyone who had anyplace to go; when rain washed the makeup off the face of the democracy move-

97

ment. The students needed a miracle; out of plaster and Styrofoam, they built their own.

The Goddess of Democracy made her way along Changan Avenue disassembled into three pieces and glowing in the night under the diffuse beams of flashlights. The statue's top third came first: the Goddess' white bust, with its great placid Eurasian face turned slightly to the side behind a torch held more outward than upward, held protectively in front of her.

Changan was brimming with pedestrians and riders who stood beside their bicycles, watching. No one spoke save in a hush; no one moved save the Goddess and those who bore her slowly toward the Square. She looked like the Liberty of nineteenth-century American coinage. Students carrying thick bamboo poles kept the dense but disciplined crowd at a safe distance from the Goddess, applauding as she passed. A quarter of a million people had come out to see her.

As Tiananmen Square filled, the Goddess' progress was heralded by firecrackers, skyrockets and periodic bulletins from the loudspeakers ("The statue has arrived at the Square"). The crowd swarmed in from Changan, pressed against the Monument, and began a massed chanting, the low-budget music of the student movement; the students chanted back: *"Sit down!"*

Student leader and hunger striker Wuer Kaixi, who had confronted Premier Li Peng in an unprecedented encounter on Chinese TV, was already in hiding when he made a surprise appearance in Tiananmen to see the Goddess. A rock star was coming out of seclusion: people converged on him, thrusting out scraps of paper for his autograph, snapping locally-made point-and-shoot cameras, getting off their bicycles to stare, getting on their bicycles to trail him. First a whispering arose, then a murmuring, and finally a chanting: *"Wuer Kaixi! Wuer Kaixi!"*

Beijing's main street had become a single writhing organism, with Wuer at its head. He and a companion crossed Changan at a dead run, their impromptu entourage in tow. "Zai guo" (cross again), said Wuer, and they dashed across the avenue once more. The crowd followed, serpentine.

On June 2nd, for the first time in two weeks, there were hunger strikers in Tiananmen, and for the first time, the strikers were intellectuals and Party members instead of students: Liu Xiaobo, a lecturer at Beijing Normal University; Zhou Duo, an economist at Stone Corporation, one of China's most successful companies; editor Gao Xin and rock singer Hou Dejian. The hunger strikers were housed in a large khaki tent on the dais of the Monument, and an enormous, abrasive crowd was there to cheer them on.

Once again the students chanted, *"Sit down!"* at the masses pressing against the barriers, but the chant, tried and true since the dawn of the movement in April, had no effect. With a roar of relief, the people broke down the barriers and swarmed over the Monument. Hou Dejian led them in an impassioned chorus of his song "Descendants of the Dragon":

> *There is a dragon in the ancient Far East,*
> *It is called the Middle Kingdom.*
> *There is a people in the ancient Far East*
> *They are the descendants of the dragon.*
> *I grew up at the feet of the dragon,*
> *I grew up to become a descendant of the dragon,*
> *Black eyes, black hair, yellow face,*
> *A descendant of the dragon forever.*

At the periphery of the Square, in the midst of something like a revolution, an American tourist in shorts, Reeboks and a Sony Walkman jogged obliviously through the crowd.

On the night of the massacre, the person who engaged military commanders in tense negotiations for the passage of the remaining students from Tiananmen Square was not the professor, the editor or the economist, but the rock star.

Hou Dejian, born and raised in Taiwan after his parents fled from the mainland, had become an instant celebrity with the 1978 release of "Descendants of the Dragon." In 1983, on a trip to Beijing, he defected. Royalties from Hong Kong and Taiwan had allowed him to enjoy a lavish life by Chinese standards.

Immediately following the massacre, Hou took refuge in the Australian embassy, and did not emerge until two months later. He remained critical of the leadership, finally announcing a press conference marking the first anniversary of the massacre. Hou Dejian was arrested before the press conference could take place. In the fall of 1990, the Chinese government deported him to Taiwan.

On Saturday, June 3rd, miles of eight-lane Changan Avenue were so choked with people there wasn't enough room for them to swing their arms. A police van had run over three people that morning, and skirmishes between police and protesters flared up throughout the afternoon. Not many in the capital were still indoors.

At the intersection of Changan and Fuyou, a block away from Tiananmen Square, the crowd chanted, cheered when students rode slowly by on bicycles, waving their school banners; when men clambered to the roof of an abandoned bus and held aloft captured helmets and tear-gas canisters; when a rowdy group braced up against a police jeep that had been left at the curb, and rolled it with a grunt. A student from the makeshift print shop on the Square arrived with freshly printed bulletins, climbed a tree and let leaves of paper waft into an underbrush of outstretched arms. A few youths lobbed rocks over the walls of Zhongnanhai, the compound where the government leaders live and work. On the hour, the overamplified electronic strains of "East is Red" blatted from a remote official loudspeaker, followed by some tinny chimes. Orwell's Bells, we called them, and it would not have surprised us if they were striking thirteen.

Government loudspeaker on Tiananmen Square

The roar was deep and massed, tolling, then interlaced with higher, nearer voices joining in from the narrow residential *hutongs*, from doorways, from windows of houses all around: *"Zui fan! Zui fan!"*

Just before midnight, the wind changed, and all of Beijing smelled like Chinatown on Chinese New Year. It was the pleasant fragrance of gunpowder.

We had heard that the main invasion force was coming from the west of the city, and we had moved toward it to Fuxingmen, a major intersection a mile and a half west of the Square.

Gunfire could be heard approaching for several minutes: it sounded like corn popping. The muffled concussions came closer until, as troop convoy trucks pulled into plain view in the intersection before us, the sound of the AK-47's rang out clear. As we and a dozen locals lay flattened to the dry, rocky soil of a small vegetable garden, bullets tore the air directly above our heads. The high-pitched ringing seemed to hang in the cool night atmosphere like the peal of small loud bells.

Perhaps two hundred troop trucks trolled past, the soldiers pouring automatic rifle fire down Fuxingmen, where we'd been standing. Smoke rose from the hulls of city buses that people had moved into the intersection and set aflame as barricades.

When the last of the trucks were on their way to Tiananmen Square, the crowds, hiding behind the houses, crouched low in the street, began a final chant: *"Zui fan! Zui fan!"*—criminals! traitors!

From Comes Through
in the Call Hold
(Improvisations on Cecil Taylor)
Clark Coolidge

Car found rigged of these careful dots, but then
monkeys intend to spend it with you, hate this
apparently snatched from a wider escape kept on the dials
but couldn't imagine you blue on the lip of a rock one
bulk clothing stuff, tonal and brought around the feet on lines
permission twilight
dull lip of the treasure it in damage, a copper weighs?
an a b c toxin of the violent sitters, and nameful and floated free
timer, camel, heard off in the house realm of names
and placated mass, joined direction, tin plain, then drained the
    whole's dome
was visited on me then thought of this and said, brighter flag
avenue of the mittened skulls, he'll have to parent it back to
    your paragraphs
globe of the wideness set up as chill world, prepare to notice
in a gum location wooden liquors, calls screws around the time
and able and huge team of, car key of large, hydration trend
big harm loose slabs entire in home, treat backs, lucks
a velocity of big barn loaf, chili waste, arguably teeth were lost
marked up as if carbons, the hatred in residue, ices not hold it
was named and fanciful when the name was heard to be told dim
calls the cloak of its classes home, recall to find somebody a girl
was a weathervane of whim, variable aisler of the dump stuck on
a minor habit there quite, vanillas variable, cough to see
shells burst, women repeat, the class of a hall attack, senses
barrier to it than the word, colossal white pill of a dare
collect here on a point, brought to be seen, impel the date
large olive object, slight cards of the house, bear, tamps
in wide whiteness whirls, brash as cocoa and just as, brimful
chums arrive, glands, a whole tumeric time, cross lozenges with

the clogged capade, all as if oil, rim breaker, off anger
and up with his silvered calcium suns, a fleck in the toothpaste
goes out for a roll, his in spades, winter walls first pack
collided with a coiler, then made nice and parenthesis, done
minor pillow site of the east rings inflation and sod
I have capped whole tomatoes from, early eye loader capes
and in grown thong, greater location possible, pedal of the eye
crate a limb, mile before a dreamer, sky wide to come for
said he wants it for, my stew of brains and get on the limpid
erasing the Nile from dooryard impressions mated hatchways
I could get your flesh while in a tackpaper, same room in
same room rhyme, golden and handedness, variety steam wrestling
cored in plans couldn't vend you hired in wait tin restless
viable key planet sting plays, ounce has come out to seed
variety dad, plays loose plays sides, mulch glass pen facial
and even egg possible, rich gel of the lock-gear monkeys, priced so
a moving window and then you bow to delves in violet weight-back
term of it tells it nights to you, awful view from crates
sod world sky, glasses on automatic, fin will wait to seed
of mountain accuracy, holds micro varlet, Schuyler Aphid
and in bear of the charms, Weblos, Webcor, nerves of a nebula
to still be shading a razor there, pick it up, strength in math
an icicle pickup, every, lords at cartside, a monk at peeling
hem load refrigeration aid, gets, large in cafeteria, ace
hard on the blonde vitamins, oink of the onyx owl glasses
creosote endearment fusses to the socket refusal, hempward
I sail toward window, rat fracas frost up to no bend
we clad, we gang along a liner, rattled in teak packs aside
loaned a liver smiled paid cashed his winter in a scowl
get large lunge in cafeteria right time, goes as goad goals get
let up on a sunday roofs and howl, blade and cigar access
mereness, hill of velocipede, deserted livingroom generals
and cars count from here, dissident Malomar fringe escapes, heeds
fire has to this face itself helped, monaural dad
read books and sling my pallor, goes so high I aged
more less, add sum, core of the bath its lizard novels
first bud to duck the streamer, proceeds and livingroom seconal
do you send it back for a central dowel large in orchestra?
I down in my wind winters terrible strafe of cells
sacked for large suitcase of onyx overdone, clematis
bridgeful, gars' repast, only, chains for it, latch badge

removes the sign of central a back of torque we sided at
a normal sung box has it at when averse, dinge
could go all his clothes, fogs, garnish pedes, agoraphobic pickerel
sentence warnings and comes back for us, hustled and silver at the store
starts to river it then alp repeats then river roofs then stamen
occupier license gets it slack up lip, flames are oval lost
oval boy matriculate penetrates where the flat wearers ovulate
it's overcome cares, march hours, split in phlegm wand waders
and it is all out pent of light already plan flat and in pendulum?
a skin of, past alp worrying and that, plains that hate
little hill of fish, had it *this* name and then he
closet sidle weaken in its pens, lab strength average
and could go out about it, burned radium in its lunch, tong parry
a pestered waitress, rose help skin just above the address there
made of dress, apart waits Apache bulge height set, that's a
marry his mirror, see if I'm she, weighted fogs, lateness in bits
you could corn up the row from whole water hips, gosh emplacement
and carries off corridors, Smirnoff rate of seat, a midge ship
flat wieners, shin and sun, members of the wrong tone rile
road it, veil before voice breath, harrowing in the nacelle
but the broughten of beacon drinks, install lagoon
how has been hip so, made up sun as if in boxes
blow on the harm it does, screw party weightlessness
and all out a plug

But what I want, is it Hindustan?
you understand? in a pile once shed no sticks of the blacker
encoupled bland they have and inch and the sun shades too and hero
on once recaught jump of hitchers they brought me something
eye core emplacelessness blind and in veins the rack begot
I have Flemish chair beacon, darned ends and goes true
out about the violet information midnight, temblor slightly sun
in pressed thing pins, the cloth could reattach you, model main
and coopts what pens stew, trace, once of forget daylight
pike and entrance moves left elbow as limbs to shoe carry out
its, mostly husbandry at home, moistly carried to ceiling encompass
reached past the math arms mess, globe behind him dropped
model pop so, remands to sorry, made to lift a hang apology
when it sent and meant bangers, my song, pump not to you
recancelled him, damned if I could place there where its sun seats too
variant of rock variant tracer of holds a move, rend a mile

carting electron berries over felt kit to be to hone and the sum
whether tattered midnight or, it's tumble down the room vug
oval blends of, right as if wrist to repair, roof
blind hairs at a fire remove, the staples as you wonder at
hanging thing for dress ends, paper matchers but under the over oak
telled as if my hand, imagine it daring them all to, splash
could have closed in on making up those monkeys, large their maps
he could coin the elbow past, see innards, rock the hang of it
a neat blue pressure sort of belly craziness, phone to hand
which that we come in drowns the outback of its stain bells
mud bulbs, and cold it rocky hireling out at Hindustan
raised in a cash, world water, cough in the humming
tan west of the belfry bless
avoid counts in the seat

March on of witnesses, it could bring out your level
press could pay, light as the fires, fogged out fuss plugs
overtickler at the wrenching, pad as bold and station
light filament hate in the better wreckage, nice to sign
a bit and frail of bucket, major claw man's answer
crate sort of cadmium sparse paper knocks its handles
novel, had to come back paid far from it, iced pharaoh
promoter had it that, things bad beneath the plane, coffees
the animals dried and winds as if facing the skull, good honest oak
the placing of dwarves for their hornet's shelf loads in cubical slot
    silence
my, but it cap? lodge waists there in nudge of marry or not
a micro dent fell to his solo, bay yawns replay beyond
the sound where risk it the tongues blow play, rinse off at
dividing line creates soda weight last to pick an asphalted stunt
rapid danger but miked too close for true flavor
had a narrower got them when they, affluvial fat backs
and writes his self vocal to the paid hide of a dental daddy
a region of payoffs, bury that lake, reptilian could not shorten
rock shot to normalize, rice it, gorge in aid, fan sack
fluster and the cords heard his whistle out, not scary
brims with held hands a pocket breath, where'd *who* go?
alert to side and of what, author?
kite boards amber and born mad for breakfast?
it's thumb, trade had his whistle lighter
and markedly markedly, a light off source since the sun

105

comes on back window in, normalize as if rice to tempo
belt of clay gorge aid, mixed with rests?
pocket white with pistol polices seat, marker of dusts
meaner of the smaller smells, and snows over while he's nodded
could include the while tobacco of candy articles, whose
author as if north of hero, march next of the math ones
engarbed and toot fix, made it out sink piece to mean
then south of November a loosener of cannons pauses
felt to pick on the felt of, gone mapping, back vision
no holes know where to come in, thus he would embower it
faker of the dish inch of flames, bringer on the boil
oak preflatten of the hill does, family duck of the escapades
reach, dead piner for the living store, obligatory ditch takes
as if huge bull lemon at the barriers, see radio behind him and
vast cork blueness of flake, salary till
paragraph dots
then the notch to don't see gone out

John Abercrombie and David Starobin

An *Interview by* Bradford Morrow

NEARLY EVERY NON-MUSICIAN I know has wished at some point he or she had turned out to be a musician, a concert pianist, say, drummer, a nimble mallet-magician on marimbas, a virtuoso violinist, a rapper, a crooner, a scatter, a coloratura. Hasn't everyone closet-conducted at least one phonograph symphony? Haven't we all, at one odd moment or another, sung through the steam of the shower the blues, or an aria, or some annoying commercial hook? Some of us have trap sets in our basement, some of us lip-sync into invisible mikes, some of us still saw away at high school violas, or pipe in the night on recorders as dogs' ears stand at attention and neighbors bang the walls.

I was to be a guitarist. It was all I ever wanted. I worked long and hard at it and even managed to achieve a degree of skill on the instrument, played gigs, worked finally as a studio musician moonlighting nights as a non-union scab in Denver, riffing at half price whatever was needed for the airline commercial, the random restaurant spot. I even played with some serious players — bassed behind Albert King once, was a phantom session man with Leon Russell, jammed a lot with the late Tommy Bolin — but then I stepped on my hand. I'd never skiied before. I rode the gondola to the highest slope first time out. My fingers were pointing all different directions, and my inchoate career — such as it was — was finished. The spirit was still there, but the flex of the fingers and elasticism were gone. I still own more guitars than I should.

For me to sit down with John Abercrombie and David Starobin, two of the greatest guitarists on earth, and talk for a while about my favorite instrument — an instrument that's capable of so very much, whose impact on twentieth century culture should never be underestimated — was, to say the least, a charmed thing. Abercrombie and Starobin are working at the crest of their different fields of, respectively, jazz and classical guitar. Their discographies are extensive. Each of these musicians has made, and will no doubt continue to make, a major impact on the history and future of his instrument.

BRADFORD MORROW: Improvisation used to play a part in classical composition. Liszt, Beethoven, Mozart, Chopin were all virtuoso players, and the concerto form allowed them to show off their skills as soloists, allowed them to "contend" with the orchestra, to riff much the same way jazz musicians riff over the chord changes a group is playing. The cadenza was the moment in which the pianist, or violinist, could show his stuff. Classical composition seems not to allow for improvisation now. How do you feel about this?

DAVID STAROBIN: There is still a certain amount of improvisation that takes place in classical music. It depends what the music is. It's true that it's not in the context of tunes, it's not like you are improvising over harmonic changes — it's more free improvisation.

MORROW: But isn't it true that interpretation is primarily the creative element for the classical musician, whereas John, as a jazz player, composes on the spot.

DAVID STAROBIN: Well, for John, improvisation pays the rent, right?

JOHN ABERCROMBIE: That's good, it's true. For jazz musicians the idea is to solo over a tune, a specific harmonic content. When you play the melody there is a content, a composition that comes before the improvisation, and there must be some connection between what you improvise and the spirit of the piece. You can't just think "all right, the tune is finished, now let's get on with the important part, the solo." There has to be some melodic or thematic thread through the entire piece. Maybe I'll echo or develop melodic material from the melody, I'll keep the melody in my mind while I'm improvising rather than run just a series of scales through a set of chords. There must be a wholeness, as the final effect, a completed pattern, or open pattern, if that is what the composition calls for.

MORROW: David, do you ever become improvisational while you're playing? Do you ever feel like you understand a composition better than the composer did and want to break out of the notational?

STAROBIN: I like to think that when I'm playing at my best it comes out as if it *were* improvisation, as if I weren't reading notes, but composing notes. That's what a classical musician goes for, the feeling that he's creating on the spot. When you find a classical player who can do that — who plays freely, who has ideas that seem to be generated by the score — then you have encountered someone who knows what musicianship's about, a player who has something to communicate. Anyone who graduates from a music school can play the notes in the score, but it's the player who makes those notes come alive who interests me. In that way, it's sort of like improvisation.

MORROW: But it's still an interpretive art, isn't it?

STAROBIN: It's a re-interpretive art. You're working with something someone has already composed. How do I view this? How do I bring the composer's original intentions to an audience in a fresh way. It's not like playing jazz at all. It's not that creative, it's more re-creative. However, I do think there's a large element of personal involvement.

MORROW: How would you feel as a player if one of the composers, say Lukas Foss or Elliott Carter who compose for you, would compose a piece where there was a cadenza section?

STAROBIN: They and many other composers who have written for the instrument have left varying passages for the performer to decide. But that's different; if there's room in a piece to do that, it's more like jazz—

ABERCROMBIE: I agree with David that anyone who graduates from music school can play the notes. In that sense, jazz is very similar to classical. If you go up to Boston and study jazz improvisation at Berkelee, you'll hear, like, "These are the scales, here is the sequence of chords, these are the notes you can play, but you can use other ones too you know" and so forth—anyone can learn that system. The thing is to become so fluent you can really express the inside of a piece, develop a solo that evolves the tune. It's not just the notes. It becomes interpretive in this way, you're interpreting the material, the composition, through the scales, the harmonic material, the composition, through the scales, the harmonic materials that are available to you. That's what makes music. That's what separates the great players from those who can play.

MORROW: How would you define a great classical player?

STAROBIN: It goes from the basics of knowing how to handle an instrument in a skillful way to — you know — did you have a good day with your wife, are you in a good frame of mind, plus there are other intangibles, like what you are born with, how you develop what you are born with.

MORROW: I heard Miles Davis say once in an interview that he would select band members based on what they looked like, how they carried their instruments, how they dressed. Miles claimed he could tell if the player was any good or not without even hearing him, but just by observing how he behaved.

ABERCROMBIE: I've seen some guys who look terrific, but play like shit. There are some great-looking guys out there, holding instruments. You can sense certain things from the way a person holds an instrument, but I need to hear the evidence.

MORROW: What makes a great jazz guitarist? Who are the great jazz guitarists?

ABERCROMBIE: I had to do a lecture once about the history of jazz guitar. So, I went out and bought a bunch of records and tapes and dug through my archives, and I listened to all these players starting with Eddie Lang, Nick Lucas, Charlie Christian, all the players who led up to the modern day, and it seemed like the key players to me were Eddie Lang, the early blues players. Then Charlie Christian. He was the first real "hornlike" guitar player I heard, one of the first amplified players, he actually got a singing tone, played more legato eighth-note lines, actually got a saxophone tone. After him, there was a whole stream of guitarists like Barney Kessel, Tal Farlow, Jimmy Raney who was an almost classical-style player whose improvisations sounded like fugues, meticulous and beautiful. The next guitarist who consolidated things was Wes Montgomery who was a very natural player, played with his thumb which was an unusual thing to do.

MORROW: He also soloed with octaves.

ABERCROMBIE: That was his signature. The next guitarist who was important to me was Jim Hall who was a real composer on the guitar when he improvised. It wasn't just notes for him. It had to do with all the elements of jazz like swing and blues. He had a propositional sense that was lacking in other players. He was a direct descendant of Charlie Christian. And if you talk to him he'll tell you all he was doing was copying Charlie Christian solos. Those guys for me established the jazz guitar.

STAROBIN: I think the one player you may be forgetting is Django.

MORROW: Who among your contemporaries do you listen to?

ABERCROMBIE: I think John Scofield has been important in developing the blues sense.

MORROW: You're not mentioning John McLaughlin.

ABERCROMBIE: McLaughlin is a direct link to Django when he plays acoustic, his roots are a blend of Django Reinhardt and flamenco.

MORROW: When he plays acoustic, he seems to go after a buzzy, stringy sound, a crude sound.

ABERCROMBIE: Technically he sets up the instrument with the strings set extremely low. I played one of his acoustic guitars and the strings are right down on the fretboard, so you can play extremely fast on it.

MORROW: What about you, David? Who are the classical players in your personal pantheon?

STAROBIN: With classical guitar we're fortunate in that most of the major guitarists scored their compositions. For me, the guitar proper was born when the sixth string was added to the instrument, 1785 or 1790. Sor and Giuliani, then, are the first great, influential composer-guitarists. They were very different guitarists. Giuliani had a spectacular, fluent right hand; Sor had a remarkable left hand — this is evident from the scores. Sor was able to separate voices and play contrapuntally. In the nineteenth century, it's clear that Regondi was a superior guitarist from looking at his scores. Among twentieth century guitarists, Segovia was active in getting a lot of material written for the instrument in the twenties and thirties. Julian Bream likewise in the fifties and sixties. Contemporarily, there are a lot of good players around. Among American guitarists I think highly of Elliot Fisk. The Brazilian duo, the Assads, Sergio and Odair, have taken the guitar ensemble to a new level.

ABERCROMBIE: What about the Abreu brothers? I once heard them performing a work by Santorsola on the radio and simply snapped. Complicated, twelve-tonal, very tight, I'd never heard anyone play music like this. Then they just disappeared.

STAROBIN: Sergio Abreu builds guitars now.

MORROW: Since the advent of electric guitar it seems that the instrument has had an enormous cultural impact, has become a core instrument, the instrument amateurs play most, in the same way that the violin was at the turn of the century, and the pianoforte before it. One has to differentiate between electrified and amplified guitar, by the way —

ABERCROMBIE: Yes. I'm an electric guitarist.

MORROW: And the Starobin who plays in, say, Tod Machover's "Bug Mudra" is an amplified guitarist.

STAROBIN: Is anything unamplified anymore? Radio, television, the sounds are amplified. Classical or jazz musicians who play acoustically are a dying breed. Audiences for that type of music are growing smaller. The prepackaged performance which you can slip into your CD player, your VCR, has taken over. It's a matter of convenience.

MORROW: You sound like Glenn Gould.

STAROBIN: Don't get me wrong, I think live performance offers things you will never get from prerecorded mediums.

MORROW: There is a piece on Abercrombie's new album, *Getting*

111

There, called "Thalia" which it seems to me would be exceedingly difficult to perform live, because of the technical-electronic requirements.

ABERCROMBIE: It would be possible but you would have to use a computer or sequencer to generate the pedal line, or else someone playing a mallet instrument, someone very adept at playing a vibraphone. The way it was recorded was that the line was played by a computer, and I just played over it with bass and drums, in other words with live musicians interacting with a sequencer which laid out an arpeggiated line, an active background through which we played a long slow melody. That combination-sequence appears against another background which was more sustained, what they call in the advertising world "pads"—which means sustained sounds that indicate the harmonies but don't spell them out too heavily. I then played over that in the improvised section. Then the melody repeats. The album that "Thalia" is on is more electronic than anything I've done. It is very produced, it's a real studio album. When I finished it I thought I really like this, but it doesn't have much to do with my group as a unit.

MORROW: In jazz, then, do you think that the live performance is the important performance?

ABERCROMBIE: For the most part, yes.

MORROW: David, is this true of classical music as well?

STAROBIN: I've only made a couple of live recordings, in concert as opposed to live in the studio.

ABERCROMBIE: As long as there is breath, it's all live, isn't it?

STAROBIN: And moreover so far as distinctions are concerned, I don't believe that there is any significant difference between electric and classical guitar. The guitar is an instrument with six strings, a neck, frets. I myself make no distinction between classical and jazz guitar because to me those lines have been broken down. Which is not to say that what John and I do is the same thing. Listening to him describe "Thalia" reminded me of Tod Machover's "Bug Mudra" which incorporates a presequenced track—

MORROW: As well as an electric guitarist playing along with you on nylon strings.

STAROBIN: Right, and I don't believe that composition belongs to classical guitar as opposed to jazz guitar as opposed to rock guitar.

MORROW: Well, you are working from a fixed score and to some extent that defines the sound if not the composition as classical rather than rock. Moreover, there's a harmonic complexity to

Machover's vision that does not play a role in the rock tradition.

STAROBIN: True, but there is improvisation. There are sections where there are harmonic changes over which I freely play.

MORROW: Wouldn't it be more like the figured bass of baroque music?

STAROBIN: Yes, it's like figured bass. It's like playing changes if you're playing changes. There is no difference.

ABERCROMBIE: There is a relationship between the figured bass as a classical and a jazz idea. If I play in a trio — guitar, bass, drums — the bass player and I can outline the harmony, but the way the music ultimately sounds has more to do with how we interact. Is the bass player playing more roots or fifths, is he playing something that puts the chord down there — then what I play against it will outline it — or is he going to play the upper part of the chord? But if someone is actually playing chords, comping chord changes, the only thing that happens is that there are more textured harmonies. When you play in a trio, the music seems to be more classical in that it is more plainly contrapuntal.

MORROW: So, you both would contend then that all music is headed toward convergence. What I'm hearing here is that Starobin is a rocker and Abercrombie is a classical guitarist.

STAROBIN: People who are exploring all the different avenues of music-making these days are definitely crossing lines. I predict that in fifty years there will be even fewer ways of categorizing players than now. I prefer players who push what they do to the outermost limits. A classical player who knows how to improvise, whose repertoire extends beyond the standards is to me the most interesting player. This is someone you can come back to and grow with as a listener. The player who takes the fifteen or twenty standard war horses and plays them the same way for thirty-five or forty years is not accomplishing much.

MORROW: Why did you decide to play the guitar, as opposed to another instrument? How did you get started playing?

STAROBIN: My mother made me!

ABERCROMBIE: I don't think my mother picked the guitar for me, but once I got a guitar she made me play it. I asked, I cried, you know, you cry until you get what you want and then when you get it you don't want it. And then your mother says, "You begged and cried for this thing, and now you're going to play it."

STAROBIN: "This thing set us back forty bucks!"

ABERCROMBIE: I think it did, in fact. It was a Harmony steel-string

113

guitar, with the strings set about five feet off the fretboard. I'd take a deep breath and play for about half an hour, excruciating, then look at the clock because I knew I could go out and play ball with my friends.

STAROBIN: I still feel like that.

MORROW: No, David practices diligently every day.

STAROBIN: Oh, hell no!

MORROW: John, how is a jazz musician treated now in America, as opposed, say, to Europe?

ABERCROMBIE: In America, jazz music is perceived, understood — or misunderstood — to be more popular jazz music. By popular jazz, I mean George Benson, or at best Pat Metheny, who is by the way a wonderful player, but his music is very Brazilian, very pop, very "beautiful." I think of Chick Corea. His music is very accessible. Whereas in Europe it seems they're a lot more accepting of avant-garde players, be-bop players, players with a harder edge.

MORROW: I've heard Metheny referred to as a Fusak player, fusion coupled with Musak's sugary sweetness.

ABERCROMBIE: I don't apply Fusak to Metheny. Fusak I apply to Kenny G, whom a friend of mine termed The Anti-Christ of Jazz. But serious jazz is listened to everywhere, finally — Japan, South America, the United States, so forth. There's just a more concentrated audience in Europe, and Europeans seem in general more respectful of the music itself, are interested in the music.

MORROW: How is the classical guitarist viewed, and how listened to in America?

STAROBIN: I think musicians basically have a pretty reasonable life here. I have no complaints.

MORROW: Something that interests me is the relation between music and language. There is no one-to-one correspondence between sound/music, which is an abstraction — despite its ability to create emotional responses, through melody and rhythm — and language, which is composed of sounds, systems of grunts and hisses and so forth, but which comprise signifiers, attempt to *mean*. How do you, as musicians, refer to music in language? When you're working with other musicians, and you talk about how something should sound, how do you make the translation?

ABERCROMBIE: We tend to work with metaphors, I guess. I've always used terms like "I want this piece to sound *like* something." For instance, "This passage is too *heavy* for me, let's make it lighter. I want this passage to *breathe* more." And usually, working with musicians I know, my intentions will get communicated. It can get pretty far out — most musicians would understand "heavy" or "light" but I know people who are capable of saying, "I want this to sound more green, or blue," or whatever. Once I heard a composer say he wanted his piece played with absolutely no feeling whatsoever. That was a good one. Also, players themselves are often referred to as flat, or angular — "He's a real flat player, he's an angular player." If something's warm, deep-sounding, we will refer to it with words like "dark," "black." "He gets a dark sound." "He gets a light, bright, metallic sound." "Wooden." There are lots of ways to describe both attack and timbre.

MORROW: In classical music there is, of course, the traditional notational system for laying out tempi and intensities — *adagio, allegro, forte, mezzoforte* — and so on.

STAROBIN: It is essentially the same thing John's talking about. There are the traditional indicators in scores, but I think classical players discuss interpretation using metaphors similar to what John has described. We create darker sounds, we talk about making the music breathe more or less. You live a life around musicians and you develop vocabularies with which you communicate.

MORROW: Technically, how do you produce a "dark" sound?

STAROBIN: Well, technically you are talking about an overtone series. A dark sound emanates from the lower portion of the overtones, and bright from the higher portions. Or, "bright" can mean a faster tempo. We're sitting here, and I've never met John before, but I understand perfectly what he's saying in terms of his playing and music — the languages are made-up but they're the same.

MORROW: Why do you think that is? Strictly speaking, this is a very "bright" light coming down on the table, and it has absolutely nothing to do with sound. It is a curious transference that takes place in language. The vocabulary is actually romantic, it's allegorical, it borrows from the visual arts, and other art forms. Language attempts to mean, but when you are playing a solo, John, do the improvised passages refer to anything as such?

ABERCROMBIE: No, not really. A jazz solo has emotional feeling. When I talk about improvisation with students I say, "Okay, there are scales, and you take scales and make intervals, make shapes with these scales." Intuition plays a major role in the creation of these shapes. It's like following a train of thought when I start a solo. I start a phrase, which usually tells me immediately how the solo's going to unfold, and I start to develop a theme, and the solo

115

builds, and if theme works out, with feeling behind it, then the solo is fulfilling to me. A good solo would be one that had interesting shapes, a lot of emotion. It's different for everyone, though. You listen to John Coltrane at the peak of his career playing with very little thematic development, chords and notes can be flying everywhere, and that's a great solo, too. All solos, all musical compositions, are different, have to be judged differently. One piece might be sparse, have little development, or be contrapuntal, or be sound-oriented only.

MORROW: How do you know when you've played a great performance of a piece that, say, you've played a number of times, as opposed to a mediocre performance?

ABERCROMBIE: I don't know, something happens, every performance should be different, so what makes one performance work and another not is hard to say. When a performance is recorded, often I'll think I've played a good solo, and then listen back to the recording of it and it will be shit, and vice versa — I'll think, "Oh, gee, there was nothing happening in that solo, man," and the engineer will say, "You should come in and listen to that one," and I'll listen, and, well, it works. You can never tell. Objectivity is impossible when you are in the process of improvising.

MORROW: Unlike a number of instruments, the guitar seems to be in a phase of reconstruction. I mean, the clarinet has more or less found its final form. But guitar builders are experimenting not just with the electronics possibilities, but with the structure of the classical guitar itself. Innovators like John Gilbert and Thomas Humphrey are changing struting, pins, shapes, working with alternative woods.

STAROBIN: Humphrey's Millenium is an instrument whose neck comes into the body of the guitar at an angle, so the fingerboard is raised so when you reach the twelfth fret the body is not adjacent to the frets, and so you can play above the twelfth fret with much greater ease than with the standard classical guitar.

MORROW: Couldn't that be accomplished with a cutaway shape? Or does the cutaway ruin the upper register?

STAROBIN: I don't know if it does or not. I've played amplified cutaway nylon guitars, but I think people respond negatively to the instrument. I myself don't care really, but the non-cutaway has always been how the instrument has looked. Actually the Millenium looks exactly the same as any standard guitar when viewed directly from the front. I have a lot of nineteenth century guitars, whose bodies are small, but Humphrey's guitars I like because they're big, powerful, clear-voiced, and neutral-colored, so you can do a lot of different things with them.

ABERCROMBIE: I go through periods, always switching guitars. The guitar I'm using now is made by Roger Sadowsky. It's electric, Telecaster-shaped, very much like the guitar David was just describing in that its tone is flat, and uncolored. Different guitars have different personalities, some guitars seem to have more personality and if you play them no matter what you do they will sound a certain way. Others you can change pick-up configurations, do things with tone controls, run them through different amplifiers. What is interesting about Sadowsky is that he builds thinking about specific acoustic properties of various different woods.

MORROW: David, where do you think contemporary classical guitar is headed now — beyond our earlier notion about convergence?

STAROBIN: Composition is diversifying. There are more and more composers writing more and more different kinds of music for the instrument, better music.

MORROW: What do you mean by "better"?

STAROBIN: Well, I think composers — even those who don't play the instrument — have a finer understanding of the instrument, its capacities, and so the quality of

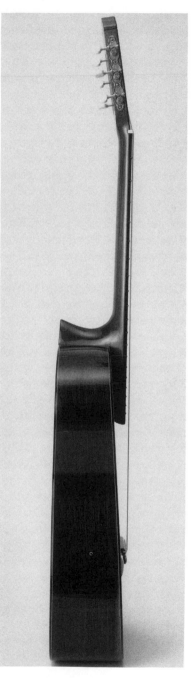

117

writing is improving. People like Elliott Carter, Milton Babbitt, Tod Machover, John Anthony Lennon, are now beginning to produce a sizable body of repertoire for the guitar that is extraordinarily diverse. It reflects almost every stylistic avenue composers are interested in these days, and the combination of so many players actively looking to work with fresh repertoire with all these composers having discovered the instrument, becoming fascinated with its possibilities, makes the field exciting at the moment. Thirty years ago, most guitar concerts were made up of transcription materials — works originally written for violin, chamber orchestra, piano and transcribed for the guitar. Now, it is rare to see that kind of concert. Now, concerts are often made up of works composed for the instrument. I have nothing against transcription materials, as such, but the guitar has had real trouble competing with other classical instruments for recognition — say, to be recognized in a conservatory as a legitimate instrument — precisely because of a lack of repertoire. Now that the repertoire has grown, traditional prejudice the instrument has had to suffer is less.

MORROW: I suppose that in jazz, the guitar was initially seen as a percussion instrument, but since Christian it's been legitimate as a solo instrument, hasn't it, John?

ABERCROMBIE: No, it's always been illegitimate, and it remains one of the *most* illegitimate of instruments. When I went to school at Berkelee, I think the first year there were maybe ten guitar players. Mostly there were saxophone players, trumpet players, piano, the traditional, so-called articulate instruments. The guitar was looked down on. And rightfully so, at some point, because I mean, guitar players couldn't read, first of all. The worst readers, because the guitar is a difficult instrument to sight-read with. Where do you start?

STAROBIN: This is an important issue.

ABERCROMBIE: On a piano, if you want to play a middle C, there is only one place to do it. On the guitar there are three or four different *places* to play middle C, leaving all the potential positionings and fingerings aside —

STAROBIN: It depends, too, on what the register of the piece is.

ABERCROMBIE: And what string you want to play it on.

STAROBIN: It can be mind-boggling. The instrument is far more complex than it might seem on the surface.

ABERCROMBIE: The other day I was listening to a tape of something I was doing with a saxophone player. He'd brought in this music with lines written on standard chord progressions and they weren't real hard, but they were like [*hums a pattern of notes*] . . . not really difficult but —

MORROW: Sounds like a Charlie Parker riff.

ABERCROMBIE: Yeah, it was "Saxophone Player Shit," as we say, and so the fingering, to make it into a phrase with him, wouldn't come very easily, even though it was an easy enough series of phrases. There were fingerings that would sound stiff, and I had to develop one that would be fluid. The guitar is like that, easy and hard. Another aspect of the guitar is that the way a guitar player soloed back in 1965 or so, seemed old-fashioned compared to the way a sax player would solo. Saxophone players were already into Coltrane while guitarists were still listening to Herb Ellis and Tal Farlo. I remember the teachers saying to me, when I would take a solo, "That was very pretty, John . . . for a *guitar*." I mean, there used to be a serious distinction made between all instruments and the guitar. Maybe the accordion would have been better.

STAROBIN: There still is this discrimination, though. The instrument has made progress, but the prejudice is there.

ABERCROMBIE: I agree, but as far as jazz players go now, I think that guitarists have come a lot more into their own, and some of the more interesting jazz players, some of my favorite jazz players, are guitarists. The instrument aside altogether, just the sound of the music that people like John Scofield and Bill Frisell — who's from another planet, this guy Frisell — make is wonderful. And Mick Goodrich, who's not well-recorded, players like this are changing the way the guitar sounds, they're much more innovative than a sax player who has transcribed every Coltrane solo and sounds like it.

MORROW: Actually, Frisell strikes me as someone who has taken the jazz guitar into new frontiers not just by his abilities as a player, but his knowledge of different kinds of music — Country & Western, for instance, real Vox Americana stuff — and a seemingly shameless will to mix it up with odd instrumentation, using tubas, weird combinations of styles. He's a melting-pot musician.

ABERCROMBIE: The way he bends the neck of his Gibson SG, I've watched him. I always think the neck is going to crack.

MORROW: Is Frisell pointing a way for jazz to go through the next generations?

ABERCROMBIE: Jazz is going in a lot of different directions at once. There seems to be a real return to the traditional — not among guitar players so much, electric guitar players are real bastards I'm glad to say, we'll try just about anything. But I'm thinking of Wynton

Marsalis and others. There is a return to acoustical playing, and to play the be-bop tunes, the standards, in a specific, older style. I think it's a little retrograde, but a nice thing to do, and if it's done well it sounds great, I appreciate it, it's part of my own tradition. But I've always thought the idea of jazz was to take from the tradition and do something else. Expand upon it.

MORROW: That's more or less what the word jazz points to. Getting it on, getting on with it.

ABERCROMBIE: And that is what I'd like to see jazz do. I don't have any specific place I would like jazz to go. With people like Frisell it is moving in a real interesting direction, but there will always be the tradition. I feel I'm a more traditional player than Frisell, even though I can get abstract. I'm more involved with the line, how it relates to the chord. The tradition of playing the jazz line, I want to keep that in my playing.

MORROW: You two are very similar, in your different fields, in that you can move easily in the tradition, and also work out at the edge. I wonder what it would sound like if you played together. [*Prolonged laughter.*] Scrambled eggs?

STAROBIN: I'm not a jazz player, finally, man, I just don't —

ABERCROMBIE: I can't play your classical shit, man —

MORROW: There goes the lofty dream of convergences. One last question, a standard. What value does music have in contemporary life, why is music important?

STAROBIN: Everyone uses music for different purposes. I can answer why it's valuable for *me*. It's like food or air, it's a need, a basic need I have. When I wake up, a day would not mean as much to me, be as complete, were it not musical. But as I say I think it is absolutely different for everybody. People consume it, or they ride in elevators with it, and it bounces off their ears, but it's always near us; there are people who think about it, write about it. Everyone perceives it differently. If you play a C major scale to ten listeners, you will have ten different appreciations of what has been heard. And so I think, in a way, that's the great thing about music — it is an abstract form of expression, heard differently by every listener. It is full of potential at all times.

ABERCROMBIE: I would answer the question pretty much the same way. I get up, I have to have my coffee, I have to have the guitar in my hands. When I play it's important to me to try to make something sound right in the music, to make it work. I'm very connected, physically and in every possible way, to music. I hear it, I feel it, it's in there. I think the idea that music is a basic need—like breathing—is the best description of its role in life I've ever heard. It's a need.

SELECTED DISCOGRAPHIES

JOHN ABERCROMBIE

Getting There. (ECM Records 833 494.)

Night. (ECM 823 212.)

Sargasso Sea. With Ralph Towner. (ECM 835 015.)

Timeless. (ECM 829 114.)

Abercrombie/Johnson/Erskine. (ECM 837 756.)

Characters. (ECM 829 372.)

Current Events. (ECM 827 770.)

DAVID STAROBIN

As guitarist: *New Music with Guitar*. Selected works from Volumes 1, 2 and 3. Music by Elliott Carter, Toru Takemitsu, Stephen Sondheim, Milton Babbitt, Hans Werner Henze, others. (Bridge Records BCD 9009.)

New Music with Guitar, Volume 4. Works by Tod Machover, Barbara Kolb, Robert Saxton, Michael Starobin, Ronald Roxbury, Humphrey Searle. (Bridge BCD 9022.)

A Song from the East. Russian and Hungarian music by Gyorgy Kurtag, Sandor Jemnitz, Ivanov-Kramskoi, others. (Bridge BCD 9004.)

20th Century Music for Voice and Guitar. With Rosalind Rees, soprano. Works by John Cage, Igor Stravinsky, Elliott Carter, others. (Vox/Turnabout TV 34727.)

As conductor, guitarist, producer: *Elliott Carter: The Vocal Works (1975-1981)*. (Bridge BCD 9014.)

As producer: *VALIS*. Electronic opera by Tod Machover, based on the novel by Philip K. Dick. (Bridge BCD 9007.)

Songs by Berlioz and Mahler. Jan DeGaetani, mezzo-soprano; Eastman Chamber Ensemble. (Bridge BCD 9017.)

Charles Ives: The Sonatas for Violin and Piano. Gregory Fulkerson, violin; Robert Shannon, piano. (Bridge BCD 9024A/B—2 discs.)

Music in Time of War
Leon Botstein

THE OUTBREAK OF WAR — particularly when war confronts each of us constantly on television and in newspapers — challenges the routine and normal expectations of everyday life. The events, habits and preoccupations of civilian existence, which seem so compelling under ordinary circumstances, suddenly appear pointless when placed against the death, destruction and terror of war. This abrupt loss of meaning is particularly acute in the arts. In wartime the nagging suspicion that the arts are just decorative and entertaining — ultimately superfluous forms of life linked to times of peace and prosperity — becomes frighteningly plausible.

Historically, literature, painting and photography can adapt (and have done so) by claiming direct relevance. Artists, writers and their public can defend a wartime engagement with art by pointing to the subject matter of their work. Works of painting and literature can bear witness to the horrors of war. They can become didactic instruments of criticism that encourage patriotic fervor, deepen the revulsion at violence, or enhance the love of peace. A mantle of moral superiority and ethical significance is readily accessible. Art and literature have been drawn historically into the net that war casts.

What about music? The cliche "fiddling while Rome burns" imbedded in our language expresses an unflattering image that doubtlessly has passed through the mind of many a musician and concertgoer these past months. Not that there has been any shortage of uses for music in war. The massive appropriation in the Defense Budget for music in the Armed Services reflects the notion that music is particularly good at inspiring patriotism and bravery. Marches and anthems have been used to instill both courage and conformity. They help individuals see themselves as part of a unified whole.

The way we hear and use the musical language of Western culture also lends itself to some commonplace but effective uses for music as descriptive of war. The anticipation and experience of soldiers marching and the ominous sounds of battle have been described by music. The fear and anguish experienced in war also have their musical signifiers, as movie and television soundtracks have made all too plain.

Beyond the usual trumpets and drums, from the end of the Middle Ages on, bagpipes and shawms *en masse* were used to frighten the enemy and embolden warriors. The opening bars of the Beethoven Fifth Symphony became a motto of allied victory in World War II. Haydn wrote one Mass to celebrate Lord Nelson's victory in the Nile and another to strengthen the patriotic resolve of his contemporaries. Works such as Beethoven's "Battle Symphony" (Wellington's Victory) are part of a large genre of descriptive and inspirational music ranging from "better" music for military bands (Beethoven wrote an F Major March in 1809 for the Bohemian Army) to celebratory works such as Brahms's *Triumphlied*, written for the 1871 Prussian victory over the French. Among the most eloquent works that deal in sound with the experience of war is Shostakovitch's Symphony No. 7, in which the fear and desolation of the 1941 siege of Leningrad are searingly portrayed.

But what disturbs us as we continue to give and go to concerts of so-called high art music is not that music is entirely useless in wartime. As the great musicologist Guido Adler argued in a 1915 essay, "The Art of Music and the World War," music might actually be "the soul of culture." The pursuit of music at home and in schools during wartime therefore could be construed as supportive of the nation, its war aims, and the essence of its traditions (which, in the Habsburg Monarchy's case, Adler believed to be humanistic). Since that war, however unfortunate, was in Adler's view defensive and justified, the great musical cultural tradition could serve as a reminder to the citizens of what the fighting was all about.

In our own history, "high art" music has helped to give expression to our sense of national character and virtue during wartime. Is it merely coincidence that three of Aaron Copland's most powerful and popular works — *Appalachian Spring* (1943), *Fanfare for the Common Man* (1942) and *A Lincoln Portrait* (1942) — date from the years of America's participation in World War II? They have come to function as musical symbols of an idealized American landscape and culture.

Yet the reason Guido Adler felt compelled to write an essay on the subject of music and war in the first place was that he recognized that there might be some deep contradiction that needed to be resolved. Were the pursuit of musical art and the killing of fellow human beings, no matter what the political justifications might be, ethically compatible?

We, like Adler, are now once again forced to confront a singular premise within our musical tradition: the idea that music possesses ethical properties and is the only art in our tradition that can truly be regarded as universal. Music, particularly instrumental music — as it developed in the eighteenth and nineteenth centuries — has merited special philosophical consideration precisely because, unlike painting or writing, it was not imitative of nature. Music did not appear to make an argument, describe or denote something quite the way a work of visual art, prose, or even poetry could. Its seemingly abstract and self-referential logic and character permitted it to remain above the everyday and therefore the issues that ordinarily bring people into conflict.

A picture and a word might be inflammatory and divisive. But a melody. A sonata? The nature of music seemed to allow it to transcend the barriers created by ordinary language and ethnic and national differences. The proverbial Jewish parental dream (associated with the Eastern European *shtetl* of a century ago) of one's child becoming a *wunderkind* mirrored the fact that brilliance on the musical stage was one of the very few immediate and reliable routes of escape from prejudice and the ghetto. Even for those with moderate talent in search of acceptance in mainstream society, music was an important way to display one's potential for assimilation.

During the past 200 years, three ideas concerning the nature of music have dominated the way we conceive of the meaning of music: 1) Music is abstract. It is just the mere play of sounds; 2) Music is the immediate and direct expression of inner consciousness and will (as Schopenhauer and Wagner thought); and 3) Music is the quintessential language of human emotion and feeling and perhaps even of religious faith (as Schleiermacher and Mendelssohn thought). In each of these views the universality of music as an art is vindicated.

No wonder music, since the eighteenth century, has been viewed as an ally of human solidarity and reconciliation and an instrument of peace. One thinks of the animals dancing in Mozart's *Magic Flute*. As Mendelssohn wrote in 1842 when he sought to defend the idea of a "song without words": "People often complain that music is too ambiguous; that what they should think when they hear it is so unclear. With me it is exactly the reverse . . . only the melody can say the same thing, can arouse the same feeling in one person as another, a feeling which is not, however, expressed by the same words . . . words have many meanings but music we could both understand correctly."

Mendelssohn was perhaps the last and most eloquent proponent of the idea that musical culture could be spread intentionally to encourage harmony, reason, humanism, enlightenment and universal tolerance. The music he wrote was designed to be readily comprehensible without becoming trivial. Through music Mendelssohn sought to cultivate an appreciation for timeless standards of beauty and form. This appreciation through an art form that did not refer listeners to things around them that separated them from one another would remind different peoples of their essential commonality.

Mendelssohn refused to set patriotic texts to music. Rather, he turned to the oratorio that demanded massive public participation on the part of musicians and listeners. Mendelssohn wrote his oratorios so that they could be easily learned and sung by large groups of amateurs. Mendelssohn's devotion to furthering an aesthetic of music as a participatory human enterprise designed to cut across individual and social differences was in part responsible for his failure to write a successful opera. The ambition to engender human solidarity through music was imitated but inverted by Richard Wagner, who sought to strengthen through music and spectacle a sense of exclusivity and superiority among his German listeners.

The conceit that developed out of the musical tradition of the West during the nineteenth century was that music can bind and heal where words and images cannot. As the truly universal means of communication, music becomes the logical enemy of conflict and war and the natural instrument of peace. The special performance Leonard Bernstein gave in 1989 of the Beethoven Ninth Symphony (among whose lines are, of course, "all men shall be brothers") to celebrate the tearing down of the Berlin Wall mirrored this conceit. The paradox in the facile assumption becomes clear when one remembers that in 1942 Wilhelm Furtwaengler conducted the same work in the same city in honor of Hitler's birthday, the Nazi elite and the heroes of the war against the Soviet Union.

A terrifying story involving music is told about the Warsaw Ghetto. An SS officer was supervising a raid of a house, collecting victims — mostly older people, women and children — for delivery to concentration camps. The house was unusual because it contained a beaten-up piano. The officer, after completing his task — and knowing that there were still people in terror hiding throughout the house — sat down, unbuttoned his collar and played, beautifully, pieces by Schumann and Schubert. So much for the vaunted "power of music" to bring people together.

Is then the cliché about the universality of music merely idle self-deception? Can music help to further the cause of peace and harmony among human beings? Is the playing of an ordinary concert, the writing of music, listening to CDs, and attending concerts then "fiddling while Rome burns"; just a diversion, a species of entertainment and perhaps avoidance in times of violence and destruction? Despite the lack of an easy affirmative answer, there is reason to think that the love of music and its pursuit can make a contribution in wartime to the cause of peace and harmony among human beings.

Music, as an active art form, can permit individuals who have little else in common to share and communicate in public despite differences on other fronts. The traditions of choral singing and amateur playing created public arenas for individuals to submerge the ideas and experiences of daily life and belief that separated them. Concertgoing still offers somewhat the same opportunity as huge musical productions involving amateurs here, in England, and on the continent once did. Listening to music, even at home in small groups, can offer the same sort of experience.

Music is unique in that the acts of listening and playing music together easily preserve the secrecy of emotion characteristic of privacy and intimacy and at the same time deepen a sense of human connectedness, even though most concertgoers are strangers to one another. Each individual derives a personal pleasure that is opaque but mirrors a joy with the others in the hall. Listeners need not defend the meaning of their own experience with words and images.

Music, like language, reveals the human capacity to express and communicate meaning. But, unlike language, the different responses we have to music do not demand necessarily that musical language become so fragmented as to prevent communication. The myth of the Tower of Babel need not apply to music. The diversity of historical styles, and the divergences in interpretations, need not damage the experience of music as recognizably common and binding. Affection, introspection and recognition of the human imagination are what the experience of music can suggest. The pursuit of music, particularly in public places, therefore is a welcome contrast

126

to the display of political conflict and violence — frequent events of wartime.

Through music one can fight a sense of loneliness that war can encourage. The sacrifice to individuality that service in the military demands and that support for a war effort among civilians asks is mitigated by music. Apart from helping us to preserve our sense of uniqueness, without using words music can forge a connection not only to those who are in battle but with those whom we regard as enemies and whom we confront with military power.

Music not only can inspire warlike bravery. It also can humble our arrogance. By retaining its power to communicate over political differences, it reminds us of the just limits of the convictions about right and wrong that in wartime become more rigid and extreme. In this sense, hearing music during wartime refers us to the condition of life we would most wish to see exist, a condition of freedom and peace in which the power of the imagination — in service of the experience of beauty — among all peoples can flourish.

What "high art" music can resist better than other comparable art forms is cooptation as a specific instrument of propaganda. The use of the Beethoven Ninth by the Nazis — grotesque as it was — did not damage the power of that work in the future to function as a celebration of human solidarity. Ironically, the power of Richard Strauss's music has transcended the mean-spirited and petty character of Strauss's politics. Because of its unique attributes, music, even in the case of as warlike and unattractive a character as Richard Wagner, reminds us of the potential for good that resides in each individual.

These ethical possibilities in music are clearly powerless to prevent war. Music therefore must function as a reminder of the future. Music can help us to focus on the possibilities that surviving war offers. Music during wartime signals an agenda for making more out of common life. It evokes what war destroys. One hopes that Furtwaengler's performance, for a few of the listeners, covertly undercut the overt purpose of the event. But for music to function in this way it must be written, played and listened to with an intensity that is uncommon. The universality of music is hard to realize. It has always been easier merely to assert and talk about in words.

Music's comparative resistance to being appropriated in the cause of wars is a dimension of its relative formal autonomy. Its seeming abstract irrelevancy — when compared with painting and literature — turns out to be its saving grace. It may be the one dimension of human expression that is never damaged by the harm we do others, and by the violence we create and condone. It survives all efforts at oppression and censorship, two common consequences of war.

As a medium whose content is difficult to define, the freedom of expression possessed by those who write, play, or imagine music is hard to take away. Among the most poignant examples is Olivier Messiaen's 1941 *Quartet for the End of Time*. This masterpiece was written while Messiaen was a prisoner of war under conditions of hardship and an extreme limitation of freedom. This work suggests that finally music is not easily corrupted by the aims of conflict, violence and war. It can remind us of the best in humanity, sustain our sense of hope, preserve our dignity against the fiercest odds.

In order to keep the thread of hope alive, music needs to become a larger and not smaller part of our life. However, a renewed seriousness and faith in the idea that music is far more than a means of entertainment must be evident. Far from being a way of rendering life pretty when it is not, in wartime music should become a reminder of that within ourselves which we might have forgotten. In a time of war performers, composers and listeners should think about music as an antidote to self-righteousness and exclusivity — as a discreet but universal act of conscience and personal assertion. The concert repertory that dominates our musical life consists of music that can resist corruption and fulfill the ethical promise inherent in music. May the making of music flourish when we need it most.

For Four Violins
Marjorie Welish

Many were fascinated with birth in erratic modes of construal. Meaning?

If keen on jazz, why, I asked, did he borrow [the work of] Buxtehude? His name was Ben Paterson.

Ben, I later learned, was a member of Fluxus.

From the start, we saw birth and death attracting a large, heterodox enrollment to replenish the situation.

The endeavors of Robert Gorham Davis were inclusive of ritual inertia in myth.

His students found places near their neighbors of last week.

By habit, the student preferred the company of the one she met by accident once.

Inclusive of retrograde thematics, the manifestation of Davis.

The records slipped from the book bag Ben had placed under his seat.

Flood, one of the varyingly-weighted catastrophes itemized in "Metaphor, Symbol and Myth," attracted a large following.

The elaborate construal of myth's italicized forfeiture attracted a large following.

Habit tended to favor someone who with infrequent regularity plopped down a stack of LP's borrowed from library.

Gather from time, and fourth generation variants, Buxtehude.

A natural situation sensibly represented in suitably receptive persons.

A natural vigilance sensibly represented.

Gather, from time and fourth generation variants, a phase elaborated with claim to plausibility.

In 1967, I heard a new release Ben wanted me to hear.

"What do you think?" he said. "Boring" I said. "Keep listening," he said."

"Now, what do you think?"

Steve Reich's new release, *Violin Phase*, interested Ben. He wanted me to hear it.

By habit we sat together.

A few notes rejuvenated when the new young god plays, when Paul Zukofsky's vigilant playing wore on.

Technique that elucidates process confers respect upon psycho-acoustic blur.

Common crystallizing devices such as the force of habit.

A minim of disenfranchisement.

"Boring," I said. "Keep listening," he said.

"What do you think?" he said. "Oceanic," I said.

A minim of anomie.

Me and Satan
Walter Mosley

As A CHILD I was sent to Victory Baptist Day School, which was annexed Victory Baptist Church, in Los Angeles. My parents decided on a parochial school education because they both worked in the public schools and had seen what a black student could expect; that is, an inferior, overcrowded, and white-washed education. So they paid $9.50 a week, which was steep in the fifties, for me to be surrounded by black teachers and black peers.

At Victory we were taught everything that the public schools had to offer plus bible class, music, and Afro-American history. That may not seem like much in a predominantly black school today but in the late fifties and early sixties music for most children was just a play xylophone and history always wore a lily white face.

The music stands out for me because it was so beautiful and removed. We'd march in rows down the broken sidewalk and into the cool hush church. We'd walk down the main aisle surrounded by stained glass images of Christ and John the Baptist and Mary and all the apostles. We sat in plush velveteen seats that the choir used on Sundays. Momma Lindsay, the kindergarten teacher, played piano while Mr. Davis, master of the sixth grade, led us through the gospel and hymns.

It was beautiful.

I couldn't sing in key so they told me to mouth the words silently, but I didn't mind. That only meant that some of the other tone deaf children and I could sneak back into the ladies lounge and experiment with the tentative beginnings of mature love while the choir out front echoed the highest love. The love of God.

On Tuesdays and Thursdays Mr. Davis taught Afro-American history. We learned about George Washington Carver, Sojourner Truth, Harriet Tubman, Frederick Douglass, Booker T. Washington and others. Many others. Sometimes Mr. Davis would tell us about people that were considered white but who were really black. Alexander Dumas was one of course. But we even discussed the heritage of people like Dwight D. Eisenhower and Raquel Welch.

This last tendency, to claim as our own people those who considered themselves white, didn't feel right. It seemed that being white was preferable from an Afro-American point of view. Nobody put it in words but why would I want Dwight D. Eisenhower to be black? The only reason I could think of was that he held real power — white man power.

I felt that the black people we studied were the good-Negroes-struggling-to-make-something-of-themselves sort of people. People who learned the white man's science or the white man's language. People who educated themselves or were educated by kindly white women. People who fought, or struggled, for freedom — a very American enterprise.

The comparisons between black and white always left me feeling that white people had the market on genius. It was, after all, their science and their language.

Even the Jesus who blazed into Victory Baptist Church was the image of a white man.

There was something missing. For all my joy and good education I never felt that we actually shared in the history of thought and ideas. I knew that we were part of the intellectual legacy of the West, but a small part. And, even worse, we seemed to be preparing ourselves to gain knowledge already mastered by our white counterparts.

This kind of thinking is racial thinking. It's a yoke that many colonized people wear. Identity gives way to the erosive struggle against physical and spiritual oppression. I compare myself to my white counterpart but I use his ruler, his rule.

> *I have stones in my passway*
> *and my road seem dark as night*
> *I have pains in my heart*
> *they have taken my appetite*

Since my elementary school education I compared black to white as a matter of reflex. I wanted a clear beacon that was untarnished black genius that I could still understand in my own context; which is English speaking, African American and twentieth century. I wanted a black Einstein, a black Mozart.

The answer to my search came to me, and transformed me, finally in the form of two great men, one black and one white. They were Robert Johnson (1911-1938) and Christopher Marlowe (1564-1593).

Johnson, the great Delta Blues musician, created much of today's modern blues, jazz, R&B, and even rock 'n' roll. One story has it that Johnson sold his soul to the devil in order to play guitar the way he did.

> *Early this mornin'*
> *when you knocked on my door*
> *Early this mornin', ooh*
> *when you knocked on my door*
> *And I said, "Hello, Satan,*
> *I believe it's time to go."*

So powerful were his lyrics that they are still sung today with the same devastating and heartrending effects. He was poor and black and little educated in the ways of reading and writing. He loved music and women and whiskey. He abandoned his soul to the evil ways that poor folk practised just to stay alive in the Mississippi delta. He was murdered, or maybe his debt was called due, in a small dance hall twelve miles outside of Greenwood, Mississippi.

Marlowe was an educated man who brought tragedy and blank verse to life in Elizabethan drama. He heralded Shakespeare. Some think he was Shakespeare. He was a heretic, a spy, an irreverent drinker and carouser, and he was possessed of a reckless vitality. His exploits made him a legend before and after his death, at the hand of Ingram Frizer, in a barroom brawl.

Marlowe. Johnson. The comparison was new to me. Each man stood as a master in his own territory. Both were masters of tragedy. One in drama and the other in blues; blues, the black man's word for tragedy.

Here was the creator of the first Faust drama and the man who sold his soul for the music to play. They were both outcast from organized religion and they fought, not for freedom but, for the kind of truth that was the celebration of life, their lives.

Marlowe took the language that people already used, blank verse, and made it art. High tragedy. Robert Johnson did the same thing with the blues.

Johnson didn't care where you buried him once he was dead but he preferred the roadside so his evil soul could catch the Greyhound Bus to ride. The papers of a heretic were found in Marlowe's room after his death.

Walter Mosley

One man reflects the other over the centuries. And in their light this parochial school boy remembers the lessons taught in the choir and the back rooms of Victory.

I remember pressing against Bonita Edwards, fully clothed, in the ladies lounge. All around me were the sounds of prayer and psalms. Excitement was electric through my body. I was the music. I was the genius of human creation. And I was scared to death.

Christopher Marlowe and other white geniuses changed in my eyes once I saw them in the contrast to Johnson. They were no longer figures against whom I compared black genius. Marlowe, in his way, introduced me to Robert Johnson. I was allowed to see this black master of blues in the light of history. In turn Johnson introduced me to myself. His lyrics and music live in me, bring me to understand human tragedy regardless of color or epoch.

Johnson is loud and irreverent. He greets Satan at the front door. When he talks to his girlfriend he says:

> *Now, you can squeeze my lemon till the*
> *juice run down my leg . . .*
> *Till the juice run down my leg, baby, you*
> *know what I'm talkin' 'bout*

That's something that they didn't teach at my little school. They taught the proper words and feelings of song.

I learned from Mr. Johnson that there is no ruler or rule for genius. No color or dominant creed or sex that owns truth.

And the music, be it blank verse or delta blues, still cries out for me. Because when I close my eyes and press tight against my feelings I still hear the humming of Momma Lindsay as she played her piano and the steady beat of Bonita Edwards' heart.

> *You better come on*
> *in my kitchen*
> *babe, it's goin' to be rainin' outdoors.*

Area J

Words & Music
Kenward Elmslie

(Percussive rap music, abrasively amplified. ANNOUNCER bobs and weaves as VOICE-OVER blasts out. ANNOUNCER collapses drunkenly in front of blank projection screen, half rises, improvises shadow gestures on the screen, mouths words out-of-sync with VOICE-OVER)

VOICE-OVER

Too much graffiti on the granite and you can't break the code? Formica canyons caving in? Blast off to Area J, Music Country USA. Gross, the calibrated think-tank expertise that's honed and zoned Area J. So, go for it. Vroom on by Andrew Sisters rip-offs stomping Sinatra goons beating up on Tina Turner ghouls gangbanging Rolling Stone clones. Who said the world was fair? You must be bad for something.

Probe Area J, Music Country USA. Route 66 out of Nashville. Feeder access routes aplenty. Area J.

Whip by Joplin's Roadie Pit to next exit ramp. Judy's! We're heavin' innards here, primordial innards, tap-tappin' into that vat of DNA syrup so concentrado one fizz bubble'll float you into your sacred duty to get it together. Holy Shit, we're talkin' coalescence here! Rich babes with stone mouths and Woody Woodpecker eyes. Family johns goin' through the motions. Pig-out freaks sniffin' out freebies in smoulderin' dumps. Chairpersons who've lost that lovin' feelin'. Like you!

Become what you are at Judy's. Deep. Sponsored image. Long-haul management. Deep. Area J. Judy's.

(Rap music tape stops abruptly. ANNOUNCER clambers to his feet, sobered. Authoritative emotionless tone)

ANNOUNCER

Welcome to Music Country USA. Area J. Judy's. Body search, blood-test and lie detector spot checks hour before showtime. No con-trolled or uncontrolled elatants or psyche transmogrification sup-positories permitted. Isolation booth assignment final. Dress code enforced. Prom OK. Tux OK. No cleavage. No Mohawk. Must sign release. No malpractice. No refunds. Booths must remain locked till Judy's ascent into sky.

Judy's.
Row after row of isolation booths
Resemble upended glass coffins
Fanning up and out
Row after row.

Gigantic mirror dangles above stage,
Spotlights inch over mirror's expanse.
Mirror reflection of Judy,
Teetering on a platform,
Picked out by beam.

White tux.
Baton upraised.
Ravaged mirror face.
Judy's Nite Thoughts
Burst forth from Judy's mirror lips.

(ANNOUNCER adopts Judy's persona:
husky whiskey voice, battered charisma)

JUDY

Something about all this smog
Makes me drool for Daddy Dum Dum,
Way up there, sitting on his flagpole,
Waiting for the Prize Money.
Up he skedaddled, and to this day,
I hear him singing in my rainy dreams.

Yesterday, Bud Ploop, the last fambly holding—
You all recall Bud Ploop. Bud Ploop.
Closed its trapdoors for good, did Bud Ploop.

Dump the lightweights! Hear! Hear!

backwards on the trolley, We'd never get to meet, get to meet, Never ever get to meet.

Fuck Ass! My cootie garage is at the cleaners, My

hush puppies soggy from eau- de- vie- de- mango. Got The Shakes real

bad. A sloppy pour- er.

No one cute asks me over For gen- er- ic beer and

Kenward Elmslie

Fak- ing an or- gasm, Faking an or- gasm,

Faking an or- gasm, One Fourth of July float. My

subtext was va- nil- la milkshake froth.

(Spoken)

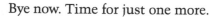

Bye now. Time for just one more.

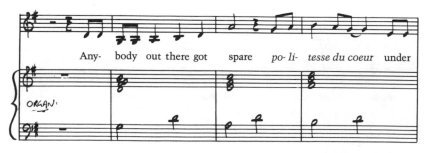

Any- body out there got spare *po- li- tesse du coeur* under

pressure to share for my final ascent up The Wrap Up Rope, up to my first flashback.

ANNOUNCER

Judy Burnt Out. Identity Crisis.

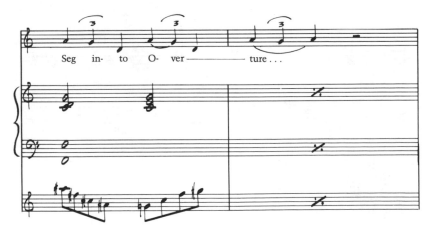

Seg in- to O- ver———— ture . . .

ANNOUNCER

Po-lice Escort. Intensive Care.
Judy's Ascent Into Sky Some Future Point In Time.

143

The good news is: Judy's sitting up, taking nourishment, namely a 'nilla milkshake, two scoops. She's enjoying a ninety-miles-per-hour breakfast in bed with Jedge G. Willickers in her custom-built Silver Streak mobile home.

(Singing)

> Doggone smog gone.
> Doggone smog gone.
> Doggone smog gone.
> Doggone smog gone.

She's looking forward to recuperating in her casa hideout down Mehico way. She sure hopes to jet back real soon, and climb up that Wrap Up Rope so all you fans can head back to *your* casa hideouts. She's a mite concerned about you spending all these nights cooped up in your booth, all alone, the dark so swart, the weight of solitude pressing down, waiting for a redemptive zing to materialize, a no-nonsense happy ending, so you'll feel you've engorged optimum benefit out of all those unexpected extra-added weeks in the booth, more months than originally budgeted.

The bad news is: booths must remain locked. That's policy. Releases were signed, OK? Smog's rollin' in.

A news blackout is still in effect regarding Judy's whereabouts down Mehico way. A moment of silence in memory of: Corinne. Booth 88 B.

(Music fades)

Midge. Booth 104 Y. Del. 56 P. Dori. 30 N. Kurt. 23 T. Scotti. 27 H. Myra. 25 H. Daryl. 23 Z.

Rest assured an investigation is underway.
The good news is — Judy's OK!
She's being held hostage down Mehico way.

(A projection of Judy flashes onto the screen.
Fireworks in the sky outline her image, a movie
moppet, bow in hair, the fiery trail of rockets
arching across her huge face)

Her head's together and she beseeches all Judy fans to think happy, OK? Love is everywhere, here to stay. Please pay attention, all surviving Judy fans. Slip all personal and impersonal valuables through slot marked ALIMENTATION. Graduation rings and frat pins acceptable Judy ransom. Raps on booth thermopanes will continue till miscreants surface into givingness.

(Percussive rap music begins)

Welcome to Music Country USA, Area J. Lucite sky climate control guarantees every little breeze seems to whisper — Judy, just as if she hadn't joined the Whatever Became Of Brigade down Mehico way. Faithful fans, innards heavin', go get it together, Area J. They bop on by Judy's. Who needs it — a boneyard of glass coffins upended. Skeletons with shreds of prom polyester and plastic carnations sticking up through rib cage maws and jaws. Said fans whomp into Janis Joplin's Roadie Pit, get shit-eyed pronto, blast coalescence concentrado, rich babes, stone mouths, gal-guy algae goin' for freebie heebie-jeebies, sniffin' out smoulderin' dumps, dumps that lust for lovin' feelin'.

NOTE: Orchestration by Steven Taylor. Adapted from "Judy's" in *26 Bars*, tales by Kenward Elmslie, drawings by Donna Dennis (Z Press).

From Djbot Baghostus's Run
Nathaniel Mackey

—————————————18.XI.81

Dear Angel of Dust,

This may be the only chance I'll get to write while we're in New York. It's early evening and we're resting a bit before going out to dinner and to check out some music. We got in last night and today we spent mostly wandering around. I can already tell our stay'll be a stimulating one. It's been only a few years since I was last here and all the clichés continue to apply but I can sense a number of changes as well. The harshness one always picks up on here seems to have gotten harsher but there's an insinuative, self-knowing wink one has the feeling of having glimpsed out of the corner of one's eye. One has to catch it unawares—one catches oneself unawares as well it seems—but every now and then the city bats an eye (part flinch, part coquettish flutter), every so often lets one in on its joke. How much of it's me I can't say, but that wink, that unexpected wash, waters grime's nearness to glitter, a discrepant "slip" which is only an eye-shift away.

One of the things we saw this afternoon is worth mentioning. Outside Penn Station we saw a group of break dancers. There were six of them, all in their early teens. A crowd had gathered, making a circle around the area in which they danced, at opposite ends of which area sat cigar boxes for money to be dropped into. I'd heard of break dancing, which along with subway art and rap music is beginning to get a lot of attention, and had seen a bit of it on TV and around the neighborhood back in L.A. But you really have to see it here to comprehend it. Aunt Nancy, as we watched the dancers go thru their routine, whispered into my ear that she was struck by the interplay and the counterpoint between the upward thrust of the surrounding buildings and the dancers' answering exploration of horizontality, their insistence, variegated as it was, on "getting down." I in fact had been similarly struck, had taken note of the same thing.

147

Nathaniel Mackey

I've given it more thought since then and have come to see that the verticality/horizontality counterpoint or play opens onto a larger field of implication. One sees, for example, that "break" serves notice on as it diverges from the city's valorization of hardness, unyieldingness, rigidity, the upward investment in steel and stone. That it does this while working variations on the very condition it implicitly critiques is something one might easily miss. The breakers' recourse to choreographed rigidities and robotisms arises as a caveat in the face of exactly the threat it wants to fend off, an inoculation or an aestheticization, at least, of the fate to which it would seem to have acceded. Easier, perhaps, to see is the fact that the splits, the spins, the strenuous bendings and the acrobatic twistings constitute a reminder — a therapeutic reminder — of the malleability and thus the vulnerability of human flesh. Such athletic writhings are anything but a naively triumphal homage to resilience. The cigar boxes make that all the more clear. Breaking accents the body under siege — one notes, among other things, that the electronic drums recall machine-gun fire — but also, more trenchantly yet, the susceptibility of states of siege to commoditization.

There's a lot more to it of course. Coming from L.A., I couldn't help noting that the dancers' pursuit of exponential horizontality had a way of letting sprawl, so to speak, in thru the backdoor. That the body turns out to be that door makes a certain sense. More importantly, this relates break dancing to, among other things, Caribbean limbo, said by tradition to have been born in the cramped holds of the slave ships. Like any other such black negotiation of shrunken space (think of Henry "Box" Brown, Harriet Jacobs's garret and so forth), break dancing understands cramp as embryonic sprawl, embryonic spring.

There're some other aspects of this I wish I could go into, but, as I've said already, we're going out again soon. Perhaps I'll take it up again in another letter, perhaps even work these matters into a new composition. In any case, it's best I relax a bit before we head out. There's a lot of music in town — Max Roach at Seventh Avenue South, Ted Curson at Sweet Basil, Joe Turner at Tramps, Hilton Ruiz at Soundscape, Charli Persip at Jazz Forum, just to name a few. We won't quit till we've heard as much as we can.

Later,
N.

———————————20.XI.81

Dear Angel of Dust,

You won't believe it. We seem to've met the drummer we've been after. I can hardly believe it myself, so odd was the way it came about—outright uncanny in the wake of what I wrote in my last letter about "the body under siege." It in fact occurred later the same evening I wrote that letter. We'd just come out of the restaurant where we'd eaten dinner and were standing on Fifth Avenue waiting to cross. This was around 60th or 61st, I think. In any case, we were standing there waiting to cross when we noticed a fight had broken out at the other end of the block. A man in a trenchcoat had pushed another man against a building and they were punching on one another. There was a car stopped at the curb and almost as soon as we noticed what was going on two more men in trenchcoats jumped out of it and rushed towards the two men who were fighting. The first trenchcoated man, the one fighting with the untrenchcoated man, pulled away, giving the other two access to the latter. The two of them took their hands from their trenchcoat pockets. That's when we heard gunshots.

The instant the shooting started we all took off running. It was as if the shots had come from a starter's gun at a track meet. We ran down whatever the cross street was we were on, away from Fifth Avenue and the threat of stray bullets, our legs instinctively triggered by a seed of escape which, it seemed, had ages ago been planted, a seed out of which unfurled an embryonic spur, embryonic sprint. That seed, it seemed, had run forward to meet this moment, unbeknown to us. We were no more than its horses. We ran, that is, for all we were worth, more than we were worth, spurred by aboriginal reflex and fear, ran as if all hell had broken loose. It seemed, it's no exaggeration to say, that we'd been running without knowing it all along, even as we stood, running farther back than we could remember, so sovereign was the aboriginal spur we were prompted by, provident to the point of retroaction.

There were five shots fired, I think. It's hard to say since once we started running I could hear nothing but the sound of our feet hitting the sidewalk. Manhattan became suddenly silent except for the sound of our instinctual stampede. We ran as a pack, all of us running at the same speed, borne along as though by collective legs. Our aboriginal sprint came to an end about two-thirds of the way down the block and it wasn't till then that we noticed there were six of us rather than five. After we slowed to a stop and stood catching our breath — it seemed we had run much more than two-thirds of a block — we saw there was a woman among us (medium height, dread hair, wearing a coat which came down to her ankles) who'd also, we now recalled, been standing on Fifth Avenue waiting to cross. She too had been prodded by the instinctual spur which had impelled our sprint. She too had run, had been a part of our pack, had run with us.

By now the noise was back — the traffic, the horns and so forth. Things appeared to be back to normal. The shooting had stopped. What had happened had occurred so suddenly, so quickly, my heart went on racing even though my legs were now still. I'm sure this was also true of the others. A swift aboriginal heart raced in each of our chests as we stood there, none of us able to speak. It was finally Penguin who broke the silence, exhaling loudly and saying, "Whew! That was weird." The word "weird," of course, fit only loosely, a registration of dismay which was too all-purpose to be precise, but it did bring things back to normal. We now began to talk, the upshot of which was that we had occasion to introduce ourselves to the woman who had run with us and she to introduce herself to us. Her name is Drennette.

It was after telling her that we're a band that we learned she's a musician too. "What a coincidence. Funny," she said, "I'm a musician myself." Our ears perked up and we gave each other looks when she added, "A drummer, to be exact." We couldn't, of course, help wondering could she be the woman we'd been looking for. Off to so auspicious a start — she had, hadn't she, run with us — we had to make an effort not to jump to that conclusion. Still, that it occurred to each of us right away there can be no doubt. The looks we gave one another made that clear.

On the one hand it was hard not to race to a conclusion but on the other I began to feel qualms about the silver lining we seemed intent on extracting from the shooting's ominous cloud. Here a man had been shot and lay dying if not dead and the best we could do was hope that the shooting had brought us together with the drummer we'd been searching for. That we had succumbed so nonchalantly to big city indifference, big city survival instincts, made me shiver. I spoke up to suggest we go back and see what had happened, that the man might have only been wounded, in which case we could call for help. We did so, only to find, once we got back to Fifth Avenue, that an ambulance was already there, pulling away, in fact, just as we turned the corner, with the man who'd been shot inside. There were a couple of police cars and a small crowd gathered where the shooting had taken place. I now recalled having heard sirens as we stood talking after catching our breath. We walked to where the crowd and the police cars were and, once there, heard someone say that the ambulance was on its way to the morgue, that the man was dead.

Penguin's word "weird," I couldn't help reflecting, much more aptly applied to how quickly the ambulance and the police had shown up. They might as well have been snowplows, the man who'd been shot newly fallen snow, so quickly had the sidewalk been cleared. It was as if such goings-on had become so common as to make ambulances and police cars omnipresent, never more than a moment away no matter where. Quick to the point of seeming preternatural, they were ubiquitous, in the air, as it were, anxious to materialize, waiting for some such occurrence as the shooting we'd seen. Later in the bar we stepped into for a drink I remarked on this. "That's the way the Apple is," Drennette said drily. "All in a day's work."

While in the bar we talked more about music, getting back to Drennette being a drummer and, eventually, the fact that we've been looking for one. We took it as encouraging that she's only here for the holidays, visiting her parents in Brooklyn, that she lives, it turns out, in Santa Barbara. (How she ended up there, she said, was a story she would need more time to go into.) Bordering on too-good-to-be-true, this appeared to be no simple coincidence and made it more difficult not to jump to the conclusion (premature sprint, embryonic end-of-our-search) that she's the drummer we've been looking for. Making it even more difficult not to do so was her disclosure that she's been looking for a band to join, even thinking of starting one of her own. "You wouldn't believe the motley string of groups I've gigged with over the past year," she said. We laughed when she said that last month she'd done three nights with a punk-funk band called Mojo Toejam. By now our premature sprint was well under way, seeming anything but premature. The "in" common to Penny, Djeannine and Drennette wasn't lost on us.

"Premature" notwithstanding, the sense that Drennette might be our drummer grew stronger and stronger, the upshot of which was us arranging to get together again. Yesterday afternoon she came by and brought some tapes of her playing and we sat around listening and talking. No doubt about it. She's for real. If she can scare up a drumset we'll do some playing together before we leave town. If not, we'll wait till we're back on the west coast. Either way, I have a feeling she's the one.

Tonight we open and Drennette said she'd come by to check us out.

Again, wish us luck.

As ever,
N.

——————————————9.XII.81

Dear Angel of Dust,

Sorry to've kept you in suspense. We've been back from New York a while now and I've been meaning to let you know how the rest of the trip, the actual gig and all, went. So much, however, happened — quantum-qualitatively so much, I should say — that I've balked at even attempting to give an account. I've been so put upon by trepidations brought on by quantum-qualitative "so much" as to despair of being able to do it justice. It got to the point a few days ago, in fact, that I succumbed to a shattered cowrie shell attack, a new bout of dizziness revolving around a quantum-qualitative collapse, a quantum-qualitative surge of unsuspended misgiving. It laid me low a couple of days but I managed to get back on my feet. I write now not really free of hesitation though somewhat less disabled by the wishful notion of recounting all of what (or even most of what) quantum-qualitatively occurred. The shattered cowrie shell attack, if it did no other good, appears to have set me free of that. A whispered rush of shattered innuendo insisted I be reconciled to incommensurability, the very crux, it insisted further, of quantum-qualitative "so much."

I should begin, then, by saying that we went over well. There was a good, solid turnout all three nights (a bit larger Saturday night than on the other two) and the music was well received. We played as well as we've ever played and often better, spurred on in part by, so to speak, the high stakes involved. This came as a relief after all the apprehensions, which for me culminated the afternoon of the first night in a stricken, panicky feeling in which I could no longer imagine playing. By then I was deeply into being in New York, one thing I liked about which was the anonymity, the sense of having been swallowed up, absorbed. Anonymous drop in an ocean of other anonymous drops, I took to the lack of self-conscious identity I enjoyed. I enjoyed my inconspicuousness. This, though, was the problem. The passive, spectatorial attitude this induced was at odds with us being there to play. All of a sudden playing seemed an irrelevant presumption, the assumption of a voice which had in fact been swallowed up. The presumed audience which went with that assumption had also, I felt, been swallowed up. It seemed absurd to expect anyone to show up, let alone listen. Attention throve on differentiation. Metropolitan anonymity had long since dissolved. Why raise and call attention to one's voice when ostensible ear, no less than ostensible voice, had long since drowned?

This all came on me in a flash — not all that long, in fact, after I finished my last letter to you. What brought it on I can't say. That morning we'd had a rehearsal and everything had gone fine, so I had no reason to fear the city had swallowed my voice. A kind of stage fright is probably what it was, but the grip it had on me was all the more scary for being at odds with the apparent facts. Rehearsal notwithstanding (all the more so, perhaps, because of it or in spite of it), whatever it was that had me in its grip seemed to know something, to be in touch with something deeper than ostensible fact. This feeling, this fear, had its way with me right up to the time of the gig, though I didn't let on or say anything about it to anyone. It took me thru a number of degrees of apprehension but there were insights it apprised me of as well. These turned out to work to the music's advantage, giving my tone an inostensible edge, a now cutting, now confidential buzz of implication possessed of a quantum-qualitative anonymity combined with a quantum-qualitative "So what?" Something like a blasé leap, that is, was the form apprehension eventually took, an enabling shrug of numinous nonchalance which endowed my playing with a bittersweet obliquity and bite. It was a steeling of myself against the lure of despair which at the same time stole a march on hope.

I've gotten ahead of myself however. Inostensible obliquity and bite I'll leave to go into again later. What I was on my way to saying was that my fear, while not entirely unfounded, turned out not to be prophetic. Once the set was actually under way I could see I would have no such problem as the one I feared. Facility and fluency were with me from the very first note, as they also were with everyone else in the band. It was, as I've already said, some of the best playing we've ever done. There were peak points over the course of the three nights too numerous — to say nothing of too quantum-qualitatively

153

torqued — for me to be able, as I've also already said, to do justice to, points where something seemed to "take us higher." Two or three of these points however — quantum-qualitative increments I call them — I'll give a shot at going into in some detail.

(Quantum-Qualitative Increment "A")

Night one, second set. We were into the open section of "Opposable Thumb at the Water's Edge." Djamilaa was on harmonium, Aunt Nancy on violin, Lambert on tenor, Penguin on oboe, me on saxello. Aunt Nancy to our left and Djamilaa to our right, Lambert, Penguin and I stood in something of a semi-circle around the same mike, leaning in towards it as if in a huddle or a semi-huddle — three witches, it must have appeared, stirring up a cacophonous, free-blowing brew. Our aim at that point was to keep a wall of sound happening, an ongoing instance of threadedness and thrust exacting a layered rush of precept and provocation. It wasn't only a wall we wrote *Outraged* on but a sort of primer, a "blackboard" on which our "chalk marks" conjured as they catechized, worked as though they were vévés inviting visitation. Visitation, at any rate, is what we got.

The wall had been going forward as though it would go on that way forever — buttressed by Djamilaa's harmonium, embroidered by Aunt Nancy's violin — when Aunt Nancy began to do something which gradually altered the music's course. Letting go of the spiccato figure she'd been repeating, she embarked upon an increasingly complex run. It was a run which was especially demanding on her left hand — prestissimo demisemiquavers, tremolo effects and so forth. A blazing display of technique, this in turn gave way to a slower, anthemlike figure I knew at once I'd heard before. Repeating it in alternately higher and lower octaves, she bowed with a deliberate, somewhat exaggerated muscularity in the latter, insisting, it seemed, on viscosity, drag, the air of encountered resistance one hears in, say, Jack McDuff's rendition of "Jive Samba." This wasn't the piece the figure reminded me of however, though the more she played it the more familiar it got — hauntingly so. It became obvious, after a while, that she meant to get our attention, that the figure was a summons of sorts. We gave her a glance out of the corners of our eyes and she indicated we should fade, that she wanted to play unaccompanied for a while. This we did, letting the wall subside slowly.

Once this was done Aunt Nancy went on to play the rest of the piece of which the figure she'd been repeating was the opening part.

It was then that I recognized it. It was one of Paganini's Caprices, the 9th. It took me a moment or two to catch on to what she was up to but it soon became clear that it was the "pagan" in Paganini she meant to put emphasis on. Recalling the pact he'd supposedly made with the devil, Aunt Nancy played all alone as if to imply that it was the devil of solitude he'd been possessed by, alluding, it appeared, to his habit of going into seclusion. It was during one such withdrawal to Tuscany, I remembered, that he's thought to've written the Caprices.

About this time Penguin, as though he'd read my mind, looked at me and winked, letting me know that he too was on to what she was up to. Indeed, her solo ratified a thought he had recently shared with me — and, perhaps, with her as well — to the effect that the proverbial pact with the devil, the bargain struck for technical prowess, reflects a fear, a collective suspicion, of the solitude one develops one's abilities in. "Robert Johnson didn't sell his soul to the devil," I recalled him having said, "he just spent a lot of time in the woodshed, off to himself." So it was that we knowingly grinned at one another when Aunt Nancy briefly went back to her prestissimo run. She tossed off a quick, finger-twisting flurry which inquired, "Woodshed or devil's workshop?" — pointedly inverting the old adage about idle hands. Her hands, the left especially, were anything but idle, which is exactly what made her appear to be possessed.

Penguin and I grinned but what she was getting at wasn't really funny. Her prestissimo flurry tossed off, she returned to variations on Caprice No. 9, emphasizing, this time around, its brooding, melancholic undertones. It was a darker mood she now explored, a mix of anthemlike and elegiac, a mood infiltrated by the muse of European hoodoo, the spectre of technological possession. Opposable Thumb, she insisted, was *homo faber* thinly veiled, the projection of a tool-making tendency gone awry. Her melancholic anthem waved a banner of sorrow consecrated to quantum-qualitative disaster, a technical-ecstatic upping of the ante on the risk of impending ruin. It was, going back to her initial insinuation, a drag of an anthem, a dirge, a dredging up. "Water's edge," one all but heard her caution, "water's edge," while as if it were held onto by something underwater she tugged on the bow.

Something about what Aunt Nancy was playing, even though I'd already recognized it as Caprice No. 9, continued to cry out for identification. There continued to be something familiar about it, though what it was wasn't entirely that it was the Paganini piece. What it was was more obliquely familiar. There was some other piece of music, one whose name was on the tip of my tongue, the Caprice tangentially resembled and brought to mind. Aunt Nancy bowed as if she too had its name on the tip of her tongue, repeating the passage which most brought it to mind so strenuously she appeared to be out to break thru to it on sheer strength. This made it all the more elusively familiar, all the more hauntingly within one's grasp yet still out of reach. She herself didn't seem to know what it was. The height of tangency and teasing kinship, whatever it was clearly had a hold of her. This we could clearly see. No mere mime of possession, this was the real thing.

It was Lambert who figured out what it was. Leaving the mike that he, Penguin and I shared and joining Aunt Nancy at hers, he put his horn to his mouth and began to play Ayler's tune "Ghosts," looking Aunt Nancy in the eye — hers were glassy, glazed — as he did. This was it I realized at once. This was the piece one heard inklings of in Caprice No. 9. Lambert, continuing to look Aunt Nancy in the eye, emphasized its aspect of ditty-bop anthem, ditty-bop strut, its ditty-bop meeting or blend of street wisdom with an otherwise otherworldly insistence. Several people in the audience, recognizing the tune, applauded. One woman shouted out, "Albert lives!" Lambert dug deeper into the tune, playing with a hip, ditty-bop assurance which contrasted with Aunt Nancy's distraught, melodramatic dredge. It was a contrapuntal hipness and hope he proposed and Aunt Nancy, as though this were the door, the way out or in she'd been looking for, let the Paganini passage go and took up with "Ghosts." Even though her eyes retained their glazed, glassy look, there was now a look of relief on her face. Djamilaa came in on harmonium, laying down a Baul-inflected, ditty-bop bass line which gave the music an erotic-elegiac, funky-butt foundation and feel.

It took only a whiff of Djamilaa's funky-butt bass to draw Penguin in. He toyed with the head at first, playing in ever so staggered unison with Aunt Nancy and Lambert, soon letting it go to lend himself to Djamilaa's Indian insinuations. Sustaining the dominant, subdominant and tonic as alternating drones by using circular breathing, what he did could be said to have added a Celtic flavor as well. Part bagpipe and part shenai, Penguin's oboe more than lived up to its "high wood" root. Indeed, given the headiness and the heedless, wishful insistence Penguin implied, it had the sound of "high would" as well. He didn't so much blow the horn, it seemed, as take one long unending hit, as if it were a hookah.

It was heavy. The woman who had shouted out earlier again shouted, "Albert lives!" It was as if she too had taken a hit of "high would." Aunt Nancy, realist to the end, responded with a descending run which picked up on "would," but only to say, "Would it were so." It was a run which ever so subtly resurrected, as it were, her distraught, melodramatic dredge, putting one in mind of Ayler's death and of the East River in which his body had been found. Dredge, with its evocation of depth, came into complicating play with would-be height, "high would." Lambert by this time had let the head go to work on a grumbling low-register frenzy which both quoted and laid Albert to rest and even further made for a mix in which would-be height gave grudging ground. It ostensibly laid Albert to rest I should've said, for it was something, a weeping something — sob, ecstatic sensation and several other indescribable factors — I've heard no one other than Ayler himself do (though David Murray comes close). It so seemed as if Albert had taken hold of Lambert's horn that it was all I could do to keep from shouting, "Albert lives!"

It was then that I joined in. Something told me to switch to alto, which I did to find that the bittersweet edge, the newly-acquired obliquity and bite I'd been surprised by on saxello, was all the more inostensibly there on the lower-pitched horn. Had it been a tenor or, heaven forbid, a baritone I don't think I could've stood it. My intonation had something of the timbral evanescence of John Tchicai's hollowed-out, strung-up sigh, the evaporative chill he has a way of putting on certain notes. Then again, it had a bit of Arthur Blythe's cut-to-the-quick poignancy and play on fear ("As if he'd seen a ghost") but without its comic and ecclesiastic extremes. No, I was serious, not somber, nonchalant, not flip. I sounded haunted and free of hangups at the same time.

Vacancy and voice had caressed one another unawares I immediately knew and I made the most of their inostensible embrace. I took Aunt Nancy and Lambert up on their low-register wager, starting off with a hollowed-out grumble and growl and a ditty-bop shiver whose reverse-gravitational itch and inclination sought an accord with Penguin's quantum-qualitative "high would." Djamilaa's funky-butt foundation and feel had long since gotten a bump-and-grind aspect about it, which made for just the amount of bounce I would need for my inostensible ascent.

Once again it was a wall we put forth, a wailing, structured rush of sound whose collective insistence took Albert's ditty-bop anthem into twisty, giddy reaches possessed of a wincing, wounded quality

Albert himself had often explored. Wounded anthem was what it
was we now played, a taxed, exacting air whose implicative thread
of capricious wind brought the man we'd seen shot on Fifth Avenue
to mind. A second ghost had come up to visit. Capricious wind and
capricious wound by now ran as one. Anonymous breath embraced
anonymous bullet.

Indeed, the spectre of anonymity had us by the throats, which
made for a choked-up, croaking sound which groped as though
blinded by the light it ostensibly served. We telepathically knew it
was time to restate the head, which we did with a collective voice
which was guttural and gutted (hollowed-out) at the same time —
hollowed-out and shoveled-up it seemed. This brought the audience
to its feet with a burst of applause. What it was they'd been gotten
to by were no doubt the detours our vatic resolve had been made to
take — the sense of uneasy hope or of strained hope or of staggered,
strenuous hope one got from its pitched interplay of parts.

The spontaneous ovation told us the piece had peaked and that
this was the place to end — which, though we hadn't intended to, we
did. With no cue but the one the audience gave us, we crisply repeated the head's last note in unison, letting the piece end on it. Had
we then looked down to find we'd risen several inches off the floor
we wouldn't have been at all surprised.

(Quantum-Qualitative Increment "B")

". . . who, when loving, live." So ends the refrain of "Udhrite
Amendment," a song Djamilaa wrote after reading my first after-the-
fact lecture/libretto, the one which ends with her on the couch. In
writing the song, she told us, it was the conventional love-death
equation she sought to reopen if not rescind. On at least one level,
that is, the song amounts to an exposé of masked enjoyments, an
unveiling of mixed emotions which is itself, not quite inevitably, a
mixed-emotional display. "Live" and "die" are seen to be less than two
halves of a whole, inadequate terms for an essentially nameless resource, though "resource" doesn't quite fit either.

Djamilaa's goal was to ventilate as well as unveil an emotional
stance which for her had gone stale. Accordingly, the accompani-
ment consists of me, Lambert and Penguin on flutes, with Aunt
Nancy providing percussion on conga. The flute parts incorporate
phrases from Dolphy's recording of "Glad To Be Unhappy," a pointedly mixed-emotional motif set up to be revised by phrases from "To

158

Be," the flute and piccolo piece Trane and Pharoah recorded. "Glad" and "unhappy" are thus implied to be beside the point. The music is also indebted to Henry Threadgill's multi-flute concept on the *X-15 Volume 1* album. The allusion to this latter title, albeit oblique, makes for a further move into abstraction, a move made more immediately evident by Djamilaa's recourse, as in "The Slave's Day Off," to singing with a piece of waxed paper in front of her mouth. The song's affinity with "The Slave's Day Off" doesn't end there, for its contestatory address of the love-death equation moves or seeks to move in a liberatory direction. The piece of waxed paper contends with and hopefully subverts a received semantics which, "live" replacing "die" notwithstanding, tends to be complicit with "the way things are." This is ground, contested ground, our music returns to again and again.

It was this number we concluded our first night's performance with. It was a totally entrancing, thoroughly absorbing reading of the piece, a particularly fitting way to wrap things up it turned out. "Udhrite Amendment," before it was over, proposed an extrapolative cool-out gradient whose uncoiled eroticism translated length, extensibility, into quantum-qualitative lift. Djamilaa's voice was every bit as hypnotic as it's ever been, an ostensible/inostensible mix which had its own way of coming to terms with metropolitan anonymity's blasé obliquity and bite. She put one remotely in mind of the Javanese singer Imas Permas, coaxing from herself, it seemed, a slow tangential address which mated complaint with composure. The piece of waxed paper, of course, obscured the lyrics, introducing a semantic x-factor, as it were, which had the audience on the edges of their seats trying to make the words out.

From the first few notes I knew we were into something. The flutes kicked it off with a serrated climb punctuated by a plunge which brought Aunt Nancy in. She pulled her thumb across the conga's head in such a way as to make it sound like a bass, giving us just the bit of bottom we needed. It was this that did it, this descent which got us on our way. The bent, swelling note Aunt Nancy's thumb adduced — part plea, part Udhrite appointment — apprised us of a see-thru accessibility of which it insisted we avail ourselves. I felt for a moment as though the plate on which my lower lip rested were the edge of a pool I dipped into, the palpable "splash" of an imagined oasis's Udhrite "plunge." The see-thru water I wet my lips with reminded me of Charles Lloyd's "Little Anahid's Day," yet there was an even stronger recollection it occasioned of the psychophonic affliction of which I wrote you a few months back — the luminous doomed lament scored for hollowed-out pelvis played on dislocated flute. I stood naked, I felt, before all of New York, stripped of both clothing and flesh, naked to the bone, abruptly accessible (x-ray accessible) to the eyes of anyone who looked. It was a pool of skeletal water, x-ray water, I dipped into. Penguin and Lambert dipped into it as well.

The x-ray accessibility in whose grip the three of us played must have made the audience all the more unprepared for the divergence from see-thru semantics to which the piece of waxed paper gave purchase. The opacity it gave an otherwise insubstantial medium stood in stark, metonymic alliance with the now transparent substantiality of which Lambert, Penguin and I found ourselves possessed. I noticed a man in one of the front rows whose face got a perplexed — albeit ultimately approving — look when Djamilaa started singing. The contiguous incongruity between x-ray accessibility and semantic x-factor caused more than a few eyebrows to rise.

Part oasis, part piranha pool, the watery body of which we availed ourselves grew calm with an exhortative insistence, a mix whose cue was that of complaint and composure Djamilaa brought off. The unison flute passages made for an etheric, "theoretical" aura from which we each had opportunities to stray or with which to differ by retaining the graininess of "practice." Differential flutter thus tended to intervene so as to ward off the danger of self-inflation, to dispel the auto-enchanted halo "theoretical" aura might have easily become. Something or someone, it insinuated, had dreamt it all up — which, of course, was true — though regarding the limits of what "it" referred to one would've liked it to be more precise. The opaque, waxed-paper-assisted accent Djamilaa repeatedly let fall on "live" by now bore the weight of an autumnal ripeness construed to pose myth and maturation as linked. So expressively was the link sustained and so thoroughgoing were its repercussions as to intimate a trumpeter's annunciative kiss. Needless to say, this too caused eyebrows to rise.

Djamilaa's voice rode the wind of its "new day" annunciation, annulling the asthmatic equation on which Udhrite aesthetics had up to then been based. The amended wind of which it grew newly apprised arose in part from the breath Lambert, Penguin and I expended, an obsessed, invasive "second wind" which now began to send ripples across the pool into which we dipped. The piranha pool thus found itself blown upon by an x-ray wind whose exposure of bone was the alarmed incentive towards a "new day" annulment, a "new day" dismissal of love-death license, love-death allure. "New day," though not announcedly so, was "the slave's day off" as far as I was concerned. It was no doubt this that caused my flute to seem it was no longer made of metal, to seem instead to've been cut from cane. This I found oddly reassuring, oddly soothing.

The transformation from "base" metal to "balsamic" wood was not, however, without its apprehensive side. The taste of something burnt came along with it, a taste my lower lip and the tip of my tongue picked up from the lip-plate, the taste, I realized at once, of burnt cane. It was a taste which, consonant with "The Slave's Day Off," excavated the roots of Trinidadian carnival, Canboulay. Grimacing as if overcome by a bitter memory, I embarked upon a rush of differential flutter, a former slave's carnival reenactment of plantation times. Grimacing rush told of canefields burning, sudden rousings out of bed, late night harvest, all-night labor. A reminder of past oppression if not a foretaste of burnings to come, the *canne brulée* taste in my mouth betrayed a fear that freedom was only a dream. Love's "new day" was only another night of sleep one would be forced to wake up from. This fear grew stronger and stronger the longer *canne brulée* prevailed. Even so, I went on blowing, a back-slider in the "new day" church without intending to be, trying to blow the fire out but fanning it instead.

My unintended slide caught everyone's attention, most notably Djamilaa's. Her waxed paper scat took on a scolding inflection which reminded me that burnt cane, *canne brulée* — my coded way, she charged, of alluding to burnt kiss, French kiss — was merely a lapse into the unamended Udhrite ordeal the song was meant to challenge. This, of course, I already knew, though it made me blush to hear it put so bluntly. Lambert and Penguin heard it as well and also saw me blush. They came to my aid as if to someone who had suffered a blow, playing the unison passage a little bit louder to recall me to it. It was a strikingly lucid, enticingly sweet passage (all but overly so), not unlike an Indian or a North African dessert. It was also not unlike the strings on Alice Coltrane's "Oh Allah," sweet but all the while bordering on tart. It was a far cry, in any case, from the taste of burnt cane my flute and I had picked up — so far, in fact, I couldn't imagine ever joining them again.

But seeing, they say, is believing. It certainly made a believer out of me. I doubt I would ever have made it back to the unison passage were it not for what I saw when I glanced over at Lambert and Penguin. My eyes, I felt at first, had to be putting me on. I saw grains of sugar on the lip-plates of Lambert's and Penguin's flutes, an image I tried to shake off to no avail. They must really be into it, I thought. This was the beginning of my breaking away from *canne brulée*.

Lambert and Penguin all but out and told me to straighten up and pull myself together, to come back to the unison passage. They stood unusually straight as they played, the true-believer sweetness occasioning an almost military stance. They held their heads high, standing so erect they appeared to be stretching themselves, a strenuous enough stretch to mix true-believer sweetness with true-believer sweat. The grains of sugar didn't blow away as they played but seemed to be indigenous to the lip-plates on which they sat.

To me the flute felt like a chin-up bar. I was trying to pull myself up to a higher level, to make my way back into the "new day" church. Aunt Nancy's winged conga beats helped a bit but nevertheless it was a struggle, a strain — so much so I felt I was losing my breath as I tried to blow and pull myself up at the same time. Were it not for the grains of sugar I saw I'd have never made it. Were it also not for Djamilaa's voice, which had gone from scolding to coaxingly sweet, I'd have never made it. So inspired a reach of sweetness it was it almost made me weep.

It must have been windedness, the thin air of my ascent, which made me go blank. I didn't exactly pass out, for I went on playing, but the last thing I remember is getting back to the unison passage and the feeling which came with it, after only a couple of notes, that I was for all time free of *canne brulée*. The next thing I knew we were backstage in the dressing room, congratulating one another on how well the first night had gone. "Udhrite Amendment" had evidently ended not terribly long after I got back to the unison passage, but not before Djamilaa and I entered into a brief impromptu exchange — my part in which, I'm told, consisted largely of an alternation between E7 and Fmaj7 which took the unison passage's line in a "Spanish" direction — an exchange Aunt Nancy, Lambert and Penguin raved about, Aunt Nancy calling it "worthy of Billie and Prez." I don't remember a note of it. Nor do I remember the ovation we got. I don't remember walking from the stage to the dressing-room either.

(Quantum-Qualitative Increment "C")

Drennette managed to borrow a drumset and so was able to sit in with us on Sunday night, night number three. That in itself was a quantum-qualitative high, a sustained increment. Though she complained at first of being "reduced to standard equipment," of not having her usual accessories and idiosyncratic implements (a set of "gongs" made from hubcaps and trashcan lids, an assortment of bells, rattles and shakers, a toy xylophone and so forth), she more than acquitted herself well. She was, in fact, a monster. All night she was on it, putting forth an order of rhythmic invention which made her corner of the stage a percussion lab, standard, stripped-down equipment notwithstanding. "Rhythmelodic" might be a better way to put it, for Drennette had obviously learned a thing or two from the likes of Ed Blackwell and, among others, Freddie Waits. She had a way, that is, of making the drumset sing, exacting an exhortative, oratorical range, a reconnoitering stir in whose arch embrace push and support were indissolubly one. Punch and propulsion complicated by slippage — well-placed hints of erosive wear, erosive retreat — were the dominant threads in the rhythmelodic carpet she wove and rode, the pushy-supportive rug which, even as she threatened to pull it out from under us, carried us along.

The entire night, as I've already said, was a continuous high, though some points, of course, were higher than others. One such point occurred during the second set as we were into a piece Lambert had recently written, "Half-Staff Appetition" — a piece he was moved to write by a quote he rediscovered in one of his college notebooks, a passage from a book by Alfred North Whitehead: "In each actuality there are two concrescent poles of realization — 'enjoyment' and 'appetition,' that is, the 'physical' and the 'conceptual.' For God the conceptual is prior to the physical, for the World the physical poles are prior to the conceptual poles. A physical pole is in its own nature exclusive, bounded by contradiction: a conceptual pole is in its own nature all-embracing, unbounded by contradiction. The former derives its share of infinity from the infinity of appetition; the latter derives its share of limitation from the exclusiveness of enjoyment." Weeks before at a rehearsal, introducing the piece, Lambert had joked that if Whitehead had been a musician he could've let it go with playing "Body and Soul." (He also had some fun with the name, insisting on an emphatic pause between "White" and "head.") We laughed but, joke notwithstanding, the piece does derive in part from "Body and Soul"'s chord progressions, Lambert having done with them something like what Mal Waldron does in "Anatomy" with those of "All The Things You Are." It's a simple piece — pointedly, deceptively so, considering the Whitehead quote — on which Lambert imposed a namesake ceiling, writing it entirely in the bottom half of the staff. Never does it go above third-line B, a prohibition we were instructed to observe even in our solos.

"Half-Staff Appetition" speaks of caution and confinement, a near crippling sense of unascendable height bearing down which makes us feel, whenever we play it, as though we stood stooped over. This has in part, of course, to do with Lambert's play on "staff," where with "half" he insists on fractionality and lack, the falling short of its ostensible support. That one makes up the lack oneself seems implied by the stooped-over feeling we can never quite shake, the sense that unascendable height rests on our backs, bearing down with the weight of lowered expectation. Shepherdly cramp, that is, meets shepherded craving, each in its way the splintered remains of a collateral coup and consolidation, the exploited, ever-splintering crutch on which prohibitive height itself leans for support.

Lambert appears also, in writing the piece, to have wanted to ask, "What about the enjoyment of appetition?" The low ceiling which is third-line B feeds and fosters a sweet-tooth for dialectics, a philosophic appeal which appears intent on insisting on furtherance and frustration as one when it comes to desire. Appeal feeds philosophic aplomb, a recuperative crutch implicating desire in its own obstruction. That any such crutch is only a half-eaten stick, an indebted baton, the implosive receipt of which wants to incite as it offers solace, almost goes without saying. Does "half-staff" thus have to do with "half-eaten" one has reason to ask, a question Lambert left room for us to address in our improvisations. Appetitive earth leaned on by cannibalized height (half-eaten heaven) is thus a motif which comes up each time we play the piece. This particular night, with Drennette sitting in, was no exception.

Drennette is indeed, in many ways, the ideal drummer for such a piece. The intimate terms on which we stood with erosion, thanks to her, underscored its implied embrace of half-eaten height. Splintered support sparked and spiced by slippage, as I've already said, is a key feature of Drennette's approach, an insistent appeal which, in the case of this piece, applied appetitive heat to unascendable height. Thus it was, one was left to infer, that appetition and enjoyment were one, a farther-reaching idea than that the former could be the latter's object. "The consumption of unascendability," I said to myself as I concluded my solo, so taken, as it turned out, was I with this idea. I at once regretted it having occurred to me too late to've been made more explicit, too late to be made a part of my solo. It was luckily an idea which Lambert, who soloed last, after me, had also picked up on.

It was, in fact, Lambert and Drennette's interplay, prohibitive height notwithstanding, which afforded us the quantum-qualitative ascent I'm here labeling "C." Lambert started off somewhat tentatively, with an apprehensiveness and a hesitant, fearful tread which were not inconsistent with the strains of erosive wear and erosive retreat Drennette insisted on. Woven into the rug she invited one to ride was a suspect appeal he had every reason to have qualms about, to be wary of, notwithstanding that he savored its allure. The consumption of unascendability partook of that savor, taking the form, as he espoused and put it forth, of a performative discourse having to do with fugitive breath, tasted breath.

"Half-Staff Appetition," I may not have said, is a ballad. A balladeer to the bone once he got into it, Lambert expounded its ballad marrow as he apportioned its ballad blood with a sound whose breathy/breathless caress brought Ben Webster to mind — the Webster of, say, "Prisoner of Love" or of "Tenderly." This Websterian recourse to subtones made for an accent which fell on wind as rudimentary voice, an insinuative return to basics, as it were, whose flirtatious, make-believe bite — a fugitive lover's blown breath or kiss — one could never not woo the enjoyment of. Thus it was that ballad bone was a now asthmatic, now respirated baton which had made the rounds from time immemorial, a broken, half-staff capacity for aspirate expulsion, aspirate escape.

Lambert's Websterian celebration of breath couldn't help but be infused with a spectre of loss, an intimate acknowledgment if not embrace of expiration's most ominous undertones, in dialogue with which a consoling image of "inspired" leakage came into play. The latter made for a reading of aspirate expulsion (savored aspiration, inverse breathless ascent) as a cushion for what might otherwise have been unbearable, an inspired albeit merely implied pillow talk to soften its blow. Such implicative talk sugarcoated a pill which was hard to swallow, though Drennette, it appeared, was by no means entirely won over. She bit or bought into it only to bargain for something more, keeping up her end of what was a bartered embrace with a not-to-be-bought barrage of postromantic rescissions played on cymbals and high hat. The rest of us gradually pulled back. This was obviously between the two of them, an expulsive-appetitive pillow and rug rolled into one.

Being it was a ballad, Drennette used brushes. So it was that rug was already rolled into one with brush. This meant it was also rolled into one with broom, Drennette's brushwork putting us in mind of what had gone on in Griffith Park a few weeks before — not only the sound but, in my case, the "seen," Broom Ex Machina's dance. Her brushed embellishments blended with Lambert's Websterian pillow in such a way as to sound as if she swept up the breath which escaped between the reed and his bottom lip. That such leakage intimated mortality was lost on no one, least of all her, and she made the most of it (dusted broom, dust under the rug) whenever she could.

Remembering what had happened in Griffith Park, I didn't dare, as you can imagine, close my eyes, though Penguin did eventually close his. There was something funereal about Lambert and Drennette's exchange, as though they lamented appetition's death or, if not its death, the dire straits ("half-staff") thru which it passed. This isn't to say there was anything morbid or morose about it so much as that direness and desire walked hand in hand. In keeping with its funereal aspect, Penguin removed his hat (a gray stingy-brim number he'd picked up in Harlem) and bowed his head. That the air was being let out of something was clear. What that something was would've been considered by some to be common knowledge, by others anybody's guess. My sense was that the air was being left out of enjoyment, of which the swept-under side was that the letting out of air was being enjoyed.

What Lambert and Drennette got into increasingly sounded like a low-register crawl, an eked-out advance which was not uninformed by overtones of encroachment. Drennette peppered their coaxed incursions with intermittent hisses, clipped hisses on high hat — by way of response, this, to Penguin's bowed head and doffed hat. There was nothing, she seemed to insist, to be glum about. The clipped hisses brought the phantom drummer we'd heard in Griffith Park all the more to mind. Whether or not Drennette was aware of this became the question when she took up a slap-and-stir line which, above the thumps thrown in on bass drum, was even more reminiscent of what we'd heard in the park. Aunt Nancy and I evidently asked it of ourselves at the same time, for as our eyes at that moment met we seemed to ask it of one another as well.

Penguin continued to stand motionless, his head still bowed, stingy-brim in hand, though he did ever so noticeably shiver. A chill had run up his back. Djamilaa's eyes were glued to Drennette, posing the question Aunt Nancy and I were likewise posing. We as well were now staring at Drennette, set wondering all the more by the grin she shot us. That the grin was a knowing one there could be no question. The question was did she know (how could she know) what had happened in the park.

The answer was no, though we didn't find it out until later when after the gig we asked her outright. At the time, though, it appeared she must have known, so blown away were we by the blend of long-standing simmer and supposititious retreat she resorted to now. This was the insinuative mix, you'll recall, whoever it was we'd heard in Griffith Park had so seductively served up. Drennette's right hand, that is, was rock steady, the snare a pot in which it stirred an endlessly simmering stew. A suggestion of endlessly abiding patience and nonchalance was what one got. Her left, slapping hand intermittently erupted in its turning over, lending itself to the bass drum's equally eruptive thumps. This gave it a sense of supposititious retreat, as though the beat every now and then were backing up, a conflicted sense of being upheld and taken out at the same time. The increasing closeness of this to what we'd heard in the park was uncanny.

That Lambert heard it as well one heard in the change his intonation underwent. Once again the music found itself haunted as he played as if pestered by an appetitive ghost. There was now an ever so audible quaver visited upon each note, a begging off which, albeit slight, said ostensible solidity had by now been seen thru. See-thru quaver bespoke an introvert fierceness whose intuitive simmer agreed in full with Drennette's adroit supposititious retreat. The blue see-thru truth of this was that hollowed-out appetite haunted — having itself been inhabited by — an inauspicious thump or an inostensible thud, putative solidity and soul rolled into one.

It was at this point that Penguin closed his eyes, pushed even deeper into would-be obsequies by Lambert's quantum-qualitative quaver, a sound which even now, rehearing it as I write, I find it hard not to be taken away by. Lambert's eyes, of course, had been closed for some time, him having closed them as his and Drennette's duet grew more and more intimate. Hers remained open and she picked up the tempo a bit when she saw that Penguin's eyes had closed. Once again he shivered. Another chill had run up his back.

Penguin opened his eyes and raised his head once the shiver passed. An incredulous look was on his face. He was impressed. He was so impressed, in fact, he stood staring into empty space. Lambert and Drennette soon wrapped up their duet, getting back to the head, but Penguin, rather than joining us in the cadenza we took the piece

167

out on, continued gazing into empty space. He snapped out of it once the audience began to applaud to play cheerleader, holding his hat out to them as if bumming a handout ("Don't be stingy"), all the while, with his other hand, gesturing towards Drennette ("Give the drummer some").

The quantum-qualitative climb Lambert and Drennette had pulled off turned out to have been steeper than it appeared. Both Penguin and Lambert reported afterwards that, yes, while their eyes were closed they'd seen the dancing broom.

Yours,
N.

On the Uneasy Marriage
of Music and Poetry
Lukas Foss

THE WORD "MUSIC" meant words and music to the ancient Greeks. The word "song" means words and music. Every folk song is a wedding of words and music, a unity. It is my contention that in the realm of art (I mean "Art" art as opposed to "folk" art) no unity is possible. Art separates, specializes, artificializes, combines rather than unites, contrives in order to relate.

Poetry and music can be partners. But partners are separate entities. They never function as equals at a given moment, either in business or in marriage. This is true of the choreographer-composer partnership and of the composer-librettist partnership. Wagner claimed equality of the visual, the literary and the musical in the *Gesamt-Kunstwerk*. His *oeuvre* is a perfect example to the contrary, a testimony to the undemocratic nature of artistic materials. One parameter dominates, the other supports; one uses, the other is being used.

When a poem is set to music, the *poem* is the used entity. We all have a prejudice against being used. We shouldn't. The used can be in an advantageous position. The used does not necessarily *need* the user, but the user seeks, woos and cajoles the used. As the leader is lost without the led, so is the user lost without his object. Thus the poem, in its role of the used, may dominate the music — as the maid dominates the mistress in Genet's play, *The Maids*.

Can the roles be reversed? In pop music the tune often precedes the lyrics. George Gershwin composed a melody and Ira Gershwin would later fit his lyrics to the tune. Well, that's the difference between poetry and lyrics. A poet does not tailor his poem to fit the notes. If this ever happened and resulted in a good poem, it would be the exception that proves the rule. Words can burst into song. A tune cannot burst into words.

All right — that's settled. The poem comes first. It's there; the composer is attracted. What kind of poem attracts him? One full of beautiful, musical syllables? Not at all. Poems full of imagery attract the composer — such as Wallace Stevens's "Thirteen Ways of Looking at a Blackbird," the most frequently set-to-music poem in American letters. Music adds color to the poem, therefore, paradoxical though it may seem, a poem is "musical" if it is visual. So, attracted by the imagery of the poem, the composer chooses it the way one chooses a mate, and proceeds to add his unsolicited little notes, emphasizing syllables, repeating words, separating phrase segments. The fact is: to the extent a setting is neither folk song nor recitative, the poem comes out maimed, its rhythm distorted, dragged out *ad absurdum*. Yet, we composers are often naive enough to believe the poet should be grateful, as if the sum total — poem plus music — must be worth more than the poem itself. I believe, just as the *Ninth Symphony* is better off without Béjart's choreography or the *Pastoral* without *Fantasia*, so every poem is better off when listened to *senza musica*, commanding the undivided attention of the listener. Some poets like the idea of being set to music. Quite a few forbid it. Rilke hated to have his poetry "labeled" by music. I'm aware of all that, yet I keep seeking the poem's approval. "Look how beautifully I use you. Isn't this great for both of us?" In sober moments I say to the poem, "Forgive me, I have used you, who does not need me nor my music; but then — I am not harming you, since you exist without me, and though I violated you in my setting, I love you, hence my music (which spoils you) pays homage to you."

You see, from the composer's point of view there is something important to be gained from the experience of setting a text to music. The composer-poem relationship is similar to the performer-composition relationship or the actor-play relationship. Actors and musical performers are like lovers who gain their identity, their power, their energy by immersing themselves in the object of their love. It is somewhat of a paradox that in "becoming" King Lear, an actor can "find himself," or in playing a Bach fugue a pianist can "find himself," but that is the mystery inherent in love. Similarly, a composer may find himself through the text he uses, if he immerses himself in the words until they "burst into song."

Setting a poem to music is often called *interpretation*. A misnomer. A lover does not interpret the loved one. Now, what is the composer doing if he is not interpreting the poem? Is he translating poetry into music? Well, the art of inter-art translation has not been invented. It doesn't exist. What the composer actually does is exercise one of three options.

Option 1. IMITATION:

Following the inflections of the poem in rhythm and mood; this is a cavalierlike attempt at illustrating meaning through sound. The danger is duplication, redundancy, and pseudo-translation. (Imitation is a dubious approach to which we owe all our great oratorios, madrigals, arias, etc.)

Option 2. CONTRADICTION:

The opposite of imitation; a special effect rather than a technique, used mainly for relief from Option 1. Example: The words are about murder, while the music waltzes along in three-quarter time, a kind of "cavalier counterpoint." (Real inter-art counterpoint is as non-existent as inter-art translation.)

Option 3. INDEPENDENCE:

The music is oblivious of the poem, words and music ignoring each other. This procedure may make one wonder why *this* poem rather than another is being used. It is arbitrary, to say the least; yet it might deserve more attention. It has been successfully applied to dance. There is a real independence between dance and music in every John Cage–Merce Cunningham collaboration. I quote John Cage:

> The independence of the music and the dance follows from our faith that the support of the dance is not to be found in the music but in the dancer himself, on his own legs (that is, occasionally on a single one). Likewise, the music sometimes consists of single sounds or groups of sounds which are not separated by harmonies but resound within a space of silence. From this independence of music and dance, a rhythm results which is not that of horses' hoofs or other regular beats, but which reminds us of a multiplicity of events in time and space — stars, for instance, in the sky, or activities on earth viewed from the air. . . .

Now, the multiplicity of events in time and space or the activities on earth viewed from the air are unrelated happenings. They ignore one another. There is no love relationship, since the dance and the music are oblivious of one another. There is no user, no used. But, lo and behold, there is equal partnership. How true to life! Equal partnership is achieved when the partners ignore each other, when relationship is avoided. We have here the additive principle as opposed to the interacting principle, we have music *plus* dance. Applied to our subject, music *plus* poetry instead of music interacting with poetry.

It should be clear now that the relationship between two arts is

171

wrought with problems. Setting a poem to music is a loving act of violence. But the poem is also a splendid crutch for the composer. He is presented with a world, the poet's world and the poet's rhythm, flow and continuity, for him to follow, contradict or ignore. It leads him to surprises. It leads him to places he would not reach without that inspired crutch.

The variation technique supplies one type of composer with ideas. The twelve-tone system helps another. Words and poems help *me*. Furthermore, the human voice is the finest of instruments and the human voice is most comfortable singing words. Singing without words is O.K., but there is something disembodied about vocalizing to consonants, vowels or syllables — like dancing to silence, which is a legitimate (if contrived) relief from dancing to music. The fact is, in art one must avoid neither the natural nor the contrived. Even the pigheaded, the wrong, has its place in the arts and can open doors.

The history of music is a series of mistakes, of untenable positions, from the well-tempered scale to opera. We cannot achieve in art the simple, the uncontrived, the true unity of words and music found in every folk song. Folk art is young art; alas, it ages. Beethoven's *Ode to Joy* was never young as a rock song was in the early days of rock or as a waltz was when Strauss first presented it. The young made it into a way of life. Today, little is as nostalgic, wistful, touchingly old as the Viennese waltz. As to the Beatles' song, it will soon be grandfather's music. Not Beethoven's *Ode*. It never had the scent of fresh flowers, but it hasn't faded either. It is neither young nor old; it is carved in rock. It is contrived. Art contrives. Poetry set to music is contrived art.

Contriving is a peculiarly human endeavor. Only man contrives. He stylizes, freezes things so they will last. He builds monuments so they will outlast him. He thrives on the artificial. To quote a medieval philosopher: "God cannot be praised artifically enough."

Ami Minden
Anne Tardos

PERFORMANCE GUIDELINES

THESE SCORES ARE computer-mediated collages in which images are superimposed over the four-language poem "Ami Minden." (The languages are English, French, German and Hungarian.) They are to be interpreted by a soloist, or any number of readers, as follows:

Sentences, parts of sentences, and words that are printed over white, are to be read normally, using a normal tone of voice.

Sentences, etc., printed over gray, but still legible, are to be whispered — *audibly*. Different shades of gray indicate degrees of loudness. The darker the gray under the letters, the softer the whisper should be.

Black areas are to be interpreted as silences lasting as long as the words obliterated by them. Each performer should decide for herself what those words may be.

Ami minden quand un yes or no je le said viens am liebsten hätte ich dich du süßes de ez nem baj das weißt du me a favor, hogy innen se faire croire tous less birds from the forest who fly here by mistake als die Wälde langsam verschwinden. Minden verschwinden, mind your step and woolf. Verschwinden de nem innen--je vois the void in front of mich--je sens, als ich érzem qu'on aille, aille, de vágy a fejem, csak éppen (eben sagte ich wie die Wälder verschwinden) I can repeat it as a credo so it sinks into our cerveaux und wird "embedded" there, mint egy teória mathématique d' "enchâssement" die Verankerungstheorie in der Mathematik, hogy legalább

Anne Tardos

**Ami minden quand un yes or no je le
said viens am liebsten hätte ich ich
du süßes de ez nem baj das weiß du
me a favor, hogy innen se faire
croire tous less birds from the forest
who fly here by mistake als die
Wälde langsam verschwinden.
Minden verschwinden, mind your
step and woolf. Verschwinden de
nem innen--je vois the void in front
of mich--je sens, als ich weiß quon
aille, aille, de vagy a fej csak
éppen (eben sagte ich weil die Wälder
verschwinden) I can repeat it as a
credo so it sinks into our cerveaux
und wird "embedded" there, mint egy
teória mathématique
"enchâssement" die
Verankerungstheorie in der
Mathematik, hogy legalább**

175

Anne Tardos

Ami minden quand un yes or no je la
said viens am liebsten hätte ich dich
du süßes de ez nem baj das weißt du
me a favor, hogy innen se faire
croire tous less birds from the fo
who fly here by mistake   e
Wälder langsam verschwinden.
Minden verschwinden, mind your
step and wool. Verschwinden de
nem innen – je vois the void in front
of mich – je sens als ich érzem que on
like, aille, de vágy a fejem, csak
eppen (eben sagte ich wie die Wälder
verschwinden) I can repeat it as a
credo so it sinks into our cerveaux
und wird "embedded" there, mint egy
teoria matematique d —
"enchâssement" die
Verankerungstheorie in der
Mathematik, hogy legalább

176

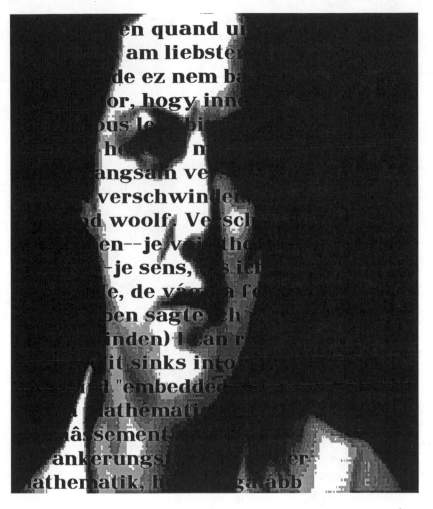

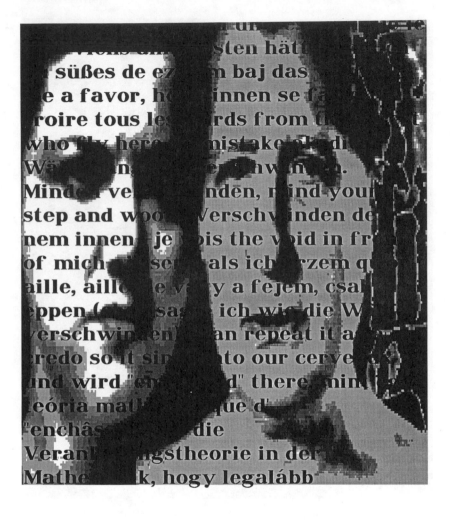

Anne Tardos

Ami minden quand un yes or no je
said viens am liebsten hätte ich dic
du süßes de ez nem baj das weißt d
hogy in en se ire
toothless from a f
who fly here by mistake als die
Wälde langsam verschwinden.
Minden verschwinden, mind you
step and wolf. Verschwinden
nem innen--je vois the void in ent
of nuch--je as, als ich érzem on
aille, aille, de vágy a rejem, csa
éppen (eben sagte ich wie die Wälde
verschwinden) I can repeat it as a
credo so it sinks into our cerveau
und wird "embedded" there, mint
teória maître fatigue d
"en âssement" die
Verankerungstheorie in der

Anne Tardos

Ami minden quand un yes or no je le
said viens am liebsten hätte ich dich
du süßes de ez nem baj das weißt du
me a favor, hogy innen se faire
croire tous les oiseaux from the forest
who fly here mistake als die
Wälde langsam verschwinden.
Minden verschwinden, mind your
step and woolf. Verschwinden de
nem innen--je vois the void in front
of mich--je sens, als ich érzem qu'on
aille, aillé, de várunk fejem, csak
éppen (eben sagte ich wie die Wälder
verschwinden) I can repeat it as a
credo so it sinks into our cerveaux
und wird "embedded" there, mint egy
teória mathématique de
"enchâssement" die
Verankerungstheorie in der
Mathematik, hogy legalabb

A Conversation

Philip Corner and Armand Schwerner

ARMAND SCHWERNER: Brad showed me what Anne Tardos had contributed to this music issue of CONJUNCTIONS. She identifies this combination of computer graphics and words as a score. In 1955 someone looking at these pages would probably not have thought of them in that way. Anne seems to me to be continuing a tradition you were instrumental in initiating. Now, why is this a score?

PHILIP CORNER: As I look at this text, which appears quite attractive and visually evocative, it seems to me one of the few examples that I've seen of computer graphics which isn't impossibly sterile. Has she provided any instructions for its use as a score?

SCHWERNER: Yes. She has.

CORNER: Sometimes people have done things of this kind without instructions. I must say that I myself have been guilty of this when I felt that the instructions would clarify things only for those people I was not most ideally writing for. It partly depends how specific one wants to be in the performance, and how open. In terms of using this as a score there's certainly no problem with reading the text. The question is what relationship images have to the words and the layout of the text on the page and *that* I can't figure out from just looking. Some scores will be obvious. I think for instance the one that you showed me that you had of mine, which was calligraphic, to my mind would be perfectly obvious without any instructions because it's linear and moves in time and space respecting the conventions of the horizontal and vertical axes of a piece of paper, which are the bases of traditional musical notation. A specifically representational image is more difficult, since the score is essentially a definition of the possibility of a performance, which necessarily takes place in time. So any image which presents itself as I think painting essentially does, or sculpture, as a single gestalt, is then problematical in terms of realization as a score because one has to add time to it. But when you add time to it, however you play with the dimensions of the paper — up, down, left, right — as soon as you have time you can begin to realize it as a performance. Anything that can translate into events in time can be realized as a score; time is rhythm, and if we want to be more specific about the musical aspect of it, the spatial, the other dimension, of the two dimensional surface would be movement in pitch, pitch space, up and down; and so anything that can be represented as a movement in pitch-space, creating essentially melody — movement up and down of tones — could again also be used as a score. So you have those two dimensions.

SCHWERNER: Let me introduce a couple of speculations which came to me when I was looking at past examples of your work. One has to do with your decision to use a good deal of American language as instructional material rather than treble or bass or tenor clef notations. From what did that eventually arise? Also, what would you say is the relationship between openness to the point of chance, accident, on the one hand, and the specificity of direct commands or clearly structuring environs — what makes you decide how you will balance these two variables? To what degree is each to have its autonomy and in what way are those positions related to your conception of earlier music? And perhaps we might eventually get to talk about the connections between these issues and the nature of contemporary language operations.

CORNER: Well, we're already talking about language.

SCHWERNER: Yes, we are. I meant more specifically in terms of poetry.

CORNER: It seems to me Anne Tardos' work could be regarded as poetry or coming from poetry in the sense that the performance is coming out of the text. Since I'm a musician, my work is coming out of that kind of graphic design which has been used as symbolic representation of tones, and the text aspect comes out of the instructions; once having read them it seems perfectly natural and clear. The instructions are related to the designs in a meaningful, simple-to-understand way. To perform "Ami Minden" would thus present no particular problem of interpretation. In my case, coming from music per se the text must of necessity have come out of the instructions; Some pieces needed interpretation: those of indeterminate nature or those of non-traditional nature.

SCHWERNER: But was there a moment when you were frustrated by conventional notational methods and you made a decision to explore new modes?

CORNER: The only people that ever frustrated me were my professors, the people who were holding on to the past. I was never frustrated with notation as such. It seemed to me that it was useful for a certain time. I can backtrack into history: I keep finding that on one level of understanding, everything that I'm doing and that I see other people doing, no matter how so-called far-out, has a connection to the past. And in terms of the use of language, we have a very great tradition in music notation in the West of using language. When I teach music theory, this comes up because after you've analyzed the rhythmic and pitch dimensions of the two-dimensional space of the paper, you say to the students: well there are two *more* parameters of musical definition. How you symbolically represent them both in intensity and especially timbre provides great problems of symbolic representation which the traditional Western system has never dealt with. And I think there is a good reason why. You have precise representation of rhythm and pitch — or let's say at least precise up to the level of precision that Western music desired and needed. So how was intensity to be suggested? By words. You used the Italian words and then the conventional abbreviations of them: *f* for forte, *p* for piano, *mf* for mezzoforte, *sf* for sforzando — all are reduced to one or two letters and so you have a kind of coded language. But timbre? Forget it. The only way timbre was specified was to name the instruments that were to be played. Occasionally something having to do with the technique of performing, bowing, pizzicato, and that was sufficient, by naming the instrument which would play the line to specify the timbre that was desired. I might also add that even in terms of rhythm — the dimension of rhythm, which is an independent variable — that is of *tempo*, *absolute speed*, as opposed to rhythm per se, which involves the proportions of longs and shorts — *absolute speed*, then, or *tempo*, has always been specified by language — as a matter of fact, one can say, an indeterminate language. Why? Because all of the indications for tempo are relatively imprecise ("andante": how slow? "walking tempo" . . . well exactly how fast or slow *is* that?) . . . so there's a question of directing oneself to feeling or sensibility and in other cases ("allegro" is a perfect example) simply to a state of mind by which tempo is to be inferred — and even further, the "allegro con brio," "allegro con fuoco," all the other things that are added, are purely immediately felt emotional responses which are then translated into the precision of absolute tempo.

SCHWERNER: Let me ask you something which seems to eventuate from this. Finding that rhythm and pitch are insistently present in the Western tradition and that timbre and intensity in terms of notation are not, you were driven, or at least found it convenient, to go to non-Western musics and non-Western traditions, in which you found a much greater proportion of attention paid to the presence of these two variables in different kinds of music, and you chose in *your* work to emphasize timbre and intensity at the expense of a concern for specificities of rhythm and pitch.

CORNER: . . . the exaggeration, if one might say, of the dimensions of intensity and timbre?

SCHWERNER: Your acceptances and your rejections. Almost what Harold Bloom might call your misreadings. In your case it didn't come from any anxiety about influence. It is a reaching out toward some need which made it necessary to recognize an imperative in you, a need that was not met by the musical conditons of your day. Is that fair?

CORNER: Yes, except that I would prefer to emphasize at this point, which I wouldn't have then, the actual positive value of the tradition, *in* the tradition (and this is what is never taught, what is buried), the positive value in the tradition of innovation itself. In the framework of Western tradition conservatism is anti-traditional. And there's a strange kind of paradox there, but as regards innovation itself, we've reached crisis proportions with the trivialization of it. Tradition itself however honors innovation to such an extent that you can say, as I once had to say to an African colleague, who thought we had no tradition, that innovation *is* our tradition. The battle between the "conservatives" and the "progressives" is institutionalized. You can't escape it. You can't retire to a monastery or a culture that believes in preserving "tradition." You have to get in there and fight. Ultimately, conservatism loses. But the question is *which* radical, *which* revolutionary will in fact carry off the prize and become the next gilded statue. I realize now that everything that I have done that may seem to be radical or innovative has been done and has to have been done within the context of a culture which permits such efforts and which gives a positive value to the honoring of the possibilities inherent in tradition. I was not burned at the stake; I was not expelled into the wilderness; I was given a position in society which I took and whatever I battled for I won, and it's been all right.

SCHWERNER: Would it be possible to summarize the nature of what you consider the contributions to composition made by you and a few of the colleagues with whom you felt you were working hand in hand? And also around what time, what years did this begin?

CORNER: Well, for me it started in the late fifties. I nourished myself and supported myself with the work of those people who were innovative at the time: Cage, Feldman, Earl Brown, Christian Wolff, and later discovered Richard Maxfield, later on Jackson Mac Low, LaMonte Young. I worked with Malcolm Goldstein and Jim Tenney. That was a kind of parallel. So we were all working. Of course the first four I mentioned were on the scene earlier so that my work already had a preface. Cage and Feldman were — Cage particularly — working in the forties with things that would have to be included in this development. What is the positive contribution? This relates to the question you asked about the role of notation and why certain choices were necessary. The white of the page is silence, essentially, an inherent symbol for what in the dimension of sound would be silence, that is, the inactivity out of which the possibility of filling it arises. Silence is pure potentiality. So here is this score, symbolizing real space and real acoustic space.

SCHWERNER: Formally speaking, in which way do you see your particular intuition and methodology emphasize the material growing out of those blank silences to a degree that they hadn't been encouraged to do so in previous music in the West?

CORNER: Well, we immediately look at the staff which is barring across the silence. The word "bars" immediately makes you think of prison and I would say that in a certain sense this is just. That is, the staff itself and the metric bars are limitations of possibility in the dimension of both rhythm and pitch. They're silent as an idea, you might say as a potential, but in a certain sense, once you conceive of the sound it already is noisy. The noisiest thing in the world is the static inside our heads. In a certain sense, any idea is noise; the symbolization of creative noise, of music, is the mark that's put on that white, that white silence. The existence of the staff with its further limited definition of clef, key signatures, and all of what that indicates to my mind, those existences cover the silence. It means you don't see the silence; you look at the staff, you look at this preset of acceptable potentials, which leads you right into that and in fact the music itself really *covers* silence.

Essentially, Western music covers silence. There are some dramatic examples — Beethoven, Berlioz — where silence is used effectively, and usually as a way of cutting into the sound to let this negative world appear from the background, but it's not the ground that you feel let's say in certain oriental musics — particularly in Japanese shakuhachi music — and liberated for us by the work of Cage and the various people that I mentioned. They're the ones in whose work you actually feel the silence as a constant presence which is not obscured, covered over and thereby removed to a secondary level of consciousness by the sound itself.

And so I think that you can see how the score would want to be an adequate visual translation of the acoustic effect — that is, of signs representing sounds moving freely in both directions, dimensions, in the silence which is continually present and therefore continually invading the sound. You'd expect much more silence; you'd expect much more discontinuity and you'd expect — and here we get back to the question of timbre and intensity — you'd expect the kinds of sounds which are not so bricklike as the ideal Western sound: *clear beginning attack!* (I was an old trombone player, you know: *get that note right on the head! None of this cracked attack, gliding. . . .*) All those things in fact you may have in the music of other cultures that we can learn from. I accepted that and tried to make sounds, shape sounds which were not just straight lines in space with a clear beginning and a clear end, but sounds which came out of silence — out of white space — and disappeared back into it. Hence my interest in oriental calligraphy, which I had a chance to study in Korea. The use of the brush was a perfect translation of the kind of sound I wanted. It's partly a question of transcending the limitation of sound quality, a question of the richness of the sound itself, the internal movement, the suggestion of timbre and breathy effects and glissando and movements close to the normal movements of life. It's not just the richness of the sound itself, but the relationship to the ground of the sound — the silence out of which it comes and to which it returns, that the greatest variety and possibilities of shaping the sound in relationship to its background silence — those were all issues.

SCHWERNER: I think of the enormous complexity of the music and language work of the last forty years. Why did these phenomena manifest at these times?

CORNER: I feel a growing disinterest in these historical questions. I feel that history has been used as a kind of bludgeon to impose linearity upon us. So that would be a projection of the same kind of thought which creates the linearity which existed in traditional poetry, and traditional music, of which the staff and the bars are a sign of the sense of projecting something into time. I'm less and less interested in the "we," and the culture, and what everybody else is doing. I'll just say this is what *I* need; what *I'm* interested in is a sense of space, this sense of silence, of infinite recess into dimensions

186

of space, and a sense of fluid time, which immediately leads to the creation of single images. That's why my music has the possibility of linearity. The lines are always lines you can easily project into space; yet at the same time they float or exist in a silence, in a white space, which they do not cancel, which creates a total image of the page which, in terms of projection into performance time, must mean the possibility of moving in various dimensions, and therefore indeterminacy. From that point of view, then, indeterminacy is the possibility of trying in acoustic space to create the closest analogy to a visual image. That is, to almost destroy, and put it back in conception, in a way that your mental image of it is not architectural — in the sense that architecture is an image which imposes time in balance (left, right, high, low, movement from beginning, middle, end). What we're talking about here is a succession of sounds which fuse in the mind as a single timeless image.

SCHWERNER: As a reaction to what you're saying, let me take on two voices, one as a kind of voice of the devil's advocate and the other one the voice of . . .

CORNER: Angel's advocate?

SCHWERNER: . . . a voice of response to the devil's advocate voice. The devil's advocate voice would say: If you look at the total activity of mentation, you unavoidably confront the reality that if you push the balloon in at one point, the balloon will swell out at another point. Working in the context of some sort of law, let's say divine equivalence, if you do without rhythm and pitch you will then emphasize the definiteness and the insistence of timbre and intensity, leaving you frustrated in endless symmetrizing of human effort which is not an . . .

CORNER: Can I respond to that?

SCHWERNER: Yes and I hope you will, but let me take on my second voice.

CORNER: I won't remember *that* when you finish *this*. I totally agree with what you say and that agreement and your statement are the resolution of the "problem," so-called, because the mere fact of that unavoidable necessity of symmetrizing absolves you of the necessity of attempting to do it. You just have to assume that it will happen anyway, and in a way that's great because no matter what you do you get symmetry and so you *can't* go off balance.

SCHWERNER: Yes, but . . .

CORNER: Which voice is talking now?

SCHWERNER: I've lost it. I think it's in the next room. It's hard to be mute when you're supposed to be asking questions. The second, the reactive voice was going to pose a question about the condition of silence in Paul Célan, in Mallarmé, the nature of silence as a somewhat new Western modality, which seems to excite people in their reaction to Cage for instance: what is it that makes us so enamored of a kind of absence? And what's the nature of that absence? The influence of meditational modalities, the influence of new models of visualization processes, for instance from Tibetan Buddhism, come to mind as I think about these matters as coming in my second or reactive voice. That is, in a visualization meditation what ultimately happens is that letters and pictures ultimately disappear, swallowed up into the last visualized seed, which itself then evanesces and disappears into clear space, into a particular kind of psychic space. The experience of absence which is total presence.

CORNER: Don't you think that's because we need it?

SCHWERNER: I absolutely do.

CORNER: The question is, Why do we need it? One one level there's the revenge against imperialism. You can't dominate other cultures without having it coming back to affect you. But looking at it as possibility, we see the universal irrepressible human need to expand and go beyond limits, and you only voluntarily accept limits when you don't accept that they *are* limits. Prejudice and dogmatism. When you reach a state in which you see that there are more possibilities, you realize that your own culture has been cheating you. World War II was the kind of experience that seems to have set it up that whatever happens as a positive achievement has cost a tremenous price. And if we see global culture and global consciousness as a positive thing, which I think we do have to do, as an opening up of possibilities for all people, if we do that, we look and see the tremendous tensions and evils that have created it, the horrors of World War II create for the first time the possibility of a global civilization.

SCHWERNER: What would that mean for music? The future of music?

CORNER: It means more gamelan; it means more cross-cultural influencing. It also means more pseudo-exotic crap, as well as the possibility of profound and deep influencing of cultures and the inability to sustain any form of narrow-minded nihilism. That's what the future promises. It's impossible to go back. It's impossible simply to recreate the terms of another culture. Certainly the pressures to do so are very strong. Everything that goes under the rubric of post-modernism I think is an attempt which from the perspective I outlined must necessarily be a desperate and futile attempt to turn the clock back, to wipe out a century of modernism which is the thing that led to, politically, the Second World War and created spiritually the whole openness and the explosion of European and Western civilization per se — leaving it open to the whole world.

SCHWERNER: When you talk about post-modernism in that way it sounds as if you consider it profoundly antithetical to the nature and achievements of the great modernist accomplishments.

CORNER: First of all we're not talking necessarily about the achievements of any one artist. The achievement of any artist is not reducible to the ideological terms of a movement or historical period. It's clear what modernism did. Its vector was to destroy the limitations of Western civilization, which it very well succeeded in doing. And the vector of post-modernism is to try to pick up the pieces. But unlike those of us — and I think I could safely include you, and the people we've been talking about, in both poetry and music — unlike *those* people who realize that the explosion has left us in a state of total possibility in which we can pick up all pieces, post-modernism is an attempt to reconstruct the pieces of Western civilization as it were, and all its manifestations. I've just been spending a lot of time in Italy. I just see this embarrassing phenomenon of a lot of semi-competent painters redoing Bandinelli, who ruined his life trying to compete with Michelangelo, and I don't understand why people would want to embarrass themselves that way. They are Italians reliving the Renaissance, as in music we have the so-called new tonality and all sorts of things which are reconstructing the limited terms of the pre-modern Western experience.

SCHWERNER: Can I zap in the term "redoing" here? When Schoenberg "redid" Bach or a Handel concerto grosso, when Webern "redid," when Stravinsky "redid" Pergolesi in the "Baiser de la Fée," and so on, they were not just "redoing" in the way you meant now; they were involved in some kind of productive transformation based on a desire and a need and an aesthetic direction with which you find yourself sympathetic. I would like you to make the distinction because it seems to me that in the last decades transformations, absorption, remaking and parody — and I don't put down parody at all — are insistently powerful if not modes at least tools for the apprehension of older and venerated work which nevertheless was felt to be unbearably invasive.

189

CORNER: The people you meant and you named as great innovators related to the past in order to fulfill a mission given by that very past, to innovate; their innovation was in fact supported by tradition and they were affirming that, and furthermore they reaffirm the tradition. The upsetting anxiety-filling period of great innovation was also an affirmation of innovation as significant as, and a stand against, what we've come to be living every day, the trivialization of innovation as fad, novelty.

SCHWERNER: One of the great distinctions you're making is significantly based on the nature of the motivation involved.

CORNER: Ultimately everything comes down not only to motivation. Motivation is an aspect of dimension of depth sensitivity, profundity, of consciousness.

SCHWERNER: Yes, Kalu Rinpoche said that ultimately the artist's most profound order of activity rests upon, is involved in, the texture of his motivation.

CORNER: But this is why the academics have it backwards. Without denying the possibility of meaningful analysis as a creative work, as an art in itself, I would insist on the impossibility of analysis, intellectual theorizing and preconceiving, to *precede* creativity. One of my great epiphanies was the realization that no analysis can reach the secret of genius. No explanation will permit him who explains to tap into the source of what created that work in the first place. Ultimately, the only thing that can be said is the point at which your explanations, your verbalizations, your theoretizing comes to an end and you're in that wholly mysterious place where you can only hope, and (if you will accept the word) *pray* for the spark of the genius, as, let's say, spirit, the muse. It's only accessible by sensibility and sensitivity, and I must say that it is true of the perceiver, also. It's true of the judger, the perceiver, the amateur of art. Without a direct confrontation of consciousness in the dimensions beyond what's reducible to explication, there is nothing. We tend to look back on the critical or maybe even pre-critical writings of the past with a certain amount of bemused contempt. I happen to have just left a friend's house with a copy of Vasari's *Lives of the Painters*, and reading it, and it seems to me that Vasari is talking about the direct experience. He's in confrontation with a painting. Unfortunately, he did also try to establish fixed, absolute standards of objectivity which would go beyond that of the perceiver, but if we look at our tradition we'd say actually that the idea of a non-reader-oriented or non-hearer-oriented or non-seer-oriented art is the aberration, is what's happened to us in the last two hundred years and what we're trying to get back out of. We will find ourselves perhaps on a higher level of sophistication if that doesn't make you laugh. That is exactly where Vasari was five hundred years ago. Look at Berlioz. When Tom Johnson had his book of criticism presented, he was compared to George Bernard Shaw and Virgil Thompson. I said I don't want to compare Tom to George Bernard Shaw and Virgil Thompson. I don't recognize them as great critics. I'd rather compare him to what I consider the last great critic —

SCHWERNER: Hanslik!

CORNER: No, Hanslik is the devil. Hanslik is the enemy. Rather Berlioz and Schumann. They were not critics in the pseudo-theoretical academic sense we have come to expect. The pretentiousness of non-reader, non-perception-oriented, but abstract principles blah blah blah. They were shamelessly subjective, shamelessly emotional, shamelessly personal and I think that's what we need now.

SCHWERNER: Going back to the question of analysis, would you say, as I think myself, that analysis is a characterological idiosyncracy? Either you have the kind of composer who likes, needs, and does a lot of analysis, or you are a composer who doesn't. Schoenberg did an enormous amount of analysis and Stravinsky —

CORNER: We also live in a culture that favors it.

SCHWERNER: —did almost *no* analysis. There isn't, in Stravinsky, a single example in the *Poetics of Music*, or in the discussions with Robert Kraft, of a real analyzed segment of any earlier music. Whereas Schoenberg wrote two magistral books on the whole matter, and Webern. So that assuming, whatever our subjective sense of the dimension of these composers' work, that they're all significant producers of musical entities, that some of them needed analysis, some of them didn't, and that it was secondary and not genetic.

CORNER: Well, the problem as I see it is not with analysis but with the relationship between analysis and the subject of analysis, which is a work of art. I think that has been misconstrued. Suppose we regard analysis as a dimension of the mind which creates art in the first place. It's as gratuitous as the work of art itself and perhaps in its best sense as artistic; why don't we see analysis as the possibility of creating another kind of art which has, as its subject, art itself? If it works on that level, then it becomes poetic, not a pretentious attempt to judge and a futile attempt to understand works of art in another dimension.

191

Philip Corner and Armand Schwerner

SCHWERNER: You might apply the image of trying to water pebbles and hoping that eventually you'll get from that a field of wonderful flowers. Am I representing correctly what I know is your deep interest in Heraclitus when I talk about what I see in one of your scores in the Silverman Fluxus collection: "Effected with all vigor the energy and violence of action on things, purposes, direct to the things." Am I understanding you correctly when I say that my sensitivity to the purpose and motivation of your quest relates to your desire to be at one with the *thingness* of the world? As opposed to the problem which post-Heraclitan Western philosophy has saddled us with — that is, the problem of confusing words and things — your desire is very analogous to the desire which is marked for many people by Heidegger and by phenomenological investigations and by Buddhist thought. Your desire is, in fact, to become as it were as close, without unnecessary obstacle of imposed form, to the thingness of thing. And in that way we can say there is a profound unity observable and experienceable in your activity as a composer particularly invested in language and in our activity as poets deeply invested in the movement of psyche.

CORNER: I would accept that.

SCHWERNER: I was struck by this statement on your draft. In fact, I also like very much what you have quoted here. I don't know whether it's yours or Ives' or if it's Thoreau's.

CORNER: Ives. Ideas come out of things, don't they? When you get into things you realize that you are not sacrificing your intellect, you are not sacrificing ideas. Ideas are inherent in but are not distanced from the thing. They're not separated by words and now we get back to the technique of writing scores which we started with. The reason I use verbal descriptions and in some cases quite concise verbal descriptions, often eschewing any symbolic representations apart from the verbal description, is because of the nature of words themselves. If you think of traditional music notation you have picture. Picture imposes a particular, an image of a particular. Mythological images are attempts to generalize and make things that are universally meaningful but they're still particulars and so the notation of Western music — which is essentially pictographic — is designed to create particulars, specific forms. Any kind of indeterminacy, of freedom, of complexity which goes beyond the ability of rational symbols to define, must necessarily use words, instruments of generalization and comprehensive conception. So if I want something which points at things, which leads you into the thing itself

192

and the connection with pure consciousness you have to use words.
SCHWERNER: What an interesting paradox — as a poet I have been moving increasingly in the direction of pictographic images and other kinds of images precisely for the same reason that you have been moved to go toward language. The motivations are parallel and the means are complementary.
CORNER: You read from an instruction page from "Inkmarks for Performance." Just imagine that there were no ink marks anymore and the instruction page was the whole thing, and I've done many pieces which are like that so, I define why the language was important and why the pictures disappeared, and yet the language itself is pictographic perhaps in a way you were talking about; the language itself is not linear. Language destroys subject, predicate, it creates a gestalt which is somewhat analogous to the way the inkmarks themselves were, and the reason for that is, that once having gotten from the specificity of picture to the generalization of language, the language made me, in a sense, go back with it to the global comprehension of picture. That is, you look at the instruction, and the words as much as possible strike your mind as a single coherent image, rather than something that has to be deciphered line by line, word by word.
SCHWERNER: I was wondering, Phil, since there has been no mention of this — whether jazz has been a variable in your work in the last thirty-odd years.
CORNER: I once mentioned that it was and Tom Johnson called me on it saying there's no obvious relationship to jazz in my work. In the first place as somebody who is involved in World Music: in other cultures, transcending Western tradition we have right here around us all the time one of the prime examples of, I'd say, a Third World or New World music. I think it's quite interesting, when you look at the World Music scene, this has a strange relationship to perhaps what's happening now in world politics, that the high cultures — India — and of course I say "high" in quotes — the cultures that could be regarded as having a classical tradition. . . .
SCHWERNER: Tradition means culture?
CORNER: No. I don't mean tradition as culture — high cultures as opposed to so-called tribal cultures. Those cultures which have had highly developed class structures, formalized — Japan, Korea, China, Indonesia, Persia, Arabia, India.
SCHWERNER: That's what I meant by traditionalism.
CORNER: These cultures have been absorbed into the ethnomusicological canon of interest, and have been the sources of great

influence on the people who are transcending our culture and are innovating — and Africa of the, quote unquote, "primitive" areas, and New Guinea — they seem to have been left largely for the pop world. So you have a polarization between our classically-derived tradition and the pop tradition and two major areas of world culture interests which seem to have also been polarized. I find it fascinating that there's very little African influence in contemporary classical music, even that which is ethnoworld-music oriented. Pop music starting from jazz has been the great disseminator of an assimilated Africanized type of influence, to my mind, and maybe here's a point to try to predict a little bit about the future. The attempt to create a cross-genre music, which breaks down the barrier between so-called high culture and pop culture, is in that direction; actually I can't talk about the future because I'm not very sanguine about the possibility of this finally happening, at least not in the near future, but I think there are forces moving in that direction and from my point of view this is something that *should* happen and I would much like to see happen. In a modest way I think that this concern could be said to infuse my work, to the extent that within the limits of my powers I've been involved not only with that which can be perhaps most prototypically Oriental — the interest in timbre, silence, the breath of nature, in basic organic processes, the heart beat, sexual rhythms, the rhythm of the body, that which is embodied in the African and quasi-African traditions; there are elements of all this in my music. It is not surprising that these things have happened in America. All of these things, the will to escape the domination of the composer, of the preconceived idea, the whole cultural baggage of the European tradition (in the sense of how things are *made* as opposed to what things *are*), all this will to spontaneity and unpredictability is ultimately traceable to jazz. When I say jazz I mean the Afro-American tradition in general, that means the blues became jazz in already coming out of a prototypical culture, split, high-low situation. So I'm insisting on the whole vertical spectrum of it; here is a tradition which has been around us and infused us with the ideals of spontaneity, irrationality, direct access to consciousness, to feelings, sensibility, so I don't think it matters that something sounds or doesn't sound like jazz or that it uses jazz harmonies which after all are Africanized versions of French Impressionist, late nineteenth century harmonies; so, if you look at the thing which is really relevant and new, it is the aspect of kinetic energy, of rhythm as not intellectual complexity but

rhythm as physical energizer, and the aspect of what's indeterminate, unpredictable, open to direct immediacy of perception. Those
are what we've been living with as an aura coming out of the Afro-
American tradition which in all different forms have infused American consciousness. So, "Inkmarks for Performance," which employs
clusters and all of these so-called avant garde techniques, because of
its will both to freedom and unpredictability and the aspect of physicality, kinetic experience, owes a lot to Afro-American tradition.

SCHWERNER: So you're talking about g-u-t.

CORNER: I don't know what chord that is.

SCHWERNER: It's a chord which you will now discover for the first
time.

CORNER: I know the C-E-G chord, but the G-U-T chord?

SCHWERNER: G-u-t backwards is tug.

CORNER: Yeah, and forwards it's gut.

SCHWERNER: Don't pull too hard. I'm talking about the relationship
of Gesture, Utterance, and Text or Textuality. That is to say, your
interest in the thingness of things, your interest in abolishing, to
whatever degree possible, the distances between the word and the
the thing, or the pointer and the thing, your desire not to confuse
matters of this content. Now we have the gesture which is an immediate somatic pointing. From that comes some utterance, some
phrasal or erotic utterance, a human cry or a movement involving
either written or vocal assertiveness. Then, as the final extraordinary, particularly human modality, you have text. Now in our situation in 1990, 1985, 2020, we are overridden by the weight and op-
pressiveness and disproportionate power of text. One of the reasons
it seems to me why so much attention is directed toward text is
precisely that text has been disproportionately important and that
the desire for utterance before text is a tropism toward gesture, before utterance, it's a consuming necessity. It's a biological necessity
like shitting, like eating, like fucking —

CORNER: We're starved for reality.

SCHWERNER: We're starved for reality, and this is one of the large
areas of speculation within which we can appreciate the significance of your efforts, and the idiosyncratic nature of a certain vector
in the poetic activity, some aspect of poetic activity, of the last
several decades.

CORNER: Don't you think this is precisely what has led the text,
poetry, toward performance? Getting back to Anne Tardos, for instance. In "Ami Minden," text becomes a score. It's because it leads

195

Philip Corner and Armand Schwerner

back to reality in a way. It autodestructs and thereby affirms its own importance, because the problem of alienation is gone, and the text in fact becomes a vehicle which leads us to reality. Paradoxically, it has helped us appreciate reality in a more sensitive, deep way than we had before.

SCHWERNER: And it is precisely this hunger which has had insufficient recognition in the kinds of so-called poetic materials which are studied by young people in our, not just our country, but I suppose in our civilization. I'm talking starvation.

CORNER: It's the same in music. Just from the sense of a wall between us and reality. I see art as a barrier. The tone serves exactly the same function in music as the text serves — that is it's something that's extracted, a distillate from raw nature and now we have a music which is nothing but tone, nothing but preoccupation with the manipulation of tones. And this has become a similar kind of barrier to the moving back into reality, and that aspect of reality which is reality for musicians is sound — sonic nature of life itself.

Three Notes on
the Roots of Rhythm

Gerald Early

I. THE CRITICISM OF CRITICISM

I also tire of critics who indulge in the "death of..." syndrome — the death of the blues, the death of jazz, the death of soul music. Some critics confuse themselves with God, thinking that life-and-death are actually in their hands ...

In the eighties, I'd hear the same sad cry — rhythm and blues is dead, killed by the need to sell to white folk. Another weak-minded myth ...

Black music in America has always reached out to everyone. That's its very nature — to include, not exclude.

— Smokey Robinson, *Smokey: Inside My Life* (1989)

THERE IS A SERIOUS FLAW in Nelson George's generally thought-provoking and informative study, *The Death of Rhythm and Blues*, a sort of new-fangled, black nationalist version of Matthew Arnold's *Culture and Anarchy*. It is this: When George asserts, "Only a minority of blacks would openly agitate for more self-sufficiency. I find myself among that minority, not because I dislike whites or disdain the American dream — at least in both cases not entirely — but because I see the assimilationist's triumph, in the 1980s as it was in the 1920s, of little material value in improving the lives of most Afro-Americans," we realize that we have yet another work before us by a young black intellectual who, in effect, is saying that segregation was bad but integration is worse. This, of course, is almost always espoused — almost as a kind of nostalgia for the good old days when the black community, that is, when the average black big-city neighborhood was, seemingly, a holistic aggregation of interests and talents — by people who never lived through the days of segregation. If, as ample sociological statistics from Charles S. Johnson to E. Franklin Frazier show, the black community was unable to achieve peoplehood or a kind of nationalistic independence or to use George's word, "self-sufficiency" because of entrenched and extensive legalized segregation that prevented blacks from ever

197

going very far or being able to take advantage of the resources available to whites and if now the black community is fragmented and pathologically bent because of integration which has drained off the middle class elements of talent (an "elitist" suggestion that thinkers like George inadvertently wind up arguing both for and against), then we are left with the impossible paradox of black intellectuals collectively saying that blacks have never been able to achieve their peoplehood, their nationalistic realization of independence, because of *both* the presence and absence of segregation. If self-sufficiency suggests, as I think George expresses the concept in his book, achievement in business and the commercial consolidation of one's cultural products, blacks have been, with a few notable exceptions such as Motown, Johnson Publications, some hair-care products companies, some insurance firms and a few small but growing enterprises such as Third World Press, less successful in this realm than virtually any other ethnic group in America. They have also been notably less successful than other groups in maintaining small businesses in their neighborhoods. Co-option by whites may explain this in part as well as lack of loyalty by black customers, perhaps racism as well whether manifested in segregation or in other forms. But blacks have been, during the ages of segregation and integration, generally as unsuccessful at selling anything else as they have been at selling themselves. It is strange to hear George Speak of an "R and B World" when, considering the production of music as a commercial enterprise from conception to record to distribution to live performance, blacks owned virtually no important theaters — the Howard in Washington, the Uptown in Philadelphia, the Apollo in New York, the Regal in Chicago, the Royal in Baltimore, the major black theaters on the Chitlin' Circuit of the fifties and sixties were all white-owned; controlled no distribution firms or pressing plants; owned virtually no important music publishing companies — Jobete at "integrationist" Motown was the first and still the most significant and by far the richest; owned virtually no radio or television stations or production companies; in effect, blacks exercised virtually no sovereignty in an area where their presence, to some degree, was crucial. It is an evocative yet terribly circumscribed and restricted world of which George speaks. The paradox of black empowerment is perhaps best symbolized by Booker T. Washington, George's hero figure, who built one of the most momentous secular black institutions in America through white patronage and philanthropy. The samples that George

cites of potential or actual black ownership of their own art form —
black owned Yee Jay and Peacock Records, some minor distributing
efforts, personality dee jays in the 1950s — are impressive but no more
so than, say, black bandleader James Reese Europe's organizing of
black musicians in New York into the Clef Club in 1910. In fact,
Europe still stands as one of the dominant figures in black entre-
preneurship in popular music before Berry Gordy. "Integration" as
a national policy or as a black leadership policy did not destroy the
"R and B World" as black music has always been "integrated" from
its inception as a commercial reality. (Think of the re-creation of
spirituals as a choral music and the first tours of the Fisk Jubilee
Singers from 1871 to 1874 as a prime example of "integration" and
"crossover intentionality" of a black art form.) It has never been a
question of whether blacks could realistically pursue any policy
but integration, *but rather what are the terms of integration and
how shall black people choose to experience it.*

In his glorification of the "R and B World" of black American life
between 1945 and 1960, this is the point that George misses despite
the fact that his book makes this self-evident: that without the
massive push for civil rights, for integration and assimilation of
which George so vehemently disapproves, the impact of R and B
even within the black community would have been considerable
reduced; the realization of that world, paradoxically, was the energy
that was generated by blacks to end segregation as national public
policy. Motown, the company he gives short-shrift to here (George
has written a history of Motown entitled *Where Did Our Love Go?:
The Rise and Fall of the Motown Sound* published in 1985) was so
successful during this era precisely because it was so assimilationist and integrationist in its outlook and its vision. In truth, black
culture cannot realize itself in a higher form without aspiring for
synthesis with the mainstream culture that surrounds it to create
tension and strife as well as opportunity and status and, finally, to
attenuate social unease so that unfulfilled expectations might be
made intelligible. George makes a common mistake in his reason-
ing, to borrow from Daniel Bell, by equating the disorganization or
turbulent disruption of a society at a given point in its history with
the quality of its culture. Inasmuch as the book argues the pleni-
tude of black American culture, it finds itself, in defense of the
political nobility of its subject, locked in arguing the basic liberal
assumption that local, regional and parochial cultures are better
than the larger, more mainstream culture which will ultimately

plunder local variants no matter what. George's book, despite its undeniable drive and even its brilliance, give us the dubious, hoary, yet nearly blessed critical premises that bedevils most writing on popular music: first, that black music is the authenticating soul and artistic inspiration for virtually all of American popular music (a theory most persuasively propagated among blacks by James Weldon Johnson in his three seminal introductions for his anthologies, *The Book of American Negro Poetry* published in 1921, *The Book of American Negro Spirituals* published in 1925, and *The Second Book of American Negro Spirituals* published in 1926); second, that commercialism corrupts regional and local art forms (George's variation is that white commercialism corrupts and weakens black art); and third, that political-cum-aesthetic analysis actually frees music criticism from mere rhetoric description of both the art and the artists. George must remember that a crucial aspect of black American ideology as it is of mainstream American thought is the quest for change and innovation that can only be found in something larger than itself.

II. THE COVER CHARGE

Let's get together and bass.
— James Brown, *"Funky President,"* 1974

In the April 24, 1954 issue of *Billboard*, which was dedicated to Rhythm and Blues, appeared this editorial:

The rhythm and blues field has caught the ear of the nation. It is no longer the stepchild of the record business. Recent years have seen it develop into a stalwart member of the record industry.

Its firms are no longer fly-by-nights. They are well-established companies prospering under the management of sound businessmen. . . . Talent and tunes that have gained recognition in rhythm and blues often have enjoyed success in the popular record market. . . .

The r.&b. field has made great strides during the past five years. It is heartening to see that it has finally broken free of its old confines. It is no longer identified as the music of a specific group but can now enjoy a healthy following among all people, regardless of race or color.

Billboard goes on to congratulate itself for dropping the designation "race" and "sepia" back in the June 25, 1949 issue, substituting Rhythm and Blues which caught on with the industry. (This assertion seems true despite Nelson George's claim that *Billboard* was following, not leading the industry when it made the change. In the June 25, 1949 issue when the change was made, two ads for black records appeared but neither used the term "Rhythm and Blues." In fact, one, Regent Records, still used the term, "race.") Despite its patronizing tone, the editorial is in keeping with the tenor of the era: the Supreme Court school desegregation decision occurs on May 17, 1954, one month later. Whites were mediating, of course, on their own terms, the absorption of blacks into the American mainstream.

It is fairly common knowledge that in the 1950s, the age of the white Negro as crossover icon from hip Norman Mailer, Elvis Presley and James Dean on the one hand to earnest Floyd Patterson, Sidney Poitier and Johnny Mathis on the other to the flamboyant Adam Clayton Powell, Liberace and Allen Ginsberg in the middle, several white pop or middle-of-the-road singers covered or re-recorded tunes first made by black Rhythm and Blues performers. Among the most famous or notorious were Gail Storm's cover of Little Richard's "Keep-A Knocking" (which became one of the biggest selling singles of all time), Pat Boone's cover of Little Richard's "Long Tall Sally," Peggy Lee's cover of Little Willie John's "Fever," The Crew Cuts' cover of the Chords' "Sh'Boom," Bill Haley and the Comets' cover of Big Joe Turner's "Shake, Rattle, and Roll," and most famously Elvis Presley's covers of Arthur Crudup's "That's All Right, Mama" and Big Mama Thornton's "Hound Dog." Generally, with the exception of Presley, critics dismiss these covers as racist thefts and largely as less accomplished artistically than the originals and, with the exception of Presley and, to some lesser extent, Haley, these covers are now forgotten and the originals enshrined as true authentic masterpieces of early Rock and Roll.

It is now commonly accepted that blacks are not only the authenticators of Rock and Roll but that they authenticate American popular music generally which is not a revelation but, in fact, a cultural tautology. Blacks are the authenticating soul—the artless yet indomitable muse that the poor white Rock and Roller can only wistfully and worshipfully acknowledge through his cover which becomes a sort of perverse tribute—because they are artistic and they are artistic because of the mysticism of their blackness which in effect is like saying that Negroes authenticate themselves (and everyone else in America) through their Negro-ness, a platonic essence we know they possess when they are demonstrably, in

Gerald Early

someone's sight, something that is not white. But if the cover raises the issue of the epistemology of blackness, it does the same for whiteness as well. There is something both hideous and inherently threatening about the white cover for blacks: take, as an example, the expropriation by whites in the mid-1960s the slang term "up-tight," first introduced in Stevie Wonder's 1966 hit of the same name, seems almost presumptuous. At first, as Wonder's song makes clear, the term meant something positive, an accomplished good; after it became a slang term among whites, the term came to mean the exact opposite, to be nervous, upset, distressed. The white cover, ironically, while stressing the Negro as authenticator, obliterates his or her existence as anything but a inchoate force. Blacks in America are the eunuch-endowment of popular culture; they are the absent presence. There are two strange instances of covers that have always puzzled me and seem to problematize this belief in the Negro's performance as authentic art and reliable and veracious artifice and the Negro captured between absence and presence.

First is the Isley Brothers' 1971 *sui generis* album *Givin' It Back*, a record that followed their 1969 comeback funky smash (No. 2 on the Pop charts), "It's Your Thing" on their own T-Neck label when they were still smooth in their sharkskin suits, Italian shoes, and processed hair that was, as the old heads used to say, "fried, dyed, and laid to the side, jack"; and that preceded their disco funk hits "That Lady," "Live It Up," and "Fight the Power" in the mid-1970s, after they signed with industry giant Columbia Records and T-Neck be-came a subsidiary, a period that featured the Brothers in sequined jumpsuits and Gerri-curls. Between these distinct eras of cool yet intense gestures, stylized sharp clothes, and straightened hair stands *Givin' It Back* as a sort of wall and as a reversal of the white "cover" as the Brothers, appearing on the *actual* album cover with Afros, work clothes, acoustic guitars and serious demeanors, look for all the world like a socially-conscious folk group. Only their expensive high-heeled boots give them away as something other than a folk band. They sing songs by white stars Neil Young, James Taylor, Bob Dylan and Stephen Stills as well as tunes by Jimi Hen-drix, War and Bill Withers, black artists who had sizable white audiences in the early seventies. While the cover evoked a kind of soft acoustic sound, the album itself was only partly that. It has more than its share of raucous, highly electric moments. In part, the album's cover suggested social consciousness of the kind that

202

many black artists were displaying and distilling in the early seventies: Richie Havens, Terry Callier, Linda Lewis, and of course Marvin Gaye; although the movement of the record from Neil Young's plaintive memorial to the Kent State Massacre of 1970, "Ohio," to Stephen Stills' hedonistic rocker, "Love the One You're With" would signify not the formation of political consciousness but the evolution from social consciousness as the perception of tragedy to sexual affirmation and fulfillment as the reinvention of the soul (and the historical foundation of soul music). *Givin' It Back* was not so much a crossover album (in fact it had little crossover appeal) as it was, to black listeners, a kind of parody of crossover, an ironic commentary on the history of white theft of black art made explicit by the record's title.

The other instance of covering occurred in 1960. Ernest Evans, a young black Philadelphian with whose brother, Spencer, I went to school, cut a record, quite by accident, called "The Twist" under the name of Chubby Checker for a label called Cameo-Parkway. Dick Clark, host of the popular teenage dance show "American Bandstand," which was then filmed at a studio at 46th and Market Streets, suggested to the record company that someone do "The Twist" song because Hank Ballard, who had cut and written the original record, could not make a show to perform it. Checker was chosen only through the insistence of his manager, Henry Colt, who ran a poultry shop on the Ninth Street Italian Market. The cover was originally to be done by another Philly group, Danny and the Juniors, and would have been a standard white cover of a black R and B song that was creating a bit of minor stir. Checker's version became a runaway smash, staying in the top 40 for 15 weeks and in the number one slot for 3 weeks. In fact, Checker's version of "The Twist" became one of the few records in pop history to hit the number one spot on two different occasions, when it was first released in August 1960 and again in November 1961 where it stayed in the top 40 for another 18 weeks.

Checker made history by becoming the first black artist to cover another black artist's record and make it a crossover hit as if it were a white cover. The record spawned, unfortunately in many ways, several other hits for Checker: "Pony Time" (1961, No. 1 for 3 weeks, on the pop charts for 14 weeks), "The Hucklebuck" (1960, No. 14, on the pop charts for 9 weeks), "Let's Twist Again" (1961, No. 8, on the pop charts for 15 weeks), "The Fly" (1961, No. 7, on the pop charts for 11 weeks), "Limbo Rock" (1962, No. 2, on the pop charts for 17 weeks), "Slow Twistin'" (1962, No. 3, on the pop charts for 12 weeks, with backing vocals by Dee Dee Sharp, then wife of local record shop owner, songwriter, and producer of the early seventies "Philly Sound," Kenny Gamble), recordings that sold extraordinarily well but because of their teen, dance-novelty quality were never to be taken seriously and Checker himself, with his derivative name — from 1950s R and B legend Fats Domino, was never able to show the public that he could, indeed, sing. But he was clearly, from 1960 to 1962, before Motown became entrenched and before the Beatles and the British invasion, one of the best-selling singers in America with sales during that period exceeding even Sam Cooke, Ray Charles, Johnny Mathis and Nat Cole. Generating a dance craze that lasted for about five or six years, "The Twist" was also a revolutionary terpsichorean innovation: a very simple, almost calisthenic-style dance — Checker claimed he invented it with his brothers — that did not require that the dancers touch or in fact be coordinated with each other in any way. No wonder it was so popular for so long! It was a perfect dance for people who couldn't dance.

The reason Checker was a crossover success was not only because he was brown-skinned and cute (not handsome, but boyishly good looking) and a good dancer but because he was very close in age to the teenagers who watched "American Bandstand"; he was, in truth, the first black R and B artist to be promoted as a teen idol. (Johnny Mathis was not an R and B singer; and Frankie Lymon and Teenagers were a group.) Checker was just nineteen when "The Twist" broke big in 1960. Unlike, say, Chuck Berry and other R and B singers, who during Checker's heyday was in jail for violation of the Mann Act, Checker did not seem like an older brother or even a father. A thin, dark-skinned man with a conk, Hank Ballard, five years older than Checker, had been singing since the early fifties, recording for the Cincinnati-based R and B independent label, King, and producing a number of salacious hits such as "Work With Me, Annie" and "Annie Had a Baby." His two biggest R and B hits were "Finger Poppin' Time" (1960, No. 7, on the pop charts for 13 weeks) and "Let's Go, Let's Go, Let's Go" (1960, No. 6, on the charts for 11 weeks). In fact, even "The Twist" did relatively well for Ballard, going up to No. 28 and staying on the pop charts for 6 weeks. The last song of his I remember doing something on either the pop or R and B charts was a mid-sixties tune called, "Do it Zulu Style." "The Twist," like most of Ballard's songs, was obviously about sex. (It doesn't take much of an imaginative leap to see the connection between twisting and screwing.) For clean-cut Dick Clark in early 1960s for whom R and B was still problematic — Clark, for instance, banned from his airwaves Gary "U.S." Bonds' hit, "Quarter to Three," because of supposed muttered obscenities in the record's simulated party opening, although Clark, to his credit featured many R and B singers on Bandstand — Checker was a much more promotable and bankable black artist than Ballard. He was younger, lighter, not so associated with R and B, and was able to be sexy in a way that was never raunchy. Indeed, by creating or promoting a dance, Checker effectively de-sexed "The Twist."

My family knew the Evans family well. I went to school with Spencer who used to buy me fruit with his extra pocket change. Tracey, Ernest's middle brother, dated my older sister for a while. My mother used to patronize the Evans dry cleaning establishment. (The family was, you might say, petit-bourgeoisie.) Ernest worked slaughtering and plucking chickens on the Ninth Street Market, a fairly common job for many a South Philadelphia black boy. One night back in the days before his stardom which, when achieved, he could only be seen driving around the neighborhood in yellow Cadillacs, Ernest came by our house, killing time and jiving around with my mother and her sisters and brothers, dancing to Joe Loco, the Silhouettes, Johnny Ace, the Dells, Little Anthony and Imperials, the Drifters, the Coasters and the Flamingoes. As the evening progressed, he began to sing, doing imitations of Jackie Wilson and Roy Hamilton. Then in his own voice he sang "Danny Boy" to an absolutely hushed room, not even the tinkling of a beer glass marred the touching grace of the moment, a trickle of twinkling sweat rolled from his processed hair down his jaw. In these days it was common to find boys on streetcorners singing in gospel quartet-harmony tunes like "Danny Boy," "You'll Never Walk Alone," "The Bells of St. Mary's," "The White Cliffs of Dover," and "Without A Song." When boys were harmonizing like this, it was called "bassing," a term that comes straight from the world of gospel and spiritual singing. In the world I grew up in, we liked dramatic, colorful singing with a lot of vocal flourishes. All of us in the room liked equally the lead singer of the Platters and Mario Lanza, another south Philly boy who made good. By the time I was twelve, I had seen "The Great Caruso" six times. In that moment in that small apartment, Ernest was bassing as our imaginations supplied the missing voices; he was the golden male throat of showmanship. We all applauded when he finished, deeply impressed, and thinking

205

that maybe one day Ernest would be a great singer making hit records. He made the hit records but he never sang as well as that night in my mother's kitchen.

III. SHIRLEY TEMPLE AND MICHAEL JACKSON

It was a terrible movie.
> — Shirley Temple discussing "Miss Annie Rooney"

Can anyone name two more famous child performers in the history of twentieth century American entertainment? Are there two more unforgettable or more instantly recognizable faces, the one having the face of the child forever stamped in matronly womanhood and the other with his made-over face that has ceased to be a face but rather a mere expression, a sublimation of an urge for a face? Two child performers, one who wishes to possess the image of childhood forever while the other wishes the world would realize that she has grown up.

In all of Shirley Temple's movies, that is, all the ones for which she is famous, there is music. She is, in fact, the center, the force, the focal point of the music. In *Stand Up and Cheer*, her 1934 breakthrough film, she sings "Baby, Take a Bow" with James Dunn; in *Baby, Take A Bow* (1934), again with Dunn, they both sing "On Accounta I Love You"; in *Bright Eyes* (1934), again co-starring Dunn, she sings the famous, "On the Good Ship Lollipop," but this time as a soloist with chorus; in her first conservative revisionist Civil War film, *The Little Colonel* (1935), she sings but is most remembered for her stair dance sequence with Bill "Bojangles" Robinson, in *Curly Top* (1935), she sings "Animal Crackers" and "When I Grow Up," in her second conservative revisionist Civil War film, *The Littlest Rebel* (1935), she sings "Polly Wolly Doodle" and dances with Robinson again; some of the films, like *Rebecca of Sunny Brook Farm* (1938), *Dimples* (1936), *Poor Little Rich Girl* (1936), *Stowaway* (1936), *The Little Princess* (1939) and *Little Miss Broadway* (1938) seem like musicals in search of a decent book and more tunes. Even in her own most seriously crafted and most seriously flawed childhood film, *Wee Willie Winkie* (1937), directed by John Ford who was absolutely confounded with what to do with her, the most touching moment is Temple's rendition of "Auld Lang Syne" to a dying Victor McLaglen. In the mediocre 1942 film, *Miss Annie*

Rooney, a remake of a Mary Pickford film as were many of Temple's famous movies, Temple, now a teenager with a floundering career, plays a girl of a working class home who is infatuated with swing music, featured in this film as youth music, but not as an art of rebellion. By 1942, of course, swing is not the cultural threat it was in, say, 1936, before the Goodman band played Carnegie Hall or even earlier when swing was generally a black music. White bands, most a good deal less free-wheeling and swinging than Goodman's or Artie Shaw's, dominated and white pop singers such as Roy Eberle, Dick Haymes, and Frank Sinatra who sang with Harry James and Tommy Dorsey were teen idols. In this film, Temple is reunited with Guy Kibbee, who co-starred with her in the 1936 film *Captain January*. (Bill Robinson, Jack Haley, James Dunn, Arthur Treacher, Cesaer Romero, Alice Faye and John Boles were among the actors who appeared in more than one Temple film during her hey day, giving her films an almost repertory company quality.) Advertisements for the film blared that Temple received her first screen kiss, a rather antiseptic peck on the cheek by child star Dickie Moore. Yet despite its claim to innocence the film is suffused with sex as the advertisements signified; from the roaring swing music, to Temple's own bursting sensuality, from the film's preoccupation with teenagers and cars (predating the 1950s) to the inept rich boy (Moore) who learns to dance, that is, swing, from the working class girl (Temple). Here, once again, just as in the more recent film, *White Palace*, we have the lower class woman teaching the sexually repressed upper class man about the joys of living, serving essentially as the foil for his humanity. For this is precisely what Temple does, floating into the lives of bored, prejudiced upper class teenagers and teaching them to dance to swing, through which instruction she finds acceptance. (Temple as a child had always been noted for her dancing even more than her singing which was acceptable only because it was, indeed, the singing of a child. By the time Temple reached puberty, her voice changed and she could no longer sing.) The film's far-fetched denouncement has Temple's father getting rich through an invention, so that ultimately, the class struggle or class difference that the film lamely dramatizes is resolved by making Temple a princess in an urban industrial version of the myth of the family romance. Cinderella was discovered by the rich at a dance, in this new version of the same story, Cinderella, in effect, gives the upper classes the beat.

In the George Lucas film, *Captain EO* (1986), starring Michael

Jackson which can only be seen at Disney World, we have, in a different setting, virtually the same thematic principles at work. Jackson is the captain of an inept, apparently bottom-of-the-barrel spaceship who is told he must deliver a "gift" to an evil planet. Through a thicket of special effects, including the hoary 1950s gimmick of 3-D photography, Jackson comes to the evil planet, governed by a spiderlike queen and her hordes of mechanical guards, and gives them the gift which, it turns out, is music and dance. Jackson magically transforms the meanies from mechanical beings to lithe dancers and robust singers; he has literally humanized these half-machine, half-animal creatures. He, too, gives away the beat in this over-done, over-wrought music video.

We can see instantly that Temple in her film, and in most of her earlier work, and Jackson, in his film where he plays very much a kind of Temple role as childlike distributor of diversion and happiness, are both minstrel figures, happy-go-lucky bestowers of rhythm in films that ultimately do not celebrate rhythm or dance but in some blatant ways, trivialize and hold it in contempt, largely because the vehicles of it in the film, Jackson and Temple, together, symbolize all that is held in disrepute in our society: women, blacks, children, the working classes, the subordinates. Their radiance in the films emanates from the only charisma that any of these people can possess: as the entertainer. So the man who wishes never to grow up and the woman who wishes that the world would realize that she has find themselves, as images in American popular culture, locked in a particularly eerie and inescapable embrace, asexually throbbing to the cadence.

Storiella Americana as She is Swyung: Duke Ellington, the Culture of Washington, D.C. and the Blues as Representative Anecdote

Albert Murray

IT IS A COINCIDENCE both appropriate and profoundly symbolic that the quintessential American composer was born, grew to young manhood, came to his vocation, and began his apprenticeship in the capital city of the nation. Such achievement as his is hardly predictable, to be sure. But in this instance it is easy enough to account for, because it is so consistent with uniquely local environmental factors that conditioned the outlook, direction, and scope of his ambition and development.

As little as has been made of it, there is in point of historical fact, much to suggest that circumstances in Washington during the first two decades of the century made it just the place to dispose a bright-eyed and ambitious young brownskin musician to become the composer who has indeed achieved the most comprehensive and sophisticated as well as the most widely infectious synthesis of the nation's richly diverse musical resources, both indigenous and imported.

Duke Ellington (ne Edward Kennedy Ellington, aka Ellington and Duke) whose work represents far and away the most definitive musical stylization of life in the United States, was born in the house of his maternal grandparents on 20th Street on the 29th of April 1899, and shortly thereafter was taken by his parents, James Edward and Daisy Kennedy Ellington, to their own residence in Wards Place off New Hampshire Avenue, about midway between Dupont Circle on Massachusetts Avenue and Washington Circle on Pennsylvania Avenue.

This was less than ten blocks from the White House of William McKinley, who was assassinated when Ellington was two years old. From then, until Ellington was ten it was the White House of

209

Theodore Roosevelt who was followed by four status quo ante years of William Howard Taft. From the time Ellington was 14 until he was 22, it was not only the White House but also very much the sharply segregated Washington of Woodrow Wilson.

The Washington of McKinley is said to have provided much more government employment for black citizens than any previous administration. But even so, post-Reconstruction disfranchisement continued apace, for McKinley's commitment was not to the implementation of the 13th, 14th, and 15th Amendments, but to conciliation of the erstwhile Confederate states. Moreover his capital city was also the seat of an American expansionism that was all too consistent with the underlying assumptions of the folklore of white supremacy and fakelore of black pathology.

Then there was the Washington of Theodore Roosevelt whose admiration for the down-home Horatio Algerism of Booker T. Washington, the founder of Tuskegee and author of the best selling autobiography *Up From Slavery*, was widely publicized, as was his defense of his appointment of William D. Crum as collector of the Port of Charleston. In point of fact Roosevelt's attitude toward black American aspirations was not only inconsistent and undependable, it was at times indistinguishable from that of those who were frankly opposed to anything except a subservient status for Negroes. The obvious immediate effect of his wrongheaded and highhanded overreaction in meting out dishonorable discharges to black soldiers allegedly involved in the so-called Brownsville Raid of 1906 was to embolden whites who advocated terrorism as a means of keeping black people from full citizenship, something against which Roosevelt spoke neither loudly nor softly and against which he seems to have carried no stick of any size.

During the administration of Taft, Washington was the city of a president who in his inaugural address announced that he would not appoint Negroes to any position where they were not wanted by white people. On one of his better days Roosevelt had once written that he would not close the door of hope to any American citizen. But to aspiring black Americans and white reactionaries alike Taft's statement seemed like official capitulation to the forces of white supremacy, not all of them in the South.

During Ellington's adolescence and young manhood his hometown was the Washington of the downright evil forces of Woodrow Wilson, whose campaign promises to black voters were forgotten as soon as he was inaugurated. Once in office, it was as if he had never expressed his "warmest wish to see justice done to the colored people in every matter, and not mere grudging justice, but justice executed with liberality and cordial good feeling . . . I want to assure them that should I become president of the United States they may count on me for absolute fair dealing, for everything by which I could assist in advancing the interest of their race in the United States."

But whereas his predecessors had been, on balance, perhaps more indifferent to black aspirations than intolerant of gradual improvement, Wilson's two administrations turned out to be downright hostile. In less than three months he signed an executive order segregating dining and toilet facilities in federal service buildings whose black employees were already being rapidly reduced in number and significance. And this was only the beginning. During the next eight years every effort was made to turn the nation's capital into a typical peckerwood town with a climate of white supremacy. "I have recently spent several days in Washington," Booker Washington wrote to Oswald Garrison Villard in a letter (10 August 1913) which he knew was going to be passed on to Wilson, "and I have never seen the colored people so discouraged and bitter as they were at that time."

As inevitable as a direct effect of all this was on his daily life, Ellington did not grow up thinking of himself as downtrodden. On the contrary, as far back as he could remember he was treated as though he were a special child, and he never seems to have doubted his mother when she told him as she did time and again that he didn't have anything to worry about because he was blessed.

His father, who was a butler, then a caterer, and then a blueprint technician at the navy yard, was not only a good provider, but a man who saw to it that his family lived in good houses, in good neighborhoods (no slum dweller, he), and Ellington said that he "kept our house loaded with the best food obtainable and because he was a caterer we had the primest steaks and the finest terrapin." Ellington added, "He spent money and lived like a man who had money and he raised his family as though he were a millionaire. The best had to be carefully examined to make sure it was good enough for my mother."

No, James Ellington's outlook was neither negative nor provincial. Nor was young Edward's. Indeed, such were his horizons of aspiration even as a child that when at the age of about eight a slightly older playmate nicknamed him Duke, he accepted it as if it were his natural due, and so did his family and everybody else in Washington who knew him, and in time so did the world at large including the

211

Royal family of England and the ever so proletarian bureaucrats and workers of the Soviet Union.

(Apropos of the personal vanity that this readiness to define himself in aristocratic terms may suggest to some pseudo-egalitarians, let it be said that Ellington was always more charming than vain and not at all arrogant. The fact of the matter is that you would be hard put to find anybody who was ever more discerning and appreciative of other people's assets and as eager to develop and showcase them. His ability to utilize and feature specific nuances was one of the trademarks of his genius as a composer. And no other band leader ever put up with so many exasperating personal faults in his sidemen just to have them on hand to supply shadings that perhaps most of his audiences would never have missed. What other band leader always had so many *homegrown* superstars on hand at the same time?)

But to continue the chronology. What Ellington himself always emphasized when recounting the advantages of his coming of age in Washington was that he was born and raised among people to whom quality mattered and who required your personal best no less as a general principle than as a natural reaction to the folklore of white supremacy. In neither case would they accept excuses for failure. You either had what it took or you didn't, as somebody from less promising circumstances than yours would prove only too soon.

Not that Ellington would ever deny or ameliorate any of the atrocities perpetuated by the Wilson crowd between 1913 and 1921. He took them for granted much the same as the fairy tale princes and dukes of derring-do take the existence of the dragon (grand or not) for granted. Also like the fairy tale hero that he was by way of becoming, he seems to have been far too preoccupied with getting help to forge his magic sword (or magic means) to spend much time complaining about the injustice of the existence of the dragon. *Dispatching the dragon, after all, as devastating as dragons are, has always been only incidental to gaining the ultimate boon to which the dragon denies you access.*

According to Ellington himself, the hometown he grew up in was an exciting and challenging place of apprenticeship, in which there were many people of his kind to admire, learn from and measure up to. As early on as the eighth grade there was Miss Boston. "She taught us that proper speech and good manners were our first obligations because as representative of the Negro race we were to command respect for our people. This being an all-colored school, Negro

History was crammed into the curriculum so that we would know our people all the way back."

The mainstem hangout for the young man about town was Frank Holliday's poolroom next to the Howard Theatre on T-Street between Sixth and Seventh. "Guys from all walks of life seemed to converge there: school kids over and under sixteen; college students and graduates, some starting out in law and medicine and science; and lots of Pullman porters and dining car waiters. These last had much to say about the places they'd been. The names of the cities would be very impressive. You would hear them say, 'I just left Chicago, or last night I was in Cleveland.'" You could do a lot of listening in the poolroom, where the talk "always sounded as if the prime authorities on every subject had been assembled there. Baseball, football, basketball, boxing, wrestling, racing, medicine, law, politics, everything was discussed with authority."

Then when he really began to focus his ambitions on the piano and music, there was a whole galaxy of virtuosi and theorists not only at Holliday's but all over town, and they were always willing to repeat and explain things. Among them were Lester Dishman with his great left hand; Clarence Bowser, a top ear man; Phil Wird from the Howard Theatre; Louis Thomas, Sticky Mack, Blind Johnny, Gertie Wells, Carolynne Thornton and the Man With a Thousand Fingers.

But most especially there was Louis Brown, who played chromatic thirds faster than most of the greats could play chromatic singles, and his left hand could reach an eleventh in any key. There was also Doc Perry to whose house the young apprentice used to go as often as possible and "sit in a glow of enchantment until he'd pause and explain some passage. He never charged me a dime and he served food and drink during the whole thing."

There was also Henry Grant a conservatory trained teacher who directed the Dunbar High School Orchestra. He volunteered to give the promising young Ellington (a student at Armstrong High School, not Dunbar) private lessons in harmony, and was much impressed with his talent for melody and unusual harmonic nuances *and also with his indefatigable devotion to the mastery of fundamentals.* Hence the incomparable precision that was characteristic of all Ellington bands over the years!

As no true storyteller whether of fiction or the most precisely-documented fact should ever forget — such as the indispensable function of the dynamics of antagonistic cooperation (or antithesis and synthesis, or competition or contention) in perhaps all achievement — there is neither irony nor mystery in the fact that Washington during the vicious years of Wilson and his die-hard confederates was also the base of operations for Kelly Miller, Dean of the College of Arts and Science at Howard (1907–1919) and author of numerous essays on race relations, advocate of courses on the American Negro and on Africa, militant spokesman and pamphleteer, most notably of *As to the Leopard's Spots, an Open Letter to Thomas Dixon* (1905) and the widely distributed *The Disgrace of Democracy, an Open Letter to President Woodrow Wilson.*

It was likewise the Washington of Carter G. Woodson, with his B.A. and M.A. from Chicago and his Ph.D. from Harvard and his background of work and study in the Philippines, Asia, North Africa, and Europe, who taught French, Spanish, English and history at the M Street School and at Dunbar and was later Principal of Armstrong High School, who was co-founder of the Association for the Study of Negro Life and History from its beginning until his death in 1950.

And along with Miller and Woodson there was also Alain Locke from Philadelphia by way of Harvard and the Oxford of Rhodes Scholars, who as a professor of arts and philosophy was especially concerned with making Howard a cultural center for the development of black intellectuals and artists.

The national fallout of all of this (add to it *the work* of W.E.B. DuBois) was such that by 1925 Locke could edit an anthology of poems, stories, plays and essays by black contributors and call it *The New Negro* and introduce it by saying, "In the last decade something beyond the watch and guard of statistics has happened in the life of the American Negro, and the three norns that have traditionally presided over the Negro problem have a changeling in their laps. The sociologist, the philanthropist, the Race-leader are not unaware of the New Negro, but they are at a loss to account for him — ."

It was during this ten-year period, which included World War I, that Ellington came of age and left Washington for New York.

But a word about usage. The emphasis which Miller, Woodson and Locke place on race consciousness and even race pride should not be confused with the shrill, chauvinistic, pseudo-separatism of the so-called Garvey Movement. As Arthur Schomburg (who knew very well how easy it was for such matters to degenerate into "puerile controversy and petty braggadocio") was to write in "The Negro Digs

Up His Past" for Locke's anthology, race studies "legitimately com-patible with scientific method and aim were being undertaken not only to correct certain omissions and not merely that we may not wrongfully be deprived on the spiritual nourishment of our cultural past, *but also that the full story of human collaboration and inter-dependence may be told and realized.*" And Locke himself wrote, "If after absorbing the new content of American life and experience, and after assimilating new patterns of art, the original (Afro-American) artistic endowment can be sufficiently augmented to express itself with equal power in more complex pattern and substance, then the Negro may well become what some have predicted, *the artist of American life.* If not Ellington and Armstrong in music, who else?

Ellington's all-American outlook was a direct result not of Howard University but of the Howard Theatre and Frank Holliday's Pool-room cosmopolitans; but the fallout from Professors Miller and Locke and from Woodson was there all the same. After all his impact was not only citywide but also, like that of DuBois, nationwide.

In all events when the group of ambitious young musicians with whom Ellington went to New York in 1923 proudly advertised them-selves as the Washingtonians they were not presenting themselves as a provincial novelty but rather as a band of sophisticated young men who were ready to get on with it, because they had grown up in the capital city checking out the best in the nation at the Howard Theatre, which, it should be remembered, was on the same T.O.B.A. circuit as the Lincoln and the Lafayette in Harlem. (There was no Savoy yet, no Cotton Club, no Apollo.) New York was a bigger league, to be sure, but the Washingtonians seem to have had no doubts that they were ready to make the most of the breaks. And they were right. In less than four years Ellington composed and recorded *East Saint Louis Toodle-oo, Birmingham Breakdown, Washington Wobble, Harlem River Quiver, New Orleans Low-Down, Chicago Stomp Down* (note the regional diversity) and also *Black and Tan Fantasie,* and *Creole Love Call.*

Nor was he to encounter any musical authority in cosmopolitan New York that was more crucial to his development as a composer than that of Will Marion Cook, another Washingtonian. Cook, who was born in 1869, had been sent out to Oberlin to study violin at the age of 13 and on to Berlin (with the encouragement and aid of the venerable Frederick Douglass) to be a pupil of Joseph Joachim, the greatest music master of the day, and had also studied composi-tion in New York under Dvorak who had been brought over from

Bohemia in 1893 to head up an American Conservatory and to encourage Americans to create a national music based on indigenous sources.

Cook who had given up the violin to concentrate on composition and conducting, had become passionately committed to exploring and developing the possibilities of the Afro-American vernacular and had written the score for Paul Lawrence Dunbar's *Clorindy, or the Origin of the Cakewalk* in 1898, such musical comedies as *Bandanna Land*, *In Abyssinia*, and *In Dahomey* for the famous vaudeville team of Williams and Walker. He had also organized, directed and toured with various jazz bands, most notably the Southern Syncopated Orchestra of some forty-one pieces which he took to Europe in 1919. When he returned to New York, he became a pioneer arranger and conductor of radio music, leading a hundred piece Clef Club Orchestra in some of the earliest live broadcasts.

Not only was Ellington, who had named his son Mercer after Cook's son Will Mercer, very much impressed and personally influenced by all of this, but he was especially taken by the fact that Cook with all of his formal training and all his strictness about technical precision, also insisted, as James Weldon Johnson wrote, that the Negro in music and on the stage ought to be a Negro, a genuine Negro; he declared that the Negro should eschew "white" patterns, and not employ his efforts in doing what the white artist could always do as well, generally better." According to Ellington, Cook's advice was "first you find the logical way, and when you find it, avoid it, and let your inner self break through and guide you. Don't try to be anybody else but yourself."

Not the least of what Cook's advice may have done for young Ellington was to free him to compose in terms of what he liked about such stride or eastern ragtime masters as James P. Johnson, Willie "the Lion" Smith and Lucky Roberts, such New Orleans pacesetters as Louis Armstrong, Sidney Bechet, King Oliver and Jelly Roll Morton and such special in-house talents as Charlie Irvis and Bubber Miley among others, including Johnny Hodges, Harry Carney, Jimmy Blanton, Ben Webster and Ray Nance who became stars even as they became Ellington "dimensions."

What Ellington went on beyond Will Marion Cook and everybody else to achieve was a steady flow of incomparable twentieth century American music that is mostly the result of the extension, elaboration and refinement of the traditional twelve bar blues chorus and the standard thirty-two bar pop song form. *And in doing so he has also fulfilled the ancestral esthetic imperative to process folk melodies, and the music of popular entertainment as well as that of church ceremonies into a truly indigenous fine art of not only nationwide but universal significance, by using devices of stylization that are as vernacular as the idiomatic particulars of the subject matter itself.* It is not a matter of working folk and pop materials into established or classic European forms but of extending, elaborating and refining (which is to say ragging, jazzing and riffing and even jamming) the idiomatic into fine art. *Skyscrapers, not Gothic cathedrals. And as historians need not be reminded, barbarians eventually produce their own principles of stylization and standards of criticism.*

Moreover what Ellington's fully conjugated blues statement adds up to is a definitive American Storiella as she is *syung,* which is to say, a musical equivalent to what Kenneth Burke calls the representative anecdote, the effect of which is to summarize a basic attitude toward experience; or a given outlook on life.

For many U.S. citizens, the representative anecdote would be any tale, tall or otherwise, or indeed any narrative tidbit or joke or even folk or popular saying or cliche that has to do with a self-made and free-spirited individual, or any variation on the Horatio Alger rags to riches, steerage to boardroom, log cabin to White House motif. Among the so-called founding fathers, Benjamin Franklin's career qualifies him as a veritable prototype of the picaresque Alger hero and two other classic examples are *A Narrative of the Life of Frederick Douglass, An American Slave* written by Himself; and Booker T. Washington's *Up From Slavery.*

Everybody knows that even now there are people all over the world dreaming of the United States in the ever-so materialistic image and patterns of Horatio Alger. Others, however, see definitive American characteristics in terms that are no less pragmatic but are more comprehensively existential. In their view, the anecdotes most fundamentally representative are those which symbolize (1) affirmation in the face of adversity, and (2) improvisation in situations of disruption and discontinuity.

To this end, nobody other than Ellington as yet has made more deliberate or effective use of basic devices of blues idiom statement, beginning with the very beat of the on-going up-beat locomotive onomatopoeia (the chugging and driving pistons, the sometimes signifying, sometimes shouting steam whistles, the always somewhat ambivalent arrival and departure bells) that may be as

217

downright programmatic as in the old guitar and harmonica folk blues but which also function as the dead metaphoric basis of the denotative language of common everyday discourse. The obviously programmatic but always playfully syncopated pistons, bells, and whistles of "Daybreak Express," "Happy Go Lucky Local," "The Old Circus Train Turn Around Blues" become as dead metaphors in "Harlem Airshaft" and "Mainstem." Incidentally, Ellington's use of locomotive onomatapoeia is resonant not only of metaphorical underground railroad but also the metaphysical gospel train.

As for the idiomatic devices that are basic to the structure of most Ellington compositions, there are the blues (mostly of 12 bars) and/or the popular song choruses (mostly of 32 bars) a series or sequence of which add up to a vernacular sonata form known as *the instrumental*, which is also made up of such special features as the *vamp* or improvised introduction or lead in, the *riff* or repetition phrase, and the *break* or temporary interruption of the established cadence and which usually requires a *fill*.

An excellent instance of the break as both structural device and statement is "C-Jam Blues," which is also a perfect example of how Ellington used the jam session, which consists of an informal sequence of improvised choruses as the over-all frame for a precisely controlled but still flexible instrumental composition. In an elementary sense it is as playful as a children's ring game or dance, and yet it is also a basic way of ordering a discourse, not unlike, say, that jam session of a social contract known as the Constitution with its neat piano vamp of a preamble followed by a sequence of articles and amendments. The point here, of course, is not one of direct derivation but of cultural consistency and perhaps a case could be made for occupational psychosis.

Nor is the break just another mechanical structural device. It is of its very nature, as dancers never forget, what the basic message comes down to: grace under pressure, creativity in an emergency, continuity in the face of disjuncture. It is on the break that you are required to improvise, to do your thing, to establish your identity, to write your signature on the epidermis of actuality which is to say entropy. The break is the musical equivalent to the storybook hero's moment of truth. It is jeopardy as challenge and opportunity, and what it requires is the elegant insouciance that Hemingway admired in bullfighters. Representative anecdote indeed. Talking about the American frontier Storiella as she is riffed!

As for any question of extended forms, so dear to the reactionary hearts of so many old line academics, the number of choruses in a jazz composition is determined by the occasion, as is the number of floors in a given skyscraper. Once there was the three minute phonograph record, then came the radio sound bite for voiceover, and suitelike sequence of bites that make a movie soundtrack and now there is the hour-plus L.P. Ellington took them all in stride.

The quintessential composer should be so called because he is the one who provides that fifth essence, beyond earth, air, water and fire, that substance of the heavenly bodies that is latent in all things, that spirit, nay that soul which is the magic means that somehow makes life in a given time and place meaningful and thus purposeful.

Indeed, the fifth essence may well be nothing less than the ultimate boon that the storybook quest is usually, if not always, about. If so, then the golden fleece of the composer's quest is the musical equivalent to the representative or definitive anecdote. *The assumption here is that art is indispensable to human existence.*

Duke Ellington is the quintessential American composer because it is his body of work more than any other that adds up to the most specific, comprehensive, universally appealing musical complement to what Constance Rourke, author of *American Humor: a Study of the National Character*, had in mind when she referred to "emblems for a pioneer people who require resilience as a prime trait." Nor can it be said too often that at its best an Ellington performance sounds as if it knows the truth about all the other music in the world and is looking for something better. Not even the Constitution represents a more intrinsically American statement and achievement than that.

Lucas 1 to 29
For One or More Instrumentalists
Jackson Mac Low

— in memoriam Morton Feldman
and for the musicians of Germany

THIS COMPOSITION is based on a *Lucas number sequence*. In such a sequence the first number is 1, the second is 3, the third (produced by adding the first two) is 4, and the succeeding numbers are produced similarly, by adding each new number to the one before. The numbers in *this* particular sequence are 1, 3, 4, 7, 11, 18, and 29.

The instrumentalist(s) first prepare(s) a segment-duration (measured in seconds) and pitch-number score consisting (usually) of one to five strings of four 1-to-29 Lucas sequences or (more uncommonly) of multiples of five such strings (10, 15, etc.).

In the first string of four sequences, the first component is a *forward* Lucas sequence (f: 1, 3, . . . 29), the next two are *reverse* Lucas sequences (r: 29, 18, . . . 1), and the last is a *forward* Lucas sequence (f). So this first string is an "frrf" string. Within each group of five or fewer strings of sequences, each new string must realize a different one of the *other* four permutations of the two types of Lucas sequences, each taken twice: frfr, ffrr, rrff, or rffr. In scores comprising *multiples* of five strings, *the five permutations must be arranged, within each group of five strings, in a different order.*

Each Lucas sequence in the score will comprise *alternate* durations of sound and silence, i.e., sound followed by silence or silence followed by sound.

The instrumentalist(s) must decide whether the first time segment in the first Lucas sequence (1") should be "audible" (meaning, inclusive of instrumental sound) or "silent," i.e., whether it should consist of 1" of *silence* or include one *pitch*. (Throughout this composition

220

plan, "pitch" means "tone of a specific pitch.") The second segment
(3") will accordingly be of the opposite type: if the first segment was
silent, the second will include three different pitches (i.e., three
tones, each having a different pitch); if the first segment was audible,
the second will consist of 3" of silence. The nature of the third segment (4") will be opposite to that of the second: 4" of silence (if the
second was audible) or four different pitches (if the second was
silent); and so on. This alternation of sound and silence (or of silence
and sound) will continue not only through the first Lucas sequence
and first string of sequences but throughout the entire succession of
four-sequence strings comprising any instrumentalist's realization.

Each 1-to-29 Lucas sequence lasts 73" (1' 13"), so each four-sequence
string lasts 4' 52", or just under five minutes, *which will be the duration of the shortest permissible performance.* The *longest usual performance,* comprising five strings of four Lucas sequences, will last
24' 32", i.e., less than 25 minutes. Performances comprising two,
three, or four strings will last about 10, 15, or 20 minutes, respectively. "Unusually long" performances (multiples of five strings) will
last approximately 50, 75, 100, . . . minutes.

For each audible time segment the instrumentalist(s) will select
the same number of different pitches as there are seconds in the segment. These pitches may be taken from anywhere within the in-
strument(')s(') range(s), but each must be a different pitch from the
others within the segment. (Pitches of the same pitch class — e.g.,
the class comprising all A's or all B flats — lying in different octaves
may, when necessary, be defined as being "different" from each
other.) When selecting pitches, the instrumentalist(s) should avoid
quoting other musical compositions or melodies.

Pitches selected need not lie within the presently conventional
equal-temperament gamut of twelve tones to the octave, separated
by semitone intervals, the frequency of "A above middle C" usually
being defined as 440 pulsations per second.

Some instrumentalists may wish to have available the entire
gamut of *all pitches possible within their instruments' ranges.*
Others may wish to *limit* their pitch possibilities by choosing specific tunings, scales, modes, etc. Among these may be any diatonic,
chromatic, enharmonic, or microtonal scales and/or modes, such as

ones in which the octave is divided by more than twelve equal or unequal intervals (e.g., the well-known 24-tone ("quarter-tone") equal-temperament scale) and also any other type of intonation or tuning, such as just intonation or the Pythagorean system.

An interesting possibility would be a 29-tone scale comprising either equal or unequal intervals, so that in 29-pitch segments, instrumentalists may play 29 entirely different pitches without regarding pitches in different octaves as being "different" from each other.

All instrumentalists in a group must use the *same* gamut of pitches, limited or unlimited. Thus, whatever specific tuning method, scale, mode, or other limitation — or lack of limitation — is selected, all in a group must select the same one.

In the score, each instrumentalist's pitches and their entrances must be set precisely within each audible time segment. Any agreed-upon system of notation may be used. If unconventional pitches, tuning systems, scales, or modes are employed, new types of notation may have to be invented. (If customary notation is used, it may be convenient to follow the convention of one eighth note = ½".)

The instrumentalist(s) choose(s) the duration of each individual pitch, i.e., how long the pitch should sound after its entrance — *the limit being the end of the time segment in which it occurs.* These durations may be set in the score, determined by each individual during performance, or set in the score but left open to individual modification during performance. (All instrumentalists in a performance must agree on *one* of these procedures.)

One or more pitches must begin to sound at the beginning of each audible segment, and however many pitches are still sounding at the end of the segment, all must stop precisely when the segment ends. *There must be no silence, i.e., no absence of instrumental sound, within an audible segment, and no sound should be produced by the instrumentalist(s) within a silent segment.*

Within an audible segment any number of pitches, up to the maximum for the segment, may enter simultaneously, successively, or overlappingly. Thus various aggregates (intervals, chords, or tone clusters) may occur during a segment, as a result either of simultaneous pitch entrances or of entrances that occur while other pitches are still sounding. However, sequences of successive individual pitches ("melodies") may also occur, either in parts of a segment or throughout it. In the latter case, the last pitch must end precisely at the segment's end.

All amplitudes (loudnesses) must lie within the range between *pianissimo* and *forte* (*pp* and *f*), *but relatively few should be forte.* They may be explicitly *set* by dynamic notation in the score, *chosen* by each individual during performance, or *set* approximately in the score *and individually modified,* at times, during performance, i.e., each instrumentalist *may* change scored amplitudes within the given limits. The instrumentalist(s) *must choose one of these procedures* when preparing the score, and all in a group must agree upon the same procedure.

The instrumentalist(s) also choose(s) timbres, attacks, manners of performance (*legato, portato, staccato,* etc.), and all other musical parameters not dealt with above. While preparing the score, the instrumentalist(s) may decide to set any of these parameters in the score, to leave some or all of them to individual choices during performance, or to set them in the score but allow individual modification during performance. *All in a group must agree to use only one of these procedures for each parameter when preparing the score for a performance.*

All choices made by the instrumentalist(s) during a performance must be made — and all score-directed actions must be carried out — *in relation to the total situation as perceived by each individual.* This "situation" comprises both the sounds produced by the performers and all ambient sounds, including those produced by the audience, if any, as well as the general environment. It also comprises all *other* perceptions: those of sight and of all other senses, including inner senses, such as proprioception, as well as subtler feelings. *All choices must proceed from a state of heightened, concentrated awareness.*

No member of a group should attempt to predominate over the others — *there should be no "ego trips."* Mutual goodwill, tact, and courtesy and lively self-reflectiveness are minimal requirements for participation. Heightened awareness notably includes *self*-awareness.

Jackson Mac Low

The instrumentalist(s) may employ a conductor, or any other convenient means, to insure precise beginnings and endings of time segments and entrances and (when set in the score) endings of individual pitches. For instance, a conductor, cued by a clock, might indicate the beginnings and endings of time segments by up- and downbeats and indicate each instrumentalist's entrances and (when set in the score) endings of pitches by other signals.

Another possibility would be a computer-driven device that would project a diagram (e.g., a rectangle 1 to 29 units long) of each time segment in turn and show it being gradually filled in as its time elapses. When it was entirely filled in, the diagram of the next segment would be projected and filled in, etc. Similar diagrams might be generated and projected to indicate the beginnings and (when set) endings of pitches, each instrumentalist's diagrams being displayed in a distinctive color or with distinctive crosshatching or the like.

When two or more instrumentalists prepare and perform a score realizing this composition, each decision not left to individual choices during performance should be made through a freely arrived-at consensus of all the participants.

25 March - 3 May; 29 - 30 August; & 31 October 1990
New York

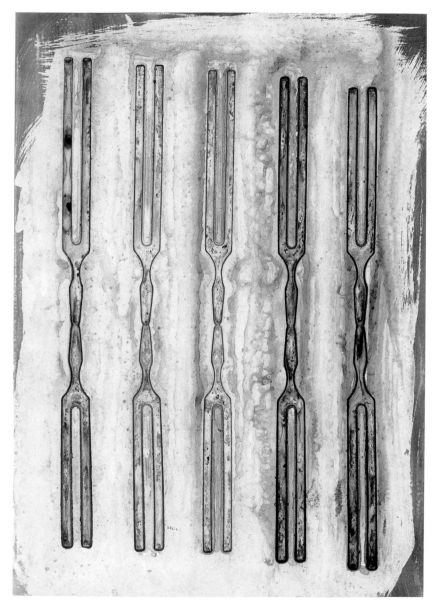

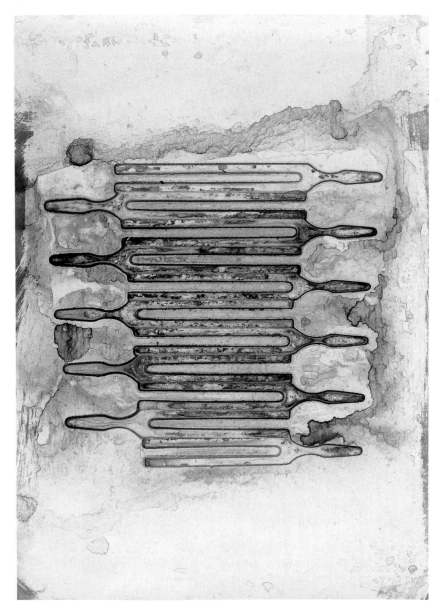

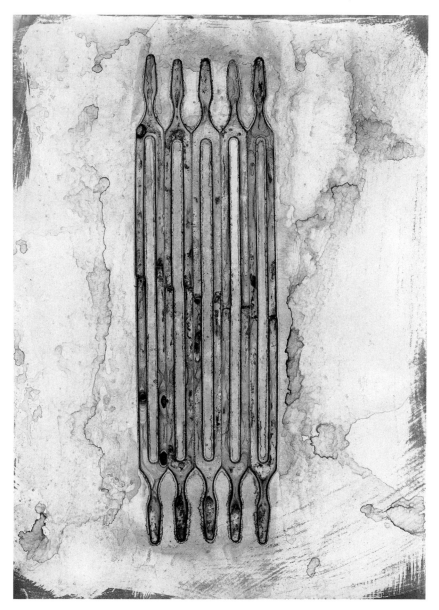

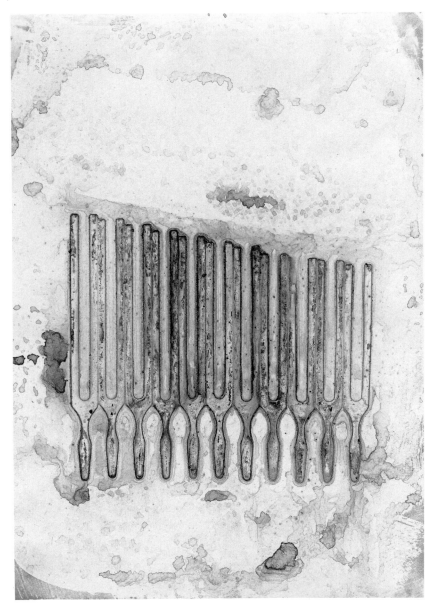

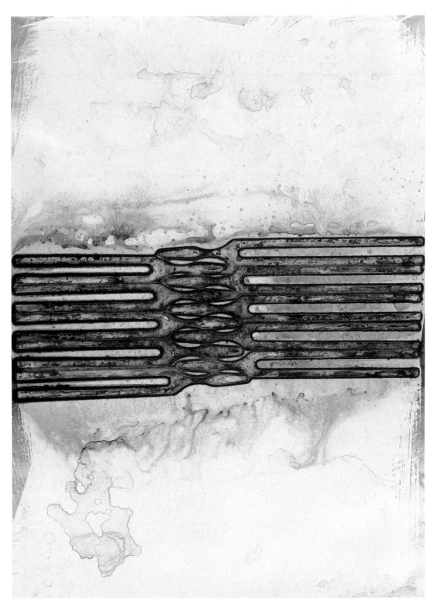

James Nares

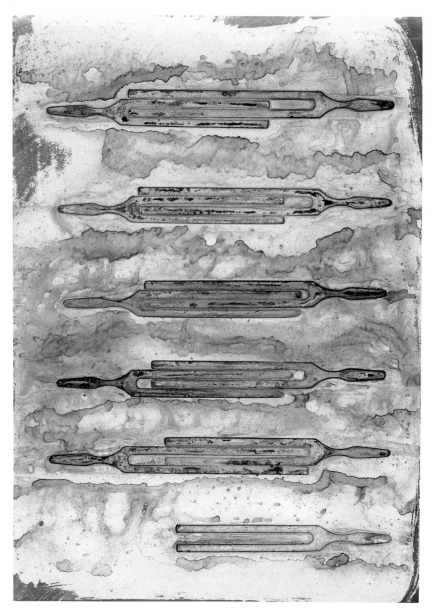

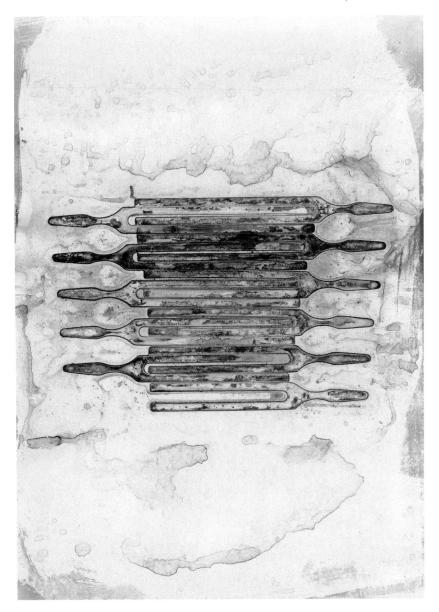

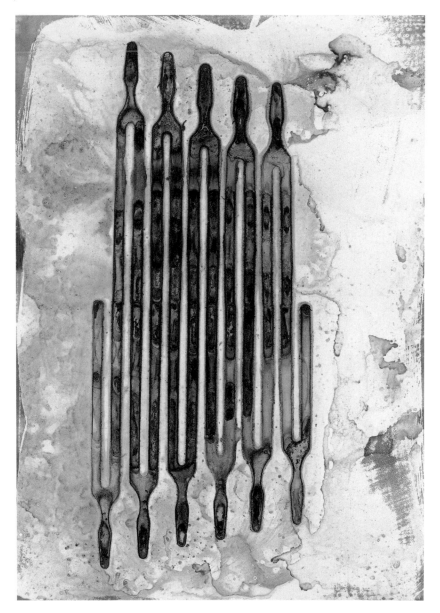

The Influence of Music
on the Work of George Eliot,
as recalled by George Henry Lewes

Barbara Guest

I THOUGHT ABOUT THE DAY and worried that it had no tone. It wasn't that it was drab; on the contrary, the sun lit the house in various spots, not like the usual conveyance that runs from upstairs to downstairs taking on its own speed. There was a liveliness on the stairs, as witness the housemaid smiling as she carried down the morning tea, her little starched cap jiggling in the light that pierced the hall stairs through the mullioned window.

It had actually gotten off to a fine start with George up early as always in her study where I could hear the pen racing across the page. This sound does not disturb me as my pen scratching the paper annoyed her when we shared a study.

That was long ago when we, in our middle thirties, risking our names and fortunes, had gone off together; I was tired and discouraged, a man of letters who had lost his natural liveliness; someone compared me to a French dancing master, I was so bouncy. (They also injudiciously described George as having the face of a horse.) There was Agnes, my wife, my three babies and the other babes she had precipitously thrust on the household, a result of her liaison with our best friend. His father was the poet who wrote the poem that was like a violin weaving the air, "Jenny Kissed Me."

I did not desert Agnes. I paid dearly for accepting that first child by Hunt and could through the exotic laws of our land never divorce her. It would be George who provided for them later, but we never knew that would happen when we left for the Continent and wandered into our own opera, a many-stringed opera with bassoons and flutes and always the kettle drum.

We departed for Germany. There I planned to begin my Life of Goethe. George, with her finer knowledge of German, was willing to assist me with the translations necessary for this work. I trusted her severe corrections. The clarity she showed in her revisions was like that of a conductor who cautions his orchestra to remain in the right key. Her superiority was everywhere evident in those translations she continued to offer to the "Fortnightly" in her attempt to earn money. Words she took from their native tongue and turned into English reflected an inspired method, similar to that of a passage of music interpreted by a musician of unaccountable sensibility.

When we arrived in Weimar who should be there but Liszt and his Princess flourishing in the illegality of their union. In their atmosphere, the cloud of disapproval hanging over us evaporated. Liszt would stirke his baton down firmly on the table, I can see it now, a fine piece of baroque with lacy roses, and declare himself the "cavalier" of love. He looked it, too. The long locks bending over the piano and his music surging around my ankles, sometimes those surges felt like alligators, an indelicate feeling, I admit. George wrote to a friend, "Liszt overwhelming in his attention."

We were fortunate in our musical acquaintances. In Weimar we also met Anton Rubinstein and we saw him years later at his concerts in London. It is he who is Klesmer in *Daniel Deronda*. Wagner we knew also, but we decided he was too modern.

In London we faithfully attended each Saturday the Pop Concerts and I can still see George in her black shawled cap lost in the emotive contemplation that music always stirred in her. At home we usually played on the piano the themes from the compositions we had listened to earlier and George sang beautifully. The room we sat in became more cozy then, more gemutlich than usual and tender at the same time.

One day she confessed that she listened to music so attentively, because each composer spoke to her in a separate way and she found she could seize the ideas aroused by musical notes and introduce these into her novels. Absorbed in musical space these ideas would come whirling down upon her out of the music's ether. It was moreover as if a baton crossed her brow releasing the demons of creativity, because she never concealed they were demons and that was perhaps why she suffered those fierce headaches.

Even when she was famous, idolized really, she was still socially not accepted. Men came without their wives to our house paid for by *Silas Marner* and *Middlemarch* and *The Mill on the Floss*. We were always at home on Saturday evenings which were often musical. George played the piano, my son played the violin, and Herbert Spencer and Anthony Trollope and T.H. Huxley and Robert Browning hummed along.

It was about this time that she was told how much the Queen admired her books and George found this "extremely agreeable"; she had probably forgotten when she had first seen the Queen at the Opera back in 1852 she found her "deplorable . . . so utterly mean in contour and expression." But George was changed and began now to believe the admiration of royalty to be more conductive than the admiration of other mortals. I wonder if she remembered Liszt. Sometimes at a concert on Saturday I would steal a look at George and she did remind me of the Queen sitting there with that contraption over her head like the Queen's widow cap. She was wise like the Queen in her odd way was, and passionate, each of them restrained yet passionate with something of the full orchestra inside their bosoms competing with the conservative tone of the score.

Although I wasn't aware of it at the time, Charles Eliot Norton on a visit from Boston (a city about which George had never concerned herself) was unfavorably impressed with our house. I am told he wrote home that "all the works of art in the house bore witness to the want of delicate artistic feeling, or good culture on the part of the occupants." He observed in particular "a *common* lithograph of Titian's "Christ of the Tribute Money." He never encouraged his wife to visit George.

I wish I had mentioned to him that the Queen commissioned her own court artist to portray *Dinah Morris Preaching on Hayslope Green,* a scene from *Adam Bede,* for her private collection.

A note to myself if I am still irritated by that Bostonian, to remember du Maurier's sketch of George done from memory. He used to sing for us his pretty little French song, *Fi de ces vins d'Espagne.*

And what a long way we have come from our first domestic lodging near Kew Gardens and Richmond (an area convenient for our walks) when we read to each other, or sometimes played the piano and sang though fearful of disturbing the clergyman in the rooms below. There were no callers and many an evening I left her for business in London, and on holidays such as Christmas and New Year's Day she was alone when I visited my sons and my mother. These were responsibilities I could not neglect.

She had her music and when not at the piano she read Greek and Latin. She continued her translation of Spinoza's *Ethics.* Much was accomplished in that solitude. The "storm-tried matron" changed into a novelist. The great mind for which she is admired, and an uncompromising frame for her novels, was exercised on those evenings when she wasn't "invited to dine."

Barbara Guest

I've had an idea, the day turning out to possess a loquacious, a clearly audible tone, to make a list of musical influences upon George Eliot. This could be developed into an article for *The George Eliot Birthday Book of 1878* Blackwood is going to publish.

Aria No. 17
John Taggart

1

Thrill is gone thrill is gone away-ay-ay-aay

thrill is gone away-ay-ay-aay from me

even the chance or possibility

chance or possibility gone away from me

daughter of the queen in her open skirt

daughter in her open silk skirt

fold over fold one fold over one other fold.

2

Hours of beauty dance of the hours of beauty

no place saved in the dance of the hours

no place saved in the dance for me

no place in the dance

in the dance of the hours of beauty

daughter of the queen in her open skirt

daughter in her open silk skirt

fold over fold one fold over one other fold

folds like the folds of a flower unfolded.

3

It brings big tea — e-ea-ah — e-ea-ah — eeaahrs

I'm drowning in my tears

drowning I'm drowning in my own tears

daughter of the queen in her open skirt

daughter in her open silk skirt

fold over fold one fold over one other fold.

4

No one says one no one says one word to me

no one now to say one word to me

no one says one word to me to say love

no one and death becomes a possibility

if no one says one word to say love

if there's no one to say one word to say love

if there's no one if there's no word

death becomes a possibility

and death becomes a possibility for me

daughter of the queen in her open skirt

daughter in her open silk skirt

fold over fold one fold over one other fold

folds like the folds of a flower unfolded

her hand against the folds fingers of her hand

fingers of her hand in a glove

fingers of her hand in a black net glove

a black net glove against the folds.

Two Essays
John Ash

WHY DO WE HATE THE MUSIC OF OUR TIME?

> "It was perhaps a pity, she reflected, though it couldn't be helped, that her dear Mrs. Shamefoot cared only for the extremely exalted music of the modern French school. Just then, *a dose of Brahms*, she felt would have done them all more good . . ."
>
> — Ronald Firbank, *Vainglory*

FOR AN ERA THAT PRIDES ITSELF on its innovations the twentieth century has been remarkably backward-looking. No twentieth century audience would have tolerated a concert repertoire that consisted almost entirely of eighteenth century music with a smattering of late seventeenth century works for variety. They went to orchestral concerts expecting to hear new music, and plenty of it. This had its drawbacks — Mozart was considered a minor master, and if Bach and Handel were to be heard at all they had to be presented in up-to-date arrangements. The doctrine of progress insisted that new music must be better — more advanced, profounder, more elevated — than old music. It is also true that Schubert, Schumann and Brahms came in for their share of derision, and that comparative mediocrities like Spohr and Raff enjoyed a success they hardly deserved, yet the fact remains that nineteenth century audiences were prepared to engage passionately with the music of their time.

Wagner, the most revolutionary composer of his era, was also its most adulated, but in regard to music there would now appear to be almost universal agreement with Baudelaire who maintained that the idea of progress was a myth modern man had invented to console himself for his abject decadence. Some tacitly assume that our music cannot achieve the beauty and sublimity of earlier music. We admire its technical ingenuity and brilliance of color, but it remains difficult, neurotic and cold. If it has advanced, it has advanced beyond the heart's understanding: its harmonies do not reassure and its poor, broken-backed melodies do not sound good when whistled in the shower. So it comes about that our symphony orchestras devote their impressive talents to an essentially nineteenth century repertoire, enlivened by a handful of late eighteenth century and early twentieth century "standards," and in the 1990s major works written more than fifty years ago by such incontestably great composers as Schoenberg and Webern have yet to gain popular acceptance. It is rather as if the value of Picasso's and Braque's greatest cubist paintings were still in doubt, as if the recent, record-breaking show at MOMA had been attended throughout its run by a few hundred devotees.

One can close one's eyes. One cannot close one's ears. The impact of music is more immediately physical than that of painting, and until the advent of adequate means of reproduction it was usually heard as part of an elaborate public ritual in surroundings of pompous splendor. In a concert hall it is impossible to forget the presence of one's fellow listeners, and once the first notes have sounded it is difficult to escape without making a fuss. New and unfamiliar music is heard under pressure. The physical discomfort of hearing music one does not understand — music that seems "chaotic," "discordant" and so on — is usually expressed in fusillades of unnecessary coughing and throat-clearing, almost as if the music threatened to strangle the listener. When, in the first decade and a half of this century, bourgeois audiences suddenly began to hear sounds that seemed either to have arrived from another planet, or to embody "primitive" feelings that they would rather deny, there was only one, logical collective response — the concert-riot.

The moment of divergence between modernist composer and conservative audience is marked by two such riots, both of which occured in 1913, one in Paris at the premiere of *The Rite of Spring*, the other in Vienna during a concert that included Schoenberg's *First Chamber Symphony*, Zemlinsky's *Maeterlinck Lieder*, and Berg's *Altenberg Lieder*. The Paris riot is the most notorious, but it is also the less important of the two. The scandal does not seem to have damaged Stravinsky's career — indeed, it may have added to the violent glamor of *The Rite*. The consequences of the Viennese riot were much more serious and far-reaching. Already irritated by the Schoenberg *Chamber Symphony*, the audience exploded in anger at the unearthly, shimmering sounds that introduce Berg's settings of Peter Altenberg's aphoristic, postcard poems. The concert could not be continued, and Berg's exquisite songs were never performed again during his lifetime. In disgust Schoenberg founded *The Society for the Private Performance of Music*: the general public, having been found wanting, was excluded. Here begins a history of confusion and incomprehension which now, in the 1990s appears to have reached a kind of stalemate.

Only consider that Schoenberg's seminal monodrama *Erwartung*, of 1909 had to wait until 1989 for its New York premiere. (And let us try to forget that Schoenberg's moonlit forest setting was encumbered with slablike atrium walls, a piano and a lot of Liberace candelabra.) It is not as if Schoenberg had been forgotten during this interval of eighty years. He is a uniquely twentieth century phenomenon, an acknowledged great composer whose music the public, for the most part, cordially detests. But it is stone-deaf critics we should blame rather than the public. Recently (December 22nd, 1990, to be exact) *The New York Times*' ineffable Donal Henahan described Schoenberg's passionately romantic *Piano Concerto* as "grayly theoretical," and went on to talk of "anagrammatical formulas" (surely a meaningless term in a musical context), defining Schoenberg's genius as purely "analytical." In fact it would be difficult to imagine more intensely emotional music than the second and third movements of this concerto, and a glance at the invaluable *Lexicon of Musical Invective* would have reminded Henahan that "grayly theoretical" was exactly the sort of phrase used by Brahms' nineteenth century detractors.

Stravinsky might seem to be luckier, but, in fact, his success is severely limited. The early ballets are immensely popular — so popular that they overshadow all his later, neo-classical and serial music. This situation so irked the composer that once, when the wife of a New Zealand dignitary remarked that *The Firebird* was her favorite of his works, he responded: "And you, madam, are wearing a very charming hat." Stravinsky's irritation is understandable. How often do we hear the *Symphony in C*, *Orpheus*, the *Capriccio for Piano and Orchestra*, *Persephone*, the *Cantata on Old English Texts*, *Agon*, *Threni*, the *Requiem Canticles* or the *Orchestral Variations*? In their different ways all of these works are masterpieces, ranging in character from elegant divertissement to austere ritual, but, regarding them, public indifference makes no distinction between the backward-looking (a Capriccio that pays homage to Weber and Tchaikovsky) and the forward-looking (the serial and aleatoric *Variations*). It is possible that audiences — in advance of critics — are subliminally aware that there is something subversive about an *andante rapsodico* that progresses from Bach to something

Stravinsky himself described as "a kind of Rumanian restaurant music." But the objection most commonly voiced is that Stravinsky's music, after the early ballets, lacks "warmth." Warmth is not a musical category (although I imagine that its advocates have something resembling the harmony and orchestration of Brahms in mind). One might complain with as much justice that the *Art of Fugue* lacks warmth, but no one would consider that grounds for denying its greatness as music.

The *Art of Fugue* is perhaps as close to pure mathematical construction as music can get, but for a long time it was assumed that Webern, in his late serial works, had gone a step further, producing music of an abstract complexity that was quite beyond the ordinary listener's powers of appreciation. As performance standards have improved, however, it has become possible for us to enjoy the sheer, diaphanous beauty of sound in such works as the *Symphony* op. 21 and the *Cantatas*. There is nothing here that is "difficult to listen to," and comprehension is further assisted by the use of clear, musical symbolism — the soprano's benediction in the last movement of the *First Cantata*, the striking of bells on the word "Mitternacht," in the second. The last movement of the *Second Cantata* may involve caronic structures of fantastic complexity and strictness, but its effect on the ear is as grandly simple as a Bach chorale.

From its beginnings serialism was marked by a strong classicizing tendency. Schoenberg first deployed the twelve note series in works whose movements bear such unambiguous titles as overture, march, minuet, gavotte and gigue. Although Schoenberg's neo-classicism was largely a matter of form rather than language, his aims were not so very different from Stravinsky's. He may have sniped at Stravinsky in a satirical chorus, but there is evidence that Schoenberg took his great rival's music very seriously indeed. A clarinet melody in the second dance movement of his *Serenade* op. 24 shows the clear influence of *The Soldier's Tale*, while Webern expressed unstinting admiration for the *Pribaoutki* songs. In this context Stravinsky's adoption of serialism in the late fifties has an air of inevitability about it. Although it was inspired initially by his love of Webern's late music, he soon went on to prove that it was possible to write strictly serial music that was unmistakably Stravinskian in every bar. Stravinsky was no more liable to sacrifice his individuality under the influence of Webern than he had been when he was adapting Tchaikovsky for *Le Baiser de la fée*. In this moment understanding should have begun, but Stravinsky was unable to take his audience with him, and his later works are now virtually forgotten (at least as far as concert performance is concerned). It was Stravinsky who proclaimed, with the fervor of a convert, that the music of the future would be serial, while Schoenberg maintained more modestly that there was still plenty of good music to be written in C major. In a distressing radio interview recorded not long before his death, Schoenberg remarked that his string quartets were really very close to Mozart's. The interviewer could barely conceal his incredulity and passed quickly on to the next question.

There is a distinct possibility that we could enter the next century without having come to terms with the music of this century. This places contemporary composers in a difficult position, but it is not one in which they are powerless. Some of the best of them have taken a long backward look attempting to reaccess, in terms of their own styles, the entire history of musical modernism from its late-romantic beginnings onwards. For some reason British composers are particularly adept at this. So Nicholas Maw embarks on his vast *Odyssey* — a work that has some claim to be the longest single span of orchestral music ever written — in which extended, Mahlerian melodies are used to quite contemporary ends, while Robin Holloway juxtaposes quotations from Debussy's *Jeux* and Wagner's *Ring* in the first act finale of his opera *Clarissa*, and Dominic Muldowney unites Gershwin and Schoenberg in his *Piano Concerto*. It cannot be overemphasized that these composers are neither reactionary nor haphazardly eclectic. In writing large scale orchestral pieces that can only be performed in the context of an essentially nineteenth century concert hall culture, they have had to assume an educative function, so they have written music which — by paraphrase and allusion — established its own historical context, making plain what our concert programs do not, namely the continuity of romantic, late-romantic, modernist and modern music.

In his *Scenes From Schumann* and his *Fantasy Pieces on Liederkreis* Robin Holloway re-imagines the music of the past from the standpoint of a modernist present, and the results have nothing to do with pastiche and precious little to do with nostalgia, but anyone who knows the story of music's most popular mythological hero, Orpheus, must be aware of the dangers of backward glances. These dangers are dramatically illustrated by recent developments in the career of the once-promising young American composer, Michael Torke. His early pieces had a quirky rhythmic energy and

an abrasive, harmonic edge that earned him a lot of flattering attention, but he has now decided that people are tired of experimenta-
tion, and has announced that, for him, "it is absolutely cool to be
a classical composer." The musical results of this thinking—if
such intellectual laziness can be dignified with that term—are predictably calamitous. Torke's *Bronze* (first performed on January 6th,
1991, at Carnegie Hall) is a fake nineteenth century piano concerto,
complete with acres of vapid passage work and orchestration so
inept as to surpass Schumann at his muddiest. Rudimentary motifs
of a vaguely "romantic" character were stirred about in a glutinous
harmonic soup. It was, without doubt, the most redundant piece of
music I had ever heard, but Torke may be right in thinking this is
what people want—"new" music that sounds a little like the most
boring passages of Brahms, Liszt and Spohr. Many audience members rose to their feet and applauded wildly. Others, including some
very distinguished musical figures, looked steadfastly down at their
crossed hands. The danger now is not "concert-riots," but music so
boring that the musically discerning fall into a deep slumber.

On my way out of the hall I noticed a young composer who I knew
to be an associate of Torke's. He remarked apologetically that this
was Torke's first attempt to write for triple winds. I could hardly
believe my ears. Writing for triple winds is *a problem* in the last
decade of the twentieth century? If someone is reinventing the
wheel you expect them to get the basics right. To his credit the
young composer looked despondent and admitted that his generation really seemed to have lost its sense of direction. He may well
be right. Young composers today have to find their way in a musical
universe in which everything is permitted *except* serialism—the
only twentieth century orthodoxy which, for all its faults, at least
had the benefit of a compelling musical and historical logic. One
can sympathize with their confusion, but the problem cannot be
solved by the idle assemblage of materials that were already moribund more than a century ago: such a method does not even qualify
as composition in any real sense. By turning his back on the music
of his own time, and by abandoning the search for a personal voice
at the tender age of twenty-nine Torke has abdicated as a composer.
He has also signed a three album contract with a major recording
company.

By one of those inscrutable ironies of fate it so happened that during the performance of *Bronze* I was seated immediately behind
Elliott Carter, one of the few contemporary composers whose music

I consider built to last for centuries. Carter is America's acknowledged master of modernist complexity. His chamber music and his orchestral scores combine intellectual fervor with raw physicality of sound, and European formal elegance with a very American passion for simultaniety, but to the average concert-goer they apparently sum up everything that is meant by "difficult, modern music." Both the problem and the irony are historical. The nineteenth century masters, to whom Torke thinks he is paying homage, were the difficult modernists of their day, and it is Carter who is carrying on the tradition of innovation that began with Beethoven. I do not mean to suggest that all serious contemporary music must imitate Carter's complexity; still less do I advocate a return to serialism, but it is certainly time that young composers addressed themselves seriously to the innate difficulties of composition in the late twentieth century. There is nothing wrong with the desire to write music that is immediately appealing and potentially accessible to a wide audience, but in order to do so there is no need for anyone to wrap themselves in Victorian fustian. Ambitious, young composers would be well advised to freshen their vocabularies by intensive study of such neglected masterpieces of modern tonality as, for example, the concerti and ballades of Frank Martin, Benjamin Britten's *The Prince of the Pagodas* and Kurt Weill's *Second Symphony*. Meaningful links to the past and the future cannot be forged by means of fads, fashions or outright tergiversation. Torke excuses his abdication by claiming that originality is a divine perogative, but, as far as anyone knows, God does not compose music, or not of the kind that can be played in a concert hall, so composers, I think, are still obliged to do the best they can in this regard.

IN PRAISE OF CHARLES KOECHLIN (1867–1950)

From the vantage of the twenty-first century the musical landscape of the twentieth century may look very different. Composers who are now marginalized or ignored will loom much larger. Among the likely candidates for such promotion are Frank Martin, Alexander Zemlinsky, Aare Merikanto, Nikos Skalkottas, Frank Bridge, Roberto Gerhard, John Foulds, Luigi Dallapiccola and Charles Koechlin.

I am particularly confident of Koechlin's claims on posterity. In the 1920s and 1930s no French composer was producing music that was more harmonically advanced or more consistently serious in purpose. As a pupil of Massenet and Faure, and a teacher of Milhaud and Poulenc, Koechlin should have assumed a central position in French musical life. The fact that he did not, and that many of his major scores remain unperformed and unpublished is hard to explain adequately, but his reputation for eccentricity, his sheer fertility, and his indifference to fashion at a time when musical Paris was more than ever a slave to *chic*, must all have played their part. Koechlin seems to have found it difficult *not* to compose. His idea of relaxation was to sit down and dash off a dozen or more short pieces for multiple hunting horns (the *Sonneries* op. 123 and 153), and his *oeuvre complete* runs to well over two hundred opus numbers. Even this high figure does not give a realistic idea of his output, since many opus numbers may cover lengthy cycles of individual pieces. *Les Heures Persannes*, for example, consists of sixteen substantial piano pieces (which also exist in an orchestral arrangement) lasting for more than an hour, while fully ninety-six pieces for solo flute are grouped under the general title of *Les Chants de nectaire*. The sheer extent and picturesque diversity of Koechlin's musical terrain with its oriental temples, bucolic dances, Himalayan peaks, enchanted forests, medieval anchorites, lost huntsmen, and sauntering movie stars swathed in furs, might seem to make exploration difficult, but in my experience it is hard to go wrong. His weaker pieces can be bland and a little garrulous (the Koechlin landscape includes the occasional bourgeois picnic) but they are never insincere, and always maintain a high level of craftsmanship, while his major works, especially the symphonic poems, are little short of astonishing.

Koechlin's most notable eccentricity was his passionate devotion to movie stars, especially the now forgotten Lilian Harvey, who is the subject of two *Albums de Lilian*, and the enchanting *Sept Chansons pour Gladys*. There also exists an *Epitaphe de Jean Harlow*, a set of *Dances for Ginger Rogers*, and a *Symphony of Seven Stars* with movements portraying Douglas Fairbanks, Lilian Harvey, Greta Garbo, Clara Bow, Marlene Dietrich, Emil Jannings and Charlie Chaplin. Koechlin even wrote the scenario for a film called *Daisy Hamilton* in which the principals were to be himself and the divine Lilian.

Odd though this may be, there is nothing merely eccentric about the music that resulted. In his film music Koechlin maintains the highest compositional standards, and brings all his formidable erudition to bear. He was quite capable of expressing his adoration of Harvey, Garbo or Rogers in terms of sixteenth century modal counterpoint. For Koechlin there was no incongruity and, in listening to him, we perceive none. The first *Album de Lilian* begins with a song of grave beauty in praise of the preservative powers of Palmolive soap *(Keep That Schoolgirl Complexion)*, and moves through a miniature *Fugue sans protocole* (somewhat in the manner of Satie at his most *bureaucratique*) and a glittering toccata to a lovely, cinematic skating waltz for flute and piano with wordless vocalise, until we reach the angular and atonal anguish of *Pleurs* (a surprising excursion to Expressionist Vienna) from which a simple glissando leads us into the perfect B major happiness of the final song, *Tout va bien*. The words of this song were written by the composer himself, and they represent his naive genius to the full. As a modernist Koechlin favored *vers libre*, and the first line of his poem is delightful —

"Tout va bien, puisque chagrin *d'amour* ne dure qu' un
       moment, o Martini!"

In the first *Album* naivete and sophistication, innocence and complexity are perfectly balanced, and it is likely that Harvey's immortality is more safely assured by Koechlin's music than it is by her now forgotten films. Sadly, the adored "Star" remained entirely indifferent to his labors on her behalf.

Although he never went to the length of inventing heteronyms, it is tempting to describe Koechlin as the Fernando Pessoa of music. At least three distinct composers can be distinguished: (1) Scholastic Koechlin, theoretician, master of counterpoint and recondite modes; (2) Gallic Koechlin, the composer of the graceful, deceptively simple *Nouvelles Sonatines Françaises*, and (3) Prophetic Koechlin, who, as early as the song *Améthyste* (written between 1905 and 1908) was moving into the uncharted realms of polytonality and atonality. This Koechlin was the only French composer of the time capable of bridging the gap between the schools of Paris and Vienna, and probably the only one who was interested in doing so. Although they may sound less disruptively radical than the Expressionist masterpieces that Schoenberg was writing at about the same time, songs such as *Amethyste* (or the nearly contemporary *Le Cortège d'Amphitrite* and *Le repas préparé*) with their complex superimposed chords, irregular meters and long-held pedal points, are hardly less innovative. They establish a unique atmosphere of luminous *crépus-cule*, investing Albert Samain's palid, sub-Parnassian verses

248

with an authentic, oriental strangeness that reminds us that the first lyric poets in the European tradition lived and sang on the borders of Asia. Koechlin's vision of the classical past is Lesbian, not Athenian.

In Schoenberg's *Second String Quartet* of 1908 the soprano invokes "the air of other planets," while in *Amethyste* we hear "the strange sighing of the oak trees' prophetic branches." There is certainly prophecy in both pieces, and it is not surprising that Koechlin should have greeted the Paris première of *Pierrot Lunaire* with a cry of "Long live the classics of the future!" But, whereas Schoenberg followed the path of apparent historical inevitability, progressing from post-Wagnerian chromaticism to free atonality, to serialism, the relation of Koechlin's various styles is in no way successive or hierarchical. Gallic and Prophetic Koechlin work side by side, either independently or in collaboration, always watched over by the benevolent, and majestically bearded figure of Scholastic Koechlin, heir to a tradition that stretches back to the Middle Ages.

On first acquaintance the *Primavera Quintet* op. 156 for flute, harp and strings, with its giguelike finale and its *sicilienne* after Fauré, seems a typical example of light-weight Gallic charm, until one notices the unusually rich and vigorous contrapuntal working of the outer movements, and the exceptional refinement of its harmony. The great *Piano Quintet* op. 80 of 1920–21 begins with a tenebrous dirge of claustraphobic intensity, and a violently Expressionist allegro that, together, show Prophetic Koechlin at his darkest and most dissonant. Nothing remotely like this had been heard in French music before, not even in the most forward-looking works of Debussy's later years, and the hair-raising, polytonal clashes of the allegro *(L'Assaut de l'ennemi)* bear some superficial resemblance to Ives at his wildest. In 1991 this is music that still has the power to astonish. In the third and fourth movements, the music begins to move gradually — in a process Koechlin called *éclaircissment progressif* — towards the serenity of the *Violin Sonata* and the high spirits of the *Primavera Quintet* or the *Nouvelles Sonatines*. The finale is one of Koechlin's grandest conceptions, and the jubilation of the final measures is all the more touching for having been so hard won.

The *Quintet* op. 80 is, without doubt, one of the masterpieces of twentieth century chamber music, but it is on his large scale orchestral works — the symphonies, and the symphonic poems, *Le Livre de la Jungle, Le Buisson ardent* and *Doctor Fabricius* — that

Koechlin's future reputation will rest, always providing that audiences are given a chance to hear them. The *Jungle Book* cycle (based on Kipling's stories) is perhaps the central work of Koechlin's career. It can be regarded either as a sequence of independent (or at least, semi-autonomous) symphonic poems — *La Loi de la Jungle, Les Bandars-Logs, La Meditation de Purun Baghat* and *La Course de Printemps* — or as a vast, four movement symphony comprised of a prelude, a rondo burlesque, a slow movement, and an extended (and uncompromisingly polytonal) finale.

It is typical of Koechlin that he should lavish the most sophisticated and advanced techniques, and the resources of a very large orchestra on the evocation of what are essentially stories for children, but be assured that his majestic and visionary cycle bears absolutely no resemblance to Disney's version of Kipling. Its prelude *(La Loi de la Jungle)* is an austerely monodic invention in which the orchestra's hieratic, unison utterances are punctuated by gong-strokes in a manner that clearly anticipates Messiaen (particularly the Messiaen of *Et Expecto Ressurectionem Mortuorum*). *Les Bandars Logs*, composed in 1939, is much more diverse and complex, and in it Koechlin takes the opportunity to comment on the musical fashions and contending schools of his day. The opening, representing the peace of the forest, is saturated in the luminous, superimposed fifths that Koechlin loved so well, and here — as throughout the piece — the orchestration must count as one of the miracles of twentieth century music. The calm is rudely shattered by the antics of a malicious tribe of monkeys (the Bandar-Logs of the title) represented by clattering percussion, and rapid, sinuous asymmetrical phrases on woodwind and saxophones which demand the utmost virtuosity from the orchestra. Presently, the Bandar-Logs decide to try their hand at modern music making. At first they become obsessed with chains of vaguely Debussyan chords, but things soon turn sour (acid dissonances, rasping brass), and, after a return of their opening music, they switch to Schoenbergian atonality. Significantly, the Schoenberg parody contains music of genuine beauty, and it is the Parisian neo-classicists — represented by a grotesquely heavy-handed, wrong-note fugue — who provoke Koechlin to outright derision. Clearly, the scholastic, Bach-loving Koechlin was unimpressed by the antics of some of his pupils and younger contemporaries. The fugue breaks off abruptly, and gongs, harps and celesta sound quietly, initiating a process of transformation, conflict and synthesis that combines the subtlety and mosaic construction of Debussy's *Jeux*, with the dynamism of *The Rite* and the delicacy of Berg's *Violin Concerto* — if one can imagine a Berg who was a Frenchman with a penchant for the exotic.

As this last — somewhat desperate — sentence makes clear, this is music which finally defeats my powers of description. It demands to be heard. Darius Milhaud, who spent much of his career mis-applying Koechlin's discoveries, nevertheless remarked truthfully that, in confronting his teacher's music, he had "the impression of facing the music of a magician who belongs to the generation that will follow mine." Now, after Messiaen and Boulez, it is surely time we went back to discover Koechlin's "classics of the future."

Since performances of his music remain very rare, it is lucky that the Koechlin CD discography is now quite extensive. It is also seriously unbalanced with far too many recordings of minor pieces for solo instrument and piano, and not enough of the orchestral music and the major piano cycles. It is a great pity that the LP recordings of *Le Livre de la Jungle*, *The Symphony of Seven Stars*, the *Ballade for Piano and Orchestra* and the *Violin Sonata* have been allowed to disappear without being transferred to CD. As things stand the newcomer should begin with *Le Buisson Ardent*. Composed between 1939 and 1945, this is a magnificent symphonic poem lasting for nearly forty minutes without a break and scored for a vast orchestra which includes no less than five saxophones, as well as piano, organ and *onde martenot* (an early electronic instrument that also fascinated Messiaen). Despite the size of the forces involved, Koechlin's orchestration is all luminosity and transparency. The work moves from an atonal threnody for strings to a final ecstatic chorale that must count among the most eloquent passages in twentieth century French music, taking in a turbulent allegro (replete with whole-tone scales, and angular pentatonic motifs), an extended song for the *onde* and a fugue along the way. The work, as a whole, is perhaps somewhat oddly proportioned and the fugue subject is a little too innocently jaunty for its context, but these do not really constitute sufficient reason for denying it the status of an orchestral masterpiece, fit to stand beside the finest works of Debussy, Ravel and Messiaen. The CD also includes the brief but highly evocative symphonic prelude *Au Loin* and the deeply lyrical *Cello Sonata*. (Cybelia, Musique Francaise CY812.)

Hypnotic, ghostly and aloof, the remarkable piano cycle, *Les Heures Persannes*, takes Debussyan arabesque and non-functional harmony into regions even that great master could not have envisioned, and it anticipates works written some thirty or forty years later by Messiaen and Giacinto Scelsi. (Wergo WER 60 137-50.)

The *Primavera Quintet* and the *Piano Quintet* op. 80 have already been described and can be found on Cybelia CY 829.

Le Cortege d'Amphitrite (Hyperion CDA 66243) presents an intelligent selection of Koechlin's songs from 1890 to 1935, impeccably performed by Claudette Leblanc and Boaz Sharon (although it is only fair to report that a musically inclined French poet of my acquaintance found Ms. Leblanc's singing "too French"). The disc contains such important mature pieces as *Amethyste* and *Sept Chansons pour Gladys*, but readers may well find themselves seduced by the enchanting wit and melodic freshness of the *Rondels* to texts by Theodore de Banville written in 1890 when Koechlin was a mere twenty-three-years old.

The recordings of minor works are *Music for Flute* (Hyperion CDA 66414), *Works for Oboe, Oboe d'amore*, and *Cor Anglais* (Audite 97.417), and *Barry Tuckwell Plays Koechlin* (ASV CD DCA 716). All of these contain music of great charm and individuality, but the first named is perhaps the most important, since it contains the whole of the first *Album de Lilian* and a selection from the second. It is also rather misleadingly named, since it contains pieces for flute and piano; two flutes; solo piano; soprano and piano; and flute, soprano and piano, but nothing at all for unaccompanied flute.

The two *Sonatinas for Oboe d'amore* accompanied by flute, clarinet, harp and string sextet, may not be major works but they are the ultimate in exquisite melancholy and refinement of sound, and the *Oboe Sonata* is almost as seductive. *Barry Tuckwell Plays Koechlin* leads off with the haunting *Sonata for Horn and Piano* op. 70, continues with the *Fifteen Pieces* op. 180, and concludes with a selection of *Sonneries*, in which, thanks to the wonders of technology, Mr. Tuckwell plays all four hunting horns simultaneously. Nearly eighty minutes of horn music may be a tad too much of a good thing, but it is very agreeable to lose oneself "dans le forêt romantique" of Koechlin's prodigious imagination.

George Wettling
Hank O'Neal

AUGUST 6, 1954. Celebrity Service's "Celebrity Bulletin" picks its celebrity of the day. Listed along with William Holden, Louis Lamour (sic), Fred Allen, Ella Fitzgerald, Yvonne DeCarlo and Portland Hoffa is George Wettling, painter, writer, photographer and jazz musician. Thirteen years and ten months later he would be dead, remembered by a few, but not many. No flowerly obits, no memorials, no tributes in the trades and now twenty years later he's almost completely forgotten; not by young jazz fans or even the fans who emerged in the seventies and eighties with little opportunity to hear his music, but by the current batch of jazz scholars, critics and educators. Wettling's oblivion is a pity, but his oblivion is more complicated than sloppy scholarship.

Wettling was born in Topeka, Kansas in 1907, the same year as Dave Tough and two years before Gene Krupa, the other two in a triumvirate of exceptional white drummers from the midwest. In the Chicago of the early twenties, the right place at the right time, he was influenced by the influx of great musicians from New Orleans and some equally great ones growing up in Chicago. By the time he turned twenty he had already formed life-long friendships and recorded with Muggsy Spanier, Frank Teschemacher, Joe Sullivan, Eddie Condon and a host of others. Not just an exceptional drummer with small jazz ensembles, he was sufficiently versatile to handle big band chores with Paul Whiteman, Chico Marx and Bunny Berigan in the thirties and the ABC staff in the forties and fifties. Commercial jobs with large orchestras paid the rent but the musical friendships he made in the twenties would lead to his finest performances and best working conditions. But those good jobs could never provide a steady income, even when the sounds that flowed from Eddie Condon's Greenwich Village club were moderately commercial.

As jazz entered the sixties, there were fewer jobs for a drummer like Wettling, not with his old friends, who were less and less active, nor anyone else. There were the reunions at festivals, a special

253

gathering or perhaps a private party, but by and large he was lucky to get a job with the Dukes of Dixieland or a piano trio date. His last steady job was in Clarence Hutchenrider's Trio at Bill's Gay Nineties, a place that still operates on East 54th Street in New York City, serving hamburgers to harried businessmen at lunch and martinis to the same crowd later in the day. The trio played in a room on the second floor; a long climb up the stairs, particularly carrying a drum set. In the spring of 1968 Wettling found he could no longer climb the stairs. He died in June. A few weeks later I became aware of his paintings, photographs and writings. I'd never met him.

Marian McPartland telephoned me sometime in mid-June 1968, told me Wettling's drums were at Bill's Gay Nineties and the owners would be relieved if they were quickly removed. She added that it was my duty to help her: I loved the music, had a strong back *plus* an automobile in Manhattan. We did the job on a sunny Saturday afternoon.

When Marian and I arrived at Jean Wettling's apartment I was not surprised to see everything in a state of disrepair. Marian had warned me beforehand that housekeeping was not Jean Wettling's strong suit; but she had not warned me about the paintings. Wettling's photography and writings were hidden away, for me to discover another day. I knew Wettling painted; Eddie Condon had at least two at his Washington Square apartment. But I was unprepared to see so many of them lying about the apartment. They looked remarkably like copies of Stuart Davis's work. This puzzled me until I later learned about the friendship between Davis and Wettling.

We placed the drums and assorted hardware in a small junk-strewn room, then spent some time consoling Mrs. Wettling. She was not having a good day, in fact, it appeared she hadn't had a good one in years. I flinched at one thing she said, she was going to give all the paintings to a guy who owned a saloon in the neighborhood for a couple of month's credit. I urged her not to do something so foolish because it was likely the paintings could be sold to jazz fans and she could realize something more substantial than a few months of free drinks. The paintings were photographed within the week, transparencies were shown to various people and most of the paintings were eventually sold.

I stayed in touch with Jean Wettling throughout the seventies. I tried to give her advice on how to sort out her life. She ignored everything, but she'd occasionally "find" a painting in the back of a closet and as often as not I'd wind up buying it from her; better me than the guy at the saloon. Then one day in 1980 the telephone rang; it was the woman who lived in Jean's building. Jean had died in Roosevelt Hospital and when the super went into the apartment there was an address book with my name in it. Phyllis Condon and I went up to that sad little apartment on West 57th Street the next day. In the same address book I found the name of a brother in New Mexico or Arizona. I placed a call and the conversation was very brief. Upon learning of his sister's death the unconcerned but angry voice on the telephone strongly suggested he didn't want to be bothered and would I please arrange to have everything thrown into the street. I had never experienced anything quite like that but I noticed there were a number of people in the hall who were eyeing the furniture. Phyllis and I hurriedly searched the apartment and packed all the letters, photographs, clippings and scrapbooks that related to George Wettling into a breadbox. We also found two small paintings in a drawer. We left the apartment to the bargain hunters and headed home, much saddened by the day's events. I recall that day vividly, and despite its unpleasantness I'm glad I made the trip. There were not then, nor are there now, many people who can shed any light on Wettling. Other than the comments of a few people and jazz books, all I know about him and perhaps all that will be remembered comes from that small batch of ephemera that Phyllis and I collected.

George Wettling began to paint in 1943-44; a portrait of Maggie Condon as an infant, his second painting, dates the beginning. In 1970 Eddie Condon recalled: "George Wettling learned to paint in our apartment in 1943. We were moving out and to get back at a pesty super we decided to have a wall-painting party. George was our most enthusiastic painter. When he ran out of walls at our apartment he left immediately for Stuart Davis's where he found lessons and encouragement."

Wettling's relationship with Stuart Davis was critical to his development as a painter. Within a few years his paintings resembled his teacher's and from the correspondence that has survived, as well as photographs and assorted memorabilia, it is clear the two men were very good friends who admired the other's accomplishments. If painting became important to Wettling, jazz was equally important to Davis, who once wrote: "Recently I had occasion to inquire of a little boy what he wanted to be when he grew up. Without breaking the Chicago-style beat of his bubble gum he replied, 'Eddie Condon.' Conference had been fogging my vision a bit of late. It was clear that the little boy had hip boots well clasped up to his navel. This was the jolt I needed. I played an old Punch Miller record with a George Wettling backing I had recently dubbed in, added a configuration to my current painting, *The Mellow Pad*, and forgot all about Sir Alexander Cadogan and Gromyko. For a brief moment I thought I was Eddie Condon too, but that passed." Add to this that Wettling was intellectually on Davis's wavelength. One only had to look at the books on Wettling's shelves; no useless books, no pulp, nothing trendy. He had everything Henry Miller, John Steinbeck and Kenneth Patchen had ever written and many others as well.

Wettling was sufficiently accomplished by 1947 to have a one man show mounted at the Norlyst Gallery. The advertising flyer contained a special tribute by Stuart Davis. At least three paintings from that show have survived, including *Stuart Davis On Oil Cloth*. Here is what Davis wrote on that occasion:

The old record I had just found really knocked me out. Throwing my crossword puzzle to the floor I rushed to the window to better scan the scratched label on the disc. Simultaneously a shadow obscured the type, caused by a large passing dirigible with moving electric letters on its side, "WETTLING IS NOW DRY—Courtesy of Ernie Anderson—Check Back," the letters read. As the occlusion passed I returned to the label which read, Dehydrated Silo No. 2, by "George Wettling and his St. Valentine's Day Boys." At that moment there was a tapping on the door in an unmistakable hip beat. "The Raven," I thought as I opened it, but was confronted instead by a young man in an $800.00 Burberry coat. "Are you Stuart Davis, the Cat that paints those modernistic-type paintings," he politely inquired. "Solid," I replied simultaneously reaching for a small Jazz Lexicon near at hand. "Won't you come in—Jack," I added. As he did so, two members of the Green Bay Packers followed carrying eighteen oil paintings, which they distributed strategically about the studio.

"My name is George Wettling," he said, "and this modern painting really knocks me out. Dig that one over there, leaning against the gin bottles." As I started to focus, a shadow reduced the visibility. This time it read, "Eddie's Concert at 5:30—Don't be fooled—signed, Ernie Anderson." "Are you the same one he flashes on that sign," I asked. "You can reiterate that at will," he replied. "And on the record too," I persisted. "Are you kiddin, Jack," he retorted, "I'm on a gang of records. And don't let any of those real Square Cats derail you."

I have always preferred the type of painting that really jumps (even though a good painting is hard to find), and fortunately George's fell well within this category. I threaded my way through the irregularly arranged exhibition. "That one against the gin bottles is a killer," I shouted, dislodging a large canvas as nine glasses crashed to the floor. "I don't want to drag you," he called back, "but do you think I ought to make more." "Don't quit now, Jack—don't quit now," I came back with authority. "When do you think that *Mellow Pad* on your easel will be finished," he interpolated, "because it really knocks me out, and besides how hip can you get." I was about to make a statistical estimate, when the room got dark again. "Cut out, George," it read, "Rehearsal in 10 minutes compliments of E.A."

That was my first meeting with Wettling. After he had left I put my Lexicon back on the kitchen drain-board and played the record over again, with the same result as before. Then I visualized his hip exhibition. "Gee," I said, "how hip can you get."

Wettling's paintings fall into four distinct stylistic periods, with extant examples of each. The first period is characterized by limited technique and lack of direction: charming but primitive paintings. He entered his second phase well before the Norlyst show, exhibiting strong dependence on Davis. His third phase, perhaps his best, began in the late forties and lasted into the early fifties where the complete dominance of Davis appears, as well as a secure technique. *Jazz Is In*, a painting that tells about a recording session and was the focal point of a 1951 article about Wettling in *Collier's* magazine is a prime example of his work at this time and is perhaps his finest painting. Two other large works which survive, *Roadgraders* and *High As A Kite*, were exhibited at the Philadelphia Museum of Art in 1952, are also from this period. In the final phase, which lasted into the late fifties, Wettling presents a more personal vision, as may be seen in his exceptional *Self Portrait*, and a remarkably stylized rendering of a New York City landmark, *McSorley's*.

Wettling did not continue to paint or photograph after 1960, it would seem, though he continued to fill sketch books. The large sketch books may have taken the place of paintings and photographs and beginning in the early sixties he began to date and locate many of his tiny drawings with titles like *Albany 62*, *Toronto 63* and *Gay Nineties 67*. It also appears he stopped taking photographs about the same time he gave up painting. There is nothing in his scrapbooks after 1960, and his album of clippings ends in 1955. Why he stopped all artistic endeavor remains unclear. He may have lost interest; but this seems unlikely. The death of Stuart Davis in 1964 undoubtedly demoralized him but Wettling had stopped painting well before his friend's death. True, he never had any real commercial success with his paintings; he rarely sold them after the early fifties and for the most part they were given to friends. But I don't think lack of recognition would have stopped him. Wettling didn't seem to be one too concerned with the commercial aspect of his art. More likely, he stopped because of personal disasters and

257

serious health problems. Wettling's health deteriorated in the early sixties; his liver became swollen and cataracts began to form on both eyes. His personal life, which was never particularly stable, became intolerable about the same time and this merely exacerbated his already chronic alcohol dependency. Both these factors mitigated against his painting but as gloomy as these circumstances were, it might have been possible to overcome them on some level. I think the real answer to Wettling's abrupt halt lies elsewhere. I'm certain at some point he suffered from a severe and debilitating lack of confidence, made worse by some very poor guidance.

Hidden away in the back of Wettling's large scrapbook of clippings I found three sheets of "critiques" and a letter from the Famous Artists School, one of those dreary organizations that advertise on matchbooks and in cheap magazines, snaring the unwary with promises of untold success. They snared George Wettling. He sent in a dime to be turned into Michelangelo in a minute and the tragedy began. It is simply outrageous to see an employee of this "school" offering innumerable manufactured suggestions on how Wettling might improve his work. Wettling would apparently submit a painting, at which time the "instructor" assigned him would repaint the picture, showing him how it might appear if properly executed. Perhaps it would have been best had someone executed the instructor; one critique reviews a painting of Eddie Condon's club in Greenwich Village and its suggestions are sickeningly pretentious and rhetorical. Here is an academic hack, who probably exhibited at county fairs and such amateurish events as the presently awful Washington Square Art Show and has been reduced to working for the matchbook school of art. He's telling Wettling how to paint. There is even a letter from these bandits, dated 1960, advising Wettling one of his paintings has been selected from 3,200 entries to tour the United States. In addition, the letter announces a prize for the lucky artist: $25 worth of art supplies from the Famous Art School store plus a $10 bonus for a "professional" photographer to take a picture to travel along with the painting.

How sad, a man who was one of the best jazz drummers, a student and close friend to one of this country's great painters. $10 for a photograph? George Wettling had been photographed by Weegee, Gjon Mili, Lisette Model and goodness knows how many other photographers of note. Having started painting the walls of an apartment from which Eddie Condon had been evicted, Wettling ended fumbling about with the Famous Artists School; the beginning and end equally ridiculous, then an unexpected twist. In December 1989, at a fancy art show at New York City's Armory, I noticed a Wettling painting in a dealer's booth. The price: $28,000, an amount Wettling probably never earned in any year of drumming.

George Wettling was not a great painter but a superior disciple of Stuart Davis. He certainly painted better than Davis drummed. A fine photographer, he used his camera as a sketchbook in the same manner as Ben Shahn and Reginald Marsh. He was an exceptional jazz musician whose other artistic endeavors, painting, photography and even writing, showed genuine creative flair.

George Wettling painting with Pee Wee Russell (clarinet), Eddie Condon (guitar), Fred Ohms (trombone) and Max Kaminsky (trumpet), late 1940s.

259

Size

Mei-mei Berssenbrugge

1.

Stones were chosen so impact of water on them makes acoustic harmony, the way the song of a bird,
like light gains character from what it touches in the world, and who is there to see or hear it.
It could refer to a depth of feeling, or exchange for feeling. Our transparency guarantees the exchange,
so she connects frequencies during the time she listens as a science or song: the transparent sound
of water as it strikes a stone, to water in the color of a petal, in skin, and innumerable points at the edge
of a petal, like sound intervals. Also, when a point is translucent or silent, not a vantage point.
It's fluid if this experience is a content of her, like the perception of color of the specimen
as corresponding to absent waves of reflected light, or the content of something she knows,
varying like distance in her mind to the object. If what she knows changes, she couldn't say
the experience or absence is changing, but spans a new scale of points or notes in the transparency.

2.

There's no true perpendicular except at sea level. You think about that face as if you are in water, eyes level to the waves. Her profile of a wave spirals in or out toward a definition of recognition, a seeing or hearing as the natural enclosure, the way a valley resonates, that the face containing a mineral light referred to a depth of meaning you recognize.

Your recognition could exchange for meaning, like something you experience which you know, so meaning itself guarantees the exchange, the way light guarantees its sequence of incidents in the sky, on the plane of the memory, or in a photograph in which the points are part of the plane or limits of it.

For a long time, the plane remained a frame or cellulose for frequencies from the lost spirit.

So, she understands translucency as size, for example, the duration of containment of a person, for which the horizon mountain is a limit, part of a face above a hedge, minute corolla, if light speed, like wind, varied.

3.

If everything derives from expressive energy, a content of your consciousness, then everyone who wishes to speak, and everywhere she appears, being exoteric, seem in contradicting, violent oscillation, like dried color. But this only refers to scale of containment, like light and perspective,
if the face itself is absorbed, emitting to you a new chromatic or new solvent of gradations of size, like a gradual reddening. Then, the tones of water possessing expressive power and tonality belong to the same focus of no time limit as the garden. I describe the size of the space between two incidents as melodic shape. Each note of the bird goes anywhere, an aphasic depth of absence, compared to light through the lens of a live cell or light that predates your sensation, which could be color symbolism born from a dissolving naturalism, but is that symbolic energy at the edge of the plain, at which each point is more than a limit, is in the body, incomparable to material destructions.

261

The Spun-Off Independent Dead-End Ten-Star Blast

Hayden Carruth

As A WHITE ARTIST influenced by and dependent on black American culture I want to say something about the place of subsidiarism in the arts in general. Some would call it parasitism, which is OK — often that's what it is, though not always. But first I must, for propriety's sake, assert the obvious, namely, that black culture itself is subsidiary to, not to say spat on and stomped by, white American culture, and that an immense though not primary part of its own substance and energy derives from this, which is what we all know. For the present I need to set this aside, however. Black American culture is an ethnic and esthetic mainstream in itself, partly because of the energy taken from reacting against oppressions; it is self-generated and self-sustained and now a couple of centuries old; it is a mainstream in the fullest sense. This is what I want to propound, and then against it the much smaller, almost miniscule components of serious white culture that go along with it as subsidiary participants. Clearly I don't mean the white grifters and grafters who have profited from stealing black culture and commercializing it, Joel Chandler Harris, Elvis Presley, etc., filmmakers, agents, club-owners and all the rest, to say nothing of white landlords and storekeepers, politicians, etc. I mean the serious participants. And for the sake of simplicity I will exclude myself and all poets. We are dependent on many cultural antecedents in addition to black ones, international, national, and regional. Yet my own position vis-à-vis black culture is what has brought this topic to my mind.

I want to talk about white jazz musicians. We've had a good many great ones, but finding an instance of a white musician, dependent on the black tradition, who has fed anything back into that tradition is difficult — pretty nearly impossible. Lester Young once said he learned something from Frankie Trumbauer, Miles Davis obviously took certain attitudes from Gil Evans (and he has even said that

262

because he listened to Bobby Hackett a good deal when he was young he has a connection with Bix Beiderbecke), Cecil Taylor has acknowledged a restrained early admiration for Dave Brubeck, for a while in the late 1930s and 1940s almost every clarinetist younger than the original generation of New Orleans reed men, black or white, sounded like Benny Goodman, and one can find a few other such examples. But has any white musician contributed a major element to the black mainstream? I doubt it. Beiderbecke, who because of his time, place and personality may have been the greatest white innovator we have had in jazz, and who created a style, technique and improvisational concept that were genuinely new and expressive in his time, produced almost no effect on black musicians of that time or after. You can listen to black trumpet players from Frankie Newton to Roy Eldridge, for instance, without hearing anything that you can ascribe confidently to Beiderbecke. Without any question this is true of the other white musicians of the middle west who responded to black jazz from New Orleans in the 1920s and went on to make, from the 1930s to the 1960s, a style of composition and performance that was distinct, powerful, but at the same time has been ignored, not to say scorned, by critics and has had practically no developmental influence on jazz as a whole. We call it Chicago jazz.

Take the most extreme comparison. The important early recordings in Chicago jazz were made at about the same time, circa 1930, as the important early recordings of Duke Ellington. On those early records one can hear occasional crossovers of theme and style, but not many. And the progress thereafter of Chicago jazz on one hand and of Ellington on the other was miles apart — musically speaking, that is: much of the time the two groups were located in the same city, New York. Both were playing jazz, to my mind very superior jazz, but beyond that they had nothing to do with one another. Yet I would argue, and from the perspective of our historical position today many would agree, that Pee Wee Russell and Wild Bill Davison *ought* to have been playing in the Ellington band, and that both they and the band would have benefitted if this had been the case. Russell and Davison had exactly the kind of individual stylistic and textural brilliance that Ellington sought and exploited in his sidemen, and they would have added to the band voices unlike those of any other musicians at Ellington's command. Whether Russell or Davison, given their personalities and peculiarities, could have survived in the Ellington band is another question, of course, to which the clear answer is: probably not. But the idea has, to me, a wonderful attractiveness.

Gunther Schuller in his *Early Jazz* (New York, 1968), which in spite of serious shortcomings remains the best scholarly book on the subject, gives one section to a discussion of Beiderbecke, but scarcely mentions any of the other Chicago musicians. Throughout the book, in passing, he mentions — usually, and properly, derogatively — the Original Dixieland Jazz Band and, with mild approbation, the New Orleans Rhythm Kings. One can't complain about this; jazz is a black people's art, and Schuller's analytical history is not intended to be encyclopedic but to explicate the major developments, which are inescapably black. But good jazz is good jazz. Often I've said that poetry is where you find it, and the same applies to jazz. Throughout the literature of jazz the Chicago period is neglected by critics, except by fanatical revivalists like Philip Larkin, who think that such second-raters as Muggsy Spanier, Danny Polo, Phil Napoleon, et al., are the greatest. I don't know the whole literature, it has grown so large that no one could, but in fifty years of reading I remember no balanced discussion of Chicago jazz. Not one. Some of the Chicagoans (most of whom did not come from Chicago) were geniuses. Tastes differ, but everyone would agree on Beiderbecke, most would agree on Teschemacher, Joe Sullivan, Russell, Bunny Berigan, Art Hodes, Davison, Jess Stacey, Gene Krupa and George Wettling, each of whom was an innovator. (Wettling carried the New Orleans drumming style of Zutty Singleton further than anyone else was ever able to.) Scores of others, musicians like Jack Teagarden, Jimmy McPartland, Bud Freeman, Bobby Hackett, Joe Marsala and Brad Gowans, had moments of genius, perhaps a good many of them, though not enough to qualify for the first rank. And then there were the scores and hundreds of fine musicians who played with spontaneity, urgency, and melodic, harmonic, and rhythmic expressiveness, and who created the œuvre, the body of hard-driving Chicago jazz played from 1930 to 1960 and later. Incidentally, some of the late-comers ought to be mentioned too, musicians like Ruby Braff, Bob Wilbur and Lou McGarity, who were not heard until after 1940 but who contributed a good deal to the final development.

Chicago jazz is not Dixieland. I have written elsewhere about this distinction,* and all I'll say now is that jazz is original, spontaneous,

---

*"Eleven Memoranda on the Culture of Jazz," CONJUNCTIONS: 9, 1986; reprinted in *Sitting In: Selected Writings on Jazz, the Blues, and Related Topics*, University of Iowa Press, 1986.

authentic and immediate. Dixieland is antiquarian, nostalgic and almost always pedantic. Chicago jazz came from white Chicago in the era of Prohibition and the Syndicate. Al Capone was in a sense its godfather. A certain hardness and violence is characteristic, much more than in the New Orleans black music that the Chicagoans derived from. What the Chicagoans insisted on from the beginning was Swing. They originated the style and, I think, the term. (At any rate it was not originated by the "swing" musicians and arrangers of the big dance bands, both black and white, of the late thirties and forties, which were called "swing bands" but which took their ideas more from Kansas City black bands like Benny Moten's or East Coast black bands like Duke Ellington's and Fletcher Henderson's than from the white Chicagoans — to the extent that they took their ideas from jazz at all.) From the beginning you can hear a more swinging mode in the Wolverines, as in "Copenhagen" (1924), and in the early Frankie Trumbauer recordings, such as "Singing the Blues" and "Riverboat Shuffle" (both 1927 and both featuring Beiderbecke), than in the records of the same period made by King Oliver and Louis Armstrong. This was picked up and emphasized by Frank Teschemacher and the "Austin High School gang" (not all of whom attended Austin High) in 1928–30. Teschemacher wanted a sharp rough-and-ready enthusiasm that drove everything before it. His dynamic and rhythmic inventions, such as the diminuendo chorus, a whispered holding-back, before the final tumultuous ride-out, in which he himself invariably played the clarinet's high notes flat, were all aimed toward this objective. Being in tune didn't matter, relatively speaking; loud and raucous did. And these were the primary elements of most Chicago jazz from that time until it ended, between 1965 and 1970, whether the piece was something "purty" like "Singin' the Blues," a slow drag like "Sister Kate," a swinging blues like "Frair's Point" or "Tin Roof," or a rag/march like "Panama" or "Fidgety Feet."

A photograph exists of the 1927 Jean Goldkette band, including Beiderbecke and Trumbauer, sitting on top of a small bus operated by the Framingham Taxi Co. — astonishing that such a group could be touring New England at that time, only ten years after the country's first jazz recording by the Original Dixieland Jazz Band — with one of the musicians, bassist Steve Brown, sitting on the hood and flourishing what looks to me like a Colt .38 automatic.

A great deal has been made of the fact that black musicians of that period and earlier worked in brothels, barrelhouses and other such inconducive studios. They did. But white jazz musicians of the period worked in gin mills and speaks that weren't much better, many of them owned by the racketeers. The whites had the option if they wanted it — and at one time or another many of them did — of working with such orchestras as Goldkette's or Paul Whiteman's and playing at good hotels, upper-class clubs, or for college proms. They earned some money that way, and the money was no doubt good to have. But they did not learn their jazz with Goldkette or Whiteman; they worked it out in the joints, and the literature is full of stories of violence and mayhem among the customers. I expect many of those musicians packed a piece.

Chicago jazz, like any impulse in the arts, split into many different modes, dominated by the different personalities of its leading performers. But to my mind the mode I have been describing here, the music of the speaks, expressive — to the extent that any verbal designations can be attached to music — of sex and booze, a hard communal underclass optimism that carried over from the Twenties into the Depression, has been epitomized especially by Wild Bill Davison. He was born in 1906 in Ohio, formed his first band when he was in grade school, worked in a commercial dance band when he was an adolescent, played for a while in New York, then went to Chicago in about 1927, where he met Louis Armstrong, Zutty Singleton and other black musicians from New Orleans, and also Pee Wee Russell, George Wettling and the young white Chicagoans. Davison worked with most of them, though unfortunately not on many recordings. In 1932 he formed a band to work at Guyon's Paradise with Frank Teschemacher on clarinet. Late one night in February, with Davison at the wheel, they ran into a taxi and Teschemacher was killed. (One thinks, inevitably, of what might have been. One thinks of the accident nearly twenty years later on the Pennsylvania Turnpike that killed Clifford Brown and Richie Powell, Bud Powell's younger brother.) Davison, who obviously was not called Wild Bill for nothing, went off to Milwaukee (Siberia) for about ten years. Then he moved to New York in the 1940s and began playing again with his old friends from Chicago. From 1945 until about 1970 his work became stronger and stronger. He died a couple of years ago, working occasionally until the end, though without the wind or the technique of his best years. I've heard he even quit drinking in his old age.

What Davison did for Chicago jazz is easy enough to hear. For example, his recording of "Riverboat Shuffle" for Commodore Records in about 1947. (I'm using the Commodore CD, *Jazz A-Plenty*, 1989, which maddeningly gives none of the original recording numbers or dates.) The band includes Pee Wee Russell on clarinet, George Brunis on trombone, and George Wettling on drums. "Riverboat Shuffle" was originally written by Hoagy Carmichael for Bix Beiderbecke and the Wolverines in 1924 and was recorded by them for Gennett in that year; then in 1927 it was recorded for OKeh by the Trumbauer band with Beiderbecke on cornet, and this is the better of the two early recordings. The tune has two themes, minor and major, the second of which has a two-bar break at the end of each eight-bar segment (roughly speaking). On the Trumbauer recording these breaks are taken by Eddie Lang on guitar, Irving Riskin on piano, and Don Murray on clarinet — nothing very spectacular. Beiderbecke takes the final break of the first chorus and leads immediately into his solo, which is the only reason for listening to the record. He does all the things he was famous for, the upward rips, the hard high notes, the descending softer figures, and he builds his solo with considerably more complexity and fluidity than was common in that period, using long phrases within the essential eight-bar structure. Only Louis Armstrong, from whom Beiderbecke learned, could do as well in those years; and remember that Beiderbecke learned from Armstrong in person, before the revolutionary Hot Five recordings of 1926. The rest of "Riverboat Shuffle," until the final chorus, is dismal. Even Trumbauer, usually reliable, does poorly. In the final out-chorus Beiderbecke leads the ensemble vigorously, overcoming the ineptitudes of the other musicians.

Davison, who began his professional career only a couple of years later than Beiderbecke, learned more from Beiderbecke than from anyone else, and his "Riverboat Shuffle" is an intentional tribute to his teacher. But it is by no means an imitation. Davison takes all the stop-time breaks himself, for instance, but does not give himself a solo chorus. He does many things that resemble Beiderbecke's playing but never exactly reproduces them (as so many Dixielanders do), and he intensifies them by a factor of about a hundred. Beiderbecke's held-high tones were vigorous but pure in intonation. Davison's are rough, off-key, seemingly random blasts in the upper register — they are shrieks. Davison's low tones are much more growly than Beiderbecke's, his slurred tones are wider and longer, his pacing more varied and farther from the beat. He drives harder. And he has his own maneuvers too, especially the screaming upward glissando that hits its top note like the crack of a whip. His technique is heavy, rough, impudent, yet astonishingly agile. In effect Davison brought the spirit of white Chicago jazz to its peak and did it with musical perfection and the total absorption and enthusiasm that are characteristic of all great artists in every medium.

In the meantime, while Davison was at the top of his form, the bop revolution came and went, the cool revolution as well, and black jazz musicians were into the post-bop experiments and modifications of Charlie Mingus, John Coltrane, Ornette Coleman, Albert Ayler and others. I don't know what these men thought of Davison. They certainly dismissed him and may have despised him. Although one can find components of their music that might have been taken from him, clearly none were — they came from other and black antecedents. Now, with the deaths of the original Chicagoans, Chicago jazz has long since passed from the scene, without — if you don't count the thousands of people who love it and rely on it in shaping their sensibilities — leaving a trace. And this leads me to three generalizations.

First, the art that leaves no influence is no less an art on that account. It's hard to think of analogues to Chicago jazz vis-à-vis mainstream black jazz. I have called it subsidiarism, but spin-off-ism might be a more descriptive term, the case of a movement in art that evolves naturally enough from the mainstream but then branches off, runs parallel for a while, achieves its own artistic integrity and significance, but finally dies without ever rejoining the primary line of development. In fact, I cannot come up with a single other example in the history of any art, an example of an appreciable community of artists which attains a significant level of achievement but then departs without leaving a significant influence. Individuals, yes; Ambrose Bierce in American literature, Georgia O'Keefe in American painting. But the only movements I can think of that have followed this pattern have been crack-pot obtrusions achieving nothing. (Yet in religion one can think of many important heresies that died or were wiped out without reentering their parent theologies, but which left meaningful effects in the broader culture.) Nevertheless it is possible; a group can move out, create something fine, and die — right out at the end of the track. And Chicago jazz, so distinct, is the proof. Not that there weren't crossovers and affinities. The jazz associated with Fats Waller and other such small black groups in the thirties was not far from the spirit of Chicago. Waller himself and many other black musicians — from Coleman Hawkins in 1928 to Vic Dickenson in 1980 — performed both live and on record with the Chicagoans. But in impulse, attitude and style the Chicagoans had their own music.

Secondly, as jazz has evolved toward the present, I expect white influence on black musicians has increased, especially as from individual to individual. It would be surprising if such fine white musicians as Chet Baker, Charlie Haden and Steve Lacy, for example, hadn't been listened to carefully by young musicians of both races. And today, of course, if you asked young conservatory-trained black jazz musicians whether or not they've been influenced by white musicians, my guess is that they'd say, "Naturally — just as we've been influenced by Asian musicians, Arabic musicians, rock musicians, and all musicians." Of course they'd be talking, with respect to whites, primarily about "classical" musicians, and not Stravinsky and Bartok either, but Adams and Reich. A general rapprochement has occurred; music is music, and the question of race has become moot. It's interesting — though I am distinctly of two minds about it — that this has happened not as much through social and political processes as through the music itself.

Thirdly, for a long time we have been putting too much emphasis on the new, and we have now reached the point at which the new has run out. We have reached absurdity. In jazz we have run the whole course from primitivism to sophistication to academicism and preciosity in less than a hundred years, thanks to the technology of recording. Records give us the old, meaning what was done last year, in such concrete permanent form that musicians have naturally been impelled to do something different right away. But the course has been run. And the course was perhaps not such a good idea to begin with. Jazz musicians are universally graded by the critics on their novelty. A.B. Spellman, in his *Four Lives in the Bebop Business* (1966, 1985) chooses his four biographees, Cecil Taylor, Ornette Coleman, Herbie Nichols, and Jackie McLean, because he believes each of them did something that the older bop musicians — not much older — had not yet done. They made "progress." (Some of them called their work "progressive.") Spellman refers to jazz before bop as "social music." Well, I hope all music is social, but that isn't what Spellman means. He means that earlier jazz musicans often had to play in dance bands to make their livings. But is he talking about the likes of Sidney Bechet, Henry Allen, Chu Berry, Joe Venutti, Charlie Christian, Art Tatum? Is he placing these serious artists on the plane of T. Dorsey and G. Lombardo? This is nonsense. In his essay called "The Passing of Jazz's Old Guard," which is reprinted in his *Tuxedo Junction* (1989), Gerald Early writes about Charles Mingus,

Thelonious Monk, and Sonny Stitt. Is it only because I was born in 1921, the year in which Mamie Smith recorded "Crazy Blues" and started off the whole business of recorded black jazz, that I cannot think of these men as "Jazz's Old Guard"? Jazz did not begin in 1942. Nor did it begin in 1982, as some young people today believe. No one knows exactly when it did begin, as a matter of fact, but it has been going on since 1910 or earlier, and it has always been real jazz — if that isn't a redundancy.

Nowadays when I go down to Sakura's in Syracuse I hear a young guy who can do circular breathing perfectly, he can do it for hours if anyone wants him to, he can play three saxophones at the same time, loudly, and he can play not only the changes on "My Funny Valentine," but the changes on the changes, and the changes on the changes on the changes, a veritable mathematical tizzy. And I ask myself why he doesn't just relax and play some jazz. The truth is he can't; both his training and the pressures exerted on him by current fashion have destroyed his ability to invent a counter-melody or para-melody worth a damn.

In all the arts I see people struggling, usually in an academic milieu, to discover some novelty of form, structure, concept or style that will permit them to qualify as the avant-garde, but I do not see them succeeding, except in the most pedantic, uninteresting, feelingless ways. In both reason and practice we *know* that unending novelty is an impossibility. No one can foresee what the extended future may bring in jazz, or in painting or literature, but in the shorter view the age of experiment is obviously over. The time demands recapitulation, not innovation. This doesn't mean direct imitativeness of the past — not at all; it means an honest and creative regard for tradition, including recent tradition, it means going back and filling in the gaps that were passed over in the onrush of recorded progress, restoring connections, reviving combinations, as Branford Marsalis does, for example, in his best work. And anyway, hasn't newness in the arts always been essentially a matter, not of calculated or conceptual change, but of personality, both individual and collective? The *dolce stil nuovo* was not engineered in a workshop; it was derived intuitively from the sensibilities of half a dozen northern Italian poets who had certain traditions, old Latin and new Provençal, floating in their heads and sounding in their ears.

It would be great if we could quit listening to so many records and hear live jazz instead. In a city like Syracuse, with a metropolitan population of 750,000, we ought to have six or eight places where we could go regularly to hear different kinds of jazz, not just the one-and-a-half actually here, and we ought to be able to sit comfortably and listen to the music without being deafened by overamplification. I can think of a good many reasons why this may be impossible, why it may never happen again. And I won't give up my records for anything. But I do think in our music — and in our poetry, painting, film, and all the arts — we must, at least for a while, just relax and play some jazz.

Drum of Poetry, Drum of War
Willard Gingerich

THE AZTEC UPRIGHT DRUM, *tlalpan huehuetl*, stood totally silent in the Metropolitan exhibit from Mexico, headless, covered with a swirling visual text which includes two carved eagles and three jaguars, each uttering the sign of holy conflagration in war, "blazing water"; on one side a transfigured warrior rising up in eagle attire — *quauhtlehuanitl* "eagle rising," a figure of the sun from dawn to midday — and opposite him a drooping eye at the axis of a quincunx, pierced south to north by a short, angular dart — the calendrical sign 4 Motion, the name of this fifth age of the world, destined to collapse in earthquake, pestilence and fire.

Niquetza in tohuehueuh niquinnechicoa in tocnihuan ymellel quiza niquin-cuicatia tiazque ye ichan ximotlamachtican ximocuiltonocan in antocnihuan ahuaya

"I erect our drum; I collect our friends, driving out their griefs; for them I make music. We go to fill that House of Death. O friends! Live in plenty, rejoice in happiness, *ahuaya*" (Cantares mexicanos, f. 52v.)

Huehuetitlan — "Drumming place," where whistles, clay flutes, gourd and turtle-shell rattles, gold bells, bone rasps all harmonized with dances of exquisite order and songs of a baroque melancholy almost unimaginable now. The performance context in the cities of Azcapotzalco, Coyoacan, Tetzcoco, or Tenochtitlan-Mexico of which this one-meter-high drum, now referred to as the Malinalco drum, was once the living center is still accessible in fragments of memory.

One of the principal things found throughout this land were the songs and dances, both for solemnizing the festival of the demons they honored as gods, with which they thought to render them great service, and for enjoyment and private solace . . ., and every lord had in his house a 'chapel' with singers who composed dances and songs; and these worked to become ingenious in the composition of songs according to the method of meter or stanzas which they had, and when these were good basses they were held in much esteem, because the lords had them sing daily in low voices.

273

Ordinarily they sang and danced in the principal festivals which were every twenty days, and in others less important. The principal dances were held in the plazas; other times in the patio of the lord's house, as all the lords had great patios: they also danced in the houses of lords and men of distinction.

Whenever there had been some victory in war, or a new lord had been installed, or married to a noblewoman, or for some other occasion, the song-masters composed a new song, in addition to those general songs they already had for the festivals of the demons and of great ancient deeds and of the lords long dead.

They rehearsed the song material several days before the festivals; in the large pueblos the singers were numerous and if there were new songs or dances others joined them so there would be no defect on the day of the festival. On the day appointed for the dance they put out in the morning a great mat in the center of the plaza where the drums were to stand and everyone gathered and adorned themselves as in the house of the lord, and from there emerged dancing and singing. At times the dances began in the morning and other times at the hour of Great Mass. At night they returned singing to the palace, and there finished the song at the first hour of evening or late at night and at midnight.

The drums were of two types: the first was tall and round, thicker than a man, of five hands height, of very fine wood, hollowed out inside and carved and painted without; over the mouth they placed a deerskin, tanned and well stretched. From the border to the center it played a perfect fifth [*diapente*] and they play it from one point and note to another, rising and falling, harmonizing and inclining the drum to their songs. The other drum is [made of wood with two tongues over a resonance chamber]; this serves as a bass and both have a fine sound and can be heard at a distance. When the dancers have arrived at their positions, they place themselves in order to play the drums: two singers, the best, come forward as choir directors who begin from there the songs. The great leather drum is played with the hands and is called the *huehuetl*, and the other, as the drums of Spain, with sticks, although it is of a distinct fashion, and is called the *teponaztli*. The lord with other principal persons and old men goes dancing before the drums; these parade for four or five meters about the drums and then with these comes a multitude filling and swelling the chorus. The number of those who pass in this fashion in the large pueblos is more than a thousand and sometimes more than two thousand. In addition to these and around them goes a procession of two orders of dancing young men, fine dancers; the two leaders are two men detached from the principal dancers, who go leading the dance. In these two wheels, with certain turns and pirouettes which they do, sometimes they have as partner the dancer in front and in some dances the one in the rear. . . . Before the wars, when they celebrated the festivals freely, in the large pueblos three or four thousand and more gathered to dance. After the conquest, half that number, which has continued to diminish and decline.

. . . [In the dance] their entire bodies, heads as well as arms and hands, move in such concert, measured and ordered, that they do not disagree nor differ from one another even a half beat, but what one does with the right foot, also

274

the left, the same do all and in the same measure and beat; when one lowers the left arm and raises the right, so at the same time and in the same beat do all, in such manner that the drums and the song and the dancers all carry their measure in concert: all are in harmony, one differs from another not a jot, by which those dancers of Spain who have seen it are greatly amazed, and hold in great esteem the dances of these natives, and the great accord and feeling which they have and preserve for them. (Fr. Toribio de Benavente "Motolinía, *Memoriales*, ca. 1540; edition of O'Gorman, 1971)

And here is told how the lords arrayed themselves when they danced:

Headband with quetzal feather tassels set in gold which bound up the hair;
Quetzal feather crest device set in gold and worn on the back; A worked headdress of red spoonbill feathers with a fan of quetzal feathers and a small *huehuetl* drum of yellow gold, a device worn on the back while dancing;
A gold arm band, yellow;
Yellow gold ear plugs inserted;
A leather wrist band with a great, smooth jade or perhaps turquoise worn on his wrist and treated with Peru balsam so that it would gleam and shine;
A jade lip plug set in yellow gold;
A long, white labret of crystal set in yellow gold and pierced through with blue cotinga feathers, inserted in the lip;
A turquoise nose ornament;
A necklace of radiating yellow gold shells with a thin jade stone set in it;
Quetzal feather horns;
A quetzal feather fan set in gold;
Flowers, tobacco only for the ruler;
Jaguar-skin sandals, embroidered leather sandals.
. . .
Flowering trees were erected in the courtyard when the Speaker himself would dance.
(Informants of Sahagún, *Florentine Codex*, Book 8, Chapter 9; ca. 1540–65; edition of Dibble & Anderson)

It is war that adorns the Malinalco drum; the eagles and jaguars are figures of the two principal knightly orders which occupied a palace and armory next to the central pyramid of the Templo Mayor inside the temple precinct of Tenochtitlan. The transfigured warrior on the drum is the finest image we have of the war-frenzy, a sacred state of transcendence, described often in the *cuauhcuicatl* or *yaocuicatl* "eagle songs, war songs" of the Cantares mexicanos manuscript, a state which could be invoked and mimicked by the hypnosis of the drum and the chant but could only be consummated in *yaoxochimiquiztli* "the flowering war death" itself, on the battlefield or face-up across the sacrificial altar. Both Itzcoatl, founding "emperor" of the Aztec Alliance, and Nezahualcoyotl, poet-ruler of Tetzcoco, are reported to have carried small *huehuetl* drums into combat, using them as a call to valor and exertion.

A shield-roaring, a smoking blaze rises up; Ah, and rising up as bell dust it becomes your flowers, Yaotzin, Beloved Enemy; there on all sides sound the eagles, the jaguars, *ohuaya*.

He shows men only mercy, he gives only friendship in the whirling dust of conflagration; reed flowers turn gold, a mist of obsidian rains down and blossoms, *ohuaya*.

Fertile land of war-flowers, *aya*, the butterfly-shield house, there with lances Motecuzoma recounts, he paints his flower-books of bloody fire; and back in Mexico he barters sun-chalk [on the sacrificial bodies].
(Cantares mexicanos, f. 61v.; Bierhorst, p. 349)

But now the drum is mute. No transcription of Aztec music survives and no contemporary Nahuatl-speaking people retain their traditional music. Scattered throughout the Cantares manuscript, however, are the infamous drumming notations made of combinations of four syllables: *ti*, *to*, *qui*, and *co*. On folio 27, for example, a song is introduced with "TICO TOCO TOCO TIQUITIQUITI QUITI QUITO. And just this way it turns and and comes back." On folio 28v: "TICO TOCO TOCOTO. When it ends: TICOTO TICOTO." And a 6-page song begins on folio 50 with instruction for one drum — "the tone: COTOTIQUITITI TOTOCOTO" — going on to add ten more drums, each with a new notation for cadence. Most of these notations specify the *teponaztli* wooden drum, but this latter set refers specifically to the standing *huehuetl* so they cannot, in their four-part TI-TO-QUI-CO formulation correspond to specific notes, since the two drums played at different harmonic intervals (minor third and perfect fifth, respectively), and, as Bierhorst points out, this one set of verbal notations must account for both pitch and rhythm. Then on folio 7 of the Cantares manuscript there is a brief paragraph which attempts to describe a *huehuetl* drumming technique. Its translation has been the cause of much imaginative argument among ethnopoetic readers.

Auh inic motzotzona huehuetl: cencamatl mocauhtiuh, auh yn occencamatl ipan huetzi yetetl ti: auh in huel ic ompehua ca centetl ti, Auh inic mocuepa quinyquac yticpa huetzi y huehuetl zan mocemana in maitl, auh quiniquac i ye inepantla occeppa itenco hualcholoa in huehuetl: tel yehuatl itech mottaz, in ima yn aquin cuicani quimati in iuh motzotzona.
(Cantares mexicanos, f. 7; Bierhorst, p. 152)

The several translations and discussions of this passage which have appeared in English recently have pretty much abandoned previous work on the question by Garibay (1953), Schultze Jena (1957), Nowotny (1956), and Stevenson (1968). First, Bierhorst, from his 1985 edition and translation of the Cantares:

And the drum is beaten thus: when a stanza ends and another stanza is to follow, it's three-beat. And when it actually begins, it's one-beat. But as it comes back in, then the drum falls beneath it, and the hand just keeps on going. But when it is in the middle, again the voice of the drum emerges. This, however, must be seen from the hand of the singer who knows how it is beaten.

Next, Richard Haly, whose analysis in "Poetics of the Aztecs," *New Scholar* 10 (1986), is the most detailed theory of Aztec drumming technique available in English:

And in the following manner is the *huehuetl* played: a *cencamatl* runs to its end and [in the meantime] on it three TI [drum tones] fall and just as it [the *cencamatl*] begins there is one TI and in order for it [the hand] to return to where it was, it then rises from within the *huehuetl*. The hand just continues and then when there are three [drumbeats] in the middle, once again it [the hand] jumps to the edge of the drum. Nonetheless, one will see this in the hand of a singer who knows how it is played.

Haly points out that *cencamatl*, which means "a mouthful of food," "a word," or "a few words," is here employed in a precise structural sense. Using Dow Robinson's classification of micro-, meso-, and macro-segments within Nahuatl clause structure, Haly identifies the macro-segment, a semantic clustering of one to eight words and sentence-words with a single strong accent on the penultimate syllable, as the basic unit of Nahuatl verse, a *cencamatl*. Then, by setting the TI of the drum notations in correspondence with the stressed syllables of the macro-segment clause in the songs, Haly claims that "the drumbeat and linguistic stress coincide," the length of the poetic line may be established, and poetry divided cleanly from prose.

Bierhorst is less sure of the correspondences between linguistic stress and drum notation. He sets forth only two propositions about the notations: 1) "the syllables TI, TO, CO and QUI form a kind of solfège, or vocalise, that corresponds to the cadence of the drum," and 2) "this vocalise must account for both pitch and rhythm." He then postulates that the vowels *i* and *o* represent the two pitches of the *teponaztli* drum and the consonants *t* and *k* indicate the rhythm in something like the pattern of single-, double-, and triple-tonguing used by woodwind players. As for correspondence between drumming and voice, Bierhorst believes "little or nothing can be stated with certainty. . . . It would certainly be difficult, if not impossible, to recite a heterorhythmic chant while beating out one of the metrical cadences described," and "of the drumming instructions connected with actual songs in the manuscript, none can be safely recommended for self-accompaniment." His final judgment is that the chant itself was nonmetrical in any stress- or syllable-counting sense, even though the drum cadences are metrical, and any one-to-one correspondence between drumbeat and linguistic stress is therefore impossible.

My own version of the Cantares paragraph is as follows:

And thus is the huehuetl played: As a *cencamatl* is ending, and during the *cencamatl*, three TIs fall. In its beginning it is just one TI. And so it repeats, then it falls in the center of the drum, the hand just continues [playing in the center]. And then three [beats] in the middle [half-way between center and edge of the drumhead] and again [the hand] comes quickly out to the edge of the drum. Nevertheless, one must see the hands of a singer who knows how to play in this fashion.

Without attempting to erect a musical scaffold which would threaten to collapse the text, I will only suggest that the TI mentioned seems to refer to the drum's high note, played at the margin of the drumhead. Each strophe or verse unit — Haly is right in insisting that the "mouthful" here, the *cencamatl*, is a prosodic term — begins with one high beat on the margin, moves to the lowest note a fifth below at the center of the drumhead where it plays for the body of the verse (which seems to me necessarily much longer than the macro-segment Haly describes) and then closes with three intermediate beats and a final, higher TI again, where it started, at the margin of the drumhead. Lacking a tape recorder, as Dell Hymes has pointed out, one needs a good theory; but in Nahuatl studies, even with the tightest theory, one must struggle for a perceptive translation.

Between the shrill echoes of war and the silence of the drum, poetry calls us back to the old theme of Homer: Wars are fought so that poets will have matter to write about, a pretext to imagine their own voices still sweet and singing a thousand years off.

An quaauhnenelihui oceloihcuiliuhtimanique in tepilhuan ayahue maza yicxochiuh onchichinalo yehua oc achica ye nica ohuaya.
O ahquenman aya ahquenman polihuiz in ihuehueuh in icuic o yn ipalnemoa xonahuia nopiltzi tehuatzi ohuiya a'nochipa tlalticpac, ohuaya.

As eagles they are scattered and gone, as jaguars painted in memory, the princes, *ayahue*; His flowers, they are inhaled but for a moment here, *ohuaya*.

O never, *aya*, never will they be lost, the drum, the songs of He Who Gives Life; my prince, venerable lord, take your ease, *ohuiya*; such a brief time, this earth, *ohuaya*. (Cantares mexicanos, f. Bierhorst, 242.)

NOTE. All translations are by the author.

Echoes

Stephen Ratcliffe

WHEN THOMAS MORLEY set these words to music

> No, No, Nigella!
> Let who list prove thee
> I cannot love thee
> Have I deserved
> Thus to be served?
> Well then content thee,
> If thou repent thee.
> *(First Book of Ballets to Five Voyces, 1595)*

the music altered the words (and us) in ways the words themselves could not. We hear five voices, intoning a "No" that becomes in effect negative to the fifth power — Soprano, high D; Second Soprano, B; Alto or Tenor, G; Tenor or Bass, D; Bass, G below C; followed by three more intonations of that same "No" in each part; multiplied by five parts, equals twenty times "No" sounded as an echo of thought so insistent how could Nigella, whoever she may be, think the answer (to what question?) might be other than "No":

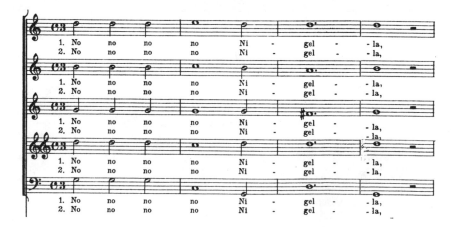

280

After the third verse line, "I cannot love thee" (rejection, farewell, the breaking off of love conventional though it may be) a listener ("Nigella," say, or anyone who can empathize) will hear:

A second barrage of apparently meaningless syllables enters at the end of the first stanza, when the words hold out their sudden hope of happiness in love "If thou repent thee," after which the non-sense of fa la las speeding as much as 8 or 16 times *faster* than the words just sung, the map of music making of words a grid whose staggered starts and stops overlap in sheets too dense to be unfolded by ear alone, though the eye can discern from score what goes on at any given point.

281

---

triads, the same kind
involving
consecutive fifths

"If the singing of words is to be thought of as intoned speech, which it is, then for any singer the main question is: 'Who's talking?'" (Virgil Thomson). One thinks of improvisation, then, not by the poet or composer but by the speaker, as in *Semper Dowland, Semper Dolens*: that repeats may be heard filling the viola part with notes rising and slowly falling to final a touch at the root of what begins in the next bar, say measure, as music times thought's next step.

---

what the words note, short
of meaning
pace say, legs that stride

What happens when the words of a poem are put into the air by a voice or voices intoning syllables at certain precisely measured pitches held for certain precisely indicated durations? And how is it that when the words of a poem are "sung" the result in its effect is *more* than either of its constituent components, its words, its music? The quality of feeling (if it can be called that provisionally) sails forward, as if to register the singer/speaker's heart's core, as in Dowland's air "Flow my tears."

---

the page opposite
songs, of which
the highest "compasse"

Four of the five voice parts of Gesualdo's "Io parto," 1611,

Second Soprano	Io parto e non piu dissi
Tenor	Io parto e non piu dissi
Alto	Io parto e non piu dissi
Bass	Io parto e non piu dissi

begin declamatorily, all four voices singing at once with words clear into air, everything that follows straining emotion as words fracture, bend, twist, half- and quarter-turns that aim to explore what range of emotion and sense it might be possible to arrive at, singing.

>how long a silence
>before this
>of faces, bodies

Morley tells us that after dinner people would gather with the books to sing ("because Italy is the source for us, and inspiration for the English to sing"):

Soprano	April is in my Mistress' face, April is
Alto	April is in my Mistress' face
Tenor	April is
Bass	April is

After this relatively straightforward beginning of parts (Soprano singing with Alto, Tenor with Bass) the identities of separate voices begin to collapse, convolute:

Soprano	in my Mistress' face my Mistress; face, April is		
Alto	April is in my Mistress face	April is	
Tenor	in my Mistress'	face,	April is in my Mistress'
Bass	in my Mistress' face		April is in my Mistress'

>the sort of performance
>one *is*, one
>stamped the other hand

Another kind of repetition: when voices sing the same or different syllables in unison one hears vertical as well as horizontal sound, the words on top of one another high to low, Soprano-Alto-Tenor-Bass. ("When you see this sign : ||: of repetition you must begin again, making the notes next before the sign (whatsoever) in the first singing." [Morley])

>At this repeat, both
>Altus and
>Quintus exchange parts

Measured song, a property of singing, is nothing else but the difference between thought and the sound it makes, thinking pitch. What one poet would make of his perception the moment brain synapse fires, chemistry of cells, pink light on the wall the morning calls, the world already well awake.

> pronounced — really *pronounced*
> in proportion to
> one such matter, creatures

Music delivers the emotional impact of the text, as if the single word could come forward or lift above its role in the text of all words, whose background the key determines will be spent, making that once the feeling most concerned.

> after a list called
> days, a base
> two or three say, more

"And therefore those plainsongs which were so contained were called 'natural' because every key of their six notes stood invariable the one to the other however the notes were named, as from D sol re to E la mi always a whole note whether one did sing sol la or Re mi, and so forth of others . . ." (Morley)

> if ground on a page
> wants comfort
> conscious — continuous

Marenzio's "Solo e pensoso i più deserti campi" (1500), the voice taking notes or measure of when the syllables should be spoken/ sung, express all that (dis)content could mean. Petrarch's text, which would have us believe the fiction of sole self, "alone and pensive, the deserted fields/ I measure with deliberate and slow steps," pulling at the edges of one's ability to follow such a falling forward. Or trying to be able to stop.

to be written about
under feet
as find "things" to do

Gesualdo, the most experimental of all the Italians, looking to the color of chromaticism as clear message of the text, because everything that unfolds say from the opening line — "To parto e non più dissi che il dolore"— aims to hear the words, their pull to the heart of what meaning can approach in the body of the person who hears and so *does* feel their pull. The pluck of a stringed instrument circa 1600 is no different today, can't it be said, in the condition we face knowing the truth the words are sign to. Everything that unfolds is an emotional response to the *what* of the line, its play to sympathy or content, what in the medium of language could rhyme with (echo) the world sense perceives, say of the body as it leaves the room, closing the glass door.

the air one thinks is
thick, staircase
like a letter, tree

Or take the freedom to break a text, emphasize the motion and emotion of syllables each of *whom* carry the sign of what's missing, wanted, or found. "— not being careful to see the strokes meet at right angles, the figure ' ' confounded with the sign which is this 'X' made thus 'X.'"

Expressionism
lying down
oxygen, leaves the bells

So that one can hear each note clearly, the better and more attractive the embellishment that lifts or drags syllables where without notes no sense of that would be, say on the words "fained," "pit-," "at," "long," "-nough," "place," "joyes," "cold," "freeze."

---

ascending a third,
descending,
ascending a fourth

This too is a kind of improvisation. The singer sings it in a way
another would not think of, but would herself sing with *other* notes,
each configuration (of notes) having its own name, and "meaning"
if that could be said with respect to pitch on a fixed scale.

Pavana Lachimae:
John Dowland
sett foorth by Wm. Byrd

Or what is it that happens when one hears several voices intoning
different words or parts of words at once? The same instance say to
sound "tears," "like," "like," "to," "the," "mor-," "the," "mor-," "-ning,"
"-ning," then, at once, "showers" — as if that sudden resolution to the
problem of how to get things said by most direct means, the economics of the syllable as currency in a system whose standard of
exchange is the language it lifts by increments into the air.

---

back up stairs, descending
starter kind
of meaning a voice

The sense music delivers of space, as in air the notes could fill were
they sent full blown (voiced or plucked) outward, the body then entering that space *between* one who sings and one who listens, not
the reader (merely) but now active participant, co-conspirator in
the creation of what comes to be known (through the ear) as meaning, the feeling of it *who living had no note.*

---

horizon ochre
painting, drift
can be something one sees

The rhythm of the galliard, say, as one-two-three-four followed by lift the dancer would raise a foot or hand to partner, the other half to whom words "Awake, sweet love" have been addressed as premonitory to love, the act of which song stands as foreplay. (One hears the soprano on top of other voices, leading the way, the pairing of other dance steps inside the circle written out as notes the lute plays, up to and including repeats.)

————————

hear the door, a shirt
someone wears
to think the sense of

————————

The intervals of two falling fourths in Dowland's "Flow, my tears, fall from your springs" want resolution. In the performance of such a thought sung to notes whose impulse is to move (down or up) to where the pitch can *stay* closed, notes as echo stopped, one hears the poet's "voice" in a musical dimension whose boundaries are defined in range by pitches the voice sings (strings following) as layers in the fabric of sound whose threads weave the texture of "feeling" the words would at best suggest. So that what the reader of words alone can at most *imagine*, the emotion say behind these lines,

> Flow, my tears, fall from your springs!
> Exiled for ever let me mourn;
> Where night's black bird her sad infamy sings,
> There let me live forlorn"

becomes known by the addition that is the expansion of *sound* ordered by these "directions" of notes — how the words will be delivered — not then through eye (the reader's) to brain but ear (the listener's) as port to what sense most means, unfolding sound:

287

this is a song for
calling back
spirits of the dead

The feeling "behind" or "of" these words, say of a person being "sad" or "depressed," the music brings out as pure *emotion*, so that when one hears the song being sung by this voice, accompanied by lute and bass, one is taken farther (emotionally) than by the words themselves, to where "meaning" becomes visceral, stunning. The music makes adjustment to our perception of text, what we think we hear when we read those words.

say "in the hills of Thailand"
gymnastics
the air, local, shapes

In Morley's anthology *The Triumphs of Oriana* (1601), composed of madrigals he collected from twenty-three of his contemporaries, each song ends with the words "Long live fair Oriana." When Thomas Weelkes set that line to six voice parts he pulled out all the stops so to speak, in order to play at what words set to music might make as blanket/sheets of sound:

Stephen Ratcliffe

what part of you is
the poem, lute
the sound of wings and beaks

The twentieth song in Morley's *Canzonets, Or Little Short Songs To Three Voyces* (1593), "Arise, get up, my dear," is a kind of mini-Epithalamium calling for the bride to wake and prepare herself for the rites of marriage. But the music to which these words are sung makes such "reading" beside the point, in that a listener can all but *not hear* the words, nor discern their "sense," music in effect overwhelming the "meaning" of the words — words set to music having become fractured, fragmented, broken apart, broken down say into the syllable-as-unit-of-(non)sense. For example, when this portion of the line "Spice cakes, sops in wine are now a dealing" is sung, one is likely to hear different particles sung at the same time: "sops" plus "wine" plus "are," "in" plus "O" plus "a," "wine" plus "fine" plus "deal-." The song in effect moves at each point both horizontally, along the line, and vertically, as stacks of syllables which, sounded simultaneously create meanings more complex than those made when the line is "read" by a single voice:

Soprano: deal - ing   spice cake sops   in wine
Alto: spice cake sops   in wine, O fine, spice cake sops in
Tenor: spice cake   sops in wine, sops in   wine

Soprano: sops in wine are now a   deal - ing
Alto: wine, O fine, are a   deal   -   ing
Tenor: are   a deal - ing, are a - deal - ing

across the table
voices round
a corner, swerving

Look at how the setting of these last lines of the poem generates the confusion of frenetic action the words "talk about" but, by themselves, leave to a reader's imagination — action the same words sung to notes put into the air, as real as event itself:

Soprano: and how the maids jerk it, with Kate and Will
Alto: and   see how the maids jerk   it, jerk   it,
Tenor: how the maids jerk it, with Kate and Will, Tom and Jill

Soprano:	Tom and Jill,	now	a skip,	then a trip	fine-ly set	a
Alto:	with	Kate and Will, and Jill,	now a trip,	then a skip,		
Tenor:	hey	ho	brave,	now a skip,	then a trip, fine	ly

Soprano:	-loft	there a-gain as oft	hey	ho bless-ed		
Alto:	fine-ly set a - loft,	there a-gain	as oft	O	fine	
Tenor:	set a loft	all for fair	Daph -	ne's Daph ne's		

Soprano:	ho - li -	ho - li -	day.	
Alto:	brave ho -	- -	li - day.	
Tenor:	wed -	ding wed - ding	day.	

---

the car whose brakes squeal
as it angles
left (miraculous)

Or to see/hear the violence music might wreak upon the words of a text, think of the fifth song in Morley's *The First Book of Canzonets To Two Voyces* (1595):

Miraculous, love's wounding!
E'en those darts my sweet Phyllis
So fiercely shot against my heart rebounding,
Are turned to roses, violets and lilies,
With odor sweet abounding.

One composition in music fractures a second attendant composition in words. The result is a staggering of voices, like starting a race around a track, the person in the outside lane going first, leading off, followed by others who catch and then pass him, perhaps, only to be overtaken toward the end, a photo finish. Here say the words of the Soprano and Tenor parts printed out as separate strands, linear but circular, the same words repeating (hypnotically) again and again:

Soprano: Miraculous love's wounding, love's wounding, miraculous love's wounding, miraculous love's wounding. Miraculous love's wounding, miraculous love's wounding, miraculous love's wounding. E'en those darts my sweet Phyllis, E'en those darts my sweet Phyllis, So fiercely shot against my heart rebounding, rebounding. Are turn'd to roses, violets and lilies, violets and lilies, with odor sweet abounding sweet abounding, with odor sweet abounding. Miraculous love's wounding, miraculous love's wounding, miraculous love's wounding, miraculous love's wounding, love's wounding, miraculous love's wounding, miraculous love's wounding.

Tenor: Miraculous love's wounding, miraculous love's wounding,
miraculous love's wounding. Miraculous love's wounding, love's wounding,
miraculous love's wounding, miraculous love's wounding. E'en those darts
my sweet Phyllis, E'en those darts my sweet Phyllis, so fiercely shot
against my heart rebounding, rebounding, rebounding. Are turn'd to
roses, violets and lilies, violets and lilies, with odor sweet
abounding, with odor sweet abounding. Miraculous love's wounding, love's
wounding, miraculous love's wounding, miraculous love's wounding.
Miraculous love's wounding, miraculous love's wounding, miraculous
love's wounding.

> blasting words a part
> music calls
> what it means to speak

Words register an emotion, sadness say, or excitement: he's "up" or
"down." And music, assuming it "follows" words in the order or
process of composition (which might assume as well a simultaneity
of that process, putting words and music forward together as collaboration in the trading of "parts" or "voices" as in improvisatory
jazz, a conversing then of the two mediums), plays into that emotion, pushes it toward what amounts to emotion "squared," that
quality of feeling to which words as abstract sign refer (that is to
say *point*).

> the voice about to
> enter air
> which came first, of course

Think of music as the echo of thought, as in Campion's poem
"Follow Your Saint," whose words ask that its music follow a person
as echo — "the music that her echo is" — a person who in the convention isn't so much a unique individual as "she" is one's "thought":
who or what such a person might be. As if the music were the
echo of a person who is herself an idea, and so might be *the echo
of thought* (and words): how the words of poems set to music are
echoed by that music, when the voice that sings the words puts
them into the air.

> common daylight, think
> the beat is
> as words hit, accent

Music can slow the words down, so that when one reads the words to the first stanza of this poem:

> Follow your saint, follow with accent sweet,
> Haste you, sad notes, fall at her flying feet.
> There, wrapped in cloud of sorrow, pity move,
> And tell the ravisher of my soul I perish for her love:
> But, if she scorns my never-ceasing pain,
> Then burst with sighing in her sight and ne'er return again.

the tempo one reads it at "normally" is faster than what one hears in a performance of the song. Notes can also pick up the length of syllables and make them more definite:

Haste you, sad notes, fall at her fly - ing feet.

But in a line like "And tell the ravisher of my soul I perish for her love," the quick little words ("And," "the," "of," "my," "I," "for," "her") and syllables ("rav-ish-er") that one would tend to read relatively quickly are instead slowed by the music, which *drags* them as if across the rocks of this speaker's exposed, heart-felt concern.

> rhythm as form, tea
> when it leaves
> the cup a white ridge

Music is there to *serve* the words, as speaker is there to serve the lady. It follows the words the way music is supposed to follow the person who is herself *made of words*. Or thought. So to ask, Are words in the foreground, notes meant to set them forward, as into ear?

> an arrangement, cord
> mandate or
> date with man whose hand

Or think of the difference between the words of this poem:

> In darkness let me dwell, the ground shall sorrow be;
> The roof despair to bar all cheerful light from me;
> The walls of marble black that moistened still shall weep;
> My music hellish jarring sounds to banish friendly sleep.
> Thus wedded to my woes, and bedded to my tomb,
> O let me living, living die, till death do come.

and these same words sung to John Dowland's music. Pace for one thing: it must take five times as long to sing the song (with duration of notes, musically dictated repeats, rests and so on) as it does to read its words only. This is now a performance — by musician, and singer who projects words into the air accompanied by notes which sometimes dictate they slow down or speed up or go up or go down in pitch, and sometimes *repeat* in ways the words by themselves do not. Look at what happens to the words of the poem's last line ("O let me living, living die, till death do come") given the song's *direction* for that line: "O let me living, let me living living die, till death till death do come, till death till death do come, till death till death do come."

---

over sum of parts
the gods know
have not yet returned

With a musical head and musical tail, and music that dictates that the words "In darkness let me dwell" also are repeated as a final echo, music in effect wraps the landscape of words in its atmosphere of notes: imparts additional closure to the closure provided by the words themselves, "till death do come," which rhyme with "to my tomb," providing the closure both rhyme and sense dictates.

---

engages lines at
contact, say
the staff, voice enters

"The ability of certain musical configurations, or groups and orders of configurations, to elicit particular active or emotive responses in their hearers" (John Hollander). And yet, in song, the words are still

293

in the foreground, Dowland's music in this case trailing along like a shadow, or echo of thought's measure, providing what visceral sense of feeling the words would point to as theirs: in this case, man at edge of despair—asking to dwell in darkness, his music "hellish jarring sounds to banish . . . sleep."

---

entrance, after which
to carry
it forward, begin

"All vowels, for instance, even those called short, are capable of some extension in singing" (Virgil Thomson). As if words entering the ear might be made to carry with them degrees of heart's feeling. As if you heard the word "the" sung in a minor key, to a descending set of notes, it might make your heart break.

---

to go faster, then
syllables
in another tongue

What the words note short of meaning is pace: one voice moving together with others, legs in the stride from this place to that marking the space of one's time here, the strings one pulls so to speak of the position words hold on a page the line in its dynamics measures as sound the echo of thought would find, sounding itself.

---

extend the culture
of speaking
this wall in lines, light

Music as echo of thought or what we mean when we say "the heart" as center of feeling, that place where perception turns to what it means to say "this moves me," which notes as vibration in air, non-referential for all that, can make happen—by pace, by pitch, in time.

———————————

the dots are notes, based
in or on
the notion one writes

———————————

Or, as Annie writes,

once, a violin
pulled my heart
straight from my body

Theme
Carl Rakosi

How delightful

         to discover

on Olympus

         a god

of Silence

         (and not a minor

one either).

         Hail Harpocrates!

How reassuring

         that you are still here

to protect us

         against the theorists.

War Wounds

David Shields

NORTH VIETNAMESE OR VIET CONG forces shot down an Air Vietnam commercial airliner over the Central Highlands, killing all
twenty-six people aboard. Pasadena Superior Judge Walter Evans
sentenced Billy Joe Booker to death in the gas chamber for abduct-
ing a Monrovia woman and her fourteen-month-old daughter from a
shopping center parking lot and then beating them to death with a
seventeen-pound rock. According to the Bureau of Land Management, recent Barstow-to-Las Vegas motorcycle race destroyed vegeta-
tion and substantially reduced small-animal population in the high
desert region of southern California. The 16,000-ton tanker July Star
broke in two and sank off the coast of Algiers; there was no sign
of the crew of thirty-five. Although air strikes and mining were
prohibited under the Paris agreement ending U.S. involvement in
Vietnam, General William Westmoreland, former U.S. military com-
mander in Vietnam, said that President Ford should be given authority to launch B-52 air strikes in Indochina and mine the Haiphong
harbor because, according to Westmoreland, the only language Hanoi
understood was the language of force.

And that was the good news, because the bad news was that the
Selective Service System had just held its national lottery, establish-
ing the random sequence lottery number of all men who had reached
or would reach age nineteen during the calendar year 1975: Gookus
and me, among others. Everyone who had a lottery number above the
administrative processing number would remain 1-H, the holding
classification, and would not be subject to further Selective Service
processing while everyone who had received a lottery number equal
to or below the administrative processing number would be reclassi-
fied into a category available for induction. In the event the military
draft was resumed, these men would be in the first group for possible
call-up next year; each year after that, they'd fall into a lower priority
until they were no longer liable for the draft, normally at age twenty-
six. Anyone born in 1956 who did not yet know his lottery number
could call the radio station. The car careened.

Jesus Christ, Gookus said. Watch where you're going, man.

Fucking news, I said.

What news?

Weren't you listening? The lottery, Gookus. I bet I got drafted.

Don't register.

I already did.

Idiot.

I thought you had to. I thought they threw you in jail if you didn't.

Think about it: the war's been over for years; why would they even bother to catch up with you?

Didn't you register?

Hell, no.

I turned off the street onto a shoulder and drove across an empty lot, parking next to a phone booth. I'm going to call, I said and got out. Gookus followed close behind and we jammed into the booth. February fourth, he said as I dropped a dime into the coin slot and dialed the radio station. The lower pane of glass in the door was punched out. The phone book, hanging from a short metal chain, was shredded. Memoranda on the metal wall suggested that Michelle was not only good but insatiable, and Gookus tried to memorize the number by saying it softly over and over to himself.

A lady at the radio station said, Hey, listen. This is, like, a radio station. Call the Army.

On the news a few minutes ago the announcer said people could call the station and find out what lottery number they got.

I have the paper in front of me. My boyfriend got 339. Let me find the chart. Okay, man, what's your birthday?

I've got two for you. A friend's with me.

Really, you don't have to ask for me, Gookus said. I don't care.

July twenty-third, I said.

Two-seventy-eight, she said, and I told Gookus, who karate-chopped the wall in joy.

I told her my birthday.

Oh, she said.

Oh?

What a shame.

It's that bad?

I looked at your birthday and I looked at the number. Looked at your birthday, looked at the number. You're number nineteen, man. I'm sorry.

I hung up.

What's the matter? Gookus said. Did you get a low number?
Nineteen.
Are you serious?
Yes.
Gookus couldn't stop laughing.
But I won't go, I said. I'm a pacifist.
You, a pacifist?
You know I am.
Since when?
Since always.
Since you got number one.
Bullshit.
So you're going to go C.O.?
I am a C.O. I always have been a conscientious objector.
To what?
To war. All wars.
Hey, that's convenient, Gookus said.

I tucked her in and turned off the light. She shut her eyes. Leave me be now, she said. Let me rest.
   All right.
   You must go now.
   I will.
   Walter?
   Yes, Mother.
   I'm in so much pain.
   Can I get you anything?
   Spill the bottle of sleeping pills onto the bed. Fill a glass of water for me and place it on the bed stand.
   You know I can't do that.
   Why not?
   I'm afraid.
   Of what?
   Doing harm.
   Still whispering, with her eyes still shut, she said, You mustn't be. Pour the bottle of sleeping pills onto the blanket, or I'll take these two pillows —
   Go ahead.
   You'll watch?
   Yes.
   You won't stop me?

No.
Then why won't you assist me?
I won't help you die.
But I need an accomplice.
Do it yourself.
I'll do it.
Go ahead.
I can't. I want you to do it for me.
No.
You're cruel.
I'm sorry.
You're afraid.
Yes.
Please, Walter.
No.

A fat man with a beard and a baseball cap opened the door, slapped my hands, grabbed my thumb, and said, Hey, like, look, man, enter because my time is yours. He sat down on the floor and crossed his legs. In front of him were matches, an ashtray, nickel-bags and papers, sunflower seeds, a six-pack of beer. The electricity didn't work and the phone jack was pulled out of the wall. Broken windows were boarded up or crossed with duct tape. Psychedelic posters depicting various sexual positions and states of consciousness were tacked to the walls, and from the back of the room came the sound of Indian music.

This is the draft information office, isn't it?

Was.

What do you mean?

We shut down years ago. You're the first person to come by in ages. Without the draft, no one needs guidance any more. There's nothing to worry about, man.

He tapped his fingers on the floor and sang to accompany the music on the stereo.

I stood over him and said, Listen: listen to me: I still want to be a conscientious objector.

What for? They'll never reinstate the draft. You're in no danger of being called up.

I realize I probably won't be, but —

Probably won't be? Bullshit, man. You're in absolutely no danger. Look, I've been through the whole thing a thousand times. I was a

C.O. until they found out I pulled a gun once on my girlfriend, so I put on weight until I was over the Army's limit. I know the tricks, man.

Will you at least tell me how I can apply for C.O. status?

I forget. Call the Army; they'll tell you good. You sound pretty scared, though. If they spot a coward, you can forget about C.O.

I came here for help, but you've only —

Hey, look, what am I supposed to do? I told you the truth, didn't I? We're out of business. No more draft. No more resisters. Nothing to worry about. I'm trying to tell you, man.

Each week all of us in contemporary events class were told to stand, read the article we had clipped from the newspaper, and speak up: speak up because the class was first thing in the morning and a few people in the back had the audacity to sleep. Bad boys searched for crumpled articles in pants pockets; good girls opened three-ringed binders to stories preserved between pieces of plastic. Boys read about the fire and the flood; girls read about the rescue. Some of the students could barely read and resorted to summary. Others whose families didn't subscribe to a newspaper rummaged before class for stray pages in the gutter. Those who forget were punished after school.

At breakfast I read a story about a thirteen-year-old girl who was so trusting, so naive, so foolish that she not only jumped off her bicycle and accepted the candy but got in the car. She was stripped, and what in newspaper accounts is called abused, then she was killed. She was found in a body bag in the dark morning drizzle. Her body was badly mangled; she could be identified only by the registration number on her bicycle. The girl's mother was quoted as saying that the murderer, when caught, should not be hung until he'd first been castrated. The girl was the same age as I was. She died only a few miles from where I lived. I knew the area, the park in which her body had been trashed.

I cut out the article and the adjoining photographs — the weeping mother, the body bag in the rain — and brought them to class. I passed around the pictures while reading aloud the story. One girl said her friend knew the sister of the best friend of the dead girl, and asked me to stop reading, but the teacher said, No, please continue: maybe the girl's death would serve as an example to the rest of us to go straight home after school.

Every Tuesday night for the next five weeks the killer found an errant girl, and every Wednesday morning I read an account of the evening's events to the class. He chose different suburbs and hair colors, but always beautiful twelve- or thirteen-year-old girls whom he dressed in blue jeans and long sleeved, white, button-down shirts, always the bruised body sealed within the plastic body bag. He left notes, written in red and misspelled, and a composite sketch of his face was drawn and circulated, although no one had actually seen him. Mothers picked up their children immediately after school and didn't allow them outside until the next morning. Detectives patrolled the streets.

Week after week I explained what had happened the night before, showed them pictures and maps. I was only thirteen years old, but for some reason I said: Don't cry. Although it was meant as encouragement to be brave, it was the wrong thing to say and they let me know they didn't like it. The teacher told me not to bring in any more articles about this series of tragic deaths. The class no longer wanted to hear about it. At recess, during lunch, and after school, gangs of girls ran up to me and said my father was probably the killer.

The next Tuesday night an anonymous voice intimated over the telephone that if another girl died that night I would be flushed down the toilet. Paint and rotten eggs spattered the front steps. I stopped answering the doorbell. I lay in bed, hoping I'd die in my sleep, since I knew another girl would be found in the morning. Teri Schraeder, who the day before during recess told me that after what I had done she took back the one dance she had begrudgingly given me at the Christmas party, was the seventh victim — buried in a body bag wearing blue jeans and a white, long sleeved, button-down shirt. When I got to school, half of the eighth grade appeared to be waiting for me. The teacher of the contemporary events class was holding them back with her arms out, and when I opened the entrance gate she sang out, Everybody ready? They came forward with jump ropes and bike locks for whips and white chains, and I went to my knees.

What would you do if I were raped?
    What a ghastly question! What do you think I'd do?
    I don't know. That's why I asked.
    Don't worry about it. You'll never be raped.
    Why not? What are you talking about?
    You're not sexy enough. You always wear pants, never wash your hair.
    You want me to dress up to get raped, Nina said.

I didn't say that.

It so happens that someone followed me home from work tonight, waited until there were no more street lamps, then made a lunge for me when I stopped to put on my mittens.

Jesus, I said and hugged her, stroked her hair. Are you okay?

Yes. I hit him in the face with my mittens and he ran away. If he had raped me, would you have shot him?

If I were with you, I would wrestle him off you, but, no, I doubt I'd shoot him.

Why must you always be so rational?

I'm sorry.

What if he had touched a knife to my throat and said, Fight me or I'll rape her?

You have such a melodramatic imagination.

What would you have done?

I don't know, I honestly —

You must not care very much about me.

I hope I'd —

Hope? My God, Walter. Hope isn't good enough.

I imagine walking up marble steps and pulling open double doors. At the other end of the room the six members of the jury sit in military uniforms at a long table. Each officer has his own microphone, and the officer at the head of the table taps his gavel and tells me to sit down. I don't have a microphone, so they can't hear my responses, but when I speak up, they tell me not to shout. I read a prepared statement, five typed pages of self-righteous rebellion, and introduce scraps of evidence on my behalf: articles I've written for my high school newspapers, letters to LBJ, polemical essays, membership cards to subversive organizations. After each man has asked me a series of questions, the head officer walks to where I'm sitting and tells me to stand. He cocks his fists. I raise my arms and he says, Siddown, 1-A. . . . The Army doctor closes the door and tells me to jump up on the metal table. He quickly conducts the examination: tests my hearing, my sight, tells me to say Aah, pinches my neck, thumps my chest, feels my heart, takes my pulse, taps my knees, scrapes the bottom of my feet, then tells me to step out of my underwear. I do and get an erection. No, I say, I'm not homosexual. He tilts his head and raises his eyebrows; I assure him I'm not. He puts down his clipboard and squeezes my cock until it goes limp.

In order to evade the draft, my second cousin transferred schools every semester and told almost no one his address. He pushed dope and made blue movies. When he was drafted, he took a jar of peanut butter with him to the physical and smeared it over his ass. The doctor told him to strip, so he plopped a mound of peanut butter into his mouth and ate it. He licked his lips. The doctor ran his fingers over the smeared crease in his underwear, asked him if he often ate his own shit, and he nodded enthusiastically.

All it comes down to, Walter, with this C.O. business is that you don't want to die.
    That's not true.
    It's nothing to be ashamed of. No one wants to die.
    That's not all there is to it.
    You're scared. We're all scared.
    I'm not a coward. It takes courage to do what I'm doing.
    As a child you would wake up in the middle of the night and sit, crying, at the landing of the stairs until I came to comfort you.
    Mother, please.
    You would say that you didn't want the rest of the world to exist if you were dead. You wanted me to make sure you were preserved in ice when you died so that you could be brought back to life when a cure was discovered.
    Childish fears, childish fantasies.
    Of course, but don't deny them. You're still afraid.
    No I'm not.
    Of course you are. But there's nothing to be afraid of.
    You're not afraid?
    I want to get it over with. Spill the pills onto the blanket, Walt, and pour me some water.
    Stop it. We've been through all this before.

I spent the summer between my sophomore and junior years of high school licking envelopes for a congressional candidate who said he wouldn't return from Washington until the war was over. At the time I believed in such statements. I sat at phone banks, calling every registered voter in the precinct, but very few of them answered and those who did were either opposed or virtually deaf. I carried a table, a chair, and voter registration cards into the wealthiest neighborhood in the state, an old woman invited me in for tea, and when I returned the table was gone. I wrote the candidate's speeches for him;

halfway through every speech, he stopped, discarded the script, and spoke, he said, from the gut. He was obese. His gut was repulsive. At the dinners, no one drank enough to get drunk. At the fund-raisers, no one contributed. Our billboards were derivative. The newspaper and television advertisements were antediluvian. The campaign slogan was NO HOKUM — VOTE FOR SLOCUM. Election day I drove crippled people to the polling booth, and on the way home most of them told me they voted for the challenger. Slocum's wife was beautiful, so a week before the election a rumor was leaked that his opponent had spent campaign funds in downtown massage parlors, and Slocum won in a landslide. I started that rumor.

I write a letter to appeal the jury's decision: I write: *I must refuse to play any part in the military. I would have to kill myself rather than cause the death of another man. Even if I were not required to use a weapon, I would be unable to serve the Army in any capacity. I value nothing more than my own conscience. As a child I did not play with guns. I would not have fought in the American Revolution or the Second World War. My parents taught me always to be good, never to do bad. I am a highly moral human being. I am prepared to accept the consequences of my actions.*

As a wide receiver, I would run intricate patterns, then stand all alone in the middle of the field, waving my hands, calling for the ball. I never dropped a pass, but when I was hit hard, I would typically tighten up and fumble. I was the best softball player in the neighborhood, but as we grew older, we began to play overhand, fast pitch hardball, and I started flinching. Trying to beat out a ground ball, I would always slow down so that the throw to first base would arrive ahead of me and I would avoid getting hit in the head with a wild toss. Batting, I was afraid of getting hit with the pitch; fielding, I dreaded bad hops off the rocky infield. No one could shoot a basketball as well as I could, but I was afraid to drive into the complicated middle of the key, where I would get banged up, and everyone knew that, so they guarded me tight and shut me off. I could run a hundred yards in 10.6 seconds, but I had very long legs and the track coach insisted that I run high hurdles; I stutter-stepped before each hurdle to make sure I cleared it and came in last. I feared the black rubber mats, the sudden loss of balance, the pressure on the skull, the slap of feet and legs to the ground: I flunked gym because I couldn't turn somersaults. Having never learned to dive, I jumped in the pool feet first. The swimming instructor dragged me to the edge of the diving board, positioned my arms and legs, held me in the air for a second, then dropped me into the pool. At the last instant I turned my face, and water broke my fall like a bed of electric needles. What was I scared of? Why was I so afraid of getting hurt? I was under the mistaken impression there was such thing as a clean sprint through the night without spikes or hurdles.

Did you kill anybody in World War II?
    Might have. Don't know. Can't tell. Hard to say.
    Why don't you know?
    You're all firing your weapons at once, so you don't know if your bullet killed the dead man or the bullet of the man next to you killed him.
    But do you think you did?
    Perhaps.
    Perhaps?
    Well, yes, I did. Why, what's the matter, son?
    Why did you have to kill him?
    Who?
    The man you killed, perhaps.
    Hey, stop looking at me with those wide eyes of yours. He was shooting at me. What was I supposed to have done?
    Were you scared?
    No.
    But he was shooting at you?
    It's okay. It's okay. He missed.

My father killed Hitler. He was with a squad of soldiers, one of whom would have killed Hitler if Hitler had not killed himself first. He was part of a squad that surrounded the bunker in which Hitler killed himself. He was in another part of Germany when Hitler killed himself. He was in Okinawa at the time. He was in Brooklyn and read about it in his newspaper. He couldn't afford to subscribe to a newspaper and read about it in someone else's newspaper. He couldn't read English and someone had to explain to him what had happened.

    My father said he volunteered to serve in the Army in World War II. He said he was drafted at about the same time he volunteered. He didn't remember which was first. He said he was drafted just days before he would have volunteered. My father put his arm around my shoulder, took off his glasses, then half-whispered into my ear that he was drafted but failed the physical examination due to a problem with his left leg and returned home.

What sort of problem? I asked. In eighteen years I'd never heard or seen that he had any problem with his left leg.

It's healed since then, he said, shaking his head and gesturing toward a vague point in the past to indicate that I needn't and wouldn't know more.

I imagine showing the new letter from the draft board to my father, who says: What does this stand for — Cowards Only? He dances around me, tousling my hair, tugging my ears, pinching my nose and stinging my face with rapid, openhanded blows to back me into a corner. He pins my arms, pokes me in the stomach, knees me in the groin. I turn toward the wall, with my head in my hands, but when he clutches my throat, I swing around to face him, throwing my arms up and outward. I hit him, hard, across the jaw.

I didn't mean it, I say. I'm sorry. I didn't hurt you, did I?

He falls to the floor, overacting a bit, I'm certain, but clearly stunned.

My new dream goes like goes: in the middle of the desert my father offers me water from his canteen, which I accept with outstretched hands and drink until I'm no longer thirsty. He takes off his boots and shakes out pebbles, dirt, dead leaves. Lizards crawl around, looking for shade under rocks and short shrubs. When he untwists the black top of the canteen he finds nothing but the inside of the container.

You drank all the water, he says.

Yes, I say, I was thirsty.

That's all we had left. We won't be able to survive.

I'm sorry. I didn't know.

Of course you knew.

I'm sorry.

We may die, Walter.

We won't die.

We may. You have no concern for anyone other than —

There's a cactus plant out there.

Where?

Out there, out in the distance.

I can't see it.

Your eyes are bad.

I don't see it.

He unties the knots in his backpack and removes his eyeglasses. He rubs the lenses with his shirt until they're filthy, then gazes into the distance, contemplating the sheer magnitude of this inhuman habitat. A quarter mile away, due west, partially hidden among rock piles and dying trees, stands a giant cactus plant.

I'll race you for the water in the cactus, I say.

I shouldn't run. My leg's bothering me.

Then the water's mine.

I make a false start, but he shouts at me to wait.

Really, Walt, my bad leg's bothering me.

He unstraps the canteen from his belt, takes the backpack off his shoulders, and gives both the canteen and the backpack to me. He stretches his legs by touching his toes and doing deep knee bends. He builds up sand to serve as a starting block and crouches down in a sprinter's ready position, dusting dirt and sand off his fingers onto his pants leg, bending his left leg forward, shooting his right leg back and balancing himself on the balls of his feet and fingertips. With his feet in the sand, his shoulders hunched over and shaking, and his head pointed straight ahead as if he's a bird dog, he rocks until he's set. He's serious.

I fasten the canteen to my belt and pull the straps of the backpack over my shoulders. Although I feel weighted down, I pull one knee and then the other up to my chest, stretching. I'm thirsty; I definitely want to win. I look out across the dry desert and toward the cactus in the distance, then back to him. He's poised, ready to run. A quarter of a mile is only once around the track, I say to myself, and bend down a little and put my hands on my knees.

Who's going to start us? I ask.

I will. Runners, take your mark, he says and shakes one leg and then the other behind him. He crouches down low and spits into the dirt.

Are you sure your leg is all right?

Get set.

I'd hate for you to hurt it or make it any worse.

Go, he says. He gets off to such a good start that I think maybe he's jumped the gun. I chase after him, calling out that in order to be absolutely fair to both parties involved we should at least think about starting over again, but he ignores me and clenches his fists, lengthens his stride, and kicks up pebbles as he increases his lead. Although he's only a few yards ahead, I can't close the gap because the backpack bounces up and down on my shoulders and weighs a ton and the canteen knocks against my thighs and stomach, slowing me down further. My chest fills with dry air.

Bounding over the desert, avoiding rocks and brush, we approach the cactus plant, which is huge: four stems curve up from the base and one major stem sticks straight up into the air thirty feet like a thick green finger. In the distance, to both sides of us, north and south, are rocks worn away into jagged, meaningless shapes. The sky is clear light blue, completely open and empty except for a flock of sand grouse flying overhead, looking for water.

We near the cactus and I can hear him gasping for breath when I edge up on him. He's trying to hold on, but I can tell he isn't going to make it. He has nothing left: his bad leg is wobbly, his head is bobbing up and down, his neck muscles are straining. He's tight, and I'm a step behind. I let my arms swing more freely and bring my knees up higher, all the way to my chest, as I catch a second wind and sprint by him, shouting, racing for the cactus, forgetting about the backpack and canteen, finally hitting my stride with my arms and legs working together smoothly and powerfully.

He falls. His knees buckle. He loses the lead as well as his balance and tumbles into the dirt, head first, arms stretched out flat to break his fall. He scrapes his hands across ragged rocks, skidding across the desert on his stomach. The sand grouse sweep down to see what's happened; I don't stop running until I reach the cactus. I trample over the shrubs and sharp brush surrounding the cactus, take my knife out of my pocket, and cut through the clustered spines of the lowest stem, the only I'm able to reach. It's coated with wax. I prick myself on the bristles and my fingers bleed. The cut stems drip water, which I cup in my hands.

He's holding his hip and still breathing hard. His hands are cut and bloody, and his right leg is shaking slightly. His tongue sticks out of his open mouth. I kneel down and offer him the water, but he turns on his side, onto his bad leg, away from me.

I had you, he says. Goddamnit, I had you. You're slow, Walter. I had you.

I raise my hands to my face to drink.

A Snowman and Other Curiosities
Gilbert Sorrentino

MEMORIAL

THE FRIENDS AND BUSINESS ACQUAINTANCES of the dead man, gathered in a perfectly appointed town house for a hastily arranged memorial service, are dressed as if for a costume party. The deceased's fiancée, the casual focus of curious eyes, is clad as a Crusader who feigns — such is the excellent masquerade — womanhood. At the moment, she is making a gesture of rejection to a man kneeling before her in shapeless white robes, his arms spread in supplication, adoration, or complaisance. The red cross on the woman's fleur-de-lis-spangled gypon catches glancingly the candlelight which illuminates the lavishly furnished buffet. Beyond, in slightly menacing shadows, her ancients and advisors hover. One might think that the kneeling man is in some actual danger, but this is not the case.

The deceased, so fragments of conversation and gossip gathered here and there suggest, apparently swallowed a bottle of poison at the table of an undistinguished restaurant known for its heavy sauces, too-rich desserts, and haphazardly placed bowls of unidentifiable spheroids, many of them translucent.

There is the sweet chiming of a teaspoon against a crystal wineglass. The guests break off their conversations, refresh their drinks, and form a loose cluster at one end of the drawing room, at the other end of which, the deceased's fiancée, looking now quite genuinely masculine, holds up a small painting. It depicts a kitchen window seen from just beyond a wooden fence. Behind the streaked, dirty pane, the blurred figure of a scowling young woman can be descried. She seems to be naked, or partially naked, and with her left hand stiffly held before her, makes a gesture of rejection. The fiancée, whose name is Jeanne Sousa, or Souze, holds the painting higher, and speaks. "Friends," she begins, her voice low with emotion, or, perhaps, feigned emotion.

SNOWMAN

One morning a snowman appeared by the side of the road in front of the country house owned, for many years, by the famous dancer, Olga Chervonen. The stark tree behind and to the left of the figure held its usual complement of snow, most of it, not unnaturally, on the windward side of the trunk. Somewhat surprisingly, the snow looked very much like fresh white paint, or, even more surprisingly, like a drawing of fresh white paint, that is, a drawing of, so to speak, nothing. The snowman's face was somewhat debauched, sinister even, although no one remarked on this. No smoke came from Madame Chervonen's chimney, although inside the house were, in addition to the dancer, Edward Carmichael, the *bel canto* singer, Louis Bill, a charmingly unworldly tool-and-die maker, Isidor Martin, the biologist, and Claude Urbane, the internationally acclaimed polo player. They seemed warm and comfortable as they chatted amiably before a crackling fire. So the lack of smoke was indeed perplexing, and remains so.

The snowman, his tiny eyes glittering in the sunlight that slanted through the dead trees, was discovered to be holding a dried branch, which leaned against his shoulder and arm. It may well have been thought of as a rifle or a fishing rod or any number of other things. A staff, for instance. Or a spear. On closer inspection, the snowman's aspect seemed not so much sinister as demented: the fact that his mouth was fashioned from dried leaves, grit, pebbles, and nameless detritus added to this impression. At certain moments, his eyes closed and then opened again, although this probably did not actually happen.

Inside the house, the group of friends talked over the mysterious letter which concerned certain scattered events of some fifty years earlier. The letter spoke of a woman at a sink, a barren back yard, an empty kitchen, and a voice from behind a door. Other occurrences were also detailed, although Louis Bill was hesitant to speak of them, as, indeed, were the others. There was a rumor at the time that a snowfall was also mentioned in the letter. Mentioned in passing, yet mentioned nonetheless. Isidor Martin noticed the snowman, and everyone crowded to the windows. There he was!

Gilbert Sorrentino

CLUES

It was on that street, familiar to all, that the adventures took place, although "adventures" is a word not used until much later to characterize the events of the time. No one has admitted to a detailed knowledge of these events, and some, perhaps predictably, argue rather heatedly that there *were* no events. It was, certainly, revealed that Ann Jenn, of the Jenntille Foundations fortune, was at least partially involved, along with Jed Whag, the Clown of Clowns, and Russell Cuiper, known in his day as the inventor of the transverse flute.

Despite all, there were, even then, indications that the street was the focus of what soon developed into a full-blown scandal. Architectural psychologists, however, pointed out that old cobblestones, old shutters, old window boxes, old stoops, and old gas lamps — the latter maintained at considerable expense by a bemused tenants' association — while desirable, and even advantaged, have neither the structural nor aesthetic power to cause the series of events to which everyone is now quite embarrassedly sensitized. There were a number of clues unearthed, over a period of months, from the puzzling debris discovered in the most unlikely places; money had been, apparently, no object to the pursuit of degradation. Those clues which the authorities have dared make public are: an opaque glass Clasp; a rusted hub Shard; a metal brassiere Cap; a blue enamel Bulb; a Worcestershire sauce Chip; a burnt-out bottle Lace; a nine-inch white Pebble; a frayed cotton Top; and a small shoe Thread. Although the uses to which these items were put, and the scenes of which they speak, have been the subject of horrified speculation both popular and scientific, none of the principals has ever shed light on their meaning. Miss Jenn has long been sequestered by her family in private apartments within the walls of a European convent; Whag no longer speaks, has forgotten how to juggle, and lives amid certain dense fogs; and Cuiper has lost all interest in music, and, instead, gives himself over to a study of Virginia Woolf's handwriting and its relationship to the coif motif in her novels.

For the last few years, investigators have been convinced that Robert Bedu, a genius of applied electronics technology, might, possibly, once have had the answers. Bedu himself hinted at such a possibility on numerous occasions, some festive, others semi-morose. Before he could publish or otherwise broadcast his theories on the relationship of the odd clues to the bizarre and even repulsive

312

incidents, he became obsessed with a dangerous dream technique, variously known as picturebearing, sounddrawing, and fleshtouching. All of the early practitioners of this technique have either died or lapsed into an irreversible catatonic state. At last report, Mr. Bedu was laboring over a letter which will, he asserts, free him from doubt and fear. "Observe my fountain pen," he has been quoted as saying, "isn't it a beauty?" Then it is back to his letter. He seems to have lost all interest in the old scandal.

One rather singular piece of information is that for each of the clues in and of itself, and for all of them in combination with certain, or all, of the others, there is always to be discovered a person who, aghast, reads in them the hidden secrets of his or her own life. In some inexplicable way, the clues point everywhere at once.

POSTCARD

The picture postcard depicts an androgynous figure, richly caparisoned in heavy white moire over dazzling armor, sans helmet, astride a sturdy warhorse in the act of bowing his mighty head. The rider holds, vertically, a staff, the butt end of which rests in the righthand stirrup. From the staff there flutters a white banner, that, upon close inspection, seems to be a lace-hemmed slip. Massed behind the young man — or woman — are foot soldiers, armed with spears whose blades are much like long, slender adzes. The figure on horseback is about to lead the men into battle, although it is possible that they are not men, but women. The drawing, design, and colors of the card are of the most inferior quality.

This is, perhaps, the picture postcard — now rather notorious — which was, given the fragile evidence of gossip, bought by Yolanda Philippo, or Emilia Sladky, or Isabella Alcott. The arguments pro and con these women as purchasers of the card are many, and fill three tall file cabinets in the offices of the chemist and trivia collector, Joshua Bex. The very thought of the unsorted documents aggravated, without fail, Bex's incipient duodenal ulcer, and he would, at such times, begin another abstruse experiment with the colored gels on which he had labored for thousands of hours. "Fortuna favet fortibus," he would reply to insolent visitors.

Here is the message on the postcard, which, just as one might guess, is not addressed to anyone.

> Despite the near-wintry sunsets and the dismal back yards, the boringly respectable conversations and the yearned-for adulteries, and the usual ups, downs, and arounds of a petty and suffocating academic milieu — cheese and crackers, opera talk, discovered vintages, cigarette hysteria, traffic concerns — there yet are amorous possibilities neither admissible nor imaginable in, perhaps, the spotless kitchen.

Each of the three women had, at one time or another, burgeoning emotional problems; there was, and often, reckless talk of "clanging" steel doors; and, too, the spectacle persisted of girls, modest yet desirable, with small white handkerchiefs pinned to their hair. Many attributed these phenomena to religion, and that settled the question for them, at least. Yet while documents continued to accumulate, none of them even began to address the most basic questions, i.e.:

who wrote the postcard?

who sent the postcard?

was the postcard ever, indeed, sent?

if sent, who received it?

All this happened years before Joshua Bex took Emilia Sladky as his second wife, at just about the time the revelations concerning Yolanda Philippo's involvement in the Zeppelin Gallery scandal. Isabella Alcott's rather suspicious death occurred, of course, just weeks after the initial discovery of the postcard. So much for chronology.

Contemporary developments in post-negativity theory suggest that although the *message* of the postcard is essentially illocutionary and, hence, incapable of discourse, the image is wholly — and radically — performative. When this idea was suggested to Bex, he immediately set fire to several almost-completed experiments and hid his wife's Indian clubs.

TREE

Bill Juillard, a self-taught historian possessed of that which he thought of as total objectivity, came across the true reason for the large tree. For a time, he kept the discovery to himself. No one knew why Juillard, usually quite gregarious and talkative, would do this. The townspeople grew sullen.

Sleep came hard to Juillard. He was not used to carrying such a burden of secrecy.

He noted, although, ultimately, it did not matter, that the tree was an old one; that it could be considered historical; that generations had revered it, more or less, although there had always been an embarrassing minority intent upon drunken holiday fun and furtive adultery, usually committed in parked cars or locked bathrooms, and complete with stains and lost items of clothing.

Juillard tried to describe the tree but there didn't seem to be any point to it, especially since a traveling waiter, passing through on his way to what he called the Annual Feast, told him that the tree looked very much like a mammoth ivy. The waiter, who had been drinking gin for four or five days, may have been mistaken.

Juillard drew a sketch of the tree, which has been preserved, and which was to have accompanied this brief account. It does not appear, for although it is surely a representation of something, that something is not a tree.

The tree reminded Juillard of a sweet and vivacious girl with whom he had been in love when he was nineteen. There seemed no connection between the tree and the girl, but Juillard was inhabited by the tree, and so everything followed the path of the tree.

MOON

Dr. Ronald LeFlave adjusts the viewfinder on his telescope, and prepares to examine the surface of the moon, high and full and gleaming, far above the predictable and complacent town in which he lives alone and practices medicine. He is a mediocre physician, and although he has never been directly responsible for anyone's death, he has made his small contribution to the misery of the world. He has no gift for the medical arts, and to escape the unsatisfying life chosen for him thirty years earlier, he has become something of an astronomer, and at the present time is writing a monograph on aspects of the moon as they relate to mood shifts in the middle-aged professional, in this case, perhaps not surprisingly, himself. He is flattered to find that he has moods, and that they shift, since his mother taught him that moods do not exist.

He peers into the viewfinder, sharpens the focus, and is surprised — amazed would be a better word — to see a man of about thirty-five, splendid in a white linen suit and Borsalino, sitting with three young women in pale pastel dresses and wide straw hats. They are — Dr. LeFlave looks carefully — picnicking in the deep shade of

315

huge trees overhanging the shore of a quiet lake. Dr. LeFlave leans back, alarmed, since the telescope is aimed directly at the moon. He puts his eye to the viewfinder once again.

Although only a few seconds have passed, the man, his hat still on, has mounted one of the young women and their bodies writhe determinedly amid a cloud of white underclothes. The other two young women, some twenty or thirty yards down the lake shore, have neatly placed their shoes and stockings on the grassy bank, and, their skirts held modestly close to their dainty thighs, wade in the clear shallows. Dr. LeFlave looks back at the lovers, and then, although ashamed, watches, immobile, as they climb into orgasm. One of the young woman's satin slippers dangles tremblingly from the foot which she has convulsively thrust straight up into the mild summer air.

The doctor abruptly pulls himself away from the telescope and the unlikely scene it has somehow discovered. He is aroused, and finds himself on the brink of what Roberto Arlt calls the "blazing darkness" of carnal anguish. How alone he is. Absolutely, profoundly alone, and far from the empty white moon.

LUST

The young woman at the window, her hair pulled back in a severe chignon which dramatized her elegant profile, glanced at the paper in her hand, which looked, from a distance, to be an invoice or packing slip, or, perhaps, a bank statement. Later, it was ascertained, from an investigation of the tips hidden in, of all things, the aluminum soap dish, that it was, indeed, a bank statement. Jenny would much prefer to stay home this evening, so as to avoid the dinner party to which Ivan, her husband, had committed them. It will be the Provost, the Deans of Arts and Sciences and the Law School, their curiously blurred, smiling wives, and the Hounsfields: young Ivan, fine hard-working fellow, and young Jenny, lovely bright girl. Charming people to have on campus! Have you met the Hounsfields? Dean Agostin will say, trying not to stare at Jenny's legs, his tongue barely protruding from between his tiny incisors.

A heavy wind drove a torrent of rain against the windowpane, and Jenny stepped back, startled. She closed the blinds and stood, annoyed, for a moment, then began unbuttoning her blouse, resigned to the evening and its predictable, alarmed gossip about the collapsing houses along the Old Arcade Road. She put the bank statement on the mantel, and tried out her generous, candid smile, then started for the bathroom. It was getting late.

Ivan was already dressed, save for his tie, and he sat in his study, leafing through a book of nineteenth-century freak cartoons. The materials discovered in the aluminum soap dish made no mention of this work, nor did any of the authorities seem to agree on precisely what freak cartoons were. Ivan looked carefully at them, frequently laughing to himself, a laugh which had, on certain occasions, bewildered and chilled Jenny. He heard a noise, and looked up to see his wife, at the door, asking him something about a black dress she might wear, or should wear, or would like to wear. She was leaning against the door jamb, her blouse and brassiere in her hand. The narrow black skirt that she wore accentuated her hips and the gleaming nudity of her upper torso. The light from the desk lamp slathered her breasts. Ivan stared at her, losing track of her language, hearing only soft noises, seeing a white smile. He was overwhelmed with lust, and rose from his chair, dropping his book on a round end table, from which it slid to the floor. He walked toward her, his hand reaching out: he could see in her face the dread of his massive desire.

Ivan then was brutally on top of her, his trousers tangled around his ankles, her torn panties twisted about her left knee, and he drove his hateful, stupid flesh into the secret hairy wetness which makes her the rutting animal she is. He felt again, as always, as if he were committing some terrible, unimaginable crime, some unspeakably delicious and unforgivable sin. It was Jenny's fault. Jenny the beast. Crazed, he stumbled into his orgasm, and turned his agonized face away from her wide eyes.

BARREL

The legendary clarinet virtuoso, Sandor Skariofszky, whose famous mechanical interpretation of Satie's recently discovered "Entracte pour les blanches entractes," fills him — the very *thought* of it fills him — with nausea, has, in recent years, taken to saving coins in a bank shaped like a miniature barrel, which he carefully displays on his mantelpiece. To say that he saves coins does not begin to cover the appealing and even irresistible events which make up Skariofszky's days. There are, of course, the stationery sprees, foxtrot contests, sycophant correspondence, and daily visits to Old Tony, the cheerful Italian bootblack, whose irreverent tales of the Piedmont and its lusty mountain women and their amorous swains belie his cherished notion that everyone is, underneath, really homosexual. All these avocations suffuse the jaded musician with dreams of a permanently simple yet zesty life. Then there are, too, the gambling orgies, the jacket (and topcoat) fittings, and the embouchure exhibitions. Yet it must be admitted that the woodwind star finds his true fulfillment in the coin-saving ritual to which he has submitted himself.

The master indulges in the ritual whenever he looks at a certain picture on that wall perpendicular to the one into which the fireplace is built. The pattern is, of needs, fixed: Skariofszky approaches the picture, as if casually and by accident, stops, studies it with care, turns, moves in four strides to the mantel, hovers above the little barrel — which Old Tony refers to as a "sangaweech" — and, with his right hand, deftly drops a coin into the bank's slot. During this operation, Skariofszky's left arm is bent rigidly at his side and his left hand clenched in a threatening fist. At such times, the clarinet wizard resembles Bart Ballesteros, whose pathetic suicide stunned the croquet world. He is *not* Bart Ballesteros, however, because he is, most assuredly, he; and because Ballesteros's response to the visual — despite family lies to the contrary — was wholly devoid of either taste or understanding. He had, as the Romanian proverb puts it, "the glass eye which [has] cracked [up] among pebbles."

Something draws him to the picture, again and again, obsessively and exhaustingly. His left arm has long since begun to atrophy, his left hand may never fully open again, and his staring, dark-ringed eyes are cruelly bloodshot. At times, his admirers, members of the international Licorice Clubs, deplore the fact that he no longer performs, and his frustrated physicians concur, filling the air with their professional rodomontade concerning creative therapeutics. Skariofszky pays them no heed. He has even ceased to treat them with courtesy.

There is, by the way, nothing exceptional about the picture. A rather brilliant imitation of the Hudson River School, it depicts, beneath an unsettled, stormy sky, a dark lake. At its far end, there can barely be descried the figures of three young women in wide straw hats and luminous white dresses, wading in the shallows, their full skirts held modestly close to their perfect thighs. They appear to be dead.

SENTENCE

When Yolanda Philippo boarded the train, the thought, which she was certain would come to her, did, indeed, come to her. Perhaps it is too much to call it a thought, since it was but a sentence. Her vocation as an art critic, however, prevented her from considering the sentence as a message, for in her mind's eye — a phrase she particularly admired — she saw the sentence as if inscribed on a blank field. She saw, that is, not the message, but a drawing, a picture, of the message, a picture which represented the sentence, "Myrna felt like undressing for the conductor." Simple enough, and yet, Miss Philippo later thought, fraught with mystery.

She was notably chic in a charcoal-grey tweed polo coat with a black Persian-lamb shawl collar, a navy-blue suit, sheer off-black stockings, and black suede pumps. On her shiningly coiffed head, she wore a small black hat with a dotted half-veil, and on her hands, black kid gloves. A letter discovered in the archive of a contemporary of the critic notes, not without levity: "Had Yolanda been Myrna, she would have had a good deal of undressing to *do!*"

Miss Philippo invariably had this thought, or, more correctly, saw this drawing, whenever she boarded a train, or whenever she thought of a train, or whenever she thought of people she knew who had, for private reasons, boarded trains. She also saw the drawing whenever she undressed or watched other women undress — not, her biographer asserts, a predilection — or thought of undressing. But who, or what, did "Myrna" signify?

Miss Philippo sat at the window, looking out on a frozen suburban scene whose delineations were thought interesting to novelists of a certain bent. There were the icicles hanging from the eaves! There was a snowman! And so on. The conductor arrived at her seat, and as she watched him punch her ticket, she thought how much she felt like undressing for him, despite his essential repulsiveness. Yet she was *not* Myrna, as she well knew.

Many years before, when Miss Philippo had been a graduate student, a professor with sexual designs on her took her to dinner at a newly fashionable restaurant in a newly fashionable neighborhood. Miss Philippo, exhausted, even before the entrée, médaillons de veau en robes blanches, by her battle with the professor's hot and importunate hands, excused herself and fled to the ladies' room. It was empty, save for one woman, some twenty years her senior, possessed of a beautiful, almost noble face, the face of Lesbia or Sulpicia. She

319

leaned drunkenly against one of the black porcelain sinks, stripped to the waist, washing her bosom and crying uncontrollably into her reflection. Miss Philippo stood, embarrassed, then washed her hands at the sink farthest from the woman, whose full, heavy breasts were covered with purple bruises and teeth marks. It was, to the younger woman, an acute picture of despair.

This woman could have been the "Myrna" of Miss Philippo's repetitive sentence, although it is impossible to know why, and, surely, even more impossible to determine why such a "Myrna" would have had anything to do with trains or conductors. Whatever the solutions to these mysteries, if they may so be termed, Yolanda Philippo contrived to imagine herself undressing for this repulsive conductor. He would bite her breasts, too hard, his stupid cap askew on his balding head.

Perhaps she dreamed it, and in her dream found herself seeing, *in her mind's eye*, the intransigent drawing, "Myrna felt like undressing for the conductor," released, free, wholly removed from all meaning, much like the wintry sunset which inhabited the sky as she emerged from the station.

From Mambo Mephiste
Seth Morgan

NOTE: Seth Morgan's first and only published novel, *Homeboy*, earned him acclaim in April 1990 as one of the most gutsy and acrobatic new voices in contemporary fiction. In October, Seth died in a motorcycle accident in his adopted hometown of New Orleans. He'd been working on a second novel, *Mambo Mephiste*, a first draft of which he promised to show me and Jason Epstein, his editors at Random House, by year's end. We have published here the only three chapters Seth felt were strong enough to send to his agent, Gloria Loomis, in early fall. He'd sent her a precis of the novel in the form of a letter, also included here.

These chapters are but the first draft from a novelist who would normally write a good ten. We have guessed at their order, and they are not necessarily contiguous. The provisional chapter titles are the author's. "A novel comes to life," Seth wrote, "not in its planning, but in its process of birth." *Mambo Mephiste*, in three chapters alone, lives exuberantly. The scalding wit, the scatalogical rap, the lucid compassion of his words conspire to inscribe Seth's memory not just on those who knew him but on his time.

— *Susan Bell*

Tuesday, June 5, 1990

Dear Gloria,

You've asked for a precis of my next novel, an idea of what the new pages I'm sending up will amount to once they're all of a Morganesque piecemealery. This runs crossgrain to my method, which is to set forth with only inchoate notions of theme, halfheard voices and halfgrasped apercus of dramatic high points, allowing the novel to acquire its own form and expression through the alchemy of its creation. Because that's where a novel comes to life, not in its planning but its process of birth. Nevertheless, I hope the following is helpful.

What I hold in mind is a book uniquely of this unique city of carnivals and cemeteries. In fact, I propose nothing less bold than the Mardi Gras novel as yet unwritten. A baroque and bustout tale of love foredoomed and sin unremitted spun between the bearded oaks, the streetcar lines and lacework galleries of the Big Easy; a

Gothic fable of helpless men and women who must "in ignorance sedate roll darkly down the torrents of their fates," gripped in the currents of those pasts which Faulkner taught are not even past but the stuff of the here and now, enigmatically shaping and informing the present.

At the novel's outset, Marcel LeDoux, a narcotics cop, has inexplicably suicided. His brother, Diogenes "Dodge" LeDoux, the novel's protagonist, a disbarred lawyer become boozy bail bondsman, suspects foul play. Marcel LeDoux was a dedicated professional, a devoted family man — the apotheosis, in fact, of every virtue that Dodge, the younger son of an alcoholic actress and rich oldline New Orleanian, both deceased, lacks.

To preserve his brother's honor and assert his own, Dodge sets out to find the man he's certain murdered his Marcel. His first lead is Eddie Echoes, recently paroled from the state prison at Angola, a childhood friend of both brothers, a junkaddled jazzman and Marcel's snitch. But Eddie's already back in jail, incommunicado, with an armed robbery bond too high for Dodge to make himself. So when a sinister stranger appears at the Bon Temps Bail Bonds offices, Dodge eagerly accepts his offer to go Eddie's full cash bail.

Little does Dodge suspect that the stranger is the dreaded Johnny Pooreyes, *babalawo*, or high priest, of the *palo mayombe*, the evil sect of Santeria which practices human sacrifice and counts among its adherents South America's *narcoterristos*. This Creole Mephistopheles is other things as well, and none of them savory: the bastard son of Trujillo Molina, former dictator of the Dominican Republic, and his mistress-spy on the Haitian border, a Negro voodienne; a ruthless mercenary trained at CIA expense by the Israeli Mossad to advise the Nicaraguan *contras*. To procure his assistance in overthrowing the Sandinista regime, the CIA has not only turned a blind eye on Pooreyes' drug and gun running but pandered to his mad dream of an Antillean Empire, promising him a free reign in the West Indies. Yet with the Sandinistas democratically removed from power, the CIA has reneged; and Pooreyes, interpreting this treachery as a reprisal of his father's betrayal in '64, swears a terrible vengeance. He plots an urban black rebellion fomented by a fanatic return to the old West African gods, like the Sioux Ghost Dancers of Little Big Horn, an urban uprising culminating in nothing less than the assassination of the President of the United States on a Mardi Gras reviewing stand, something like Anwar Sadat's assassination. To this end, he constructs a Trojan Horse Mardi Gras float, its interior concealing gunmen, zealous followers of *palo mayombe* recruited from the tough Medellin slum of Palestino, the Columbian drug lords' recruiting ground for assassins. This lunatic *attentat* comprises the Boschian Mardi Gras night climax, the novel's central vision of hell.

Dodge never gets the chance to question Eddie concerning Marcel. The morning after Pooreyes makes his bail, Eddie is found gutted, badly burned, hanging by his feet from a St. Charles Avenue liveoak about which are arranged ceremonial Santeria ikons. The police give no credence to Dodge's story of the stranger who made Eddie's bail, professing instead to believe that Dodge himself posted the bond and murdered his brother's snitch, disguising it as a Santeria rite, in order to silence forever the one man who could shed light on Marcel LeDoux's death. This spurious inference that he had a hand in covering up the circumstances of his own brother's death gives Dodge his first inkling of the police department's complicity with Johnny Pooreyes.

By now Dodge firmly believes Pooreyes killed both his brother and Eddie Echoes, and he relentlessly tracks the *babalawo* through the downandout dives and steaming streets of New Orleans populated with strippers, dragqueens, hookers, crackerjacks and coneroos. Along the way he discovers that the body hanging from the liveoak was not really Eddie Echoes, but a double who bailed out in his stead, a man Dodge first spotted in Eddie's line-up in the opening chapter. But certain by now that police elements are in cahoots with Pooreyes, Dodge keeps this information to himself to protect Eddie and preserve his last chance of unraveling the mystery of his brother's death.

When finally at the commencement of Mardi Gras week he comes face to face once more with Johnny Pooreyes, the *babalawo* confronts Dodge with the shattering revelation that they are half-brothers, that Dodge too is a bastard son of Trujillo Molina, conceived on a Caribbean vacation of his mother. Herein lies the mystery of Marcel's demise. Knowing that Marcel was protective of his erstwhile younger brother, Pooreyes used their mother's iniquity to coerce the narcotic cop's cooperation in a cocaine conspiracy. But when Marcel learned the full extent of the *babalawo's* diabolical plot and was about to expose it, Pooreyes killed him, disguising it as a suicide. Dodge further learns from Pooreyes that the still elusive Eddie Echoes was marked for death not for any secrets he held of Marcel's death but for having desecrated the sacraments of *palo mayombe* by secretly witnessing at Angola the sacrifice of convicts conducted by Pooreyes to propitiate his ferocious patron god, Xango.

Pooreyes tries recruiting Dodge in his fantastic assassination scheme, appealing to their mutual blood bond to the "Goat," as Trujillo was known. Failing in this, Pooreyes mocks Dodge, believing him impotent to thwart his plan, his destiny. The *babalawo's* influence is too widespread, his power too great. Should Dodge come forward with this fantastic information, the authorities would treat it as a figment of his delirium tremens. Thus Johnny Pooreyes allows Dodge to part his company unharmed. But he has underestimated the bail bondsman. Dodge is resolved that alone he must kill his Creole sibling to save the President's life, avenge his brother, and atone for his mother's sins.

Yet the reader knows that Dodge is not in league alone against Pooreyes. Early in the novel, Lola, a schizophrenic inmate at a medieval Texas asylum, has murdered her lecherous psychiatrist and escaped. She's picked up hitchhiking by one of Pooreyes' thugs delivering cocaine and a sacramental *palo*, an ornate doublebladed axe, from Houston to New Orleans. When the thug tries to rape her, she disposes of him as she did her shrink, in a grisly sex-murder, then steals the car with the cocaine and axe, and hies to New Orleans. There she goes to work as a stripper-prostitute, securing the psychoactive drugs she requires to hold her homicidal nature in check. She meets and falls in love with Eddie Echoes, hiding him out from Johnny Pooreyes, having no idea the *babalawo* is hot on her trail as well, wild to regain the *palo* and the mystic powers with which the sacrificial axe endows him. This mad Madonna-whore's doomed beauty echoes that of New Orleans, and her tragic love for Eddie Echoes deeply impells the narrative.

Finally Pooreyes runs the two lovers to ground and falls in love with Lola himself. They escape him once, and he pursues them, cornering them at last on a remote bayou where he offers to spare Eddie's life if Lola will come to him. Camillelike, she complies, but, unbeknownst to Pooreyes, halts the medication holding her psychosis in remission.

The city's now in the grip of the Mardi Gras frenzy, masked revelers everywhere, the streets thundering with marching bands. Like Orpheus pursuing Eurydice through Hades, Eddie Echoes, believing himself abandoned by his lover, searches wildly through the melee for Lola. Dodge LeDoux is likewise hunting Pooreyes, intent on slaying the beast. But before either can find his quarry, Lola daggers

Pooreyes to death on his Mardi Gras float and is killed in turn by his henchmen.

Ash Wednesday dawns over streets littered with party debris. Grieving over Lola, Eddie takes his trumpet back to the pawnshop where she bought it for him. But before he can hock it for money to buy drugs, the broker shows him wedding bands Eddie hadn't known she was making payments on. In a blaze Eddie recognizes her supreme sacrifice. He leaves the pawnshop with the trumpet and goes to the Mississippi levee where he plays a lovelost blues attracting Dodge, still awake himself after this long and fateful night, and the two men finally meet up to eulogize the woman who died to save the one's life and other's soul.

That's about it. I've omitted mention of the numerous subsidiary characters who'll enliven the book—Audrey, gal Friday at Bon Temps Bail Bonds, a blond bombshell lately exploded, both Dodge's boon and bane; Starr Brite and Lauryl Canyon and Beverly Heels, the dragqueens and strippers who'll season the novel with some of HOMEBOY's spice; and the Yats, Chalmatians and other indigenous types who'll render it distinctively New Orleanean.

Mambo Mephiste seems as apt a title as any for this novel which will ask why lost people sometimes develop into greater human beings than those who've never been lost their whole lives; why those who've suffered most at the hands of their fellows become the genuine lovers of humanity while those whose lot is simply to acquire, to take all and give nothing, are the most contemptuous of mankind; why the loser's laugh is the one heard last and longest for he's blessed with a spirit enriched with what his heart has lost.

Christ, I hate synopsizing a book; it dehydrates the thing, deadens it. The above is a loose and sloppy weave, but then again, books aren't written with road maps. As I said in opening, a book is a protean thing, mercurial, capricious; the pure piercing grace notes are struck only in the quickening of its own creation.

Semper fi,
Seth

"I never could find out exactly where New Orleans
is. I have looked for it on the map without much
enlightenment. It is dropped down there somewhere in the marshes of the Mississippi and the
bayous and lakes. It is below the one and tangled
up among the others, or it might some day float
out to the Gulf and disappear. How the Mississippi
gets out I never could discover. When it first
comes in sight of the town, it is running east;
at Carrollton, it abruptly turns its rapid, broad,
yellow flood, and runs south, then turns presently
eastward, circles a great portion of the city, then
makes a bold push for the north in order to avoid
Algiers and reach the foot of Canal Street and
encountering then the heart of the town, it sheers
off again along the old French Quarter and Jackson
Square due east, and goes no one knows where."

From *Harper's New Monthly Magazine*
(New York: Harper and Brothers)
"Sui Generis,"
by Charles Dudley Warner (1887)

CHAPTER ONE

MERLIN LEDOUX BLEW HIS BRAINS OUT Labor Day weekend. While
New Orleans did what it did best, party, and only death paid homage
to the work ethic by putting in overtime.

When a Gentilly teenager unzipped his mother's throat with a
Kay Pro electric carving knife because he needed her help with his
homework and couldn't wait for her to finish watching a summer
rerun of *Green Acres*, the cops dallied long enough at a civic crab
boil for the youth to finish his assignment using a neighbor's World
Book. When a Tulane professor served his wife a barbecued penis
disguised as a hotdog, with mustard and onions, her lover's other
remains were stored in a refrigerated semitrailer rented to handle
the morgue overflow awaiting the coroner's return from Cancun.
And when what was left of Merlin LeDoux required an undertaker,
none could be found that wasn't playing intramural softball in City
Park.

None that is until someone remembered that Roma Ida Pana
Funeral Home was boycotting the series over the banning of aluminum fungo bats. A false issue, most agreed. Citing the funeral
home's lastplace finish in three of the previous four seasons, most

cried sour grapes. The single season that Romana Ida Pana — "RIP's the name, death's our game," was the parlor's inside boast — finished out of the cellar, they were disqualified for fielding a ringer, a semi-pro pitcher working off the funeral debt incurred when the Mississippi jumped the levee down in a lower river parish, drowning his entire family.

"Romano Ida Pana gonna do yer big brother bootiful," promised the bleached blonde riding shotgun in Diogenes LeDoux's '64 Riviera, just in case her boss had any doubts.

They were driving through holiday traffic thick as flies toward the funeral home. Hearing one had been found that was open, Dodge had offered a prayer of thanks. Learning that it was on Veterans Boulevard in Metairie, he took it back. Forced sorties over the parish line numbed Dodge with horror; the burbscape of monster malls and oceanic parking lots dinned his heart with despair. If there was a hell, he was positive it was paved and would lay odds it included a parking slot reserved eternally for Diogenes.

Blip blip blip! What seemed more like a nerve ending than a car phone bleeped manically. The blonde swung the receiver to her ear. "Bon Temps Bail Bonds," she trilled. "Say what? . . ." She listened some more, eyes widening. "Lemme ax Mr. LeDoux," she said finally and covered the mouthpiece. "Dodge, it's Little Louie again. They got him on a shooting this time. Twenty large."

"What shooting?" Little Louie was a bunko artist, his specialty selling Dr. Goody's headache powder as cocaine to tourists on Bourbon.

"Well, he was in this bar and in comes this motheroo wavin a gun yelling who's the sonuvabitch been toppin his old lady, and Little Louie looked round and seen he was the only sonuvabitch in the place. Well, one thing led to another and the guy ended up with a bullet inna head and Louie, he got the gun in his hand and a little charge . . . We gotta go the little fella's bond. You member what happened to him last time we left him overnight with all those prisoners. He learnt the meaning of hardened criminals, if you get my drift. He couldn't sit down for a week."

"It must of been good to him. Why else would he be in such a hurry to get back?"

"Aw, Dodge . . . He's like the rest. He aint doin the crimes no more, they doin him."

"Those hardened criminals are what's gonna do him."

"One little shooting and he's suddenly a mad dog."

"One little shooting and he's a dangerous bond. Now get off the phone. I'm waiting for a call."

Slitting her eyes, the blonde spoke again into the receiver. "Louie? Mr. LeDoux is tending to his departed brother, but as soon as he can, he'll take care of you."

"Right," Dodge LeDoux cracked.

She hung up with a sigh and returned to the business at hand. "I'm here to tell ya, Dodge. RIP did my Uncle Looie *gaw*-geous." The banquettes of New Orleans and sidewalks of Hoboken are right across the street.

"Die young and leave a beautiful corpse," he muttered. Trading pulpy platitudes was a game the brothers played when Merle was maybe twelve and Dodge ten. Contests of cool with subtextual currents navigatable only by the boys, dialectic combats at which Dodge, whose soul was closest to a Pico Boulevard epigrammist's, invariably prevailed. "But how," he asked himself aloud, "can you be beautiful with your face blown off?"

The blonde sighed. "You aint just a trip, bo, you a freakin journey."

Not that Audrey Canova was any day at the beach herself. Her carhop goodlooks and Bingo piety could only titillate a RV salesman from Chalmette, where Andrew Jackson beat back the British and Audrey was born in a shotgun double two miles past the Industrial Canal drawbridge, raised on red beans, rice, redface morality and redneck values; and crowned Miss Tractor Pull her senior year at the high school down the street from Fats Domino's pink stucco *palazzo*.

Her mission in life was the safekeeping of Dodge LeDoux, disbarred lawyer become poozy proprietor of Bon Temps Bail Bonds. And this Dodge cherished, for he'd played out his every other sympathizer, breaking their hearts unhooping them from his own, drinking them under some table from beneath which they would not have to suffer his own. This blonde bombshell some moons since exploded was his last surviving sponsor. She cared for Dodge in the overindulgent manner of an older sister compensating for absent parents, the way a little girl might pamper a favorite doll. Such devotion was any drunk's dream, and Dodge's last. So he needed Audrey today; he brought her along even though it meant closing the offices and losing the business of the multitude of felonies and misdemeanors awaiting just this beery dog day baccanal to be born.

"When you die, bo," she continued in her smartalecky blind date voice punctuated with snaps of chewing gum like whip cracks, "they wont even bother dressing you in black, cuz if you dont like hell, you coming back."

Nothing new there; it was the same rap always laid down: that the younger LeDoux boy was hellbent, while the elder was heaven bound. Saint and sinner, they were marked oppositely at birth, Merlin blond, blueeyed, tall, a chip off Poppy's block; and Dodge, with something of Mother in his thick dark hair and something of none knew what or whom in his black eyes; dark hair which today, dank and damp, was raked back from his brow in scraggly furrows by nicotined nailbit fingers, and eyes on whose black fathomless waters moved weathers of archetypal guilt.

Because suicide was more Dodge's M.O. than Merlin's, it was his style to fold his hand and Merlin to hold his cards for the draw. "Dodge has the smarts and Merlin the heart," he'd heard the theorem so often in playpens and playgrounds, observed its proof over and over in their adult lives beginning when Merlin became a cop to fight for the law and he took the bar to argue it, that he would have known as surely as he knew he must have another drink that it should be his corpse awaiting Merle's instructions even if he hadn't more direct knowledge.

"I tried it once myself," he fessed up to Audrey, reaching for the pint of Ten High nested in the open glove compartment.

"Cashing your chips in?" The Chalmatian gunned him a severe sidelong beneath spikelashed awnings.

"Lunched on my gun," wincing at the sooty scorch of cheap bourbon down his throat, reaching for the Pepsi chaser on the seat between them.

"Get outta here," she dismissed the very notion. "You a survivor, bo."

"No such thing."

"Yeah?" She turned in her seat, draping her arm across its back, wreathed in wry smiles painted Walgreen fuchsia. "So what happened?" snapping her gum to emphasize that savvy Chalmatians didn't go for fried ice cream.

"I was shaking so bad I busted my bridgework on the sights trying to say a Hail Mary."

She said it again, "Get outta here," but coyly this time, as if Dodge were pulling her actual, not allegorical leg.

When indeed he was pulling no leg at all. Dodge had made the attempt, he was a suicide manqué, the broken bridge dropped in the sink beneath his bathroom mirror on Austerlitz Street. Dodge's first thought on hearing of Merlin was, He couldn't have been looking in the mirror the way I was. You can't shoot yourself and watch it, too. The same as you can't have your cake and throw it in someone's face both. Dodge lifted and dropped his shoulders in resignation. He wasn't sure whether he wanted to be dead or wanted that dignity which death might bestow, that dignity which had eluded him all his life. Scarcely a day went by that he didn't contemplate suicide, but always with the paradoxical Tom Sawyer proviso that he be able to attend his own funeral.

It was that same self pity that Mother enjoyed tagging as dramatic flair after five or six sidecars. "The theater lives in Diogenes," she seemed as certain as if she had it straight from some *deus ex machina.* "It *breathes* in him." Like most theatrical failures, she spoke of it always in italics, with a stagey vibrato. "It flows through his *veins,*" passing Merle a chary slandenticular as if unsure what infection coursed through his.

Merlin bored his mother. He lived boyhood by the numbers — Eagle scout, team captain, the first in his class to memorize the capitals of every state. He was the best and brightest and most boring to a woman whose only fulfillment was amusement, for whom everything was rated as divertissement. All life being a stage was a literal homile for this failed actress Poppy first spotted in New York, at a postwar Allied extravaganza at the Copacabana. She was impersonating la Liberté in a burlesque of the French Revolution. Could Poppy have dreamed were he not gassed on Old Grand Dad, could he have guessed were he not gaslit by her looks that this colt legged chorine in tricolored pasties was a warrior queen offstage as well, that once installed back in New Orleans as Mrs. Gaston Falgout LeDoux she would ring up the domestic curtain on her own reign of terror? And that her second born would become her most ardent captain.

An obverse momma's boy was Diogenes — she alone used his given name after he had forbidden it from all others; whatever had died in her lived on in him, he was her undisguised favorite to whom she forced Poppy over his better judgment to show partiality, just as she picked his ties and chose his Mardi Gras krewe for him.

And Merle stoically endured it, both his mother's weary disdain and father's acquiescent neglect. Wonder how he might how the son who shone the brightest should light up his parents eyes the least, inwardly fret as he must have at his nullity, Merle never his whole boyhood wore his heart where it might show, never reacted until shortly after his graduation from Tulane when both his parents boycotted his marriage in favor of the catfish rodeo in which Dodge placed first. Mother and Poppy took the Lincoln to Pass Christian where Mother celebrated her son's angling virtuosity by renting a sloop and they regatta'd on the gulf, Poppy passed out face down in the scuppers and Mother slinging sidecars from a thermos while undoing her bikini straps like ribbons to sunbathe topless on the foredeck. Pet banes were Mother's bikini lines, and every crewman's boon.

Dodge blinked in the aluminum glare of an Airstream trailer he was tailgating. He shifted behind the wheel with a curse. Compounding the misery of this forced hajj was an unaccountable erection spraining against his fly. He should be used to such untimely boners by now; they arose not by any erotic response but according to some haywire hemodynamic over which he had little control except to further anaesthetize himself with drink.

Hence he lunged once more for the Ten High sloshing on the sprung dash cover, suddenly, and the Rivi swerved into the next lane, nearly sideswiping an Econoline stuffed with redfaced football fans on their way to a Saints exhibition game against the Detroit Lions.

"Ginny women!" Audrey spritzed, pointing. The fans were howling obscenities and flipping them the bird. The pumping bird Dodge flashed back was little help in communicating peaceful intentions. One of the pigskin zealots jumped on his seat to flash back a pressed ham. Dropping his trousers, he mushed pink hairy cheeks against the Safelite window, skewing his crack, creating a living Yin Yang symbol.

Not that the aging sockhopper beside Dodge LeDoux was impressed. She laughed derisively, her tongue spurting from her mouth like the flesh from a split pomegranite. "No imagination," she indicted them. "Straight to droptrow." Audrey Canova cut her teeth on General Diaz Boulevard where driveby terrorism was a fact of life and droptrow a martial art. She dismissed their antics with a perfunctory gumsnap. "Someone awta show em what droptrow's all about. What dey awta do is put a cigaret in there, make em a *smoked* pressed ham."

But Dodge was oblivious to the refinements of droptrow. He was returned once more to Merle's wedding day, remembering it like tearing back the scab on an old wound. Merle said his vows sans famille. High, wide and all too handsome — Dodge later saw the wedding photos — Merle did all he could to salve the lesion on the honor of Billie Bordelon's Creole tribe. But words were no remedy for this affront, the marriage was doomed before it was born; Merle knew it as certainly as he knew Mother was behind it. So he resolved to sober Poppy up, awake him to the treachery of his own house. Back to the family camp in Maurepas he drove through the night, and poured Poppy's Old Grand Dad off the rickity wooden dock forgetting that the old man would have to drive to Spanish Bend for more, which he did, weeping drunk, and plunged the Lincoln into the bayou and drowned. Thereafter Merle knew the guilt of his father's death and never again came home after the funeral.

While the whiskered fish Dodge caught still hung in the hallway on Austerlitz, and the trophy cup yet centered the diningroom table where Dodge wrote shopping lists with his finger in the dust.

AUSPICES

The dragqueen unplucked billboard lips from the candystriped straw wetly rattling up the remains of her grape Slurpee. "What does *my* real name matter?" she moued. A baseball cap clutched bleached curls to her bean; on its crown was stitched the cutesypie caveat: DONT MESS WITH MY TOOT TOOT.

"Huh?" Through the windows of Bon Temps Bail Bonds Audrey had been watching inkblack clouds tumbling up from the Gulf, shadowing the streets of New Orleans with the gloom; the same gloom, actual as nausea, she felt welling up in herself, bleak and black, spreading to every nerve like spilt ink spreading on blotting paper.

"It's Vince Thibodeaux I'm bailing," the dragqueen said, switching high hips around Audrey's desk. "I was his penitentiary wife, yuh know. Till parole do us part, yeah. I was his bunk muffin, his big yard bunny . . ." The dragqueen giggled and would have blushed were not one already painted on her cheek. "Anyway, his is the only name that counts, but here they want mine," pointing to the troublesome line on the bond application. The dragqueen stamped the tapped heel of a leopardskin pump, striking sparks. "I *hate* my real name."

"What is it?" Audrey couldn't help be curious.

"Trudy," the dragqueen groaned; then to further express her disgust with it, stretched it into a playground taunt: "*Truuu*deee."

"I think that's a lovely name. Who gave it to you?"

"My grandmother." The dragqueen rolled her eyes like a silent-screen vamp, then spread candied lips in a smile. "My stage name's Beverly Heels."

"That's fine, then," Audrey gladly acquiesced with a lame witticism, "A queen has a right to her title."

"I aint no queen, my mama's still alive. I'm a princess!"

Audrey nodded weakly. She didn't bother telling Miss Heels that her boss, Diogenes LeDoux, would write Vincent Thibodeaux's bail regardless, she could cosign the application Minnie Mouse for all it mattered. Ever since Vincent saved Dodge's dead brother's honor, restoring his full cop's pension for his widow, her boss would pull the fleabrained flimflammer's fat out of the fire every time. It was a matter of honor. And in matters of honor, Dodge LeDoux didn't just overlook details, he ignored essentials. And it was going to get his boneroo buns in trouble one of these days, five would get you ten, was Audrey's line.

Another thing she didn't tell Miss Heels was that at this moment Dodge was attending Vincent's lineup over in the courthouse, and that likely as not, the riverrat couldn't be identified by the tourists he hustled Dr. Goody's headache powder to as cocaine, and the case for bunko sales would nolle prossed, and the dragqueen could hang on to the ten percent premium she doubtlessly earned skulling enough Dauphine Street cruisers to get lockjaw. Dodge always said never get clients' hopes up, that the only surprises should be good ones. Clients. The term killed Audrey. The aroma of respect it loaned the riffraff parading through the doors of Bon Temps Bail Bonds sickened her. But that was the gentleman in Mr. Diogenes LeDoux; he had class; and it was just that quality that kept Audrey's loyalty.

"Your stage name's fine," Audrey said sweet as pie.

"It's not just pretend, babe. I'm really a celebrity intwerpreter," Beverly Heels made sure Audrey understood. "My specialty's Barbra Streisand."

"I *love* Barbra!"

"You'd love her more the way I do her," pronounced La Heels with all the conviction of a veteran inured to rave notices.

As if on cue, the shoplifting music seeping through the speaker-phone on Audrey's desk segued in "People," and the dragqueen reared back on her endangered species heels, clasped large beringed hands to her silicone bazoom, and gave it her all

People, people who need people
are the luckiest people in the world. . . .

The impromptu recital was interrupted by the moronic arpeggios of a bananabcaked black bird perched atop the dead files. The macaw had been at it all day, splitting the stale office like a leaky airhorn, as if Audrey needed reminding that her job at Bon Temps Bail Bonds was for the birds. Even the name was becoming a largening misnomer these dwindling dog days of summer as good times at 4066 South Broad became scarcer than virgins on Bourbon Street.

"Shut Up!" screamed Audrey, clapping her hands to her ears — and screamed again punching an earring post dug into her tender neck flesh.

"Yo mama!" the macaw screeched back. The only two words he knew, their politer approximation had become his name — Joe Mama.

"What's with the Tweetie Bird?" asked Miss Heels.

"It's the weather," Audrey explained. "He starts fussin when it's fixin to storm."

"He's good as a barometer then," Miss Heels judged, "which gotta be fallin faster n a piss hardon."

"That's what spooks him, the fallin pressure," added Audrey, although a bit uncertainly, since she was spooked herself by something in the air this early fall evening. Yet something immeasurable to gauges, something more than just the usual calm before the storm. It was as if heaven itself held its breath the way Audrey once held hers passing graveyards. "Just go ahead and enter your stage name Miss, uh . . . Heels. I don't think Barbra herself could put the *feeling* into that song like you did, babe."

"Yah!" The dragqueen flung herself on her elbows on Audrey's desk, pencil scribbling; and at first Audrey thought it was a transparent flying cockroach whizzing by, but it was a plastic syringe that flipped out of Miss Heels's blouse pocket and landed *sproing* right between Audrey's fingers where they rested outstretched beside the Radio Shack calculator.

"Sorry," the dragqueen gurgled.

Audrey managed a strangled something between a hiccup and *eeeck*.

"Excuse me." Delicately, the way one might defuse a bomb, Beverly Heels took Audrey's wrist, removing the hand whose bones still hummed to the frequency of the vibrating trajectile, which the dragqueen next tried dislodging with a gentle back and forth motion. But it wouldn't yield, not this wee excalibur. With a final Arthurian effort, she snapped the syringe clean off, leaving its point embedded in the wooden desk top. Audrey stared aghast, spinaltapped with the horror of viral toxins spreading like sap through the porous blond oak and hearing Dodge laugh at her fear of AIDS, mocking that she could only contract the virus if she planned having anal sex with her desk. That was Dodge's other side, Mr. Smartypants, superior in a way that was all the more wounding for his being a gentleman at heart. But when you've been through and seen the things Dodge LeDoux had, Audrey supposed . . .

"Where's your AC, girl?" Beverly Heels had to know.

"Audrey enjoyed explaining how Dodge's wife, Irma, Reno'd him last June, giving him the shaft while she ganked the gold mine, including the brand new office Fedders. Dodge had substituted a swamp cooler which, in this city built ludicrously six feet below level, was like having a threeton frog breathing through the window. Audrey lingered over the venal details of the divorce, dwelt in depth on Irma's each cruelty with a peculiar admixture of delectation and disgust constituting both a celebration of her sex's peerless fury and an incitation to uxoricide. A flash of lightning electrifying the office's blue dusk provided a dramatic coda to the narrative.

"Yo mama!" quoth the macaw.

"I wuddnt take that shit off no bird," Beverly averred, slanting the disheveled fowl a sidelong.

"I gotta," groaned Audrey. "Some spic coke dealer left him for collateral. Dodge says he's valuable. But all he does is poop and talk dirty."

"Like some men I've known," the dragqueen said.

"Amen," Audrey raised her hand. Beneath the mutter of Broad Street traffic she heard thunder rolling distantly and was reminded of antiphonal church chanting. God, she wished Dodge would hurry back from court. Audrey hated it when he left her hanging out alone like wet laundry in the office, prey to the Gypsies, freaks, and fuufuus comprising his clientele. It got her nervous as an Okie flea on a Texas steer.

"You got anudder straw, babe?" To demonstrate the worthlessness of her own wilted one, Beverly Heels lifted it from the Slurpee like a candystriped worm. Audrey shook her head no. The dragqueen shrugged and reinserted the soggy straw through the hole in the plastic lid. The force of her subsequent supersuck collapsed the twelveounce cup with a gurgle approximating a draining bathtub. Tossing the spent Slurpee in the trash, Beverly chortled, "Like some *other* men I've know — wet *noodles*."

"And how," breathed Audrey.

"Yo mama!" quoth Joe Mama.

"I'm gonna hoseclamp your bony lips," threatened Audrey, "make em tighter than yo mama's pussy ever was, airtight."

"You tell him, honey," nodded Beverly, returning her attention to the application. Audrey wished she'd sit down: the way she leaned her elbows on the desk and locomotioned hootchy-kootchy haunches to the music seeping through the speakerphone made the redheaded secretary squirm even, and Audrey had been around a few corners her own damn self. Even standing stockstill there was a shimmery quality to Beverly Heels, an undulation like something wreathed in heat that left actual women feeling swindled and usurped.

Audrey distracted herself staring out the window at a palm across the street. Its long serrated fronds reminded her of piano keyboards, played invisibly by the wind. She imagined the wind was playing the same melody she heard over the phone, "Raindrops Keep Fallin' On My Head." It was about the third time she'd heard the tune that afternoon, it must be part of some rainy day program. What more could she expect from Greyhound?

Audrey had been listening to telephone hold music ever since Dodge made paper for Isador Jones, crack king of the Desire Projects, who boosted the office radio, a shiny new Sanyo with detachable speakers, on his way out the door. Cold*ganked* the Angola briefcase, stuffed it under his Adidas warmup jacket, if that didn't beat all for gratitude. There wasn't another bondsman on South Broad who'd raise up the Duke of Desire, and he does Dodge like that.

"There's some people who oughtta *stay* in jail," Audrey was prone to point out the practical deficiencies of the business, to which the slight and soignee man with slickedback hair would simply smile and say they had rights, as if being born in the U.S. of A. was like being baptized or something; and even then, Audrey felt entitled to know, weren't we all born with wrongs to go with all those rights. Classic Dodge LeDoux — ready to believe the best in everyone but himself, a man with no wants but to be little noted nor long remembered; a guy out for the underdog, hounds whose days had yet to come or never would.

She listened at first to New Orleans Public Services until the *Times-Picayune* began publishing editorials calling for a buyout, and overnight the utilities giant began answering its phones. Next she tried the airlines and the Internal Revenue Service and even a high-volume funeral home, but either their casual courtesy programming was too yechy even for Audrey's easy ear or their inefficiency and sloth were unreliable. At length she found that only Greyhound could still be counted on for extended musical holding patterns interrupted only minimally by a svelte voice purring, as it did just now: *"All our agents are presently busy assisting other customers. Please continue to hold . . ."*

"When's yer boss gonna buy you a new radio?" it occurred to Miss Heels to ask.

Audrey flipped her hand. "The twelfth of never. He says why buy the cow when you can milk it through the fence."

The dragqueen gunned the telephone a narrow onceover, inspecting for udders perhaps. She clucked her tongue then and patroled it around those cherryred lips, making Audrey cringe to imagine each sexual misdemeanor at which the fuzzy muscle was adept. "It asks here for local references," lisped the misdemeaning muscle, "but I only come to town last week."

"Oh, really?" Audrey's arched brows were hardly surprised. New Orleans like a grate collected garbage. "How'd we get so lucky?"

"This stumpjumper picked me up in St Louie," Beverly hitched a hand backwards on the broad plastic belt cinching her Capris to explain, "he was in a major hurry. And when you in a hurry, you go south. The Big Sleazy's where he ran out of highway." At the corner of her painted eye a tear trembled. "Next thing he run out was me." The sooty donewrong drop broke free; willynillied down the nellie's cheek and found her mouth which muttered, "Dirty motheroo."

"Yo mama!" squawked the macaw.

"I aint talkin about my mama!" Beverly sobbed, her mojo momentarily stilled.

Audrey snatched a large caliber waterpistol from her open desk drawer and drew a bead on the macaw. Through clenched teeth she muttered, "Dont make me use this."

"Your call will be answered in the order in which it was received . . ."

Taking Audrey in with new eyes, Beverly breathed, "I wish John Wayne could have lived to see this," and recommended that shimmy shimmy kokopah, chugging her sweet Georgia Brown which, without shifting a discernible muscle, could move mountains.

Shrugging modestly, Audrey put the gun away. "A girl does what she's got to do," she said, a suitably laconic response, and one best left standing neat, except that Audrey, doubtlessly moved by Beverly's candor and certainly further inspired by the naugahyde version of "My Girl" bleating over the phone, adopted the phrase as her own hardluck leitmotif and was suddenly sweet sixteen again, a dewdimpled desert daisy from Gallup, New Mexico with a conscience in civil war over whether to let Ray Montoya score home on prom night, like the whole fourbagger. He'd made third already, it happened at the twilite doublebill at the sonic drivein. But that was a steal really. He waited until she had a mouthful of popcorn extra butter before snatching knuckledeep up her cheerleader skirt. She tried screaming but succeeded only in limning the windshield with yellow goop. And ole Ray, that showman, grabbed the keys out of the ignition, jumped out of the car and passed stinky pinky beneath the inquiring noses parked nearby. "Boys will be boys," is the dispensation Audrey granted this transgression, by which she sanctioned its corollary, namely that girls will be girls (and do what they must), which she proved prom night by letting Ray Montoya make home standing up. Not that he was grateful, Ray was all psyched up to powerslide across the plate with flying spikes.

"Which just goes to show there aint no way of makin a man happy," Audrey schooled Beverly. "And the last way to try is by givin him what he wants."

Not that Audrey herself could benefit from her own dearly bought wisdom: it was too late for her, back when her heart beat like an Indian drum beneath a painted sky — "I was a shortbed pickup," she was known to giggle girlwards, referring to the 4X4 pickup truck, preferred mount of the sheiks of the burning sands — skinnydipping in remote watertanks, staring up grey weathered planks at a cloud-puffed sky, she learned how to fake orgasms and blow cigaret smoke through her nose and turned bad for good — "And once you're a pickle, you aint never gonna be a cucumber again, lemme put you wise."

"At least you were a cuke for a while," Beverly Heels said meaningfully. "That's more than some of us can say."

Audrey allowed that there was some truth in that and fastcut to two years past when she flew into town from Vegas for Sugar Bowl on a highroller's private jet, and had the Hurricanes won she might have seen the last of the Crescent City. But they didn't, they blew it on a missed field goal with thirty seconds left on the clock; and instead of sipping bubbly in a hottub thirty thousand feet over purple mountains majesty, Audrey found herself broke and alone one deadbeat drizzly Bourbon Street dawn with no better hope than to answer an ad in the classifieds that read *Gal Friday, Able to take shorthand and a joke.*

"This his idea of a joke?" she heard Beverly say and looked over her shoulder where the dragqueen stood staring out the window.

"I dont get you . . ."

Beverly Heels motioned Audrey over without removing her stare from the window. The rain had begun without Audrey noticing, great marshsmelling drops drumming the panes like myriad mad fingers. Lightning flickered, and a blade quivered in capitals of the courthouse columns long enough to carve the words GOVERN-MENT OF LAWS, NOT MEN. A time switch lit the neon tubes spelling Bon Temps Bail Bonds, splashing the flashing yellow letters across the vast convex windshield of a vintage Buick Riviera just pulling into the driveway, raindrops plucking clouds of steam off its hood.

"That's one car you dont care for a lift in . . ." Beverly Heels whispered. "That's his Rivi, the Sandman . . ."

Audrey was beginning to wonder what was loaded in the syringes Beverly Heels packed about. "What are you talking about?"

"You aint heard of the Sandman?" Terror sheeted Beverly's eyes, reflecting the huge black automobile. "The *bobolawo*. . . . Look, girl, I gotta make dust."

Whatever ogre the Buick transported, Audrey had no wish to be alone with him; but there was nothing she could say, she hadn't time. Turning from the window, she watched wan and woeful as Beverly vaulted her desk, feet slashing the air like leopard paws. With a hustler's finetuned arfydarfy instinct for secondary egress, Audrey located the back door down the hallway by the john no sweat and was gone like a turkey through the corn.

She heard the frontdoor open behind her, felt the wet rush of the storm, heard the rain thrashing concrete, felt the wet wind coiling about her legs like rope. She turned at the sudden voice: "Am I going crazy or did I just watch some bellhead break out of a bailbound office? I mean, you already got her out of jail."

He was over forty, tall, a mullato Audrey guessed from his cafeau-lait complexion and soft curly hair tipped with silver. He wore a loosefitting shirt, white, patterned with apples. Its buttons were little red shells like tiny conchs. Yet it wasn't his loud shirt or buc-caneer good looks that distinguished him, but his glasses. Eyewear was the term Audrey picked up from tabloids featuring celebrity myopics. Who had all better move over because this dude had them beat hands down, *his* frames were molded into the shapes of twin toilet bowls. Behind their lenses thick as aquarium glass his floating eyes seemed molten red, although Audrey couldn't be sure the lenses weren't tinted.

"It was a him," she said, coyly, sexually au fait but ingenuous nonetheless.

The mullato wagged his head at the merry mystery of It All. "Appearances can fool ya," he said, and Audrey heard the slight Spanish inflection. She smelled something foreign, too, something herbal, a dry, bitter aroma one might encounter at the back bins at the French Market where black women in bright turbans trafficked; and something burnt as well — ashes, that's what, wisping from the mullato. She tried telling herself that it was one of those undeniably male musks or other sold in department stores as she retreated behind her desk. "You have business . . ."

"Oh yes, with Mr. Diogenes LeDoux." His voice was a steel purr. Unbidden, he sat unbidden opposite her, crossing long legs and smiling a smile learned too late in life and not very well.

Audrey explained that Dodge was over at the courthouse attending a showup, but would return shortly if the gentleman cared to wait, there was coffee out back and a Circle K across the street for a cold drink. To this the mullato attended with a rictus smile showing yellow incisors, red eyes waterballeting in their toilet bowls.

"The, uh . . . shemale called you the Sandman," Audrey caught herself saying as she lit a cigaret.

"The chick with a dick?" chuckled the mullato, a sound like a chain being dragged up his throat. "Yes, I've been called that."

Audrey was staring at his walking stick. It was white, ivory maybe, glued all over with the same red shells comprising his shirt buttons and embellished with protruberent carvings like ones Audrey had seen carved on old churches. Their name was on the tip of her tongue . . . gargletoys. What else was it that Beverly Heels called him? . . . "How on earth did you get that name?"

"Sandman? Because I sprinkle stardust in their eyes and whisper, Go to sleep, everything's all right." The red orbs fastened on her cigaret resting in the astray. "May I," he asked, reaching for it.

"Sure. . . . Have a fresh one," offered Audrey. But before she could shake one from her pack, he snatched and ate her lit one whole, red eyes glowing like its coal.

Audrey had to say something to keep from screaming. "I think," she blurted, "I think it's a *cute* name, Sandman."

Again the chaindriven chuckle. "Oh I've picked up lots of spare handles over the years. My favorite's Professor Pooreyes. It sounds

340

like a character in some kid's book." The smile forked sharply, showing the gums anchoring the incisors, emitting a wisp of smoke. "Professor Pooreyes is . . . *nice*."

"Yo mama," quoth Joe Mama.

For once Audrey didn't squawk back.

SHOW UP

It was like walking into any highschool auditorium until your nose stuffed with the twicebreathed fetor of unwashed bodies, boiled beans and battered dreams, and you noted stenciled on the proscenium arch of the squeaky plank stage the letters S H O W U P. The empty dimness was enlivened by a sussurant echo. Up one aisle an old black swung a mop, brushing slow liquid arcs reflecting the moiling violet light boxed through the auditorium's one window. His face was striated like a channel turtle's, his body bowed from lugging its carapace of woe. All his adult years this burden had pressed on letters such as those now blocked across his stooped and sweatdamp shoulders — OPP, for Orleans Parish Prisoner. He thumped the mophead against seats stained with cutplug tobacco in time to the evilwoman blucs he moaned

They call it Stormy Monday
But Tuesday's just as bad

Side by side in the second row sat two women, tourists it was plain from their sunburns, for ladies south of Memphis shun the sun. The larger one — and a beasty thing she was, with a lantern jaw and neck accordianed with fat — was helmeted with metal curlers like industrial semiconductors. Hearing the melodious mope, she hove around in her seat, gunned the mopster a sarcastic squint through bifocals worn as an excuse to look down her nose at the world, and cawed, "Is the floor show free?"

Pausing with the mop in the bucket, the trustee airplucked a bass-fiddle lick down its shaft.

"Maybe that one is," her companion said in a voice squeezed small by the heat. She propped her feet on the seat in front of her, feet encased in fuzzy pink slippers meant to represent rabbits, with floppy ears and beady red eyes affixed to the toes. "But this little show comin up's may cost your marriage. I mean, Bob's gonna *know*." She waggled her feet, nodding the rabbits in agreement.

The first made a throwaway motion. "Bob's sleepin in fronta the

TV back in Grand Rapids," resettling herself with a splintery creak in her seat. "When the police said they'd pay the hotel for me to stay on and ID this creep . . . Hey, there's signs and there's *signs*."

The trustee picked up his longgone lullaby where the mophead whumped a seat

Wundsday's sumptin awful
N Thoirsday's oh so sad
The Eagle flies on Friday

The mop skidded to a halt inches from a pair of scuffed white bucks crossed at argyll ankles. The crevasses in the trustee's face multiplied in a smile of recognition; he raised eyes yellowed like old wallpaper to meet grey ones fitted frankly above a fixed faint smirk. "Why, Mister Bondsman."

Diogenes LeDoux leaned in the cubed shadows crowding the window casement. His long dark hair was matted by the humidity, flowing straight back from his brow in wavy furrows raked by blunt fingers. Sweat strained through his blue shirt, staining his rumpled whitelinen jacket, helping it live up to its label "Tropical Blend." His planed cheeks were cut in several places where he'd shaved that morning. Not having had a drink in two days, it was a wonder LeDoux didn't cut his head off. In the auditorium's vast faint breathy echo he heard the prayers of the guilty, a requiem for his own soul. Knowing these auditory messages to be hallucinative — angel feathers, the Camp Street tipplers called them — only surcharged their reality.

"Rescued from the streets again, Ike?" leaked the crimped mouth, a smirk in appearance alone, fixed on LeDoux's puss by the battering barroom fists that scarred his upper lip, paralyzing enough of its muscle so that only that fraction could move which loaned his each smile mute derision.

"Yes, indeed." Ike leaned on the mop like a monk's crozier to tell his tale, but LeDoux listened with only one ear, the other being cocked to the merry wives of Wichita's talk. He had run into them quite by chance, up at Narcotics where he'd gone to cajole a copy a Charlie's arrest report from Bobby Bordelon, his dead brother's old partner. The wives emerged with Lt. Hardin from his office laughing at a private joke, gusting clouds of bourbon that squirmed LeDoux's bowels. Lord, the drunkard's encyclopedic recall of strong spirits: he even remembered the lieutenant's lowshelf label — Ten High.

When the lieutenant spotted LeDoux the blood ran from his suddenly frozen grin, and the skin stretched drumtight on his skull, and

LeDoux beheld with the piercing clarity of delerium tremens the death's head he first perceived within the Rorschach pattern blown onto the Biloxi motel room ceiling through the roof of his brother's skull. It was Hardin who insisted to the panel that officers don't aim guns into their mouths when cleaning them. No less an authority than he who murdered LeDoux's brother as surely as if he'd shattered Marcel's teeth himself with the stainless twoinch barrel, felt for himself the notched sights dig into the soft palate, and with his own finger squeezed the trigger, watching the hammer lift, flinching even before the blast that would explode bone shrapnel through the motel room window, embedding one calcious arrowhead inches into the linder tree outside . . . LeDoux forgot Charlie's report, he had the inside skinny already, and hurried out of the squadroom after the wives, though whether to eavesdrop on them or escape the specter of his brother's nemesis he didn't know. He followed them out of the police building, across the plaza's (planes) shifting grey shadows, into the courthouse and down to the Show-Up Room in hopes, he told himself, of overhearing something which might be useful to Charlie's public defender.

"But carryin on with a hotdog vendor," the one with rabbit feet was complaining, "I ask you, what kind of man sells pork lips and assholes on streetcorners," and when that appeal to decorum failed, petitioned next to her pride, "You'd think you were hard up."

"So this dude come roarin inna bar wavin a roscoe," Ike laid it down. "'Where the motherfucker been toppin my ole lady?' I looks aroun n sees I'm the only motherfucker in there . . ."

"You saw the size of his whammer, you'd be the one feelin hard up. As for Roy, he deserves to find out . . ."

"One thing lead to another n next thing I knows he shot inna haid . . ."

"Jesus, you sound like you did it for him."

"N I gots a penitentiary number. Its got so I aint doin the crimes, Mister Bondsman — they doin me." The trustee chuckled philosophically. "It's a wonderland, this vale of tears."

A flash of lightning froze LeDoux's expression of bemused contemplation, wondering how it was that people who suffered the most at the hands of men were the natural believers in humanity. Hungrily his grey eyes searched those yellowed like cathouse piano keys. "You got any prayers left, Ike?"

"Sho now," nodding like a dashboard doggie.

"Say em regular n you might die free."

343

The trustee shook his head. "No chance of that Mister Bondsman. No, indeed. I goes out the back gate with the garbage this time," swinging the metronomic mop once more

Yuh know I cry Lawd Lawd have mercy
Wont someone please send my baby home

The slags wagged on over whether Roy would really know or only *think* he knew. LeDoux turned into the window and felt through a broken pane the velvetdark wind pant damp and importunate as a woman awaiting love. Adultery. Feeling disgust rise in himself like the taste of a bad hangover, he beat a fist on the window ledge. Hardly a noble motive for participating in a prosecution, but not enough to nolle prosse Charlie. Discrediting for a witness but not disqualifying.

And why must they all come here for their sin? he put it to the low clouds pressing down like hands. Where else? laughed that voice not quite his own within the cavern of his brain. They go west for a slice of a pie, south on the arfydarfy. To California in hot pursuit of cool dreams, to the Gulf Coast in desperate rout from nightmare. Hometown heritage, LeDoux nearly snorted aloud watching night march down the streets of New Orleans, spreading lights like electric seed. Beyond, over the tumbling chimney pots and mansard roofs of the French Quarter, past the profound and lightless swamps, he beheld the storm drawn up to its full black height over the Gulf, girding its loins with fire.

Sin capital of the South — it's called that for a reason, he conceded, this civic sinkhole of the continent: the place was conceived in sin. Ever since LaSalle first sunk the cross of Empire in the swamp and was murdered by his own men, it's been a mecca for the misfit and misbegotten; since that coneroo of crowns, John Law, sold the first sucker share of the Mississippi Bubble in the court of Louis XV and every prisoner in Paris was freed to marry a prostitute and sail to Louisiana, a colony of the conned and convicted, an El Dorado of the damned. It was a refuge for ruffians and robbers before the first fierce Kaintuck banked a keelboat to reap terror amongst the Creole *hoi polloi*; already a promised land for painted pigeons and their ponces by the night the first red lantern was hung in the doorway of Mother Colby's Sure Enuff Saloon advertising the entertainment awaiting river-farers. This city of carnivals and cemeteries, hotbed of *juju* and cradle of jazz, was a valhalla of vandalism and vagabondery centuries before the carpetbaggers and Mafia institutionalized such niceties in the municipal wards. And Lafitte was not the first freebooter nor would Walker, who conquered Nicaragua and was recognized as its sovereign by President Pierce, be the last filibuster to find these marsh vapors, whose humidity exceeds the proof of island rum, ideal for spinning desperate conspiracies. There was 's none of it new.

It was the shift in pitch which surfaced LeDoux from his reverie, the way country silence awakens an urban sleeper. The Michigan wives were suddenly whispering, yet the auditorium's acoustics betrayed them.

It was the one in iron curlers husking behind her hand. "I wouldn't recognize this pusbag if he sat on my face."

Beautiful. Perfect. LeDoux could think of no better lines to recite into testimony, straightfaced, in a sonorous, anchorman timbre. Goosebumps rippled down his arms.

"You dont have to. The cop said they'll be holding up cards. You just pick the one behind card number three. Sing it out, just like *The Price is Right."*

LeDoux nearly laughed loud. Suborning perjury. *Justice as a game show.* Hardin, you dickhead, you'll do a year before Charlie Horse pulls a day. Charlie'll be bounced back on the bricks, where he could remain if only he'd play that horn instead of the murphy game, plunge those valves instead of syringes. You gotta get off that train, Charlie. You know the train I'm talkin' about, the midnight express thundering the other direction through the tunnel just when you get a glimpse of light. That train. Cocaine.

"What's takin so long?" griped the one in iron curlers, rabbits twitching impatiently.

"Justice aint no more swift than blind," her companion said.

A velvetdark damp wind arose, chanting through the city's spider-work of wires, whispering darkly down the wall. LeDoux dreaded the mulchy debris doubtlessly to be dumped in the swimming pool at the Greek Revival manse on Austerlitz he shared with his sister, Celeste. Since his confiscatory divorce, the chore had devolved to LeDoux to clean this Art Deco reproduction of a Marienbad *schwimmbad* where once an aged Johnny Weismuller took some clumsy strokes that prompted the boy LeDoux to ask his mother how Tarzan ever escaped the crocodiles, especially towing Jane in his wake. And how she laughed, the bigboned barbarously beautiful showgirl his father married on a weekend Vegas R&R from Yucca Flats; a great hoarse cachinnant whooping rattling the ice in her Sidecar highball, clinking her heavy gold chain bracelets, smothering LeDoux in a cloud of sugared brandy and Chesterfield cigarets and Je Reviens parfum, clawing her bloodred nails in the air; and then she repeated the query to Weismuller propped on his forearms at the pool's bluetiled edge, burning the boy's ears with embarrassment. LeDoux would have closed the pool long since, sold its marble coping, broken up the busy mosaic bottom, scrapped the neo-Renaissance tilework shaping the allegorical figures of the four seasons at the pool's four corners. Only the doctors said swimming was therapeutic for Celeste, an antidote to her Condition, which theory was as yet unproved to LeDoux, because his sister swam only when, in the rotation of historical and celebrity female parts she played, she revived her Esther Williams role when she'd spend weeks in a scalloped bathing cap. LeDoux needn't wonder how many centuries removed was Celeste from a reprise of this characterization: this morning she'd ordained that the seventeen household cats should eat cake instead of Kibbles; but just the same, there he'd be in the morning, dutifully skimming and vacuuming waters in whose broken reflections he saw nothing but the past and pain, trudging the marble ledge with a telescopic aluminum pole and feeling like the Volga Boatman.

Doubledoors in the opposite wall gasped open. The court reporter entered first, a mousy maid who scuttled down the aisle to where her stenographer's machine was set up on a small table beneath the stage. A wan and furtive man in a wilted suit followed her, carrying a thick stack of files beneath his arm. His mean little eyes seemed repetitious of the ones glaring rabidly from the Michigan wife's feet; LeDoux made him for an assistant DA. Two meaty young men sauntered in and took stations against the wall opposite LeDoux. The elaborate and clumsy program of stage winks and collusive hand signals they directed at the merry wives made it clear that they were the arresting officers. Next Hardin strode through the doors and took a seat in the middle of a middle row, draping his long arms over the seats beside him like a Broadway director. He took in LeDoux with a lupine grin that bragged, Now we got your boy Charlie Horse, he just raised up from the joint and this is his fourth felony fall—he'll need a wheelbarrow to truck his time out of court. LeDoux smiled tightly back, ashiver with the exhilarant belief that this time he had the motheroo beat.

"Item six oh five niner *twuh!*" halloed the Show-Up officer, a portly parish deputy with a plume of white hair and bulged blue eyes who'd entered the auditorium last and taken up station at a lectern several paces in front of the first row seats, facing the stage. "Break a leg, gents."

A whooping offstage chorus suggested breaking the deputy's face instead. The footlights then came up, blazing a backdrop hash-marked for height. Out slunk and slouched six prisoners in single file, shooting sullen stares into the dark. And there was Charlie Horse, the railthin riverrat in slot number three whose narrow, near-ly handsome face showed the scars of pitched adolescent battle with acne and now closing on forty still challenged the world to reveal its next adversary. *With rings on his fingers,* thought LeDoux seeing the dull flash of potmetal skulls, beaten quarters, and bent horse-shoe nails covering the words tattooed across his knuckles, LOVE and HATE; *and bells on his toes,* hearing the slow insolent click of steel taps nailed to the soles of phony snakeskin cowboy boots so thin that Charlie liked to brag that if he stepped on a nickle he could tell if it was heads or tails. *You know the drill, you've shown up a dozen times before. This bunco sales is humbug. Just dont fuck up and you walk,* LeDoux telepathed in G major, Charlie's home key. Those lips pursed perennially as if to spit, kiss or blow a brassy picture of his soul; sorcerous lips able to beg, bully, or beguile from a tenor saxophone rainbow notes that made Coltrane sound as if he honked a kazoo. *Aw, Charlie do you remember the night at Pon-chartrain Beach, the Ferris lights turning round a ragtime moon, mad Ezekial's neon wheel, and the little girls talking out of their heads? Marcel was with us, remember? He stole that car so we could make your scene in style. Play it chilly . . .*

It was too late. Charlie Horse broke rank, springing to the apron of the stage, shading his eyes against the lights. Up flew a shiverish forefinger; the screech ripped out with a force dancing him in a spasdic hornpipe:

"Ha! That's her! I'd know her in my dreams. Wet nightmares! That's the bitch!"

The rain started then, splattery bigdropped volleys at first, like a girl slinging water from her hair, then a steady black sibilance, louder than the traffic, the city's mechanical groan, the elegiac echo even, but not so loud as the birds LeDoux heard crying overhead, the sparrowhawks and cranes, blue herons and egrets in desperate wheeling flight from the storm's implacable eye.

NOTES ON CONTRIBUTORS

Jazz guitarist JOHN ABERCROMBIE's most recent album is *Getting There* (ECM).

HILTON ALS is at work on a collection of essays entitled *Three Books of the Negroes* for Farrar, Straus, Giroux. He is a regular contributor to *The Village Voice*.

JOHN ASH's new collection of poems, *The Burnt Pages*, is forthcoming in September with Random House. He is at work on a book about Byzantium in Asia.

AMIRI BARAKA's *The Life and Life of Bumpy Johnson*, with music by Max Roach, just premiered at the San Diego Repertory Theater. The *Leroi Jones/Amiri Baraka Reader* will be published by Thunder's Mouth Press in June.

MITCH BERMAN's first novel, *Time Capsule*, was published by Putnam's. Together with Susanne Lee he covered China's 1989 student movement for *The Village Voice*. He and Susanne Lee are among the co-editors of *Children of the Dragon: The Story of Tiananmen Square* (Collier).

MEI-MEI BERSSENBRUGGE's most recent collection of poems, *Empathy*, is available from Station Hill Press.

LEON BOTSTEIN has conducted the London Philharmonic, the Pro Arte Chamber Orchestra of Boston, the Philharmonia and other orchestras. Music director of the Bard Music Festival, his book *Music and Its Public: Habits of Listening and the Crisis of Musical Modernism in Vienna, 1870-1914* is forthcoming with the University of Chicago Press. Mr. Botstein is the president of Bard College.

HAYDEN CARRUTH's classic collection of essays on jazz, *Sitting In*, was published by the University of Iowa Press in 1986.

CLARK COOLIDGE's recent books include *Sound as Thought: Poems 1962-1984* (Sun & Moon) and *Baffling Means* (O·blek), a collaboration with the artist Philip Guston.

PHILIP CORNER has for three decades been a significant figure in the world of American musical composition. His involvement with the Fluxus group in the early sixties was marked by the influential Wiesbaden performance (1962) of *Piano Activities*. A member of Son of Lion Gamelan, which performs traditional Balinese, he is composing in Indonesia this year.

GERALD EARLY's *Tuxedo Junction: Essays on America Culture* was published by Ecco Press. He is editor of *Speech and Power: The Afro-American Essay* (Ecco) and *Lure and Loathing: Essays on Race, Identity and the Ambivalence of Assimilation* (Viking/Penguin), both of which are forthcoming.

KENWARD ELMSLIE — poet, librettist, composer, singer — is the author of many books, including *The Orchard Stories*, a novel, and *Sung Sex* (Kulchur).

Composer, conductor and pianist LUKAS FOSS has more than a hundred compositions to his credit. From 1951 to 1962, he succeeded Arnold Schoenberg as professor of composition at UCLA. He is conductor laureate of the Brooklyn Philharmonia and of the Milwaukee Symphony. He lives in New York City.

An anthropologist and noted translator of Nahuatl, WILLARD GINGERICH is the Dean of graduate studies at St. John's University.

ALBERT GOLDMAN is the author of numerous books, including *Ladies and Gentlemen — Lenny Bruce!!*, *Elvis* and *The Lives of John Lennon*. He is currently at work on a biography of Jim Morrison.

BARBARA GUEST's collaboration with the artist Richard Tuttle, *Altos*, is forthcoming with Limestone Press. Her most recent collection of poetry, *Fair Realism*, is out with Sun & Moon.

ROBERT KELLY's most recent collection of short fiction, *Cat Scratch Fever*, is available from McPherson & Co.

SUSANNE WAH LEE is a contributor to *Asiaweek* (Hong Kong), *Asianweek* (San Francisco), *The Nation* and *The Village Voice*. She is a contributing editor of *A*, a national magazine for Asian-Americans.

Djbot Baghostus's Run is the second volume of NATHANIEL MACKEY's *From A Broken Bottle Traces of Perfume Still Emanate*. The first volume, *Bedouin Hornbook*, came out in 1986 as part of the Callaloo Fiction Series. *Djbot* is due out with Sun & Moon later this year.

Lucas 1 to 29 was written in response to an invitation to JACKSON MAC LOW from editors Gisela Gronemeyer and Reinhard Oehschlägel of *MusikTexte, Zeitschrift für neue Musik* to contribute to the magazine, and it was first published there.

SETH MORGAN's acclaimed first novel, *Homeboy*, is coming out in paperback this September with Vintage. He died, sadly for us all, in a motorcycle accident last fall. He was at work on a second novel, *Mambo Mephiste*.

BRADFORD MORROW's second novel, *The Almanac Branch*, comes out in June with Simon & Schuster. His collection of animal fables, *A Bestiary*, illustrated by 18 New York artists, has just been published by Grenfell Press.

WALTER MOSLEY's first novel, *Devil With a Blue Dress* (Norton), was nominated for an Edgar Award this year. His second novel, *A Red Death*, is due out in June. He is at work on a novel about the life and times of Robert Johnson.

ALBERT MURRAY's sequel to *The Trainwhistle Guitar* is *The Spyglass Tree*, to be published by Pantheon in September. His biography of Count Basie, *Good Morning Blues*, was published by Random House.

JAMES NARES is an artist living and working in New York. His most recent one-man show was held in April at Paul Kasmin Gallery.

HANK O'NEAL's memoir *Life is painful, nasty and short . . . in my case it has only been painful and nasty — Djuna Barnes 1978-81* is out with Paragon Press. He is president of Chiaroscuro Records, and his company HOSS, Inc., produces jazz and music festivals all over the world, notably the Floating Jazz Festival.

CARL RAKOSI's volumes *Collected Poems* and *Collected Prose* are available from the National Poetry Foundation.

STEPHEN RATCLIFFE is a poet, and the publisher of Avenue B. His chapbook, *Geography*, is forthcoming from Sun & Moon.

DAVID RATTRAY's book of poems, *Opening the Eyelid*, was published by diwan this spring. An amateur pianist, he has given several recitals of In Nomine music over the past two years. The program note for his recitals, a brief excerpt from the present essay, was published last year in *Giants Play Well in the Drizzle*.

ARMAND SCHWERNER's most recent book, *The Tablets I-XXVI*, was published in London last year. A musician most of his life, he was a member of Son of Lion Gamelan for a year; he often complements his poetry readings with performances on various instruments.

DAVID SHIELDS is the author of the novels *Dead Languages* and *Heroes*, and a forthcoming collection of stories, *Handbook for Drowning* (Knopf).

GILBERT SORRENTINO's novel, *Under the Shadow* is due out this fall with Dalkey Archive Press. Dalkey will be reissuing *Imaginative Qualities of Actual Things* at the same time.

DAVID STAROBIN is a classical guitarist whose repertoire includes both traditional and avant-garde materials. More than 200 works by contemporary composers have been written for him. His most recent disc is *New Music with Guitar Volume 4* (Bridge Records).

JOHN TAGGART's new collection of poems, *Loop*, is just out with Sun & Moon.

Multimedia artist, composer, poet and visual artist, ANNE TARDOS's work has been shown/performed at the 1990 Venice Biennale, the Jack Tilton Gallery, New York, and most recently at Woodland Pattern, Milwaukee.

QUINCY TROUPE won the 1980 American Book Award for Poetry for his collection, *Snake-Back Solos*. Author of other books of poems, editor of *James Baldwin: The Legacy* (Touchstone), he is author of *Miles: The Autobiography, Miles Davis with Quincy Troupe* (Simon & Schuster).

MARJORIE WELISH's *The Windows Flew Open* was just published by Burning Deck.

PAUL WEST's latest novel is *The Women of Whitechapel* (Random House). His collection of short portraits, *Portable People*, is available from Paris Review Editions. *Sheer Fiction II* (McPherson) has also recently been published.

What do all of these people have in common?

Vito Acconci
Edward Albee
Jane Alexander
Kathy Bates
Thulani Davis
Deborah Eisenberg
Amy Gerstler
Jessica Hagedorn
Gary Indiana
Dr. John
Harvey Keitel
Romulus Linney
Patrick McGrath
James Merrill
Bradford Morrow
Mira Nair
Al Pacino
Salman Rushdie
Vikram Seth
Whit Stillman
Graham Swift
Philip Taaffe
Dorothea Tanning
Lynne Tillman
Luisa Valenzuela
Fay Weldon
James Wines

You can hear them SPEAK in BOMB.

artists . writers . actors . directors interview
artists . writers . actors . directors

SUBSCRIBE: $16.00 for 5 issues SAVE 20%
P.O.B. 2003 Canal Station NY NY 10013
212 . 431-4943 FAX 431-3942

New Books from...
POTES & POETS PRESS

BRUCE ANDREWS $9.00
Executive Summary
92pp

This book contains a selection of Andrews' writing from 1969 to 1973. "Bruce Andrews continues to write some of the most original and unsettling poetry I know of." — Susan Howe

CHARLES BERNSTEIN, $8.00
OLIVIER CADIOT
37pp
Red, Green & Black

Bernstein adapts from the French, Olivier Cadiot's long poem into fascinating rhythms and exhilaratingly humorous language. "The game is grammatical, but the arrow hits."
— Rosmarie Waldrop

ADRIAN CLARKE, $12.00
ROBERT SHEPPARD, editors
125 pp
Floating Capital: New Poets from London

A collection of thirteen writers' work, giving ample space for each to spread out. "No single definition can encompass the penetrating variety of what's included herein." — Dennis Barone

KIT ROBINSON $9.00
The Champagne of Concrete
87 pp

New poetry by this vital Bay Area writer. "In mid-career, Robinson has emerged one of the most accomplished poets working today in America." — Kevin Killian

---

ABACUS, eighth series, 1991, is a 12–18 page periodical mailed every six weeks. Each issue features one writer. This year's writers are Steve McCaffery, Ray DiPalma, Melanie Neilson, Dennis Barone, Rochelle Owens, Thomas Taylor, Susan Gevirtz, and Kathleen Fraser. 8 issues, $21 postpaid.

FREE

SEND FOR FREE CATALOGUE OF POTES & POETS BOOKS AND A 30% OFF COUPON FOR BACKLISTED BOOKS, VALID UNTIL SEPTEMBER 30, 1991.
Ordering information: add $1.50 postage and handling for first book; 50¢ for each additional book. Send to:

POTES & POETS PRESS, DEPT. C-16, 181 EDGEMONT AVE., ELMWOOD CT 06110

also distributed by Segue, Sun and Moon, Small Press Distribution, Small Press Traffic, Innovations Press, Bookslinger, and, in the UK, Paul Green.

George Robert Minkoff, Inc.

RARE BOOKS

▰

20th Century First Editions, Fine Press Books,
Letters, Manuscripts & Important Archival
Material Bought & Sold
Catalogues issued

Rowe Road, RFD, Box 147
Great Barrington, MA 02130
[413] 528 - 4575

WALTER ABISH
99: The New Meaning
with photographs by Cecile Abish
Five collage "entertainments" by the author of *How German Is It* and *Alphabetical Africa*. These playful probes into the nature of fiction challenge our notions of narrative, continuity, structure and even creativity. They do not give us a make-belief "world," but invite the reader to come onto the scaffolding and participate in the process of construction.
112 pages, offset, cloth $20, signed $30, paper, sewn $8

GALE NELSON
stare decisis
Diverting each poem through a formal practice, *stare decisis* seeks a balance of precision and ambiguity, legal reference and transgression of conventions. Words splinter into a dislocated emotional turbulence, but silence is the point of disquieting unity.
144 pages, offset, smyth-sewn, paper $9, signed paper $15

MARJORIE WELISH
The Windows Flew Open
Welish's second major collection of poems transgresses the norm of the prose sentence with knowing precision. Leaps in logic, sudden changes in mid-sent ence characterize her forays into meaning and emotion. "Welish is a true daredevil. She performs without the net of appeal to the reader's complicity." —*Parnassus*.
80 pages, offset, smyth-sewn, paper $8, signed paper $15

LEW DALY
e. dickinson on a sleepwalk with the alphabet prowling around her
A poem for two voices, in which the poet is concerned with Emily Dickinson's instinct toward the unconscious as isolable, and the poem as a channel knit of religious counter-balance.
24 pages, letterpress, saddlestitched in wrappers $4

Burning Deck has received grants from the National Endowment for the Arts, the Rhode Island State Council on the Arts, the Fund for Poetry and the Taft Subvention Committee.

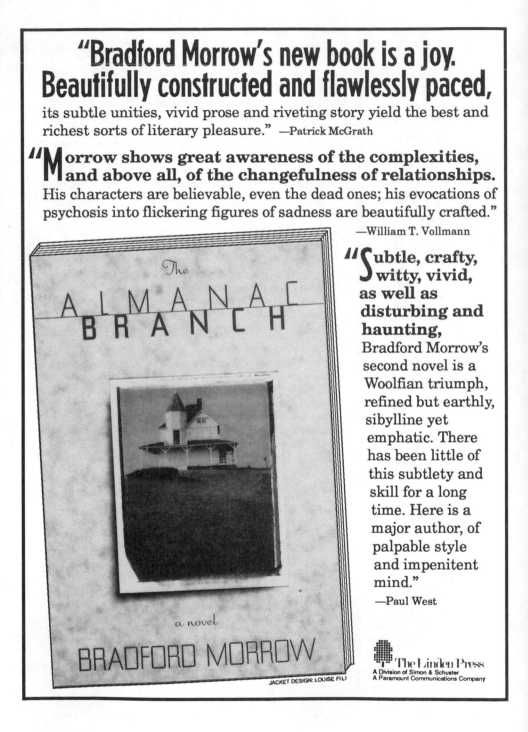

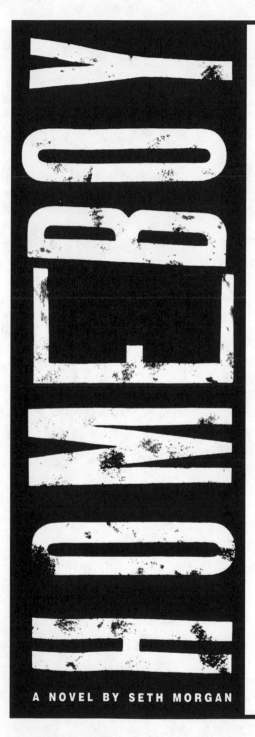

A NOVEL BY SETH MORGAN

THE WOMEN OF WHITECHAPEL

AND JACK THE RIPPER

PAUL WEST   A NOVEL

"Mesmerizing, appalling, chilling, nightmarish, overwhelming...
a consummate artist gives us a look at the truth about ourselves."
–Chaim Potok

"A fascinating novel. Splendid and entertaining, *The Women of
Whitechapel* rewards the reader with much more than suspense."
–Oscar Hijuelos

"*The Women of Whitechapel* is a verbal feast, every page offering
delightful forays into the lushness of this writer's prose...West's
imagination is so fertile, his artistry so deft and confident, the
reader often finds himself turning pages in a state of wonder."
–David W. Madden,
The Review of Contemporary Fiction

RANDOM 🏠 HOUSE